Jewish Public Culture
in the Late Russian Empire

THE MODERN JEWISH EXPERIENCE
Paula Hyman and Deborah Dash Moore, editors

Jewish Public Culture in the Late Russian Empire

JEFFREY VEIDLINGER

INDIANA UNIVERSITY PRESS
Bloomington and Indianapolis

This book is a publication of

Indiana University Press
601 North Morton Street
Bloomington, IN 47404-3797 USA

http://iupress.indiana.edu

Telephone orders 800-842-6796
Fax orders 812-855-7931
Orders by e-mail iuporder@indiana.edu

LIBRARY OF CONGRESS CATALOGING-IN-PUBLICATION DATA

Veidlinger, Jeffrey, date–
Jewish public culture in the late Russian empire / Jeffrey Veidlinger.
p.   cm.   — (The modern Jewish experience)
Includes bibliographical references and index.
ISBN 978-0-253-35287-3 (cloth : alk. paper) —
ISBN 978-0-253-22058-5 (pbk. : alk. paper)
1. Jews—Russia—Intellectual life. I. Title.
DS135.R9V43   2009
305.892'404709034—dc22
2008032577

1   2   3   4   5   14   13   12   11   10   09

CONTENTS

ACKNOWLEDGMENTS

I greatly appreciate the assistance and support I have been given from numerous friends, colleagues, and organizations during the writing of this book.

I have benefited enormously from all my colleagues at Indiana University in the Robert A. and Sandra S. Borns Jewish Studies Program, the History Department, and the Russian and East European Institute. In particular, I am grateful to Matthias Lehmann, Ben Eklof, and Dov-Ber Kerler for their thoughtful comments on significant portions of this book. I welcome the opportunity to share ideas regularly with Steve Weitzman, Shaul Magid, Mark Roseman, and Dror Wahrman. I am privileged to hold a chair established in honor of Alvin Rosenfeld, a friend and colleague who has done much to promote Jewish public culture in our day. My graduate students, Jolanta Mickute and Nicole McGrath, gave an early draft of this manuscript a close read, and Larisa Privalskaya and Ryan Kilgore stepped in at the last minute to serve as research assistants.

I have presented aspects of this book at numerous scholarly conferences and workshops over the last few years. These opportunities to interact with scholars in related fields have helped me formulate my ideas. I therefore thank the participants of the "Revolution of 1905: A Turning Point for the Jews?" conference at Hebrew University; the "Jews and Russian Revolutions" conference at Stanford University, the "Translation and Yiddish Culture" conference at the University of California, Berkeley, the "Yiddish Theater Revisited" conference at the University of Washington, and the "Klutznick Symposium on the Jews of Eastern Europe" at Creighton University. I also thank the Midwest Russian History Workshop, the Indiana University Modern European History Workshop, the American Association for the Advancement of Slavic Studies, and the Association for Jewish Studies. Brian Horowitz, John Efron, Jeremy Dauber, and Marci Shore have provided particularly useful comments, as has the anonymous reviewer for Indiana University Press. I would also like to acknowledge with sadness the passing of John Klier and Jonathan Frankel, both of whom have influenced and supported my own work as well as the entire field of Eastern European Jewish history.

Janet Rabinowitch has been supportive of this book since I began writing it. I am fortunate to have such an expert editor working with me and greatly appreciate all that she and the staff of Indiana University Press have done. Kate Babbitt's attention to detail and thorough copyediting have made my prose more clear. Scott Taylor of IU Graphic Services prepared the map, and Jesse Cohen of the YIVO Institute for Jewish Research assisted me in selecting photographs.

Several organizations provided much-appreciated financial support toward this project. I was fortunate to receive an ACLS/SSRC/NEH International and Area Studies Fellowship, a summer stipend from the National Endowment for the Humanities, a grant-in-aid of international travel from the REEI-Mellon Endowment at Indiana University, and research fellowships from the College Arts & Humanities Institute and the Research and University Graduate School at Indiana University.

Portions of this book were previously published in other forms. Much of chapter 9 appeared as "The Historical and Ethnographic Construction of Russian Jewry," *Ab Imperio* no. 4 (2003): 165–184. Segments of other chapters have been published as " . . . Even Beyond Pinsk: *Yizker Bikher* [Memorial Books] and Jewish Cultural Life in the Shtetl," *Studies in Jewish Civilization* 16 (2005) 175–189; and "Jewish Cultural Associations in the Aftermath of 1905," in *The Revolution of 1905 and Russia's Jews,* ed. Stefani Hoffman and Ezra Mendelsohn (Philadelphia: University of Pennsylvania Press, 2008). I thank these publishers for permission to republish these materials.

Finally, I would like to thank my family. My father, my brother Daniel, and my uncle Louis Greenspan each read the manuscript and provided useful comments. I thank my wife Rebecca and my daughters Naomi and Leah for their love and support. I dedicate this book to Rebecca and, with apologies that Jewish history just doesn't have many princesses, to Naomi and Leah.

A NOTE ON TRANSLITERATION

This book discusses people and places that existed in multilingual environments. Proper names varied depending upon personal inclination and audience and were expressed alternatively in Hebraic, Cyrillic, and Latin alphabets. Even within these alphabets pronunciation varied vastly, most notably between Hebrew (*loshn koydesh*, the Holy Tongue) and Yiddish, and even within Yiddish between numerous dialects. I have tried to balance an authenticity of expression with the consistency expected of a scholarly work.

In the text, I have transliterated Hebrew names and terms according to the Ashkenazic pronunciation that would have been used by the individuals discussed in this book. Thus: *oylem ha-zenik, bitl toyre, kheyder, seyfer.* However, when using familiar Hebrew words, I have adopted the common English spelling. Thus: Torah, yeshiva, Haskalah, Hanukkah, Hasid.

I have transliterated most foreign words according to the Library of Congress system for Hebrew and Russian, and the YIVO system for Yiddish, all without diacritic marks. Familiar Russian names ending with -kii have been rendered in the more familiar -ky (Dostoevsky rather than Dostoevskii; Gorky rather than Gorkii). Other names have been rendered differently depending upon the primary language of activity of the individual and the individual's own usage: thus Mendele Moykher Sforim's proper name, Sholem Yankev Abramovitsh, is rendered according to a Yiddish transliteration system; Osip Rabinovich's name according to a Russian transliteration system; and Solomon Rabinowitz, Sholem Aleichem's proper name, according to the personal stationery he used while living in New York. When in doubt I have used *The YIVO Encyclopedia of Jews in Eastern Europe* as an authority.

For most geographic place names located within the Russian Empire, I have used the official Russian name that was in use before World War I. I have made an exception for place names located within the Kingdom of Poland, in which case I have used the Polish name. I have also made an exception for the transliteration of common English names where they exist (Moscow rather than Moskva and Bialystok rather than Belostok).

I recognize that this system is imperfect, but its imprecision accurately reflects the ambiguities of living in multiple languages and with multiple alphabets, an experience shared by the protagonists of this book.

INTRODUCTION: JEWISH PUBLIC CULTURE

Speaking before the All-Russian Zionist Congress in Minsk in 1902, the Zionist thinker Ahad Ha-Am (One of the People), the pen name of Asher Ginzburg (1856–1927), identified two strands of national culture: objective and subjective. He defined objective culture as "the concrete expression of the best minds of the nation in every period of its existence" and subjective culture as "the degree to which culture is diffused among the individual members of the nation, and the extent to which its influence is visible in their private and public life."[1] It was subjective culture—the penetration of rituals, beliefs, and ideas into the broad public—that he believed was essential for the consolidation of a national identity.

Using similar ideas but different terminology, this book examines institutions of Jewish public culture as keys to understanding the transformation of Jewish society that occurred in the late-nineteenth- and early-twentieth-century Russian Empire. I understand public culture to refer to how public life is culturally articulated; it is the systems of collective representations that underlie a social structure. Public culture is about perceptions of public life, about "social imaginaries"—that is, the ways that ordinary people envision the world around them.[2] The concentration on public culture, like Ahad Ha-Am's subjective culture, is intended in part to relocate scholarly emphasis from the professional producers of cultural products to how those products are received as well as to the participatory role amateurs and common folk play in creating culture. The notion of public culture, then, seeks to decouple cultural studies from the hierarchical distinctions between elite or high culture, on one hand, and popular or mass culture, on the other. Certainly professional artists have an impact on the shape and articulation of public culture, but this study emphasizes the cultural points of intersection between disparate groups, the public spaces—both physical and metaphorical—that can be inhabited by both seamstresses and celebrities.

Insofar as the generalized networks of collective representations that constitute public culture are intangible, they can be approached only through the intermediary of specific artifacts, performances, and institutions. Such artifacts can include film, television, radio, and other media of modern mass culture; costume, cuisine, and folk art; statues and monuments that decorate urban squares; or voluntary associations. Clearly the mass media, which has attracted so much attention from recent cultural critics, is of limited use when discussing a time period that predates the technological advances that brought radio, television, and the Internet into the homes of modern individuals. Folklore and folk songs, while promising direct access to public culture, can also be interpreted only second hand through the eyes and ears of those who collected, compiled, and often reworked them to conform to aesthetics that were sometimes alien to the folk. Since Jews historically lacked their own town squares in which they could erect statues and monuments, the study of urban landscapes also has particular limits within the study of Jewish public culture. Instead of engraving their national myths in stone and erecting memorials of their legendary heroes in bronze, Jews in the early-twentieth-century Russian Empire tended to enact, express, and debate their public culture through everyday rituals and marked performances within the realm of the new public institutions that were being established on voluntary bases throughout the empire.

These public institutions, formed by private individuals and groups, included economic organizations such as joint-stock ventures, credit associations, mutual aid societies, and artels as well as social and humanitarian groups, such as societies for the protection and defense of orphans, widows, and the poor.[3] But it is cultural associations, defined in accordance with contemporary classification as organizations with the goals of raising the intellectual and aesthetic levels of the adult population, that are the focus of this study. Although contemporary sources generally grouped together cultural and educational organizations, I have sought to decouple the two, focusing only on the former. Thus, schools, universities, and adult-education courses are beyond the purview of the current study. Instead, this study focuses on libraries, literary societies, drama circles, theaters, musical groupings, and learned societies. The remaking of society that characterized the modern era required the construction of an entirely new system of myths, the articulation of new legends, and the enactment of new ritual behavior. In the Russian Empire these processes took place for the most part within cultural associations, which became in turn the preeminent institutions for the expression, presentation, and encapsulation of Jewish public culture.

This book also limits its discussion of public culture to secular culture. That is not to say that Jewish religious life was unimportant. On the contrary, most early-twentieth-century Russian Jews lived predominantly in a religious world: they regulated their lives according to a religious calendar, tried their best to follow the commandments of Jewish law, and had faith in their religious traditions. But growing numbers were beginning to spend more time in secular pursuits. When the protagonists of this book spoke of culture—whether in Russian of *kul'tura,* in Yiddish of *kultur,* in Polish of *kultura,* or even in Hebrew of *tarbut*—they meant it in a secular sense.

Several different types of sources, both institutional and personal, can help in efforts to interpret public culture. Official organizational statutes, membership statistics, annual reports, newsletters, and other publications all reveal a particular organization's public and official persona. The larger organizations discussed in this book have their own archives full of such data, and the sections of this book that deal with these organizations draw upon that material. Obtaining information about smaller-scale organizations and societies in the provinces, which usually left much shorter paper trails, is more difficult but can be accessed through other sources. One of the most important means by which we can discern the ways that ordinary individuals remembered their experiences of Jewish public culture is through memoir literature. Many of the leading cultural producers and activists of the era were prolific writers, producing multivolume memoirs. Despite the sometimes inflated roles they assign themselves and the factual contradictions and inconsistencies that made their way into the narratives, these sources can communicate the perceived meaning of events and perceptions of ideas in a personal and evocative way.[4] While this type of memoir literature is limited in that it tells only the stories of the elites—those who found it necessary to write their memoirs—it can be supplemented by the memoirs of ordinary folk recorded in hundreds of memorial books (*yizker bikher*). These books were compiled in the aftermath of the Holocaust to memorialize the destroyed Jewish communities of Eastern Europe.[5] Survivors of a city or township were encouraged to write short descriptions of life in their hometown as they remembered it. In this manner, thousands of ordinary people whose memories would not otherwise have been deposited in the historical record were able to leave their reminiscences in print for posterity. When we supplement the autobiographies of famous figures with the memoirs of ordinary folk, a more complete picture of Russian Jewish public culture emerges. Although the vast majority of these recollections tell of the interwar period, many depict the last years of the tsarist empire. Written long after the period they describe, these accounts are subject to vicissitudes of memory, but, combined with other sources, they provide a richly textured layer of context that would otherwise be inaccessible. Despite the impact of nostalgia and (willful or

inadvertent) forgetting, memoirs convey a sense of the ideals and myths—
the public culture—that defined the era.

The imperialist expansion of the Russian Empire in the late nineteenth
century meant that a large number of Eastern European Jews were brought
under the rule of the same state and, despite residency restrictions, were
able to communicate and interact with each other to a degree not matched in
the twentieth century. The Partitions of Poland of 1772–1795 had brought
what would become the provinces of Volhynia and Podolia under Russian
rule. As part of the 1812 Treaty of Bucharest that concluded the Russo-
Turkish War of 1806–1812, Bessarabia, including the city of Kishinev, was
ceded to Russia. The Kingdom of Poland, originally created as a Russian
protectorate under the name of the Duchy of Warsaw by the 1815 Congress
of Vienna, gradually became incorporated more formally into the Russian
Empire, and by the early twentieth century it had lost virtually all of its
independent political features. Although Jews were largely restricted to
living within the Pale of Jewish Settlement and the Kingdom of Poland,
they were permitted to move around within these areas. By the early twentieth century, several categories of Jews were also permitted to live outside
the Pale, many of whom congregated in St. Petersburg. The conglomeration
of such a large territory under the same state structure allowed for a freer
flow of people and ideas than would be possible later in the twentieth
century. After World War I, these territories were divided into numerous
independent states. These states often gave their own Jewish populations
greater freedom of movement and expression, but the new geographical
divisions made cross-border interaction increasingly difficult.

Pre–World War I borders tended to be more porous than they would
become in the postwar world. Thus, those Jews living in the Russian Empire
were able to have extensive contact with neighboring Jewish communities
on the other side of the border. The Jews of the Russian Empire were heavily
influenced by personal, institutional, and ideological ties with Jewish communities in neighboring lands, particularly Austrian Galicia and Bukovina
and Romanian Moldavia. Metropolises like Iasi, on the Romanian side of the
River Prut, and Lemberg, Tarnopol, Drohobycz, and Cracow, all located on
the Austrian side of the River Zbruch, played important roles in the cultural and intellectual lives of Jewish subjects of the Russian Empire. Border
towns like Brody, which divided Austrian Galicia from Russian Volhynia,
and Czernowitz, which rested near the border between Austrian Bukovina
and Russian Bessarabia, became major centers of cross-border cultural
exchange. Jews crossed these borders to attend universities outside Russia,

where admission policies were less restrictive for Jewish students; to pay homage to the courts of Hasidic rebbes; to arrange marriages; to trade goods; to seek employment; and to emigrate. Traveling musicians, itinerant theatrical troupes, book peddlers, and public speakers also frequently trekked across these borders, helping forge a common public culture.

Recognizing the transnational characteristics of modern Jewish cultural identity and activity, this book is about Jewish culture in the Russian Empire. Since the vast majority of the Jewish population within the empire lived in the Pale of Settlement and the Kingdom of Poland, these regions are the primary focus of the book. The imperial capital of St. Petersburg, where much cultural activity was centered and where the largest Jewish cultural societies housed their headquarters, also plays an important role and is the focus of the final two chapters. Inasmuch as they partook of the cultural developments and opportunities coming out of the western borderlands, references are also made to smaller Jewish merchant communities scattered throughout the empire. The territorial coverage of this book is both vast and diverse. The cultural experiences of Jews in the northern city of Vilna, the "Jerusalem of Lithuania," were very different from those in the Black Sea port of Odessa in the southern territory of New Russia, even though both were multinational metropolitan centers. But Jewish life in the Volhynian town of Novograd Volynsky, known in Yiddish as Zvhil, was also very different from that of the neighboring village of Gorodnitsa. And even within a single city or town different individuals experienced their lives uniquely. The assimilated Jewish residents of Novograd Volynsky lived very different lives than the Yiddish masses of Zvhil, even though they inhabited the same town. Other variations in the ways public culture was experienced abound. For instance, while the new culture could be enjoyed by both men and women, who intermingled—often for the first time—in modern cultural settings, public culture was nevertheless gendered. None of this is remarkable. The same can be said for any large state structure. Even in early-twenty-first-century America, where mass media connects every community, life in small towns is experienced differently than in large urban centers. Each town and city has its own character, differentiating it from neighboring locales, and even within small towns numerous different communities can be found interacting with each other.

What is more remarkable is how in the waning years of the Russian Empire, a cohesive Jewish community was imagined despite the enormous chasms that still separated individual centers. Small-town provincial Yiddish newspapers reported on a Jewish world that would be recognizable even to those who read the Russian-language Jewish periodicals of St. Petersburg. Similarly, memoirists in town after town told their stories within similar frameworks, drawing upon recognizable motifs and coming to analogous conclusions. Almost everyone imagined themselves on the stage when itinerant theaters came to town, and countless youth discovered in the community library whole new worlds opening up before their eyes. Undoubtedly these commonalities are partly products of memoirists replicating established patterns and prototypes, but they caught on because they were perceived as being true and as accurately representing the authors' personal experiences. Explaining how this sense of cohesiveness came into being is part of the agenda of this book.

Chapter 1, "The Jews of This World," provides historical background to the story and introduces some of the major themes of the book. The rest of the book is divided into four sections, each of which is in turn divided into two chapters: the first generally looks at the formal production of culture on a professional level and the second addresses the dissemination, reception, and amateur production of culture on secondary levels. The first pairing of chapters deals with Jewish reading habits. Chapter 2 looks at the most widespread cultural organization—the public library. The local library was one of the primary means by which the average Jew came into contact with the cultural movements and modernist ideologies of the early twentieth century. In the first decade of the century, librarianship became professionalized in Russia as journals of library science were established and librarians' conferences took place. The Jewish community, which had traditionally placed great importance on books, soon participated in these professional trends in librarianship. The Jewish community, however, already had a well-developed system of libraries in the forms of the *besemedresh, maskilic* private libraries, and Bundist or Zionist underground libraries. When the Society for the Promotion of Enlightenment among the Jews of Russia took it upon itself to oversee the development of a network of libraries throughout the Pale of Jewish Settlement, it was forced to challenge the existing network. The battle was not merely one of library ownership but cut to the very heart of the fissure within Jewish society between accommodation and resistance to political authority.

Chapter 3 turns its attention to the most popular books and tries to suggest some ways that a typical Jew in the Pale of Settlement might have read these books. The period of late tsarism saw not only a transformation of the types of books Jews read but also a revolution in the way books were read. Using circulation statistics from Jewish libraries, discussions of

reading habits in biographies, and publication statistics, this chapter inves-
tigates Jewish reading habits in the early twentieth century. As modern
notions of leisure infiltrated the Russian Jewish community, Jewish readers of fiction no longer had to hide their chapbooks behind their Talmud
folios but were able to openly engage in the literature that was becoming
a staple of Russian youth culture. Despite the goals of library activists,
Jewish readers preferred Russian-language bestsellers and popular fiction
to the polemical writings of the intelligentsia. They appreciated particularly books that shed light on Jewish life and valued books that promised
social advancement and cultural acceptability.

The next chapter pairing looks at literary societies and their impact.
Chapter 4 traces the development of the Jewish Literary Society and the
Lovers of the Hebrew Language society, first in the imperial capital and
then in smaller provincial cities throughout Poland and the Pale of Jewish
Settlement. The chapter highlights the conflicts over language and organization that accompanied the formation of each of these groups and looks at
the relationship of these societies with the state structure and local officialdom. Chapter 5 looks at the most common means by which literary societies disseminated their ideals to the populace—through the sponsorship of
spoken-word events, such as public lectures and readings. This chapter
examines the impact these events had on Jewish modes of speaking and
listening. Spoken-word events can be understood as cultural performances
that united the community under a single roof while at the same time
invoking fissures, primarily through the choice of the language in which a
performance takes place.

The next chapter pairing turns to more complex forms of cultural
performance, particularly theater, drama circles, musical societies, and
orchestras. In the aftermath of the 1905 Revolution, as the infamous ban on
Yiddish theater was relaxed, Yiddish drama circles and theater clubs proliferated throughout the Pale of Jewish Settlement. Chapter 6 examines the
development of professional theater both in the metropolises and among
itinerant theatrical troupes in the provinces. Chapter 7 looks at the role
amateur drama circles played in opening up new social networks and helping individuals develop the skills that were valued in the emerging modern
society: self-confidence, charisma, oratory, and cultural literacy. For community audiences, theater was an accessible means of being introduced to
modernist culture. Theater often challenged traditional social hierarchies,
as the lowliest beggar could suddenly become a local star and heartthrob
by shining on the stage. At the same time, klezmer bands, fire brigade

orchestras, and other groupings of musicians entertained provincial audiences. This chapter looks at grassroots musical and theatrical groups to demonstrate the transformative role they played in modernizing Jewish national culture.

The final pair of chapters turns its attention to the imperial capital, St. Petersburg, and focuses on more elite learned societies. Chapter 8 traces the formation of one of the most important elite voluntary associations of the period—the Jewish Historical and Ethnographic Society (JHES). The JHES provided a realm in which the leading Jewish intellectuals of the period could meet for social and intellectual exchange. Although the society was dedicated to the study of history, in its discussions and deliberations the problems of contemporary Jewish society were debated and solutions for the future proposed. Through public forums such as public lectures and the periodical *Jewish Antiquities,* the JHES interacted with educated members of Jewish society, influencing public debates and helping formulate ideological programs. Chapter 9, "Public History: Imagining Russian Jews," discusses several interpretations of Russian Jewish identity that were articulated within the Jewish Historical and Ethnographic Society. The leaders of the society sought to adopt the existing political borders of the Russian Empire as the limits of Russian Jewry and were thus compelled to incorporate into the Russian Jewish community the non-rabbinical Karaite Jews and other non-Ashkenazic Jewish communities of Central Asia, the Caucasus, and Crimea, as well as sectarian communities, such as the Subbotniks. At the same time, they largely excluded Galician Jewry, who, despite a close cultural relationship with the neighboring Jews of the Pale of Jewish Settlement, found themselves on the Austro-Hungarian side of the border.

The conclusion looks at the impact of the Great War. Changing borders, war, revolution, and migrations disrupted the grassroots organizing that had characterized prewar Jewish life. As the dust settled and the empires fell, Jewish public culture was transformed again, this time under the influence of the new global movements that sought to radically build this world anew.

Jewish Public Culture
in the Late Russian Empire

The Pale of Jewish Settlement and the Kingdom of Poland

1

The Jews of This World

In 1910, Jewish cultural critic A. Mukdoyni (Alexander Kapel, 1878–1958) wrote of the "this-worldnik" (Yiddish: *oylem ha-zenik*) who "takes advantage of and enjoys with great appetite all the pleasures of life."[1] "The old generation with its great asceticism has died out," he declared "and a new generation has arisen, new people with little desire to struggle against the pleasures of this world."[2] During the turbulent revolutionary period that marked the last two decades of the Russian Empire, as hope engendered by the promise of the tsar's 1905 manifesto was tempered by the violence and destruction of the pogroms that followed, many of the five million Jews across the vast Russian Empire abandoned the messianic faith that had inspired Jews for generations. Many traded in messianic longings rooted in rabbinic, kabalistic, and folkloric traditions for new forms of eschatology. Some believed that the working class would usher in a new utopian world, destroying the old in its wake. Others placed their faith in the "ingathering of the exiles," the mass migration of Jews to Palestine, where they would rebuild the land of Zion and in turn be remade themselves. But the "this-worldniks," the Jews of *this* world, rejected all projects of utopian reconstruction. For them, happiness was not to be found in any world to come but rather was to be sought in *this* world. The "this-worldniks" accused their fellow Jews of suffering silently on this earth like Yitskhok Leybush Peretz's (1851–1915) fictional protagonist Bontshe the Silent, who had become so docile in life that he could only ask for a fresh roll of bread and butter upon reaching the heavenly world to come.

The Jews of this world, by contrast, focused their energies on bettering this world through institution-building, cultural enrichment, leisure, and self-edification. When they looked to the biblical prophets, they drew inspiration not from the messianic and apocalyptic dreams that ignited the imaginations of the Zionists and socialist revolutionaries but rather to Jeremiah's exhortations to the Babylonian exiles about quotidian life:

> Build houses and dwell in them, plant gardens and eat the fruit they produce. Take wives and have sons and daughters; take wives for your sons, and give your daughters in marriage, so that they may bear

sons and daughters; multiply there and do not decrease. And seek the welfare of the city where I have sent you into exile, and pray to the LORD on its behalf, for in its welfare you will find your welfare. For thus says the LORD of hosts, the God of Israel: Do not let the prophets and diviners who are among you deceive you, and do not listen to the dreams that they dream, for it is a lie that they are prophesying to you in my name. I did not send them, says the LORD.[3]

Just as Jeremiah urged the Babylonian exiles to ignore the apocalyptic prophets and instead to build houses and plant gardens, the Jews of this world urged their followers to live life to its fullest in the here and now.

Jewish learning had traditionally denigrated entertainment and leisure for its own sake as a waste of time that could have been spent studying Torah. Both homiletic literature of the yeshiva and works of Hasidic pietism urged readers to abstain from worldly pleasures. *Bitl toyre,* literally the annulment of Torah but a term that was more broadly used to refer to any activity other than Torah study and divine service, was regarded as among the most troubling—and most prevalent—of sins. Young people were always considered to be particularly susceptible to the sin of *bitl toyre,* and ethical literature repeatedly reminded parents of the obligation to keep their children away from external temptations. The still-widely-read twelfth-century *Seyfer khsidim* warned against socializing with friends and engaging in amusements.[4] The *Kitser shulkhan arukh,* or condensed code of Jewish law, stated that "all the necessities of life should be performed for the sake of serving your Creator, or for the purpose of doing something that will bring about the performance of His service."[5] The enormously popular *Mesiles yeshorim* (Path of the Upright) declared that "there is no worldly pleasure that is not followed by some sin in its wake."[6] The writings of twentieth-century Galician rabbi Hanokh Teitelbaum warned of the gravitational pull of material things and engagement in this world, a force so strong, he argued, that it prevents the soul from rising upward.[7]

If we are to believe contemporary accounts, the taboos against leisure were not confined to homilies and legal codes. Around the turn of the century, *maskilic* writers (proponents of the Haskalah, the Jewish enlightenment) began mocking what they regarded as this traditional attitude. In his popular Hebrew novella *Le'an?* (Whither?), Mordechai Ze'ev Feierberg (1874–1899) satirized this rejection of leisure when his fictional protagonist Nakhman is chastised by his father for playing with his peers upon returning from *kheyder* (Jewish primary school) one summer day: "A Jew is forbidden to fill his time with recreation in this world," his father scolds him. "In this world you must study and serve the Lord. God forbid that we should squander our time with false vanities. . . . All joy and any delight are Satan's work, to drown us in the vanities of this world and to deprive us of our share in the world to come. We are forbidden, son, forbidden to be merry in this world."[8] Bundist activist and writer A. Litvak (Khayim-Yankl Helfand, 1874–1932), who credited the Jewish socialist Bund (The General Union of Jewish Workers) with having introduced the Jewish worker to modern culture, painted a similar portrait of the "cultural nourishment" of a traditional common Jew:

> in his youth—a story book, a heart-rending novel by Shomer [the pen name of Nokhem Meyer Shaykevitch, 1849–1905, a popular Yiddish novelist]; later, from Sabbath to Sabbath a tiresome chapter of psalms or a bit of the *Khayyei Adam* [Man's Life, 1810, a code of rabbinic law geared toward the educated layman] without comprehension. His leisure: a glass and some cards, and even this measured and weighed in good manner; for the frivolous: a dance class. A couple of times in his life he would go to the circus. He would live a married life. When he gets older the greatest joy becomes to nap through Sabbath and holidays, either at home after a meal or in the study hall listening to a preacher. . . . The Jewish worker was obtuse and superstitious; he did not see past his own nose; he got no pleasure from his deeds, but trembled in deadly fear of committing a sin.[9]

Both Feierberg and Litvak conveyed a general sense that the traditional Jewish community had failed to embrace the pleasures and edifying potential of modern culture. But both also write with explicit political motivations: Feierberg, writing in 1899, months before his untimely death and barely two years after the first Zionist Congress, had come to believe that the future path for Jewry could lie only in Zionism and a revival of Hebrew culture. Litvak, on the other hand, who wrote his memoirs in American exile in 1926, had believed since his involvement with Bundist circles in Vilna in the 1890s that Jewish life could be remade only through Yiddish culture.

The sense that the older generation was unwilling to partake in the opportunities of this world and lived only for the next was widely shared. Peretz's short story "Di toyte shtodt" ("The Dead Town") can be seen as a satirical portrait of contemporary Jewish life. The story tells of a whole village of corpses, Jews "who never really died because they never really lived."[10] The entire community walked the streets like zombies, existing in this world but living only in the next. Yiddish writer Zalman Shneour (1886–1959) mocked the older generation in similar terms in his poem

"Yene velt" ("The Other World"). Speaking in the voice of his childhood teacher, who scolds the children for peering out the window to gaze at the world, he wrote:

> It's all nonsense! Nothing more
>
> A simple vestibule to the other world.
>
> What do you want from a world that is a vestibule?
>
> Be quiet, little Jews, be good and pious
>
> And learn with zeal. Do not forsake
>
> The other world![11]

For these writers, the joys of the Sabbath, religious festivals, and daily *avoyde* (service to God) were no match for the newer modes of secular leisure. Whereas Judaism had long urged its adherents to enjoy their lives for the sake of the world to come, many who were living fast-paced lives in the modern era had chosen not to wait that long for their rewards. It was these Jews, the Jews of *this* world, who created, enjoyed, and consumed modern Jewish public culture.

The "this-worldniks" rejected what they saw as a traditional mindset and embraced the more modern notion of cultural leisure. Many of these found inspiration for their views in contemporary Russian literature. Sanin, the hero of Mikhail Artsybashev's 1907 novel of the same name, characterized the hedonistic ethos of the first decade of the twentieth century in much the same way that Ivan Turgenev's Bazarov and Nikolai Chernyshevsky's Rakhmetov had come to symbolize the nihilism and communal asceticism of earlier ages. "We all agree that man isn't created to suffer and that suffering isn't the goal of human aspiration," Sanin declares. "In other words, gratification is the goal of life. Paradise is a synonym for absolute gratification and everyone more or less dreams of paradise on earth."[12] Sanin's lust for pleasure in this world and his protest against the morality of asceticism and sexual abstention resonated among the youth of the time. For a generation reared on the merits of sexual abstinence (whether as preached by Russian novelist Leo Tolstoy or in the writings of Hasidic storyteller and homilist Nakhman of Bratslav), the new morals Sanin and his ilk advocated were nothing short of revolutionary.

These morals were reinforced by modern Central European culture, as portrayed in the plays of Arthur Schnitzler and the writings of Otto Weininger. The new European culture was almost always associated with Jews. In the best-selling Russian novel of the period, Anastasiia Verbitskaia's

Kliuchi schast'ia (Keys to Happiness), the Christian heroine's Jewish love interest, Mark Steinbach, represents the decadence of modern liberalism. His learned appreciation for highbrow art is simply unable to bring about the joy in life that his young lover craves. Similarly, the Jewish student Soloveichik's suicide in *Sanin* comes about as he realizes the futility of intellectualism. If literature is a reflection of life, then these books reveal a troubled society in flux, with cultural modernism at its center. Widespread disillusionment with the apparently stagnant political realities of the inter-revolutionary era fed into a general retreat from public politics among the youth of the period. Some embraced worldly pleasures for their own sake, others sought to harness leisure for broader cultural and intellectual edification.

Among the latter group were those who sought to reorient the public's enthusiasm for leisure toward what they regarded as more productive cultural activity, to foster among the public a sense of *kultur'nost'* (cultural refinement). In his 1904 essay "Flesh and Spirit" ("Basar ve-ruah"), Ahad Ha-Am explicitly linked the materialism of those who live only for this world with the general project of cultural enrichment. He argued that in its "original form," in the times of the Temple, Judaism embraced neither the extremes of hedonism nor the extremes of asceticism. Instead of searching for answers within oneself—either within the individual flesh or the individual spirit—Jews found meaning in the well-being of the community as a whole. Ahad Ha-Am believed that despite some medieval and modern relapses into asceticism or hedonism, Judaism maintained a balance between the flesh and the spirit that allows for "the uplifting of the flesh by the spirit"—that is, for the pursuit of cultural and spiritual enrichment as both individual and communal objectives. These ideas, shared in some form by many leading liberal intellectuals, stimulated a movement to channel the "this-worldniks" into productive activity, to use their desire to uplift the flesh for the benefit of the spirit.

At first those intellectuals who ventured into the world of culture for its own sake did so hesitantly and usually anonymously for fear of public censure. The most reticent were those who chose to write in Yiddish, the colloquial spoken language of Eastern European Jewry, but those who wrote in Hebrew, the language of prayer and the written language of letters, or in one of the co-territorial languages, such as Russian and Polish, were also wary of public opinion. Nokhem Meyer Shaykevitch, who in the late 1870s signed his first Yiddish novella under the pseudonym "Shomer," continued to use the appellation long after his identity was revealed. Through the more than 200 novels and stories Shomer published in Yiddish, he came to epitomize the type of *shund* (trash) literature that flooded the reading market. When in 1864 Sholem Yankev Abramovitsh (1835–1917) decided to publish his first novella, *Dos kleyne mentshele* (The Little Man), he was concerned that publishing in Yiddish for a mass readership would tarnish his growing reputation as a serious Hebrew man of letters, so he presented the novella as the work of Mendele Moykher Sforim (Mendele the Book Peddler). By the time Sholem Aleichem elevated Abramovitsh to the status of a national celebrity, proclaiming him the *zeyde Mendele* (grandfather Mendele) of Yiddish literature, Abramovitsh was already known in Yiddish circles simply as Mendele, as he continues to be known today. Sholem Aleichem, for his part, was born Solomon Rabinowitz (1859–1916) but adopted the customary Yiddish greeting Sholem Aleichem (Peace Be Unto You) as a pen name when he began writing in the early 1880s. Over the course of his storied career, Sholem Aleichem became a household name within the world Jewish community. The pen name became so closely associated with the person of the author that his wife would sign her letters "Mrs. Sholem Aleichem," and when the writer died in New York City his gravestone was marked with the name Sholem Aleichem. Recurring characters in his stories, like Tevye der milkhiker (Tevye the Dairyman) and Menakhem Mendl, came to typify the world of Eastern European Jewry. Other writers adopted folksy names in order to disguise their elite backgrounds and assert populist credentials. Asher Ginzburg was a distinguished community leader and scion of a wealthy Hasidic family when in 1889 he published his "Lo zeh ha-derekh" (This Is Not the Way) under the name Ahad Ha-Am (One of the People). The populist writer and ethnographer Shloyme Zaynvl Rapoport (1863–1920) settled upon the quixotic pseudonym S. An-sky, possibly in part because it has the ring of an anonymous appellation. Those active in the illegal Bund had good reason for disguising their identity: Ayzik Meyer Devenishki (1878-1919), for instance, was known by his party name "Comrade Aron" before adopting A. Vayter as a pseudonym when he started writing for Yiddish periodicals. The Bundist Khayim-Yankl Helfand adopted the name A. Litvak in 1905, after his return to Vilna from Siberian exile.

The practice of adopting pseudonyms became so common that we can assume that those who used their given names did so in a conscious effort to expose themselves to public opinion. Historian and cultural activist Simon Dubnow (1860–1941) began writing Russian-language articles anonymously in 1880 before experimenting with the pseudonyms S. Mstislavskii,

Externus, Kritkus, and a few variations of his initials. In 1889, though, he began consistently using his given name for the publication of scholarly articles, although he retained Kritikus for his literary reviews. In the early 1890s, Dubnow began asserting himself as a public intellectual by calling for the collection of Jewish historical documents and the redefinition of Jewish historical understanding. His ambitious "Letters on Old and New Judaism," which he began publishing in 1897, helped establish him as an original thinker. In these articles, Dubnow chose to use his given name as a deliberate attempt to enter the public sphere as a genuine interlocutor willing to take responsibility for his words. Yitskhok Leybush Peretz is rare among Jewish writers of his age in that he never adopted a pseudonym, using his given name from his earliest publications in both Hebrew and Yiddish. His short stories in Hasidic style and fables with socialist morals earned him a reputation as one of the leading Yiddish writers of his day. Peretz merged his literary work with public activism, holding court for young writers at his Warsaw home and openly advocating on the public stage for his pet projects, including the promotion of Yiddish literature and theater, Jewish music, and relief work. Peretz's support helped launch the careers of numerous writers, including the roommates Sholem Asch (1880–1957), Hersh Dovid Nomberg (1876–1927) and Avrom Reyzen (1876–1953). Hayim Nahman Bialik (1873–1934) also used his given name throughout his career. His first poem, "Al ha-tsipor" (To the Bird), was published in 1892 and earned him a reputation as a talented Hebrew poet. His 1903 epic poem "Be-ir ha-haregah" (In the City of Slaughter), about the recent Kishinev pogrom, was widely interpreted as a call for action and attack on Jewish passivity. From Odessa, where he lived from 1900 until 1922, Bialik was widely acclaimed as the Hebrew national poet. Whether they chose to use their given names or pseudonyms, all these figures shared a desire to stimulate public engagement with culture and to elevate the status of secular culture within the Jewish community. Those who openly presented themselves with full accountability to the public, though, could claim to be acting as modern citizens as well.

Voluntary Associations and the Public Sphere

Theoretical understandings of the public engagement with culture through voluntary associations have been greatly enriched by the writings of Jürgen Habermas. Habermas's inquiries into the institutions of early modern bourgeois society, particularly newspapers, salons, coffeehouses, and theaters, suggest some ways that cultural associations have impacted the public sphere. The notion of the public sphere, he writes, "may be conceived above all as the sphere of private people come together as a public"[13] or as "a realm of our social life in which something approaching public opinion can be formed."[14] The institutionalized *idea* of the public sphere—not to be confused with the more complex reality—is characterized by organized and ongoing dialogues regarding matters of common concern that are commoditized in such a way as to become accessible and general. The concept of the public sphere urges historians to look anew at the importance of voluntary associations as formative institutions in the modernization process.

Certainly the application of the concept to an autocratic polity like the Russian Empire is problematic.[15] No sphere of public debate in imperial Russia was empowered by the fundamental legal rights—the infrastructure of a civil society—that necessarily presage the formation of an autonomous public sphere capable of producing free and unconstrained public debate. Even after the October Manifesto of 1905 guaranteed freedom of assembly in theory, the state continued to regulate and interfere with voluntary association in profound ways. Yet the realignment of public life that voluntary associations produced was probably the most noticeable change generated by the Revolution of 1905. Voluntary associations dedicated to the spread and dissemination of cultural activities took the initiative in modernizing Russian culture, at times bringing the culture of Russia in tune with contemporary middle-class customs in Western Europe and at other times resisting the allure of bourgeois values. These developments profoundly influenced the subsequent development of Russian culture and society.[16] Numerous case studies of select organizations and organizational modes within the late Russian Empire have found the language of the public sphere to be instructive, at the same time recognizing the complex social, cultural, and political forces underpinning the era.[17] Despite imperial Russia's lack of an autonomous civil society, it certainly had a lively participatory public life, often with a political impulse.

As Habermas's critics have pointed out, even the eighteenth-century bourgeoisie was constrained by self-censorship, social mores, and access. In essence, there has never been a truly unconstrained public sphere, only greater and lesser degrees of constraint.[18] Historians have often pointed to the exclusivity of the eighteenth-century public sphere from which the notion of civil society originated. They have shown that the public sphere was always restricted on the basis of class, gender, ethnicity, and a multiplicity of other variables.[19] The public sphere, these historians have contended, should be viewed more as an arena of conflict and negotiation where numerous public spheres compete for space. Thus they have posited either a multiplicity of public spheres, each acting according to its own interests, or a "spatialization" of the public sphere, a space actors can enter and exit at will. The public sphere then becomes an arena open not only to bourgeois men but also to other groups, each of whom are able to express their own distinct interests while simultaneously acting as members of society in general.

One of the first scholars to study Jewish communal institutions in the Russian Empire was Isaac Levitats, who examined fifty-two statutes and reports of Jewish voluntary associations as well as thirty-three minute books of *khevres,* brotherhoods sanctioned by the Jewish communal authorities, from the late nineteenth and early twentieth centuries. Levitats noted correctly the correlation between the new voluntary associations and the older *khevres* but emphasized the distinctions between the two rather than the continuities. "The essential difference between the *hevrah* [sic] and the new association," he wrote, "was that the one was heaven directed, the other earth directed; the benefits of the first were largely spiritual, while those of the second were practical. From this flowed another difference: the *hevrah* [sic] was monolithic whereas the association was of different types."[20] Levitats's stark differentiation indicates the degree to which the association was conceived by its members as a radical departure from the confines of formal and traditional communal institutions. Yet it is overly simplistic to view the voluntary association as simply the heir of the *khevre.* The two forms of sociability coexisted and overlapped in membership, merely serving different needs of the community.[21] Christoph Gassenschmidt provides a more detailed consideration of the role that voluntary associations played in modernization. He sees the interrevolutionary development of Jewish cooperative movements and vocational training institutes as "major breaches into the traditional Jewish world" and "indicators of a rapidly modernizing Jewish society."[22]

Jewish Modernity

The role that parochial ethnic and national identities play in modern multinational state structures has been the subject of much recent thinking. Despite its general association with the elite aesthetics of the Central European metropolises, modern public culture was represented by far more than avant-garde secessionist movements, risqué cabaret, and atonal musical experimentation. It also had a revolutionary impact on the ways that common people interacted with each other in the public arena, enjoyed their newfound leisure time, and conceived of themselves and their roles in society. Certainly different individuals experienced modernity in a variety of ways, depending on their place of residence, social status, religious and ethnic identification, gender, and personal inclination. But there are also meaningful commonalities in the experiences of modernity. At least in the major urban centers of Europe, modernity brought increased personal mobility (both in the ways that individuals physically navigated around the city and to the city and in the ease with which individuals could migrate between occupations, professions, and even social status), innovative technologies, improved literacy, shifting social and cultural mores, mounting political engagement, and new conceptions of time and leisure.

Another commonality within modernity was the position of Jews in conceptions of modernity, whether by their actual participation or merely by evoking that participation. Throughout Europe, the Jewish Question was—and continues to be—somehow central to any discussion of modernity. Whether the Jews are conceived of as being central to the modern project or merely incidental, it is difficult to discount—for better or for worse—some relationship between Jews and modernity.[23]

It has often been noted that one of the reasons Jews contributed to the modernist movement in the ways they did was because they alone among urban intellectuals were barred from participating in the conventional arenas of public debate—universities, government bureaucracies, municipal councils, private clubs, and parliaments. Instead, they were forced into alternative public spaces, such as cafés, theaters, libraries, and informal circles that were not bound by the conventions of tradition. It was within these liminal spaces—which were beyond the reach and often under the radar of aristocratic and confessional authorities—that the secular and individualist notions of the modern began. Like George Simmel's "Stranger," European Jews were able to see the modern world from a new vantage point—that of the outsider. This point of view differed significantly in Berlin, Vienna, Budapest, Munich, and St. Petersburg, but each of these metropolises shared a cosmopolitan composition and outlook and each experienced the impact of innovative technologies—faster motion, increased mobility, newfound time for leisure, and, in the eyes of many, a greater proclivity to decadence. One could hardly live in these cities without witnessing the profound transformations and in the process be transformed oneself.

But in the Jewish shtetls of the Russian Empire, outside the European metropolises where an emergent bourgeois class defined political values and transformed the public sphere in its image, modernity was more difficult to discern.[24] In fact, the obsession that many had—and continue to have—with equating Jews and modernity was accompanied by a countervailing tendency among Jewish intellectuals to heap scorn on their own community for its perceived failure to modernize and keep pace with its non-Jewish counterparts. Whereas many among Russian society at large saw the Jews as agents of modernity, Jews themselves were more likely to express exasperation and shame at what they saw as the backwardness of the shtetl.[25]

The Yiddish daily newspaper *Der fraynd* (The Friend), for instance, reported that the need to coordinate activities among educational institutions was discussed at a 3 January 1908 conference of cultural activists from the capital and the provinces. Among the topics on the agenda was the need to integrate art into education and to spread the message that art was not just for elites but also for the masses. This message resonated with Jewish activists, and the Jewish press would play an integral role in promoting it. As the article proclaimed, "Speakers represented all the peoples of Russia up to the absolute smallest—Kalmyks, Kirgiz, Tatars, Buriats, and Yakuts from Siberia, even the Votiaks and Cheremish were not forgotten. . . . Only one group was forgotten—the Jews."[26] This sense of inferiority and of being left behind in the great national awakening was at least partially responsible for motivating the Jewish community to legitimize cultural activity among its members.

That is not to say, however, that the shtetl had ever been somehow hermetically sealed from the impact of modernity.[27] Despite the static portrayal of shtetl life propagated in American popular culture, whether in the simple old-worldness of Broadway's Tevye, Marc Chagall's fantastical paintings, or Mark Zborowski and Elizabeth Herzog's classic anthropological study *Life Is with People: The Culture of the Shtetl,* Russian Jewish society was if not wholly modern in terms of technological access then at least modernizing in terms of societal organization and thought. Although he is more often portrayed as a nostalgic product of a world gone by or as a simpleton whose ardent faith and naiveté epitomize the Old World, Sholem Aleichem's Tevye—the quintessential shtetl Jew—actually wrestles with feelings of personal and social alienation wrought by the introduction of modern ideas into the shtetl. In his personal anxiety, he bears a greater resemblance to the archetype of the angst-ridden, alienated victim of urban modernity—Kafka's Joseph K—than Broadway or Hollywood would care to admit. Chagall's "House in Vitebsk," which graces the cover of the1962 Schocken Paperback edition of Zborowski and Herzog's book, also power-fully demonstrates the impact of modernity on Chagall's native Vitebsk. The famous image of a horse and cart floating through the sky alludes to the movement and mobility the modern age facilitated, while the charm-ing home it leaves behind presages nostalgia for a world that was already perceived to have been left in the past.[28]

Jewish Public Culture in a Multinational Empire

Philosopher Charles Taylor has argued that when cultural homogeni-zation and institutional modernization challenge national difference, the public sphere emerges as a "space for recognition."[29] Within this space, individuals should be recognized not only as individuals per se but also as members of those groups with which they identify, including national entities. To deny individuals a national identification is to deny them an integral aspect of identity. Collective rights, which many liberal thinkers believe accompany individual rights, can be asserted in a variety of forms, ranging from full self-government to public cultural recognition. Identity politics—to use a modern term—need not be completely submerged by the public sphere.[30]

By the early twentieth century, a group of Jewish activists had come to a similar realization. In his "Letters on Old and New Judaism," Simon Dubnow called upon Jews to demand both individual civil rights and collec-tive national rights in their countries of residence. As Dubnow explained, the Jews do not require territorial sovereignty, either in Palestine or in the Diaspora. Their national identity, based on spiritual and cultural affini-ties, is of a higher type than that of nations whose identities rely upon territorial possession. "Political or territorial independence of the Jews in every country, as we have seen, is impossible," he wrote. "The conversation should be only about national-spiritual independence; that is about our attempts to preserve and develop our native originality in the spirit of our historical evolution, our religious, communal and educational institutions, our language and our literature."[31] Dubnow, one of the most articulate spokespeople for Jewish nationalism, imagined Jewish autonomy not in terms of territorial sovereignty or a nation-state but rather in terms of a collective cultural and spiritual identity realized in a delimited space within a multinational public sphere. Multiculturalism in this manifestation is about place and standing, or visibility within the larger society. Thus, "cultural nationalism" can be polycentric, individualistic, and liberal, allowing for choice and acceptance of difference. Like modern proponents of liberal nationalism or cultural difference, Dubnow and many Jewish activists of late-tsarist Russia believed that national cultural development is compatible with civil society and can take place within a public sphere. The development of national consciousness and collective identity need not be the exclusive domain of clandestine political parties and elite intellectuals, they argued, but rather can take place legally and openly through cultural activity. They believed that by encouraging the formation of institutions of public culture, Russian Jewry could transform itself from a confessional estate into a secular nation despite the legal and political impediments to full civic emancipation. In concrete terms, this meant the right to use one's own languages and form one's own distinct learned societies, schools, journals, newspapers, and other institutions of public culture.

Dubnow's conception of liberal nationalism was shared by Ahad Ha-Am, Martin Buber, and others who sought to harness the this-world-niks' love of life for the collective benefit of the nation.[32] Buber and other "cultural Zionists" had been filling the pages of the Zionist weekly *Die Welt* with articles encouraging the formation of groups of Jewish artists and patrons capable of establishing stable institutions and a unified Jewish cultural community. In his formative article "Gegenwartsarbeit" ("Work in the Present"), Martin Buber wrote, "We see the essence and the soul of the movement in the transformation of the people's existence, in the education of a truly new generation, in the development of the Jewish tribe into a strong, unified, independent, healthy, and mature community."[33] Whereas for Buber all Gegenwartsarbeit was in preparation for eventual emigration to Palestine, the primary proponent of cultural development within the Diaspora for its own sake was Dubnow, whose theory of autonomism was formulated most elaborately in his "Letters on Old and New Judaism." In his fourth letter, structured as a polemic against cultural Zionist activists Max Nordau and Ahad Ha-Am, Dubnow wrote, "A spiritual nation demands spiritual-national rights: recognized communal autonomy, the right to have its own special social or educational institutions (such as parochial schools with instruction in their native language and literature) and the general right to original internal development."[34] Both the "spiritual cultural Zionism" of Buber and the "spiritual nationalism" of Dubnow concentrated on cultural work: reform of education, renewal of social institutions, economic betterment, and the promotion of literary and artistic creativity. Although there were numerous differences in how exactly these were envisioned, Buber, Dubnow, Ahad Ha-Am, and other cultural nationalists all regarded the development of a public culture as at least as important (if not more so) than political activity alone. As Dubnow wrote in what would become the platform of his Diasporist Folkspartay:

> We must leave aside the tedious politics of waiting; waiting for civil equality, for the enlightenment of the anti-Semites, or for the good will of the Turkish sultan. Our program is a program of action, of persistent day-to-day and often-unacknowledged work on ourselves, and at the same time a feasible battle for our human and national rights that can actually be won. Every effort in the present is a step toward the future. Every local organization provides strength to our national movement, every institution that supports our legal autonomy, every school imbued with the Jewish national spirit, every new circle for the study of Jewish language, history and literature—each brings us closer by one step to an internal renaissance. This great national-cultural work has already begun, but it has not yet been given a universal and defined plan.[35]

The types of cultural activity Dubnow and Buber promoted differed in many respects from those that the "this-worldniks" enjoyed, but by sanctioning cultural activity as a legitimate and worthy path toward spiritual and national self-realization, both transmitted modern secular European values to the Jewish community, stimulated the formation of institutions of public culture, such as schools, learned societies, journals, and newspapers, and validated Jewish life in this world. Public recognition in Dubnow's model, then, is predicated on cultural expression.

Jews in the Russian Empire participated in the project of constructing a public culture in conjunction with numerous groups around the world, each of which sought recognition in its respective public spheres. By the beginning of the Great War, cultural distinctness was becoming one of the primary means of asserting group identity and claiming collective rights. As Dubnow, Buber, and Ahad Ha-Am predicted, national sovereignty was becoming increasingly dependent on cultural production, and cultural production (as well as consumption) was becoming increasingly institutionalized, mediated by cultural organizations such as theaters, libraries, and learned societies.[36]

The Russian Legal and Political Context

Throughout the early nineteenth century, freedom of assembly was severely limited in Russia; formation of any private association was forbidden unless it was personally authorized by the tsar himself. The only allowable institutions were confessional and corporate societies within the structure of existing communities. In the Jewish case, these took the form of *khevres,* which were operated and administered by the *kahal* (Jewish communal authority) as a whole. Although the *kahal* was officially abolished by an 1844 law, the community retained several legal responsibilities, thereby necessitating that some of its institutional framework be retained. Every Jewish community needed a *khevre kedishe* (burial society) in order to bury its dead, and most also had a *khevre lines tsedek* to visit and assist the sick, a *khevre koyne sforim* to purchase holy books for the study hall, a *khevre mishnayes* or *shas* to study Jewish law communally, occupational *khevres* to function as Jewish guilds, and often many others. The formation of private organizations outside the corporate structure of the formal Jewish community, however, was forbidden without special dispensations. In Poland, even the *khevre* itself was proscribed in 1822, and the 1844 law formally disbanding the *kahal* placed the status of *khevres* in judicial limbo. Nonetheless, in both Russia and Poland, they continued to function, providing integral institutional infrastructure to the Jewish community.

Freedom of association remained anathema to the tsarist authorities throughout the century. Even the Great Reforms of the 1860s and 1870s, which among other things emancipated the peasantry, instituted universal conscription, reformed the judiciary, and allowed for the creation of *zemstvos* (elected regional diets), failed to alleviate the most noxious restrictions on freedom of assembly. They did, however, allow for the formation of select associations deemed to serve the interests of the state provided that their charters were approved by the relevant ministry. The most important Jewish voluntary association formed during the period of the Great Reforms was undoubtedly the Society for the Spread of Enlightenment among the Jews of Russia (Obshchestvo dlia rasprostraneniia prosveshcheniia mezhdu evreiami v Rossii, OPE). Formed in St. Petersburg in 1863 with the ostensible goal of spreading enlightened ideals among the Jews of Russia, in its early years the OPE sought to convince the Jewish community to acculturate itself into Russian society by adopting the Russian language and abandoning the most parochial of Jewish practices and customs. The leaders of the OPE hoped that ultimately such reforms would persuade the authorities to extend civil rights to the Jews.

The largely patrician leaders of the organization embarked upon this goal by funding and sponsoring educational endeavors (including providing scholarships for Jewish students to study at Russian universities) and assisting in the establishment and maintenance of Jewish elementary- and secondary-level educational institutions that taught the Russian language. The OPE also supported the publication of Russian-language pedagogical materials. Toward the end of the century, the membership of the OPE expanded into wider circles of the intelligentsia, and the organization began to embark upon broader cultural programs in Hebrew as well as Russian. Among the programs it supported was the Jewish Historical Committee, which would evolve into the Jewish Historical and Ethnographic Society. Toward the beginning of World War I, the OPE further expanded both its membership base—it established some thirty branches throughout the empire—and its activities. Acting as an umbrella organization for numerous advocacy groups, the OPE began to accept Yiddish as a legitimate language of enlightened expression and began funding even broader cultural activities, such as libraries. The OPE's activities, however, were always constrained by both the watchful eyes of the tsarist police and the conservative leanings of its elitist leadership.[37]

In the four decades after the Great Reforms, the state came to rely increasingly on private initiatives to meet the humanitarian and economic needs of the population. Voluntary associations, often attached to the *zemstvos,* took the lead in bringing doctors, teachers, and agrarian scientists to the countryside, and private philanthropic associations provided much-needed relief after the famine of 1891. At the same time, changing work habits and home life allowed a growing middling class and aspiring bourgeoisie to partake of leisure activities, while the simultaneous increased concentration of people in urban centers facilitated the creation of cultural institutions designed to accommodate larger publics. The state's legislature did not enact a comprehensive legal code governing voluntary associations until after the 1905 Revolution, but in the waning years of the nineteenth century, the Ministry of Internal Affairs issued a series of regulations codifying the treatment of the growing number of societies. Even these regulations, which aimed to decentralize authority over voluntary associations, did little to alleviate the bureaucratic and legal impediments to their formation and operation. The Ministry of Internal Affairs gave local authorities the right to permit voluntary associations to be established, provided that the association submitted a charter for advance approval. Local authorities also retained the right to close down any society conducting activities that were not envisioned and articulated in its charter. Central and local authorities could also liquidate societies that "appear dangerous to the well-being of the state or the moral direction of society," as the 1899 legal code stated.[38] All associations were also required to obtain prior approval from local authorities for all public activities (lectures, performances, etc.), even when such activities were included within already-approved statutes. These laws left ample room for local officials to intervene at will to harass individuals and societies with which they disagreed or about which they had suspicions. Despite these impediments, within two years, there were thousands of voluntary associations throughout the empire.[39]

In the chaos of the turbulent revolutionary years 1904–1905, even the restrictions of earlier regulations were blatantly ignored and voluntary associations proliferated, many with explicit political programs and demands. Spurred on by Russian military difficulties in the war with Japan and perceptions that Nicholas II was politically incompetent, discontented elements of the Russian population pursued a wide array of means to bring about political reform. Savvy political actors had begun forming oppositional political organizations in the last years of the nineteenth century. The zem-stvos served as central sites of political party formation in the early years of the twentieth century. Their role in gathering people who were developing professional identities apart from their estate origins was crucial in the formation of a "third element" with liberal views and demands. The liberal intelligentsia and professional classes, though, were forced to confront not only the tsarist autocracy but also a variety of opposition groups. The greatest threat was posed by the peasant-based Socialist Revolutionaries, who sought the confiscation of noble estates and redistribution of land to the peasantry. The two major Social Democratic parties—the Mensheviks and the Bolsheviks—would have to wait another decade for their moment in the sun.[40]

On Sunday, 9 January 1905, a group of peaceful protestors marched to the Winter Palace to call for the convocation of a representative assembly, equality for all before the law, and freedom of assembly, press, and speech. The protestors were met with lethal gunfire that killed 130 and wounded nearly 300. The government's resort to violence in the face of a relatively calm protest unleashed a wave of unrest that lasted for over two years and eventually forced the hand of autocracy. The most immediate result of Bloody Sunday was a breakdown of governmental authority. Labor unrest, peasant rebellions, urban hooliganism, student demonstrations, soldier mutinies, national insurrections, and anti-Jewish pogroms all contributed to the breakdown of authority during this turbulent period. Labor and student unrest continued over the summer and fall, culminating in the October general strike that stalled the railways, thereby preventing the regime from demobilizing soldiers to Manchuria, let alone mobilizing the force needed to quell the rebellion. The strikes compelled the tsar to issue his October Manifesto, which allowed for a Duma (assembly) of elected representatives and promised freedom of association, press, and speech.

The October Manifesto was met with excitement and trepidation. For the Jews of Russia, the manifesto represented a partial realization of their dreams for broader civil rights and the hope that these rights would be extended still further. However, the wave of pogroms that accompanied the manifesto soured the optimism of the Jewish community. As *Der fraynd* noted in its 25 October 1905 edition: "The first days of Russian freedom have become days of sorrow for Russian Jewry. It has been a long while since the Jews in Russia have lived through times as difficult as those accompanying the celebration of Russian freedom."[41]

The exact terms of the tsar's capitulation were not articulated until the following spring, when he issued a revision of the Fundamental Laws of the empire, partially taking into account the new political realities. Published on the eve of the Duma's convocation, these laws retained an altered aristocratic State Council as a counterweight to the Duma and affirmed the tsar's "supreme autocratic power" by providing him with controlling authority over foreign policy and the administration of military and domestic matters as well as legislative veto power and the right to appoint and dismiss ministers. The tsar also reserved the right to dismiss the Duma and declare martial law. Although they were far from allowing full freedom of assembly, the revised Fundamental Laws ended confessional restrictions on the formation of voluntary associations and shifted the requirement of approving charters from local governors to provincial boards.

The 4 March 1906 Temporary Regulations on Societies and Unions was the first legislation to recognize the right of private individuals to form societies without prior approval provided that they submitted a charter of statutes to the Ministry of Internal Affairs in advance. The Ministry of Internal Affairs then had two weeks to object if the society's actions appeared to "threaten social order and peace." Thus, although the society did not need prior approval per se, the ministry was still given the legal opportunity to prevent a society from being formed. Religious organizations and several other categories of societies were excluded from the charter. The regulations created provincial and local boards that were responsible for overseeing the opening, registration, prohibition, and closing of local and provincial societies.[42] These half-measures were sufficient to release pent-up social, political, and cultural activity. Thousands of new learned societies, trade unions, libraries, professional organizations, political parties, consumer and credit cooperatives, and other voluntary associations were formed over the next decade.

Jewish Politics in the Duma

When elections to the Duma were held in the spring of 1906, the liberal Kadets (Constitutional Democrats) received a plurality of votes (largely thanks to the radicals' boycott), allowing them to form a government in alliance with the centrist Trudovik Party. Twelve Jews were elected to the Duma, mostly as members of the ruling Kadets. Among the leaders of the Kadet Party was Maksim Vinaver (1863–1926), who was not only Jewish by birth—as were a number of elites in the Social Democratic parties—but also by sentiment. Vinaver was an active member and leader of numerous Jewish organizations and continued to play a prominent role in the formation of Jewish voluntary associations and the advancement of Jewish public interests. However, his faith in the Duma (and that of many others who believed an elected parliament would be a panacea) was dashed. Despite the Duma's grandiose calls for universal suffrage, civil liberties, and agrarian reform, Prime Minister Ivan Goremykin declined to submit important legislation to the body, forcing it to debate trivial legislation or declare empty platitudes. The Duma also failed to address the Jewish Question—the question of whether civil rights should be extended to the Jews—until it was shocked into action by the Bialystok pogrom of June 1906, which left eighty-two Jews dead and finally galvanized liberal public opinion. The Duma's newfound demands for equal rights resonated within Jewish society. The era of hope, however, was short lived. Before Jewish emancipation could even be debated on the Duma floor, Nicholas disbanded the Duma.[43]

The Second Duma, convened in March 1907, was a great disappointment to the Jewish population. Despite its more left-leaning composition owing to the participation of the radical parties, it counted only four Jewish deputies among its members and showed even less sympathy toward the cause of Jewish emancipation. It too was unable to work within the confines the tsar established, so in a coup d'etat in June 1907, Nicholas disbanded the Second Duma as well. With the Second Duma's dissolution, the tsar also ensured that future dumas would be more cooperative by changing the electoral laws to reduce representation from workers, peasants, and national minorities. The Third Duma, which served a full term, from 1907 to 1912, had only thirty-six non-Russian representatives, of whom only two were Jewish. The coup d'etat of June 1907 ensured that no future duma would be capable of modernizing Russia or ameliorating Jewish political discrimination under the tsarist regime.

Scholars have long seen the duma period of 1905–1907 as a seminal era for Russian political party formation in general and Jewish political activity in particular.[44] In his comprehensive study of Jewish politics in late tsarist Russia, Jonathan Frankel writes of the increase in political activity following the 1905 Revolution that "the Jews felt that there was no escape from the Russian arena, that they had no choice except to participate."[45] Whereas Frankel looks mostly at socialist and Zionist political movements, noting the radicalization of their positions in the post-1905 period, Christoph Gassenschmidt observes similar developments in a splintering and proliferation of Jewish liberal parties. He notes that after the Revolution of 1905, "a Jewish public had come into existence in form of a wide range of Jewish newspapers of various political views," so that "by the end of 1906 the representation of Jewish interests had developed into a kaleidoscope of groups and parties."[46] In the immediate aftermath of 1905, Jewish political actors committed themselves to parliamentary politics. According to Gassenschmidt, "Jewish Liberals perceived the creation of a public space as the opportunity to join the Revolution, and bring forward specific Jewish demands more effectively."[47] The era of political activity, though, was cut off in its infancy.

From Proclamations to Playing Cards

Following the restrictive electoral and parliamentary laws of 1907, many Jewish activists came to believe that parliamentary politics was futile. Those who still believed in political activity found it difficult to be active again. A. Litvak complained that "the masses ran away from the movement, turning the unions and the activists into a joke. . . . The masses suddenly became 'clever.' They became eager for practical things and chased after crass entertainments. They became crude and profligate or gray and indifferent. Dance classes replaced the unions and playing cards replaced proclamations."[48] The most obvious evidence of the disenchantment with political activity among the Jews was the declining membership of Jewish parties.[49] The September 1907 closure of the Jewish Bund's daily newspaper *Folkstsaytung* (People's News) marked for many the beginning of "the years of reaction." Vladimir Medem, who was working at the paper at the time, recalled that

> the reaction began gradually. One cannot say precisely when it began, but every day it felt like things were going further downhill. After the momentous shocks of 1905 and 1906, a great weariness began to set in. All of us who were at the center of the movement felt and saw the various signs. Our finances wore out, organizational life weakened, the number of people we had in our movement fell, the mood became desperate.[50]

The gloomy mood was shared throughout the cultural and political community. "In the year 1908," wrote Sofia Dubnova-Erlikh, Simon's daughter, "there only remained scant vestiges of the earlier achievements. A dark gray cloud hung over Russia."[51] But, she continues, "The years of societal renaissance awakened in the circles of Jewish workers a strong desire to learn, a desire so strong that even the reaction could not extinguish it completely."[52] Having rejected political activity, many Jewish activists and common folk reoriented themselves toward what the Poles called "organic work," or economic, social, and cultural development.[53]

With the state unwilling and unable to help by enacting broad legislation, Jewish activists took it upon themselves to transform their society step by step through the politics of small deeds. Many activists believed that instead of changing their world through parliamentary action or lobbying authorities, inward-directed grassroots activity provided a more hopeful future. Empowered by the March 1906 Temporary Regulations on Societies and Unions, Jews banded together in voluntary associations to build a viable Jewish culture that could withstand political enfeeblement. As one Lodz-based columnist in *Der fraynd* wrote of this period: "Lodz is fertile soil—societies sprout up here like mushrooms."[54] In the words of Dubnow, from 1908 to 1911, "everywhere one noticed public animation; in gatherings everywhere people discussed not only cultural, but also political themes, until the authorities took notice."[55]

At a series of conferences between December 1906 and 1908, diverse groups of Jewish activists with varying political and social goals announced their intentions to dedicate their resources and efforts to legal cultural activity. At its 1908 party congress, the leadership of the Bund agreed to embark upon a "new form" of activity that would eschew illegal political organization in favor of cultural development. The following year, the party encouraged its members to join legal nonpartisan cultural societies and associations.[56] The Bund's resolution echoed a similar decision made by the All-Russian Zionist Organization at its Helsingfors Conference of December 1906, when the organization officially endorsed Buber's program of Gegenwartsarbeit, calling for the promotion of Zionist and Hebrew cultural activity within the Diaspora. The Helsingfors Conference also coincided with the formation of Dubnow's Folkspartay, which sought to secure national minority rights for the Jews in the Diaspora and advocated in its party platform the promotion of Jewish cultural activity.

The most celebrated of these conferences, though, was the Czernowitz Conference in September 1908, when over seventy activists met at the Hotel Bristol, where even the non-Jewish head porter spoke Yiddish, to declare Yiddish a national language of the Jewish people and to advocate the promotion of Yiddish cultural activity. "The Czernowitz conference gave a great stimulus to cultural work on the Jewish street," recalled Dubnova-Erlikh.[57] The following year, at a conference of Jewish activists in Kovno, Bundist representatives proposed a resolution declaring the "satisfaction of the cultural needs of the Jewish masses" to be the "chief goal of the community."[58] Although the resolution was ultimately rejected, it is indicative of how important many activists at the time felt cultural affairs were. Jewish intellectuals had begun to see within Jewish culture a possible source of inspiration and the raw material of national rejuvenation.[59]

It was a culture as well that, first and foremost, was intended to be public. Yiddish theater, which was first performed in the basements of seedy pubs in the 1840s, gradually emerged out of the basement and into outside beer gardens in the 1880s, and then by the first decade of the twentieth century was being performed in imperial theaters in the Russian capital. Jewish musicians were transformed from an outcast group forced to beg on the streets for sustenance into respectable members of a profession, who would perform in modern European suits or even as uniformed members of fire brigade and military orchestras. Jewish historians, originally entrusted with the task of writing apologetics to justify Jewish residence, began to assert proudly a national identity. All shared a fundamental belief in the public expression of Jewish culture and identity.

The writer and ethnographer S. An-sky may have expressed these sentiments best in his highly influential 1908 article "Jewish Folk Creativity." Jewish folklore, he argued, is distinct from that of other nations because it is based on inner feelings and beliefs rather than external entities, it places more emphasis on spiritual achievements than physical heroics, and it is based on the actions of humans rather than divine beings. In other words, it is a folklore of *this* world rather than the next. An-sky's message was clear: Jewish denigration of worldly activities could be offset with a long-standing countervailing tradition of direct engagement with *this* world.[60]

~⊚ 2 ⊚~

Libraries:
From the Study Hall to the Public Library

In 1918, Soviet Yiddish writer Yekhezkl Dobrushin portrayed a scene enacted in cities, towns, and shtetls throughout the Pale as young enthusiasts banded together to establish libraries. "It was not long ago, ten years ago. A small-town young man established a Yiddish library. He brought Mendele, Peretz and Sholem Aleichem to the shtetl for the first time. He outfitted a bookcase and quietly put it under the prayer room (*kloyz*) in the school (*talmud toyre*). Then, like a Passover meal (*seyder*), he had a public celebration (*yontef*) and delivered a holiday sermon (*droshe*): 'Look at the bookcase' a young speaker exclaimed, 'it will be our new Torah case (*orn*), from upstairs in the prayer room the divine spirit (*shkhine*) will come, because the new Jewish Torah' is here."[1] Through his use of religious terminology (*kloyz, seyder, orn, shkhine, Torah, droshe,* and *yontef*), Dobrushin not only highlighted the spiritual role that reading played for the community but also portrayed the new secular library as a surrogate study hall (*besmedresh*). Libraries, in Dobrushin's portrayal, were supplanting traditional life and traditional forms of reading.

Lending libraries are often credited with democratizing culture and ushering in the modern era. Richard Altick was perhaps the first to show that "the democratizing of reading" brought about by the establishment of lending libraries "led to a far-reaching revolution in English culture."[2] Lending libraries, particularly those geared toward the lower classes, opened up whole new worlds to their patrons. This was as true for the turn-of-the-century shtetl as it was for Victorian Britain. Jewish memoirs from the Pale are rife with descriptions of libraries and the transformative role they played in shtetl society. Both leading intellectual luminaries and more common folk tell of how libraries helped open their eyes to a larger world. "It did not take long for several of us small-town more developed youth (of course those of us with talmudic education and religious upbringing) to begin to see for ourselves a new world with entirely different horizons," wrote one.[3] "The small-town folk became familiar with the larger world," wrote Dvoyre Kutnik, whose father ran a small library in Luninets

(Minsk Province). "It opened their eyes and they realized that there is a whole world with problems outside of Luninets and even beyond Pinsk."[4] In the town of Zastavye (Grodno Province), "the crowded little room of the library became [the youths'] own cultural center, their first school; it opened a window for them to the larger world of progress and civilization."[5] In towns still awaiting the arrival of electricity, movie houses, and radio, the library provided one of the only windows to the outside world. If modernity was characterized by speed, noise, crowds, and secularism, most Jews in the Russian Empire were far from modern. Aside from the railroad, most of the physical manifestations of modernity may have been absent, but the library provided a glimpse into the world of the modern as seen from the perspective of Dickens's London, Hugo's Paris, Schnitzler's Vienna, and Dostoevsky's Petersburg. Like most Europeans, they experienced the modern age vicariously but passionately.

Precedents: Reading Circles, Private Libraries, Clandestine Libraries, Book Peddlers, and Teahouses

The first Jewish libraries maintained by public funds were storehouses of religious texts collected in the *besemedresh* (plural of *besmedresh*) of the synagogues and yeshivas that could be found in every Jewish settlement. Since at least medieval times, wealthy Jews had been encouraged to donate books to the synagogue. By the seventeenth and eighteenth centuries, significant libraries were attached to Jewish schools in several Italian cities as well as in Salonica, Smyrna, and Amsterdam. Polish and Lithuanian study halls had basic book collections by the eighteenth century, and in the nineteenth century Jewish societies for the acquisition and preservation of books existed in several Polish towns. Galician *maskil* Joseph Perl wrote of these libraries that "there is no Jewish community in Galicia that does not have one or more study hall, prayer hall, and synagogue, in which can be found collections of important books, organized in open cabinets, and to which everybody in the community, including the youth, has free and complete access. . . . There are books there that have not even been checked by the censors."[6] Citing Perl's words, Jewish historian, former rector of Hebrew University, and former Israeli Supreme Court justice Simha Assaf declared on behalf of all Jews: "We can be proud of this, that we were the first to establish public libraries in every city and township."[7] Although the *besmedresh* libraries were invariably closed to women and probably had more modest collections than those envisioned by Assaf, these libraries certainly served a role similar to that of modern public libraries for their constituents.[8]

In the last quarter of the nineteenth century and at the turn of the twentieth, freethinking young Talmud students began smuggling into the *besemedresh* of the yeshivas the new literature of the Haskalah. Khayim Rabinovitsh of Derechin (Grodno Province) recalled of the first years of the twentieth century:

> In those days, suddenly among the newly arrived bookworms (*prushim*) in our *besmedresh* there appeared a certain type of youth who would hide various profane books under the Talmud on his stand. I remember one of these bookworms, a relative of Rabbi Leyb Luner, a young man, a child prodigy, who brought to Derechin all kinds of Hebrew books and Russian journals. . . . From time to time he chatted with us about worldly and scientific things and would give us one of his books to read.[9]

In the Lithuanian town of Mir, a group of young enlightened thinkers who had left the city's famed yeshiva formed their own secret library in the late 1890s. To avoid applying for a permit, the founders of the library camouflaged their institution as a bookstore, even putting false stamps in the first books.[10] The disenchanted yeshiva student who immersed himself in secular literature instead of the talmudic study in which he was supposed to be engaged is one of the most common motifs in Yiddish and Hebrew *maskilic* literature and memoirs. As Avrom Reyzen put it, "Among the poor yeshiva students there could always be found one or two young men with a zest for life for whom Talmud study was only for show; in the *besmedresh* they used to read worldly books or would study the Russian language instead."[11] Most of those who came upon secular literature in the late nineteenth and early twentieth centuries did so through a system of mentorship. These mentors often evolved into proprietors of lending libraries as their circles of influence expanded, rippling through the local yeshiva.

In his autobiographical *Hat'ot Ne'urim* (Sins of Youth), S. An-sky described his role in establishing such a circle. He would arrive in a new town and play the part of a pious teacher in order to make a living, but the aspiring youth of the village nevertheless "understood immediately, I was not as pious as I made out, and wordlessly, but with expressive glances, they hinted that they wanted to establish contact with me. . . . After the first two boys, others also so idealistically inclined came. Soon they formed a peculiar club of six or seven. They usually assembled at my place Fridays late at night when the town slept soundly: the visits were so furtive and conspiratorial, the discussion conducted so quietly, that for the several months I was in the town no one learned of these meetings. When I became better acquainted with my comrades and became convinced that they could be trusted, I began to lend them my secret books, even the most precious and most dangerous, *Sins of Youth*."[12] The autobiography of the *maskil* Mosheh Leib Lilienblum, *Sins of Youth,* became such a formative text in both An-sky's life and the lives of those in his circle that he borrowed its title for his own autobiography. These informal circles in which like-minded individuals met—often in secret—to share ideas and later to share books were common sources of early lending libraries in Russia.

Around the country, students formed small reading groups and lending libraries in private residences, where they freed themselves from the exclusive study of canonical Jewish literature and exposed themselves instead to the writings of the Russian intelligentsia or the Jewish *maskilim*. Mikhal Rubensteyn wrote of Ivenets (Minsk Province) that "the shtetl was far from a train and from a large city. Besides the *kheyders* there were no educational institutions in the shtetl, so the youth decided to educate themselves. In the evenings, they would meet in the attic of Ber-Yesheyhu Rabinovitsh's house, where they would read newspapers and books in Yiddish, Russian or Hebrew and have discussions on various themes."[13] Most of these clubs remained small in scale. In the lending library Avrom Kotik helped establish in the 1880s—this time at a Warsaw gymnasium rather than a shtetl yeshiva—a group of mostly Jewish students pooled their books and lent out volumes to others. The library was kept in one student's room, and a large table with chairs was set up as a reading room and seminar room.[14] Whether under the guidance of mentors or through their own initiative, growing numbers of students in both religious and secular institutions were clubbing together for the purpose of sharing, distributing, and discussing literature.

The more daring ventured into the large municipal Russian libraries, where they immersed themselves in the literary climate of the Russian intelligentsia. In the late 1870s, Dubnow discovered in the Mogilev public library the writings of nihilist Dmitri Pisarev and radical writer Nikolai Dobroliubov.[15] Yitskhok Leybush Peretz recalled his first visit to the city library of Zamość (Lublin Province), held in the attic of a house near the castle. He portrayed his entrance into the secular library as crossing a divide between the Jewish and Gentile worlds: "One doesn't just suddenly rush from the Jewish to the Gentile *besmedresh,*" he wrote.[16] Here again, the secular municipal public library is imagined in Jewish terms as a *besmedresh*. His description of the visit is rife with biblical imagery, borrowing in one case the image of the pillar of cloud and pillar of fire that led the biblical Israelites through the desert to the Land of Israel:

> I forced myself to step over the threshold. Sweat formed on my brow. This was a strange house to me. No Jews lived here, maybe by happenstance, or perhaps because of its proximity to the castle. The house was new—at that time the newest—and had a lit stairwell, which was at that time the only lit stairwell in the city. I climbed up. A good sign—a lit path. So I climbed in light. One floor, then the second—a landing to the attic. The daylight was extinguished. I became a little uneasy. But, "None who go to her come back." [Proverbs 2:19] There was no return. . . . The pillar of cloud! The pillar of fire! Both guide through the desert! I turned the key. A grinding noise in the old lock and my heart trembled. Yet the door was already open. I tore open the shutters and I was in "their" *besmedresh*.[17]

Metaphors of light, freedom, and life permeated his description of the municipal library, which he contrasted with the dark and dank *besmedresh*. Peretz's description of the public library contrasts starkly with Feierberg's fictional account of the traditional *besmedresh*: "He comes to the *besmedresh*. The shadows of the night have not yet disappeared completely from the hall. The lecterns are black, scattering darkness. The corners are full of shadows, and out of this shadow, from one of the corners, a dark form moves, and a soft and sad voice trembling in the silent air disturbs the awesome stillness and fills the house with dark sorrow."[18] In *maskilic* Jewish lore, the darkness of the *besmedresh* was often contrasted with the shining light of the public library.

Proponents and supporters of the new library movement were also always quick to make the comparison between the old *besmedresh* and the new public library, viewing the latter as a natural successor to the former. In his plea for the establishment of Jewish public libraries, Avrom Kotik called for new secular books to be treated with the same reverence and respect accorded to holy books. "The old book, the *seyfer*, has its own library that has already existed for some hundreds of years; every *besmedresh* is a library. The new book, the book that is not only for the learned, but also for the common Jew; the book that is not religious but secular, this book still does not have its own resting place. There are not yet suitable places where these books can be collected and preserved with love."[19]

Jews often constituted a majority of the members of libraries funded by public organizations and a majority of readers in municipal libraries. For instance, in 1905, 87 percent of readers at the Pushkin municipal library of Bobruisk (Minsk Province) were Jewish, even though the total Jewish population of the city was only around 20 percent.[20] The library of Gomel had 1,588 readers in 1903, only 27 of whom were not Jewish.[21] These Jewish majorities could sometimes use their influence to establish Jewish sections within the municipal library. In 1902, the Jewish community of Oster (Chernigov Province) requested assistance from the OPE in establishing a Judaica section in the local *zemstvo* library.[22] In April 1903, the general assembly of the municipal public library of Kharkov voted to establish a Jewish section, "despite the shrill outbursts of some homespun anti-Semites." The 25,000 Jews of the city, where there was no other Jewish lending library, could borrow books from the municipal library for the regular fee or use its reading room for free. A commission of local Jewish students, teachers, "doctors, and their wives" was established to oversee the Jewish section.[23]

Jews were not always able to take advantage of Russian lending libraries established in the 1890s. Typically, these libraries tended to be subscription libraries that charged between 25 and 50 kopeks a month plus deposits of 1–3 rubles. Further, they rarely held books in Yiddish; the few libraries that were free were for the most part prohibited by law from doing so. Hostile librarians or officials could also make the municipal library an unwelcome place for Jewish readers. As of 1906, the Jewish community of Shavli (Kovno Province) had been unsuccessful in persuading the management of the Pushkin library to establish a Jewish section.[24] In some cases, Jewish membership on the library board was limited by official fiat. When the city of Brest-Litovsk (Grodno Province) received permission to establish a library in 1904, for instance, the permission was contingent upon an emendation to the library's statutes that would limit Jewish membership on the governing board to a maximum of one-third, even though the vast majority of those who drew up the petition were Jewish.[25] Perhaps this was one of the factors that led to the establishment of a parochial Jewish library in the city, which by 1908 had 693 members (519 men and 179 women) who each paid a 15-kopek monthly membership fee.[26]

Other readers obtained their books from the libraries of private individuals who opened their doors to the public, or at least parts of the public. These private lending libraries (*chastnaia publichnaia biblioteka,* or *biblioteka dlia chtenia*) modeled themselves on the reading rooms many booksellers established in the back of their stores throughout Moscow and St. Petersburg in the first two decades of the nineteenth century.[27] Within the Jewish community, private libraries had also long been a popular source of enlightenment. Since talmudic times, wealthy Jews had been encouraged to lend out books to students and to make their collections available to the community. Medieval responsa literature is rife with queries about individuals who lend out books, while ethical wills of the period often instructed the estate to lend out the deceased's private library. The twelfth-century *Seyfer khsidim* encourages its readers to "lend books to people who learn Torah for its own sake. Lend books to poor people before lending them to the wealthy."[28] With the advent of printing, private Jewish libraries became more widespread, particularly in the Ottoman Empire, where Hebrew printing flourished.[29]

In nineteenth-century Russia, wealthy Jewish book collectors and *maskilim* often opened their private libraries to the community as a whole or more often to select individuals who shared their literary inclinations. Each of these libraries had its own forte, depending on the interests and caprices of its owner. For instance, the St., Petersburg library of Baron David Gintsburg, one of the richest private Jewish libraries in the world, was known for its collection of medieval Arabic works as well as contemporary French, German, and Italian literature. The library, which Gintsburg opened up to the *maskilic* elite of the capital, was designed to be a showcase of his literary and aesthetic inclinations: "Among the large and tall cases in the large and tall parlors there were in various directions and angles sofas, chairs, and divans, in Amfir style with soft pillows covered in silk and lace. Among the modern, one also noticed exquisite pieces from centuries gone by. Everything in the large parlors where the books could be found reeked of wealth and comfort."[30] One imagines, however, that the design was intended in part to intimidate visitors. The landscape of Gintsburg's library made it clear that it was closed to the common reader.

Osip Mandelstam famously recalled his father's study in similar terms. The study included not just a bookcase, as Mandelstam titled the chapter in which he describes it, but also "a handmade oak armchair bearing the image of a balalaika and a gauntlet and, on its arched back, the motto 'Slow but Sure'—a tribute to the pseudo-Russian style of Alexander III. Then there was a Turkish divan completely overwhelmed with ledgers . . . [and] the penetrating smell of tanned leather; and the webbed kidskins thrown about the floor, and the pudgy chamois skins with excrescences like living fingers—all this, plus the bourgeois writing table with its little marble cal-

endar, swims in a tobacco haze and is seasoned with the smells of leather."
As for the bookcase itself, Mandelstam wrote,

> I always remember the lower shelf as chaotic: the books were not
> standing upright side by side but lay in ruins: reddish five-volume
> works with ragged covers, a Russian history of the Jews written
> in the clumsy, shy language of a Russian-speaking Talmudist. This
> was the Judaic chaos thrown into the dust. . . . Above these Jewish
> ruins there began the orderly arrangement of books; those were the
> Germans—Schiller, Goethe, Kerner, and Shakespeare in German—in
> the old Leipzig and Tübingen editions, chubby like butterballs in
> stamped claret-colored bindings with a fine print calculated for the
> sharp vision of youth and with soft engravings done in a rather classi-
> cal style. . . . All this was my father fighting his way as an autodidact
> into the German world out of the Talmudic wilds. Still higher were my
> mother's Russian books—Pushkin in Isakov's 1876 edition.[31]

In this passage, Mandelstam sought to convey his parents' progression
from the chaos of talmudic modes of reading to the decorum of bourgeois
approaches to world literature. This decorum, though, lay solely with the
art of storing and displaying books and not at all with the act of reading.

Another of the most famous private Jewish libraries in the empire was
that of Matityahu Strashun (1817–1885). The son of Shem'uel Strashun,
Matityahu was a prominent and learned member of the Jewish community
of Vilna, former head of the Central Charity (Ha-Tsedakah ha-Gedolah),
which functioned as the Jewish communal authority in the city, and an
avid bibliophile and book collector. He played an active role in virtually
all aspects of the Jewish community in Vilna, including the founding of
enlightenment schools, the promotion of enlightened book publishing, and
charity works. He even served as a member of the board of the National
Bank in Vilna.[32] His home was a gathering place for the learned members of
the community and a site of pilgrimage for visitors from abroad. When he
died childless, he left his library of over 5,700 volumes to the community.
The library was officially opened in 1892 in Strashun's former home but
was not initially open to the general public. Realizing that the current space
would not suffice, in 1899 the Central Charity decided to build a structure
to house a communal library, which would include all the books from the
Strashun collection as well as other books that it henceforth acquired. The
library was registered in the name of the rabbis and officials of the Central
Charity and was authorized to hold books in Russian, Hebrew, Yiddish, and

German; it was forbidden only to hold books in Polish, owing to continued tsarist anti-polonization campaigns.[33] The library was open to the general public every day (including the Sabbath and holidays, but not the High Holidays) and was funded by the Central Charity. The new library building was completed in 1901. At its official dedication on 14 April 1902, a choir sang Psalm 30, the hymn in honor of the dedication of Solomon's Temple, and the hymn "Ma Tovu" ("How Goodly"), which was traditionally recited upon entering the synagogue.[34] The hymn begins with the refrain "How godly are your tents, O Jacob, your dwelling places, O Israel. As for me, through Your abundant kindness I will enter Your house. I will prostrate myself toward Your Holy Sanctuary in awe of You. O Lord I love the House where You dwell and the place where Your glory resides." The repeated references, both explicit and implicit, to the Temple could hardly have been lost on the gathered crowd. If small-scale libraries, like that portrayed in Dobrushin's story, were imagined as surrogate *besemedresh* and syna-gogues, then the great Strashun Library of Vilna could only be likened to God's own Temple.

The success of the library was facilitated by its exceptional director, Khaykl Lunski, who served in that capacity from 1895 until the library's destruction by the Nazis in 1941. Lunski was an Orthodox Lithuanian Jew who had studied at both the Slonim and Mir yeshivas and was at ease in both Orthodox and secular circles in the Vilna Jewish community. In addi-tion to serving as the Strashun librarian, he was also a collector of folklore, collecting primarily stories about the famous rabbis of Vilna and the Jewish neighborhoods of the city.[35] Lunski's writings on the library convey the dual role the library served, straddling (like Lunski himself) the traditional sacred realm of Torah and the modern world of scientific knowledge: "On a Jewish street," he wrote, "on the courtyard near the large synagogue there stands a two-storied house. This house is the temple of the spirit, the palace of wisdom, the pride of Vilna. Young and old, learned and wise, writers and scientists, are drawn to this house to acquire from it Torah and knowledge. This house is the Vilna Jewish community library of the great learned and wise man Matityahu Strashun."[36] These sentiments were echoed in a 1909 recollection of the library: "It was a spiritual center for all the wise men of our generation, all the young men who thirst for the glorious past, and all those who seek the word of God and the wisdom of Israel throughout the ages. The spirit of the Jewish people fluttered among the walls of the grand building, and those who came inside felt that they were entering a genuine Jewish atmosphere."[37]

On a much smaller scale, private libraries were established in town after town, often by the local intelligentsia who served the community as teachers and administrators. "In the shtetl," recalled a resident of Lenin (Minsk Province), "one could find educated and well-to-do men who owned private libraries."[38] A. I. Paperna recalled that in Kopyl (Minsk Province) as early as the 1850s, "Besides the library in the *kloyz* in Kopyl there were many private libraries on a smaller scale. Every prosperous and self-respecting resident had in his house books, which were accessible to him and appropriate to his taste."[39] There was even a private woman's library in the town, containing mostly Yiddish books. Memoirist Yekhezkl Kotik of Kamenets-Litovsk (Grodno Province) recalled borrowing *maskilic* literature in the 1860s from a friend whose wealthy father had a large private library. When he and his friends exhausted that library, they began ordering books from the library in Bialystok for a borrower's fee. After devouring the books they received, they would ship them back and order a new consignment from a handwritten list.[40]

Memoirs of those who established private lending libraries portray them as surrogate public libraries that were open to the masses and even served as a second home or source of enlightenment for the aspiring poor. They are often presented as the only place working folk could receive a respite from the drudgery of their daily lives or escape into the fantasies of the written word or use the library as a stepping-stone to self-education and a better life. Dvoyre Kutnik of Luninets, for instance, recalled of her father's library that:

> Every Friday afternoon in our house visitors came from among the seamstresses, servant girls, clerks, and workers—shoemakers and tailors, who would remember, coming from the baths, to stop by Avrom Hershl the teacher's to take a book home for the Sabbath. . . . The library had a great influence on its readers.[41]

For most people, the establishment of a private lending library in the shtetl was their first introduction to modern notions of public culture. Falek Zolf provided a colorful and typical description of the impact that the establishment of the first library in the shtetl Zastavye had on the community:

> It was a summer Friday evening, after candle lighting. Zastavyer proprietors, all shampooed, cleansed, and dressed up in their Sabbath clothes, arrived with hurried steps to the *besmedresh* in order to welcome the Sabbath. First they glanced between the washstand and the holiday calendar at a long announcement that had been mounted there,

written with a very fine hand with rounded letters . . . : Whoever is thirsty and yearns to drink from the fountain of wisdom and understanding, must come to our storehouse of books, that which is called in the local language, a library, that we have opened for you in the house of the widow Tsipe-Dvoshe, who lives under the mountain on Kobrin Street. We have assembled there for you a storehouse of spiritual nourishment: holy books and secular books in numerous languages: in "jargon," in the holy language, and also in Russian.[42]

The placard was signed only "the spreaders of light and wisdom among the people." According to Zolf, the announcement was received with a mixture of bemusement and consternation. "Around the large announcement there soon gathered a cluster of Jews. All stood with haughty heads, looked one over the other, read again and again, tried to make some type of sense of the strange proclamation with its Turkish Hebrew, and simply could not grasp the motive, the true meaning of the words."[43] Those who understood the meaning, though, recognized it as the work of the *maskilim* from the city and sought to put an end to it. "The next morning in the *besmedresh,* as they prayed, the pious God-fearing proprietors raised a great fuss, a cry, that they must once and for all thoroughly eradicate the unclean (*treyf*) clan that seeks to spread heretical views. It could still threaten to, God forbid, lead their children into sin."[44]

Over time, however, the library became integrated into the community and became a favorite gathering spot for the youth.

Every evening, at sunset, when the pious, God-fearing Jews would go to the *besmedresh* to say the afternoon and evening prayers, to study a page of Talmud, a chapter of the Mishnah or to say a few psalms, the youth of the shtetl, dressed up in their Sabbath and holiday clothes, would stream into their dear storehouse of books, to the library which could be found, as the proclamation had announced, in the home of the widow Tsipe-Dvoyre, who lives behind the mountain. Of course there was not a single parent who did not fight with their son or daughter and attempt to convince them with good or bad arguments not to go there to the heretic's. But it did not help. The word "library" was like a magical incantation, a siren that enticed people there, and no force in the world could keep them back.[45]

Similarly, in Briansk, a group of young intellectuals established a library in 1905 in the attic of a private home despite the objections of established members of the community, who feared it would lead to heresy, and the local book peddler, who feared it would detract from his business. "There one could find many Yiddish books. Mendele Moykher Sforim and Sholem Aleichem were very popular. Young Jewish women were frequent visitors and good readers of the popular Yiddish books. They were no longer satisfied with the story books (*mayse bikher*) that they used to get from book peddlers. . . . When the library opened, all the customers of the book peddler came to take out books. Workers and genteel children all patronized the library." By 1910, "a book from the library could be found in every home in Briansk."[46]

But private libraries were not a solution for everyone. Many of the poor felt uncomfortable (or were made to feel uncomfortable) frequenting the homes of the wealthy to use their books. "In some of [the private lending libraries], one could from time to time read a book, but it was not convenient for us young people from poor families to call upon the well-to-do aristocrats very often. One read what came into one's hands."[47] Even in the homes of the most generous benefactors, private libraries accentuated class differences, alienating those who were forced to rely upon the beneficence of their wealthy neighbors. In addition, many private libraries were established with deliberate political or social agendas that did not always coincide with those of the constituents they sought to serve. The storybooks and popular European fiction most readers devoured with the greatest relish served no explicit political agenda; they were read exclusively for entertainment. These books could rarely be obtained from the private libraries of the intelligentsia.

Popular fiction and storybooks were more often obtained from the traveling book peddlers who set up their carts in front of the synagogue. Yekhezkl Kotik remembered that "once booksellers used to travel around the land with a nag, much like that described by Mendele Moykher Sforim. Their wagons, which they would set up in the courtyard of the *besmedresh,* would be full of various holy books and story booklets (*sfoyrim un mayse-bikhlekh*). At night they would put themselves up at some cheap inn, and then in the morning, at prayer time, the bookseller was already in the synagogue courtyard standing again with his horse and wagon. Sometimes, for a few rubles, some bookseller would rent a table at the door of the great *besmedresh,* on which he would spread out his books. Meanwhile, his partner (sometimes he would have a partner) would take the rest of the books around to the neighboring villages."[48] "There was no book shop in Kopyl," recalled Paperna. "Stores, shops, taverns, all commercial establishments in general were intended primarily for the Christian public, and the local or surrounding Christians, being illiterate, did not need books. The need for books came exclusively from the Jews, and their demands in this matter were completely satisfied by the wandering book peddler, who arrived several times a year on his emaciated jade, overburdened with a troublesome carriage filled to the rim with books. . . . Stopping in the synagogue courtyard, he would take off his smock, unharness his horse, and, after feeding her some oats, spread out his wares."[49]

Ostensibly the book peddlers sold primarily religious literature, much of which could be purchased in installments. Yekhezkl Kotik recalled how he formed his first "association" in the late 1850s in order to buy the Slavuta edition of the Talmud; each of his friends donated four kopeks a week toward the purchase of the volumes.[50] However, it was an open secret that underneath the moral literature and talmudic editions hawked by the peddlers one could find popular storybooks and lowbrow fiction as well as various odds and ends. The variety of merchandise carried by the typical book peddler was made famous by the author Sholem Yankev Abramovitsh, whose alter ego Mendele Moykher Sforim recounted that "I trade in staple books, that is with Bibles, daily prayer books, High Holiday prayer books, penitential prayers, women's prayer, and such books. . . . Aside from the basic stock of books I also carry prayer shawls, fringed undergarments, tassels, phylacteries, shofars, amulets, mezuzahs, wolf teeth, charms, sparkling children's shoes and skull caps, and sometimes also brass and copper works."[51] Another observer recalled, "They would come with their goods straight to the *besmedresh* in the late hours of the afternoon, take out their wares and spread them on the table next to the stove: the Book of Rom'l, Pentateuchs, prayer books, collections of women's prayers, elegies, prayer books for after meals, Stories of the Baal Shem Tov, Hagiographies of Tsadiks, and wondrous tales of the Ari and his holy disciple, Hayyim Vital. Among the holy books and pamphlets could also be found wonder tales for women in Yiddish translation, books of Yehoshua Mazakh and Ayzik Meyer Dik."[52] Whereas Kotik and his friends purchased Talmud editions from the book peddler, others sought Yiddish popular novellas and stories instead. Avrom Slutsky recalled that "from time to time a traveling book-seller would come to the shtetl. People would buy from him a novel by Shomer [Nokhem Meyer Shaykevitch] or one of Elyokem Tsunzer's stories, or stories and jokes about Hershele Ostropoler. This type of literary work would from time to time be read by one of us at a gathering (*farzamlung*) of boys and girls."[53]

The propensity of young men and women to spend their leisure time reading aloud in groups easily facilitated the formation of informal gatherings, like that described by Slutsky, which often evolved into formal reading groups or book clubs—and eventually lending libraries. In Slutsky's case, the gathering, which began with popular storybooks, soon took on a more serious political orientation when the group secretly subscribed to a Bundist journal. Sharing the cost of a subscription required a more long-term financial investment than splitting the cost of a romance novel, and the conspiracy of subscribing in secret required trust and commitment. Slutsky also made a semantic distinction between the nascent ad hoc gatherings and the more committed group of subscribers: he referred to the former as a *farzamlung* and the latter as a *krayz*. Although both words are derived from Germanic stock, the use of the term *krayz* (circle) mimics the Russian usage of the word *kruzhok* (circle) to refer to an informal grouping of intellectuals. By adopting the Russian usage of the term, the author and the Yiddish language in general alluded to a Russian influence in both terminology and the activity itself.

It is very possible gatherings evolved into circles because of politically motivated intervention. Committed Bundists traversed the countryside in order to infiltrate existing circles and propagandize among them or, when such circles could not be found, to establish them independently. Reading circles and libraries were the key to the Bund's massive propaganda drive. Workers' clubs and socialist political organizations often organized clandestine libraries, many of which were small scale and itinerant. The libraries were the nuclei of the Bund's local organizing. In smaller towns, the library often *was* the Bund organization or at least preceded the founding of an organized chapter. With legendary flare, Avraham Yaron told of the formation of the Bund in Goshcha (Hosht, Volhynia Province), a small shtetl near Rovno: "On a beautiful summer day in the year 1910, Moyshe the tanner's blind mare stopped and would not go any further. Her mangy long ears heard the noise of a new song. A song of freedom and uprising. Singing the song was a group of workers in the tannery. Thus, the first organization in Hosht, the Bund, was founded. . . . They had brought to Hosht the first worker's literature and founded a workers' library."[54] In order to avoid detection, the workers' library in Hosht "was not kept in a single place, but wandered around from one member to another, under the strictest supervision."[55] In his memoirs, L. Berman described the well-developed system of illegal workers' libraries that existed in Dvinsk (Vitebsk Province). A central library purchased books that were sold legally in the marketplace but were banned from free libraries and secretly distributed them to the smaller workers' libraries, exchanging books several times a week in secret locations.[56] As Bundist A. Litvak wrote: "It was not enough to create a Jewish working-class reader; we had to remember that this reader has to have something to read: the reader grows together with the book. Workers' libraries went together with the first workers' savings banks. The library committee always had an important role in the network of every organization. Beginning with a few dozen books that lay hidden somewhere in the attic of a house, to building the library from a circle or a vocation, and ending with a relatively rich library such as one of today's Gresser or Borokhov clubs, a long chain of caring and hard work extends simply to put a book in the hands of a worker."[57]

The Bund worked not only to establish places for workers to read and obtain books but also to reform the reading habits of workers. Activists complained that the typical worker skimmed through books, "often reading only the short lines, the dialogues, skipping over the descriptions, rushing to find out the ending of the story."[58] The Bund strove to show workers how to quench their thirst for knowledge. Litvak explained, "He taught the Jewish worker to look at a book with proper respect; not like an ignoramus, like a children's game to waste away the time, but like a deeply serious thing that can teach, educate and show the way to a proper life, even if it must be endured as a sacrifice."[59]

Library proponents established reading circles to disseminate the "proper" interpretation of literature to the workers. Librarians were instructed to question readers about the books they read before providing them with new literature.[60] In the library of Wyszków (Warsaw Province), "When a reader returned a book in exchange for another one, the librarian had the right to test him to see whether he had indeed read the book, and if so, whether he had understood it," even though the librarians were not professionals but were simply "the most competent members of each group."[61] Similarly, in the library Avrom Kotik established, the better-read students acted as librarians, recommending the works of the Russian radicals to the less experienced.[62] Before lending books from his Slobodka (Kovno Province) library in the 1890s, Moyshe Shmuel Shklarsky would "deliver a sermon for the children about the importance of reading books, then distribute to each of them a book according to their taste."[63] It was taken for granted that Shklarsky himself was best suited to determine the tastes of his readers.

Other small libraries were established as teahouses or coffeehouses. The coffeehouse library was a staple of Central European public life, a place where locals and travelers would go to catch up on the latest news and browse through the daily papers. It was in just such a coffeehouse, in

Vienna, that An-sky set his story "Am ha-sefer" ("People of the Book"), which explores the nature of Jewish assimilation in German lands. Although Russian teahouses were not as widespread as Viennese coffeehouses, teahouses in Russia had an advantage: whereas free libraries were subject to severe restrictions on the acquisition of books, teahouses and taverns, where books and periodicals were available for free perusal, were exempt from these laws. Zionist teahouses in particular took advantage of this legal loophole. The goal of one teahouse established in Grodno in 1900 was reported "to be a house for the Zionists in our city to gather here occasionally in the evening to discuss subjects of interest relating to national affairs or literature etc. over a hot drink." Those who gathered there were encouraged to speak in Hebrew, and the teahouse subscribed to several Jewish newspapers in Hebrew and Russian.[64] In Slutsk (Minsk Province), the Zionist organization Kadimah (Forward) reported in 1903 that it was in the process of establishing a teahouse that would subscribe to ten newspapers.[65]

In practice, each of these types of libraries existed in multiple forms and alongside the others. As one memoirist related of the town of Korelichi (Minsk Province) in the late nineteenth century, "Everywhere libraries were established. Older boys and girls used to meet there. The serious youth began to read about sociology and political economy. The majority, though, threw themselves into belles lettres in Russian, Hebrew or Yiddish. Novels from world literature began to be devoured and the girls salivated over Shomer's work."[66]

The Public Library Movement to 1905

The public library movement reached Russia after it had already begun to impact Western Europe and North America. By the turn of the century, public libraries with reference reading rooms and circulating books had already been established throughout the United States, Britain, and Western Europe. Many cities had a central library with branches in the suburbs and a means of distributing books to neighboring environs as well. American libraries also functioned as cultural centers, sponsoring public lectures, entertainments, and exhibitions of various kinds.[67] In Russia, however, the development of a public library movement was hindered by extensive legal restrictions. The 1865 Statute on Censorship and the Press forbade the establishment of any lending libraries or reading rooms without permission from the local gubernatorial authorities. Applicants were required to submit a statute of by-laws to the authorities describing the management and resources of the library. The decision to approve or reject the statute was then dependent on the whims of the authorities. Letters and chronicles in educational journals of the period provide ample evidence of the difficulties entailed in this process. Many local authorities feared the repercussions of allowing the masses access to reading material and modern ideas; others simply had little interest in educating the general public.

In response to the establishment of several free public libraries, the Rules Regarding Free Public Libraries of 1890 stated that free libraries were obligated to register with the authorities. Additionally, the 1890 rules added the clause that free public libraries were only permitted to carry books that appeared in the newly instituted *Catalog of Books and Periodical Literature for Free Public Libraries,* which would be published by the Ministry of Education. Thus, whereas libraries for which admission was charged could carry any book not specifically banned by the censors, free public libraries were restricted to carrying only books specifically approved by the censor. This list amounted to less than 8 percent of all books that went past the censors. Free public libraries were thereby forbidden from carrying books that were being openly traded in the marketplace and, as many activists pointed out, were available even in taverns and teahouses. Subsequent enactments modified the precise terms of the laws but failed to diminish their restrictions and sometimes even expanded them.[68] Library activists often complained of the capricious and arbitrary enforcement of these laws, the bureaucratic impediments in the way of establishing and maintaining libraries, and the severe limitations placed on library acquisitions. These laws remained in effect until February 1906.

The first efforts to establish public libraries and reading rooms on a mass scale in Russia began in the middle of the 1890s.[69] In 1894, the St. Petersburg Literacy Committee embarked upon a campaign to subsidize the establishment of reading rooms and encourage local *zemstvos* to do the same in villages and towns throughout the empire. Thanks to the support of the Moscow, St. Petersburg, and Kharkov literacy committees, by 1898 there were probably about 3,000 local lending libraries in Russia, although many had only a minimal number of books and most were affiliated with a school.[70] By 1905, a group of library activists had emerged in Russia who believed that libraries played an important role in education and in the spread of civic consciousness and enlightenment to the lower classes. These individuals were inspired by the American and British examples and sought to emulate the efforts of their colleagues in the English-speaking world. Over the course of his career, Nikolai Rubakin, the most prominent of the library activists, published hundreds of articles, books, and guides on reading for both professional bibliographers and simple readers in search of guidance.[71] His three-volume *Sredi knig* (Among Books), the first volume of which appeared in 1905, was unmatched as a catalog of Russian books.[72] A self-styled Department of Self-Education based in St. Petersburg, of which Rubakin was a member, disseminated reading lists for those interested in self-education on a variety of topics. Others published handbooks of library operations detailing the legality of libraries as well as techniques for cataloguing, binding, circulating, and accessioning materials. With the increased professionalization of library science in Russia, a Librarianship Section was established within the Russian Bibliological Society in 1903 that sponsored lectures and seminars on library affairs. Throughout the first two decades of the twentieth century, these organizations helped inform the general public about reading techniques, provided guides and advice for choosing books, and disseminated information on the technical aspects of library science to would-be specialists throughout the empire.

Yet despite the enthusiasm with which they were organized and the modest successes they enjoyed, Russian public libraries developed unevenly. In 1900, the average library was small, possessing only about 400–500 books, serving between 150 and 200 members, and lending out about 1,600 books a year.[73] Without municipal taxation, it was difficult to raise the type of funding needed to develop public libraries on a mass scale. Local *zemstvos* were forced to rely upon subsidies from literacy committees in the larger cities and private donations, of which even the most generous could not compare with the type of funding American libraries received from private philanthropists and municipal tax dollars. Even libraries that achieved some level of financial success were hindered by the extensive legal restrictions on their holdings and on their ability to develop as free public spaces dedicated to the dissemination and advancement of knowledge.

The legal and economic situation was even worse for the Jewish population. Despite its relatively high level of literacy and the cultural value it placed upon books, the Jewish community lagged behind in the establishment of secular public libraries.[74] One of the primary impediments was that the list of approved books for free public libraries did not include even one book in Yiddish and only a few in Russian on Jewish subjects. Thus, prior to 1905, free public libraries were proscribed from holding Yiddish books and limited in their holdings of Russian or Polish books on Jewish topics. Further, Jewish readers, who were on average poorer than Russian readers, were more likely to need free libraries. Another impediment to the establishment of public libraries among the Jewish population was ignorance about how to obtain official permission coupled with a general distrust and fear of the local authorities. Many among the educated Jewish elite also had little inclination to make secular books accessible to the general population. Rabbinical authorities rightly regarded the dissemination of secular knowledge as a threat to their guardianship of scripture—all the books they believed the people needed were available in the *besemedresh. Maskilim,* for their part, valued the ideology of the Enlightenment but often had little interest in disseminating this ideology to the broad masses.[75]

In 1905, according to information collected by the OPE, there were 108 legal Russian-Jewish libraries in the Russian Empire.[76] Of these 108 libraries, only thirty-seven were truly public libraries in the sense that they were registered in the name of a public institution, such as a Jewish mutual aid society, a Society for the Aid of Indigent Jews, a synagogue, a hospital, or another public institution. Seventy-one libraries were actually private lending libraries; that is, libraries registered in the name of private individuals but open to the public. The relative ease with which private individuals could establish a lending library and open it to the general public made this type of library a practical option for many communities. In Mogilev Province, for instance, nearly three-quarters of all Jewish libraries open to the public—including both those that charged admission and those that were free—were registered to private individuals.[77] Once they became established, many of these libraries functioned independently of the formal owner and became in many ways indistinguishable from libraries established by public institutions. Often their collections were formally transferred from the private individual in whose name they were registered to a public organization. This occurred in Melitopol (Taurida Province), for instance, where the large and successful library was originally started on the initiative of the Melitopol rabbi, A. Bragin, and registered in the name of S. Y. Bragina, presumably a female member of Rabbi Bragin's family. The library received start-up funding from the local Zionist organization and supported itself by hosting theatrical shows and lotteries and soliciting donations from nonprofit societies and local financial institutions. After two years, ownership of the library was transferred to the Society for the Aid of Indigent Jews, under whose auspices the library grew to become the largest in the city and one of the most successful Jewish libraries in the empire.[78]

However, libraries registered in the name of a public organization tended to be more open and more stable than those that were privately owned. For instance, whereas three-quarters of public libraries had reading rooms, only one-third of private lending libraries did. The legal status of private lending libraries was also precarious; they were dependent upon the standing of the individual in whose name they were registered. For instance, a library in Novoselitsy (Bessarabia Province) that housed some 800 Hebrew books as well as Russian books was closed and its books were confiscated by the local authorities after the individual in whose name the library was registered left town.[79] Private lending libraries were also subject to the whims of their owners, who often had specific political or social agendas to promote that may have been at variance with the ideals of the society at large. Finally, private lending libraries were less likely to attract donations, upon which all libraries were highly dependent. For many activists, these problems underlined the need to have libraries registered in the name of a Jewish communal authority or some other public entity rather than the name of a private individual.

One of the leading public Jewish libraries registered to a community institution was the Odessa Jewish Clerks' Library. The library was established in the mid-1870s as part of the Odessa Jewish Clerks' Mutual Aid Society. This society had been formed in 1863 as clerks and other white-collar workers in the city sought financial independence from the synagogue's mutual aid society. Its library was part of a broad project to enlighten the members of the society in order to make them more competitive in the marketplace. It was also designed as a social space for business networking and communal activities. By 1882, the library had over 1,100 books and subscribed to sixteen periodicals. Thanks to a large donation of some 500 Jewish books in 1885, the library had been able to significantly expand its Hebraica collection and establish a separate Hebraica department. Three years later, it established a Judaica department as well. In the late 1890s, Simon Dubnow and Ahad Ha-Am took an interest in the library and helped transform its Hebraica section into the second-largest collection in Russia, after that of the St. Petersburg Public Library.[80] At the turn of the century, the library had well over 10,000 titles, nearly sixty journal subscriptions, and 1,500 members. In both scope and ambition, though, the Odessa Jewish Clerks' Library was atypical.

The OPE and the Library Movement

The most noxious restrictions on library acquisitions were removed in the aftermath of the 1905 Revolution. Laws of 2 December 1905 and

28 February 1906 allowed all public libraries to acquire any book permitted by the Committee of Affairs of the Press, the government's censor. Censorship in general was also reduced in 1906. Most important, preliminary censorship was curtailed for books. Pamphlets and periodicals were still subject to preliminary censorship; materials that contained slander, falsehoods, promotion of class conflict, and praise of criminal activity were still banned; and foreign books, dramatic works, and several other categories of publication were still subject to preliminary censorship. Many libraries also still required local authorization to function and remained under the supervision of local authorities. Despite these continued restrictions, libraries were able to function with considerably greater ease.

Over the next five years, regional *zemstvos* eagerly embarked upon campaigns to establish Russian libraries throughout the countryside by organizing conferences on the subject and subsidizing library formation in their districts.[81] Professional associations, journals, and conferences were established in the imperial metropolises. The Russian Society for Librarianship was founded in 1908; the first Russian journal of library science, *Bibliotekar'* (The Librarian), was founded in 1910; and the first All-Russian Librarians' Conference was held in St. Petersburg in 1911 and attended by some 350 participants.[82] The total number of libraries in the empire had risen to about 19,000 by 1912 and 24,000 by 1916.[83] Still, most libraries (80 percent, according to one 1914 survey) were connected to schools and many remained small-scale affairs.[84]

In the period of reaction that followed the assassination of Stolypin in 1911, new restrictions were put into place. In 1912, libraries affiliated with primary schools, most of which were run by local *zemstvos*, were placed under the authority of the Educational Committee of the Ministry of Enlightenment and numerous other libraries were closed. Three years later, authority was restored to the *zemstvos*, but the regulation of books remained in effect. Nevertheless, in the seven years from 1906 to 1912, an infrastructure of libraries emerged with the potential to develop into a network of public libraries that would have been competitive with, if not equivalent to, the network that already existed in the English-speaking world.

The Jewish library movement also benefited from the post-1905 climate. Jewish library activists followed their Russian colleagues in arguing for the systematization of Jewish library science and the promotion of Jewish public libraries. Among the most prominent of these activists were Avraham Kirzhnits and Sofia Kotsyna. Kirzhnits (1888–1938), the director of the acclaimed Bobruisk Jewish Library, wrote extensively on the technicalities of librarianship and the particular challenges Jewish libraries faced. He believed that clandestine Jewish libraries and private lending libraries failed in their mission to serve the public and urged these libraries to take advantage of the registration process to establish themselves as legal communal institutions. As a member of the Library Commission of the OPE, he advocated the professional training of librarians and was one of the authors of the OPE's *Handbook of Jewish Libraries,* a widely disseminated handbook containing important practical, legal, and technical advice on establishing a library.[85] Kotsyna (1873–?) had been the leader of the Moscow OPE Library Committee since 1899 and was the author of numerous articles on reading. She was also an early proponent of the use of film projectors as an educational tool.[86]

These activists sought to institutionalize library science by establishing professional library societies, journals, and congresses and sought to legalize clandestine libraries through official registration. They called upon the OPE to encourage the formation of legal Jewish libraries by subsidizing them, disseminating information, and convening a conference of bibliographers. They placed enormous faith in the library movement and felt that books had the potential to both preserve Jewish tradition and adapt Jewish life to modernity. As one activist wrote, "If our fathers and grandfathers saw in books the key to understanding God and His commandments, then the young generation of Russian Jews, having joined general European civilization together with the recently developed but quickly matured Jewish proletariat, search within books for solutions to all their problems, be they of a cultural, national, or political nature."[87]

Despite almost constant demands throughout the OPE's existence to take a leadership role in library affairs, its involvement throughout the nineteenth century was episodic at best. When the central organization did involve itself in library affairs, beginning in the mid-1890s, it did so only as part of its project to develop primary schools. Even in 1905, when a unit was finally formed with the express goal of assisting in the development of libraries, it was established as a department of the School and Education Commission of the OPE rather than as an independent commission. With St. Petersburg showing little interest in libraries, the Moscow branch of the OPE jumped into the fray, establishing a library commission in 1896. Originally the commission sought to help establish Russian-language libraries in OPE schools in Moscow, but in two years it expanded its mandate and began subsidizing public and private lending libraries as well as school libraries. It increased its subsidies tenfold from 1896 to 1899; its total annual subsidization reached nearly 3,000 rubles by the end of the century. It soon expanded its activities throughout the Pale of Jewish Settlement, concentrating on the provinces of Mogilev, Vitebsk, and Chernigov. In the first years of the twentieth century, it also began publishing and disseminating catalogs of Russian-language books for use in Jewish libraries and Jewish schools and began to take an interest in libraries as sites for adult education.[88] Toward the end of the decade, it doubled its funding for library affairs from 5 percent to 10 percent of its annual budget.[89]

In 1904, the central branch of the OPE in St. Petersburg responded to the challenge the Moscow branch posed by allocating 1,000 rubles for subsidies for fourteen preexisting libraries. It still declined to take an active leadership role in organizing new libraries and disseminating information, however, and the high level of subsidies allocated in 1904 was short lived. The St. Petersburg branch provided less than 500 rubles the next year and did not reach the 1904 level again for the rest of the decade. Both Moscow and St. Petersburg put stringent restrictions on their subsidies and made them available only for the purchase of books. Lack of books, though, was only the smallest of problems most libraries faced. Books could be easily obtained through private donations, but most libraries lacked sufficient funds to hire library staff or build appropriate storage facilities for the books they already owned; few benefactors who donated their private libraries to a community or institution made provisions for the maintenance and accessibility of the books they provided.

Nevertheless, by 1905, St. Petersburg had recognized the importance of libraries, making time for discussions of library affairs in its annual meeting and conducting a systematic investigation of the state of Jewish access to libraries throughout the Pale. The issue of public libraries was one of the factors that led the OPE to revamp its central mission. The library movement challenged the OPE to meet the masses on their own level. Ordinary people, its members believed, would be most willing to read literature in an easily accessible language. Previously the leaders of the OPE had equated enlightenment with Russian-language skills. OPE schools had sought to teach Jewish students Russian literacy, and the libraries affiliated with these schools reflected the Russian emphasis. As the OPE looked toward the Jewish masses and Jewish adults, though, it realized that the most effective means of making an impact was through the Yiddish language. Thus, at the same meeting at which library affairs was elevated to a central mission of the organization, the leaders of the OPE recognized the importance of making Yiddish-language books available, admitting that Yiddish had to play "a prominent role in the matter of enlightening the Jewish population of Russia."[90] In response, the Moscow branch began to include Yiddish and Hebrew books in its catalogs.

Local branches followed the leadership of the central organization, leading to a proliferation of libraries throughout the empire. Within five years, OPE libraries had been established or reopened in Shklov (1908), Slutsk (1909), Voronezh (1909), Kovno (1909), Orel (1910), Vilna (1910), and Gomel (1910). From 1905 to 1910, the number of libraries in Mogilev and Vitebsk provinces doubled. During the same period, branches of the St. Petersburg Jewish Literary Society, which was not affiliated with the OPE but shared some of its goals, established about twenty-five libraries. Existing libraries were also enlarged as a generation of *maskilim* passed away and left their private book collections to the community library or, in some cases, to the large research libraries of the metropolises.[91] The St. Petersburg OPE library, which was, according to one observer, "formerly a modest synagogue library" was growing "not by the day, but by the hour" into a major research library, thanks to the gifts of generous estates. Library zealots imagined the library of St. Petersburg competing with Oxford's Bodleian Library and the New York Public Library as a center of research for Judaica.[92]

In 1910, for the first time, the OPE recognized "libraries and reading rooms as one of the most important factors in the activity of spreading enlightenment" and it declared that one of the society's goals was "the systematic and organized opening of networks of libraries and reading rooms." It encouraged local branches to open libraries and reading rooms, and in regions where the OPE did not have a branch, it called on local cultural or charitable institutions to assume the task. The St. Petersburg OPE promised to aid library development by compiling and distributing catalogs and other relevant information. The OPE declared that library fees had to be affordable, librarians had to be paid, and that books should be collected in "Hebrew, Yiddish, Russian, and other languages, depending on local conditions." The decision to promote Yiddish-language book collection reflected the continuing rise of the Yiddishist factions within the OPE.[93]

The first All-Russian Librarians' Conference, which was convened by the Society for Librarianship in St. Petersburg in the summer of 1911, provided further impetus toward the increased involvement of the OPE in library affairs. The Jewish Literary Society decided to send a delegation of

Jewish librarians, for which they sought nominations from local libraries. Of the 200 libraries the Jewish Literary Society contacted to participate, though, less than thirty responded. In the end, eighteen Jewish delegates attended, for which they needed special temporary visitors' permits to visit St. Petersburg. Others who sought to attend failed to receive the requisite permission from the Ministry of Internal Affairs. The conference debated issues of local management and demanded an end to the continued restrictions upon the establishment of libraries. The Jewish delegation fought for declarations that stated that a library's holdings should reflect the nationality of the local constituency and that libraries should include books in the national languages of the local population. The Jewish activists were adjusting to the new language realities and demanding the right to use minority languages in general and Yiddish in particular. The Jewish delegates also met among themselves and resolved to facilitate better access to libraries and library science throughout the Pale by establishing a central bureau for library affairs with branches in Moscow and St. Petersburg and by publishing catalogs of books.[94] For the most part, though, the Jewish library activists were disappointed by the small turnout of Jewish librarians.

When they returned from the conference, the Jewish delegates urged the OPE and the Jewish Literary Society to take leadership roles in the promotion of Jewish libraries. The OPE responded by appointing a Library Commission that included Kirzhnits and Kotsyna. It entrusted the commission with the task of collecting statistical information from provincial libraries and dispatching instructional information, primarily in the form of catalogs of books.[95] The Library Commission's first meeting, which was held in St. Petersburg in January 1912, was attended by thirteen individuals, most of whom came from within the city environs.[96] Residency restrictions prohibited delegates from the provinces from attending the conference in St. Petersburg. As usual, the Jewish elites of St. Petersburg were forced to discuss among themselves how best to serve the provinces with little input from those they sought to serve.

However, the movement spread rapidly to the provinces. Other branches of the OPE took the cue and began working to promote the establishment and maintenance of libraries. The Kiev branch sponsored the collection of information on libraries in Kiev Province. The newly established Perm branch persuaded a municipal library to open a Jewish section and funded subscriptions to Jewish periodicals for the section. Other OPE branches, such as those in Eletsk (Voronezh Province) and Pinsk (Minsk Province) were rebuffed in their efforts to open libraries by local authorities that refused permission.[97] The Moscow OPE also stepped up its efforts, subsidizing a record number of libraries in 1911–1912 and even more the following year. By 1912, the Moscow OPE was spending almost as much money on subsidies to libraries as it was on subsidies to schools.[98] Local library activists kept abreast of the activities of the OPE's Library Commission through the press and newsletters and responded favorably to its creation. Many provincial librarians welcomed the opportunity to pose queries to the commission and hoped that a central organization would provide much-needed leadership and guidance. Local librarians dispatched some 300 letters from the provinces to the Library Commission; nearly half asked for assistance in navigating the legalities and technicalities of establishing a library. However, when the Library Commission put together a conference for provincial librarians in October 1912, few responded to its invitation. Those who did attend the conference debated the level of involvement the OPE should seek with regard to provincial libraries. The meeting revealed an emerging schism between the desires of provincial librarians and the officials in the central offices of the OPE. Although local branches freely admitted needing financial and informational assistance from St. Petersburg, they resented interference from the St. Petersburg elite. In particular, many provincial library activists took exception to the OPE's policy of favoring public libraries.[99] Many towns had successful smaller-scale private lending libraries that were being neglected in favor of official public libraries. Largely in response to these concerns, at its general assembly in December 1913, the OPE called upon local branches to "render all assistance toward the legalization of existing libraries and reading rooms," hoping to level the playing field.[100] It also continued to promote the establishment of reading rooms in libraries and began to advocate for the establishment of libraries geared specifically toward children. Between October 1912 and March 1914 at least twenty-eight new libraries were legalized, half of which were registered in the name of individuals. By early 1914, the Moscow OPE was subsidizing fifty-eight libraries.[101]

In addition to the legal libraries, numerous clandestine libraries, often founded by worker or Zionist organizations, remained in existence throughout the Pale. In keeping with its commitment to legal cultural development, the OPE fought against these libraries. One of its primary weapons was the rational argument that clandestine libraries represented a waste of resources because of extensive duplication of titles and space. If the Bund established a library in town, for instance, the local Zionists were sure to follow. Nearly half of the towns with a clandestine library had more than one such library, often with a significant overlap of collections. The OPE advocated that these libraries be converted into legal societies with formal charters. Supporters of this strategy argued that it would be possible to air political differences during open member meetings. The OPE sought to discourage the formation of numerous competing libraries within the same city by refusing to distribute subsidies to more than one library in a single town or city. This followed the OPE's policy of acting as an umbrella organization that oversaw the entire Jewish community.[102]

However, not everyone agreed with the OPE's emphasis on legally registered Jewish libraries. While most activists agreed that legal libraries were the ideal form of library organization in theory, others felt that relying upon local authorities to grant permission for the establishment of libraries would in the end be a lost cause and a waste of resources. Opponents of the OPE conjured up images of vast storehouses of books in beautiful buildings remaining locked up as the petitioners waited in vain for approval from the authorities. The Jewish population of Russia should have learned by now, these critics contended, that only fools would rely on the generosity of the Russian authorities in granting permits. Even after a permit was granted, the local authorities retained the right to close a library on a whim. The OPE, its critics advocated, should instead be using its resources to help private libraries or existing municipal and temperance society libraries. Scarce resources should be devoted to institutions that already existed and were providing valuable services rather than to pipe dreams.[103]

Internal Functioning of Jewish Libraries

Most libraries supported themselves through monthly membership dues and readers' fees, which were set by a general assembly of the library's members. The members also typically elected a governing council to handle the day-to-day administration of the library. Dues typically ranged between 5 and 15 kopeks per month—about the price of a paperback book—with reduced rates for children and for those who only read Yiddish books; these were generally assumed to be members of the working class. Libraries could charge additional fees for access to periodicals and new releases. Many libraries also made exceptions for readers unable to pay the fees. For example, the Kamenets-Litovsk library waived the dues of fully 30 percent of its members. Some libraries charged readers' fees for circulating books outside the library, although they usually made exceptions if a deposit could be given. The OPE recommended reduced deposits for students, children, and readers of Yiddish. Borrowing periods ranged from ten to fourteen days for regular holdings and three to five days for periodicals and new releases. In the library of Fastov (Kiev Province), for instance, members had the option of paying three rubles a year for full membership privileges—roughly half the price of an annual newspaper subscription—or paying monthly fees for the privilege of using the reading room. There were several gradations of monthly fees, depending on the number of books the reader wished to borrow.[104] Many lending libraries charged a nominal admission fee of about one kopek for entrance to the reading room, which usually contained a few noncirculating current newspapers, reference works, and the most popular books, although exceptions were made for members, children, and the indigent. A very few libraries, such as one in Kiev and a few in Kherson Province, were completely free.

Although membership and readers' fees were the primary means of support for most libraries, fees were waived for 20 to 30 percent of the readers in many Jewish libraries. Subsidies from the OPE, charitable organizations, and private donations helped improve the situation but never completely eliminated the financial difficulties of most Jewish libraries.[105] OPE subsidies were simply not enough to replace the type of funding American libraries received from municipal taxation and Russian libraries received from *zemstvo* funds.

One of the solutions proposed was to fund Jewish libraries through the *korobka* tax, a tax levied on kosher meat and certain other products, to fund Jewish communal needs.[106] This was already being done in some towns but was usually very controversial as *korobka* funds were invariably too limited to subsidize all activities within the Jewish community. The town of Orsha (Mogilev Province), for instance, had a large debate in January 1911 about allocating funds from the *korobka* to the library, which was in a serious financial crisis. It was eventually decided to allocate 50 rubles toward financing the library out of a *korobka* budget of 5,505 rubles but not without objections from the Society for the Aid of the Indigent, which regarded libraries as a luxury that was less important than providing basic food and shelter for the needy.[107] As of 1911, Jewish libraries in Bobruisk, Orgeev (Bessarabia Province), Melitopol, and Kovno were receiving *korobka* funds and others were in the process of applying for them.[108]

The key to a successful library was the librarian. However, nearly half of all librarians were unpaid. One survey found that in Vilna, Grodno, and Bessarabia provinces, only eighteen of forty-three libraries had paid staff.[109] Those who were paid received only modest compensation. The librarian of the small shtetl of Zakharino (Mogilev Province), for instance, received only one ruble a month; most received less than twenty-five rubles a month.[110] Typically librarians also held another job; some served as important community functionaries. Librarians were drawn largely from the ranks of the intelligentsia and were either members of the liberal professions, students, or teachers. Nearly three-quarters of librarians were men; most were young. Few librarians had received any professional training.[111]

The need for librarians to hold multiple jobs limited the number of hours libraries could be open. A typical Jewish library was open for two to three hours in the evening, six evenings a week. Most were closed on Friday evening but opened again on Saturday. Those with paid staff could usually afford to be open every evening, whereas those that relied upon voluntary staff could typically open at most two or three evenings a week.[112] The library of Kamen Kashirsky (Volhynia Province) established a monthly membership fee so that it could hire a few librarians who would staff the library every Sunday, Tuesday, and Thursday from 6 to 10 in the evening.[113] Typically, Friday afternoons and Saturdays were the busiest times. On Friday afternoons, patrons stopped by to pick up a book to read over the Sabbath, and on Saturdays, when the shops were closed for the Sabbath, patrons gathered in the reading room and library for social and leisure activities. On winter Saturday evenings, when the Sabbath ended earlier and outside activities were limited, libraries became a central gathering place for young men and women. Some, like the Riga OPE library, were open only eight months a year, from September through May.[114] In the summertime, many potential patrons preferred a walk through the fields or a dip in the river over a visit to the library.

Library Membership

Russian Jewish libraries in the early twentieth century typically had between 100 and 400 members, although several libraries in major urban centers were significantly larger. The Melitopol Jewish Library for the Aid of the Indigent had over 2,200 members, the Odessa Clerks' Library over 1,300, the Vilna Library of the OPE nearly 1,000, and the Odessa OPE library over 800.[115] The average Jewish library in the provinces of Mogilev and Vitebsk had 270 members. In many cities and townships, the library was the largest Jewish communal organization outside the synagogue. The membership levels of legal Jewish libraries were generally higher than those of Russian libraries, which averaged less than 200 members per library.[116]

In some towns, up to a quarter of the literate Jewish population were members of the library. According to the 1897 census, the city of Orgeev had a Jewish population of 7,100, of whom some 1,500 were listed as being literate in Russian and an additional 1,200 as literate in another language, presumably Yiddish or Romanian. The city's Jewish library boasted 564 members, meaning that about 20 percent of all literate Jews were members of the library.[117] Similarly, nearby Kolorosh (Bessarabia Province) had a Jewish population of 4,000 and a library with 443 members in 1904.[118] Based on Jewish literacy rates for the locality, we can assume that the Jewish literate population of the town was approximately 2,000, meaning that nearly a quarter of all literate Jews were members of the library.[119]

More commonly, though, the public library did not reach even 10 percent of the literate population, although even this would be an accomplishment envied by most librarians today.[120] Even in the much-envied British library system of the era, only 3–8 percent of the total population of most towns were active borrowers.[121] Although only a small proportion of the overall population joined a town or city's library, for each registered member, two or three additional people made use of the library's resources. Membership cards were often transferable to family members, and individuals who borrowed books often shared them with two or three other readers before returning them. Russian bibliographer Nikolai Rubakin assumed that membership figures could be multiplied by four to arrive at the total number who used a library's resources. Nevertheless, Rubakin estimated that in the 1890s only a minute fraction of the total population used Russian public libraries. Even among the most educated 10 percent of the population, nearly three-quarters would never use any public library resources. Those who could afford it maintained their own private collections. The one-quarter of the elites who did use public libraries used them only haphazardly and episodically.[122]

Available statistics suggest that Jews used their libraries in an equally sporadic manner. Only a small minority of residents of most cities were members of the library, and many of those who visited libraries did so rarely. In Odessa in 1910, 85 percent of the visitors to the library borrowed only one book, 12 percent borrowed two books, and only 3 percent borrowed three or more books.[123] About 40 percent of visitors to the Riga OPE library in 1910 were one-time visitors.[124] But those who did come regularly read extensively. In both Vilna and Voronezh in 1912, the average reader requested twenty-one books over the course of a year.[125] In Gomel the same year, the average reader requested nearly nineteen books.[126] These figures compare favorably with non-Jewish Russian libraries. For instance, the average reader in the public library of Kharkov borrowed ten books in 1911.[127] Unfortunately, statistics that would indicate the median number of books borrowed and which groups borrowed the most books are unavailable. However, given the high proportion of one-time visitors to those libraries for which such statistics are available, it would seem that a small number of readers borrowed very large numbers of books while the vast majority of readers were content with far fewer books. Most Russian peasants and urban Jews in the late nineteenth and early twentieth centuries had little time for leisure reading. Young people went to school if they were able to do so and when they were out of school, they worked at home, in the fields, or at the family store. But in between the demands of home, school, and work, growing numbers of young men and women found time to read, either alone in a comfortable corner or at a public library among friends.

The library was predominantly the domain of youth. A 1911–1912 survey of twenty-three libraries found that 55 percent of the readers were under the age of twenty.[128] Fully three-quarters of a typical Jewish library's members were under the age of thirty and about 15 percent were under the age of twelve. Students inevitably constituted a plurality of readers, usually from one-third to one-half of the total membership of any given library. Yet only a fraction of all students visited libraries. One observer estimated that of approximately 10,000 *kheyder* students in Mogilev and Vitebsk provinces, less than 800 had visited a library within the year. These figures are similar to those of Russian libraries in the early 1890s, although in general Russian libraries had an even larger percentage of students than Jewish libraries.[129] The intensity of reading also decreased with age. In Gomel in 1903, for instance, the youngest age group (7–12) visited on average twenty-two times during the course of the year, students aged 12 to 15 visited eighteen times, those aged 15 to 18 visited thirteen times, and those aged 18 to 25 visited nine times. Those older than 25 visited on average eleven times. Students borrowed on average nearly twenty books a year, whereas workers borrowed on average only nine.[130]

In one survey of libraries, nearly half (42 percent) of those who were not students were classified as people without defined occupations. Among those whose occupations could be determined, the largest group was comprised of workers and artisans, who constituted 10 percent of the overall readership. Working-class membership figures distressed many activists, who regarded the working class as the group for whom public libraries would be most beneficial. Public libraries had to compete with smaller-scale Bund libraries and workers' cooperative libraries that were specifically geared toward the working classes and may have been more attractive to them. Yet activists could be pleased that public libraries were by no means being monopolized by members of the intelligentsia and the liberal professions; these two groups constituted only 7 percent of the total readership. Teachers were foremost among the members of the liberal professions most likely to frequent libraries, followed by medical professionals, technical engineers, and lawyers. Those engaged in the creative arts, such as actors, musicians, writers, and artists, lagged far behind. Even white-collar workers constituted only a modest proportion of library readers. In Odessa, students outnumbered clerks even in the clerks' library. However, members of the intelligentsia and liberal professions may have constituted a larger percentage of the library readership in smaller libraries.[131]

Although Jewish libraries catered overwhelmingly to Jews, some also had a significant number of non-Jewish readers. The large library established by the Society for the Aid of Indigent Jews in Melitopol, for instance, counted 30 percent of its readers as non-Jews. Its enviable collection of over 10,000 books made it the city's leading library.[132] Among the thirty-two libraries surveyed in Mogilev and Vitebsk provinces, Christian readers accounted for 6 percent of the membership.[133] In Kovno, the community library reading room welcomed an average of 58 people per day, of whom 70 percent were Jewish, 13 percent Russian, and 12 percent Lithuanian and Polish.[134] This suggests that in at least several cases, Jewish libraries were more attractive than non-Jewish libraries, either because they had more comfortable reading facilities or superior collections of books or both.

It is difficult to determine in aggregate whether men or women were more likely to frequent libraries, as the figures vary immensely by library. In Kovno, only 23 percent of the members of the Abraham Mapu Library were women.[135] In Aleksandriia (Kherson Province), 34 percent of the adult members were women.[136] In the Melitopol Library and the Odessa OPE Library, women constituted 43 and 42 percent of the library membership, respectively.[137] Women accounted for only 27 percent of library visitors to the Riga OPE library. On the other hand, women accounted for 60 percent of the library's adult members in Shklov, 58 percent in Orgeev, and 52 percent in the Odessa Clerks' Library.[138] Among the surveyed libraries in Mogilev and Vitebsk provinces, 53 percent of the members were women.[139] Several libraries that provided statistics on the gender breakdown of their visitors did so only for adults, making it difficult to determine if the gender distinc-

TABLE 2.1.

Readers in Selected Jewish Libraries in the Pale of
Jewish Settlement by Occupation, 1911–1912, by Percent

OCCUPATION	PERCENT[1]
Students	58
Workers and artisans	10
Clerks and white-collar workers	7
Liberal professions and intelligentsia	7
Merchants and industrialists	4
Undefined occupation	20

Source: A. D. Kirzhnits, "Bibliotechnoe delo u evreev i zadachi Obshchestva
Prosveshcheniia (Vnutrenniaia organizatsiia evreiskitch bibliotek)," *VOPE,* no. 13 (March
1912): 8.

1. Percentages are greater than 100 because some individuals were counted in
more than one category.

tions held for younger visitors. In any case, Jewish women used libraries
at a much greater rate than Russian women had used Russian libraries a
generation earlier, when men often constituted 90 percent of a library's
members and on average there were three to four times as many male members as female.[140] Even by 1912, one survey of Russian libraries in Kharkov
Province found that only 20 percent of borrowers were women.[141]

The number of Jewish women who used public libraries takes on a new
dimension when looked at it in relation to the number of literate women.
In Orgeev, for instance, where women constituted 58 percent of the library
membership, only half as many women (891) as men (1,752) in the town were
literate.[142] Thus, whereas 37 percent of literate Jewish women in the city
were members of the library, only 14 percent of literate Jewish men were.
In Melitopol, women were also more heavily represented among library
members than their literacy rates in the city would suggest.[143] Similarly, in
the province of Mogilev, where women accounted for 53 percent of library
members, Jewish women accounted for only 40 percent of the literate Jewish
population.[144] Literate Jewish women were visiting public libraries in much
greater proportion than Jewish men. This contrasts with the situation in
Germany, where women were far less likely than men to frequent Jewish
reading halls, although they often borrowed books to take home.[145]

The resources of Jewish libraries were also being used extensively. A survey of forty-four Jewish public libraries conducted from 1908 to 1912 showed that on average every book was circulated 3.7 times per year. If we remove the four largest Jewish public libraries, which were essentially research libraries with many holdings that rarely circulated, then the figure is raised to 4.7. By contrast, estimates on average book circulation in Russian public libraries for the same period range between 0.8 and 2.0 times per year. Thus, the resources of Jewish libraries were being used about three times as much as Russian libraries. It is important to remember, as well, that the figures may understate the number of times each book was read because circulated books were sometimes read in groups or shared among several readers. On the other hand, not everybody who took a book home ended up reading it, although those who went through the trouble— and expense—of borrowing a book probably did at least glance through it, if not thoroughly read it.

Distribution and Typology of Jewish Libraries

In 1911, according to statistics compiled by the OPE, there were a total of about 300 legal Jewish libraries in Russia. On average, there was one Jewish library for every 17,500 Jews. Within the Pale of Settlement, the ratio was slightly better at one library for every 15,000 Jews. This statistic compared unfavorably with Russian libraries; a 1914 study estimated one library for every 9,300 persons across much of Russia.[146] Some provinces, like Kharkov, Moscow and Vladimir, boasted one library for every 4,000–5,000 persons. Yet even Russian libraries within the Pale of Jewish Settlement were overcrowded: Kiev Province was the least served in the empire with one library for every 25,000 inhabitants.[147] The comparison with Russian libraries was even worse than the statistics reveal due to the higher rate of literacy among Jews. The number of actual readers (as opposed to simply inhabitants) each Jewish library served in comparison to Russian libraries was therefore even higher than the statistics imply. Jewish library proponents aimed for a ratio of one library for every 8,000 persons.

The distribution of Jewish libraries was also uneven. Kiev Province had only one library for every 31,000 Jews and Vitebsk Province had one for every 23,000, whereas Taurida Province had one for every 3,000 and Ekaterinoslav Province had one for every 6,000. The territories of New Russia, where secular Jewish culture had made the greatest inroads and where secular Jewish communal associations had begun to appear as early as the 1860s, were the best-served regions.[148] Only in Taurida was the Jewish population better served than the general Russian population, and some of the best Jewish libraries could be found in Odessa and Melitopol.[149]

Poland saw the most dramatic growth of Jewish libraries in the interrevolutionary era. Contemporaries observed that before 1905, Jews in Poland had been content to use municipal libraries or libraries in Polish gymnasia, but as a result of increased anti-Semitism in the post-1905 period, they felt less welcome in Polish libraries. The growth of Jewish libraries in the region was stimulated by the strong Jewish nationalist movements that advocated the establishment of separate Jewish institutions and sought to distance Jewish communal life from Polish life.

The library movement was least developed in the Russian interior and the eastern provinces of the Ukrainian regions of the Pale. Even in some towns with Jewish populations of five thousand or more, complaints about a lack of Jewish libraries could be heard. One such town, Glukhov (Chernigov Province), had apparently no secular Jewish cultural institutions whatsoever: "You don't hear living Jewish words for years on end," complained one resident, noting that local and gubernatorial authorities would not permit the establishment of a Jewish library.[150] Farther from the center of Jewish life, good Jewish libraries were even more rare, even in locales with relatively large Jewish populations. Baku, for instance, had a Jewish library but it did not have even the most popular Jewish books. According to one observer, "There is no Mendele Moykher Sforim, no Sholem Aleichem, no [Sholem] Asch, no [Avrom] Reyzen, no [Hersh Dovid] Nomberg, in general nothing. You can find Russian books, but you would be searching in vain here for Russian-Jewish books."[151] Suggestions to ease distribution problems by forming small traveling libraries of thirty to fifty books never fully got off the ground.[152]

Perhaps even more important than the number of new libraries was the growing percentage of those that were registered in the name of a public organization rather than a private individual. Whereas only 36 percent of the libraries surveyed in 1905 were registered in the name of a public organization, 55 percent were in 1910. This was largely a function of the increased ease with which voluntary associations could be established under the March 1906 Temporary Regulations on Societies and Unions. In addition, among libraries registered to public organizations, increasing numbers were being established by voluntary associations with specific educational or cultural (as opposed to economic or health) mandates. According to Kirzhnits's calculations, 69 percent of all public libraries in 1910 were

TABLE 2.2.

Growth of Jewish Libraries in the Russian Empire, 1905 and 1910

REGION	1905	1910	GROWTH	PERCENT GROWTH
Northwest Pale	31	86	55	65
Southwest Pale	28	64	36	56.25
Southern Provinces	25	79	54	68.3
Kingdom of Poland	6	42	36	85.7
Baltic Provinces	2	9	7	77.6
Internal Region	8	11	2	27.0
Total	100	291	191	65.3

Source: A. D. Kirzhinits, "Bibliotechnoe delo u evreev i zadachi Obshchestva Prosveshcheniia," VOPE 11 (January 1912): 14.

established and run by cultural or educational societies; in 1905, only 21 percent had been. Most in the earlier period were established by mutual aid societies or societies for the aid of the indigent; for these groups, a public library was a secondary concern.[153]

A typical case was that of Tiraspol (Kherson Province), where a Zionist benefactor established a private library in 1906. While the library was initially successful, its founder departed soon after and the library declined in his absence. Two years later, a new group of local barristers drew up a charter and received permission to establish a Russian Jewish Library and Reading Room Society, which quickly drew 100 members.[154] The increased role cultural associations were playing in the formation of libraries was the result of a new level of professionalism. Organizations whose primary purposes were distributing aid or caring for the sick were hardly able to dedicate a significant portion of their resources to their libraries. A mutual aid society's primary raison d'être should not be—and legally could not be—maintaining its library. Library proponents, like Kirzhnits, believed that the most productive way to manage a library was through a library society—that is, a society whose sole purpose was to establish and maintain a library. Barring this ideal situation, the next best alternative was to have a library established by a literary society or a branch of the OPE. Those who advocated more libraries frowned upon libraries established by mutual aid societies or political movements on the ground that they lacked the necessary institutional framework. Nevertheless, many societies for the aid of

TABLE 2.3.

Official Registration of Jewish Libraries
in the Russian Empire, 1905 and 1910

	1905	1910
OPE	2	9
Literary, musical, or dramatic society	0	18
Professional society or union	0	6
School	0	4
Public	0	2
Library society	0	2
Society for the Aid of Indigent Jews	14	22
Synagogue administration	10	9
Philanthropic society	1	3
Mutual aid society	5	10
Official Jewish communal authority	6	75

Source: A. D. Kirzhnits, "Bibliotechnoe delo u evreev i zadachi Obshchestva Prosveshcheniia," *VOPE*, no. 11 (January 1912): 20.

the indigent regarded the cultural enlightenment of the poor as one of their responsibilities, and the statutes of societies often stated so explicitly.

Proponents of library societies could point to the M. A. Kulisher Library of Fastov, southwest of Kiev, as a model. It was established in early 1911 by the newly formed Society of the Fastov Public Library–Reading Room. By the end of the year, it held about 2,300 volumes in Russian, Hebrew, and Yiddish and subscribed to ten periodicals of general interest and seven Judaica periodicals. The library had 1,230 members (including both full members and subscribers who received limited borrowing privileges), a remarkable number given that the total Jewish population of the town was only 10,000. The success of the Fastov library, though, was rare among those established by library societies, and the Fastov example was not without its problems. The library's charter, for instance, prohibited it from hosting evening events and lectures.[155] In addition, because they had no political agenda, nonpartisan libraries, like the Fastov library, were vulnerable to manipulation by members of the board who sought to impose their own ideological leanings onto the organization. Within a year of the Fastov library's founding, the governing board split in a very public way over the role the library should play in local Jewish life. The tipping point came when one of the board's members sought to discontinue the library's subscription to the popular Zionist weekly *Razsvet* on the grounds that the journal was "chauvinistic."[156] The issue, which was picked up by the paper, cut to the very core of the fissures within contemporary Jewish life. Some believed that libraries should promote the spread of Russian culture and literacy, thereby preparing the next generation to partake in Russian civil society as citizens of the liberal state they hoped would come into being. Others had little faith in the Russian future and preferred to prepare the youth for life in a Jewish state, where the language of the Diaspora would be repudiated along with its customs. The latter condemned the former as accommodationists, and the former condemned the latter as national chauvinists. Often these frictions were so intense that it became impossible for organizations to balance the two viewpoints under a single roof.

Ultimately, many of the most successful Jewish libraries did not resemble the OPE's vision at all. The Odessa Jewish Clerks' Library, for instance, was established only as part of a larger Clerks' Society whose primary goal was not cultural enlightenment. Indeed, it was significantly easier to establish libraries as part of existing organizations; the charters of many societies included a clause that specifically envisioned the establishment of a club or library for its members. For those without such a clause, it was far easier to amend their charters than it was to establish a new separate library society.

The Period of Reaction

In the period of reaction that followed the assassination of Stolypin in 1911, the growth of Jewish libraries slowed along with that of Jewish cultural institutions in general. Legal impediments once again hampered the spread of reading, and local authorities were more willing to deny permission to establish libraries and to close down existing libraries. Of the nearly sixty towns and villages that Kirzhnits visited in Vilna, Grodno, and Bessarabia provinces in 1912, he found seventeen where a Jewish library had been closed, usually by administrative fiat. Other unofficial libraries were unable to obtain formal legalization.[157] The Slutsk OPE library was closed in late 1911 by administrative fiat after five banned books were discovered in its collection.[158] The Kiev OPE reading room was also closed in 1912. The library remained open as a public lending library for several months, but in the spring of 1913 it began to limit its use exclusively to members of the local OPE branch, thereby depriving students (who had constituted its largest contingent) and the general public of access.[159] In its heyday, it had been, in the words of its supporters, "the only Jewish library in the city that serves the interests of the local Jewish population."[160] Among the libraries most seriously hit were those established by library and literary societies and by the OPE. Associations who had broader economic or hygienic mandates weathered the storm better, as did the libraries attached to them. The library activists who put their faith in the Russian government's beneficence regarding cultural development were forced to concede that the social consequences that would ensue if hospitals, orphanages, or indigent aid societies were closed ultimately protected their attendant libraries. In contrast, the autonomous libraries they had championed simply could not withstand the pressures of the reactionary period that followed the assassination. Other libraries were repressed on the grounds that they were being used as illegal political arenas. These accusations were often based on truthful information; since 1910, the Bund had been encouraging its members to seek positions on library boards and the executive committees of other cultural organizations in order to use them as instruments of propaganda.

Blocked from establishing their own libraries, Jews sometimes united with Christians to establish a general library in which a Jewish section could then be set up. This occurred throughout Grodno Province in Belsk, Kobrin, and Pruzhany, all cities with Jewish populations of approximately 15 percent.[161] *The Handbook of Jewish Libraries* recommended that when local authorities refused permission to establish a Jewish library a general municipal library should be established instead. Once a municipal library was established, a Jewish section could legally be opened without securing additional permissions. This loophole, which had been recognized twenty years earlier, continued to be used into the revolutionary period. As early as 1906, activists had advocated establishing Jewish sections in municipal libraries, noting that municipal libraries could become "a new arena for the spread of Jewish literature."[162] Although select Jews had always used municipal libraries, as it became increasingly difficult to establish separate Jewish libraries after 1911, organized or semi-organized Jewish groups increasingly turned toward municipal libraries as sources of enlightenment. Jewish communal institutions sometimes supported this goal. In Orgeev, where Jews constituted a modest 13 percent of the population but 50 percent of the public library's members, the library received 120 rubles a year from the *korobka* tax. Twenty percent of its holdings were Hebrew- and Yiddish-language books.[163] Advocates of using municipal libraries urged the OPE to donate books on Jewish topics to such libraries around the Pale. They argued that rather than establish parochial libraries, Jews should be encouraged to use existing libraries and use their funds to purchase books for these libraries rather than to maintain separate buildings. The presence of books chosen by the OPE on Jewish topics in municipal libraries would also benefit Christian readers, as it would provide them with reliable information about Jews to replace the libelous rumors they were fed by the anti-Semitic press.[164]

Not all municipal libraries, though, were willing to represent Jewish interests; some actively opposed the efforts of Jewish members to influence the library holdings. In Berdichev (Kiev Province), where in 1914 over 70 percent of the population of 80,000 was Jewish, the municipal library turned down a request by its many Jewish readers to form a Jewish section on the grounds that such a section would harm the reputation of the library.[165] When the members of the Pushkin Public Library of Voznesensky (Kherson Province), where 40 percent of the population of nearly 20,000 was Jewish, decided to open a Judaica section in 1907, the librarians stalled by refusing to subscribe to Jewish journals or to purchase Jewish books. After two years, the library finally subscribed to one Russian-language Zionist periodical in the face of popular demands but continued to stonewall about other Jewish literature. Thus, although the library's users were 90 percent Jewish, the library reportedly held only seventy-six books of Russian Jewish literature in its collection of over 7,000 volumes and only eight titles in Yiddish. The situation was similar in Bobruisk, where the public library held only thirty-one Yiddish-language titles of its approximately 8,000 volumes, and these had been donated rather than purchased with library funds.[166] The main public library of Kishinev was closed on Saturdays, the day Jews were most likely to visit a library, according to one complainant, "for the sole reason of depriving Jewish readers of the opportunity to use the books."[167] Despite repeated attempts by Jewish activists to force the library to open on Saturday, it remained closed. Notably, by 1908, both the free municipal library of Kishinev and the Russian-Jewish library of Kishinev had been closed by official fiat, making it very difficult for the Jews of Kishinev to gain access to libraries.[168] In Kharkov as well, by 1911 there were complaints that the Jewish section of the municipal library was being neglected, although the neglect was blamed on the apathy of the local Jewish intelligentsia rather than official resistance.[169] Even the largely successful public library of Orgeev was not free from religious tension. In 1910, a group of Christians offered to subsidize the library with the condition that it subscribe to a series of right-wing and anti-Semitic newspapers.[170]

While many of those who frequented libraries tended to regard them as lively centers of conversation and socialization, many library proponents believed that libraries should be used for quiet reading and study: "A library should be built in the center of the region it serves, preferably on a quiet street, where there is little noise and drinking," advised the *Handbook of Jewish Libraries*.[171] Library activists imagined libraries as a respite from the hustle and bustle of the city, a place where weary workers could escape the daily grind in order to quietly meditate and study with a volume of enlightened wisdom. "On Saturday and holidays as well as in the evenings, when these people [artisans and merchants] are free from their usual obligations, the only place where they can go amid the wretched cultural life of the provinces not only to rest their souls, but also to become *au courant* with current political and social life, to find answers to all the questions that interest them, is the library reading room," wrote one library proponent.[172] Such individuals believed that the working classes could be persuaded to choose books over vodka and that the library could replace the tavern as the center of working-class leisure.[173] Jewish library proponents repeatedly called for libraries to remain open on holidays, Saturdays, and winter nights in particular so that the people could spend their leisure time reflecting upon the written word rather than frequenting clubs and taverns, where they would become engrossed in the spoken word of their peers.

Yet many readers welcomed the idea of bringing the sociability of the tavern into the library as the best of both worlds. Memoirs of the period recall the liveliness of the library with great pleasure. Those who patronized libraries often described them as bustling centers of intellectual and social exchange, where the mostly young men and women who frequented them could meet in a realm beyond the strictures of traditional religious society. An evening at the library was a communal activity. In Baranovichi (Minsk Province), for example, the library established by the Jewish Literary-Artistic Society was housed alongside a small theater hall in the second story of a private residence. "It was located in the very center of the city," said one former resident, "and everybody could feel at ease and at home there. . . . In the years before the First World War, [it] was the lively nucleus of social life in Baranovichi and the only place in which cultural activity was concentrated. Here theater performances, concerts, anniversary celebrations, Hanukah celebrations, and traditional Purim balls would take place, as well as literary evenings and other activities."[174] Similarly,

the major Jewish library in Kamen Kashirsky was, in the words of one former resident, "the cultural center of our shtetl. There the youth would get
together, regardless of political affiliation" and meet for literary chats and
meetings.[175] In Zabludov (Grodno Province), the library was "like a culture-
club, where people used to go to exchange books, read a newspaper, or
play a game of chess or dominos."[176] In the Zastavye library, "people read
with great diligence, sometimes alone and sometimes in groups, and what's
more, sometimes in pairs, boy and girl. . . . Outside, in front of the library,
in the light of the moon, the youth became acquainted, they held meetings
and the occasional *rendezvous*. Night after night, hand clasped hand, eye
kindled eye, young heart spoke to heart."[177] As one of the few public spaces
in which the sexes could freely intermingle, the public library was also a
place where young men and women could lose themselves in romance.

The image of the library as a social space was not new to twentieth-
century public libraries. In the early years of the nineteenth century,
maskil Joseph Perl, for instance, had said that many visitors to the *besmedresh* enter "under the pretext of studying, but they spend their days, and
very often part of the night, wasting time with gossip and smoking."[178] A
generation later, Paperna described the Kopyl *kloyz* "as a substitute club:
at dusk, between the afternoon and evening prayers, the people loved
to gather around the stove (the stove was large and between it and the
northern wall was a warm, cozy corner), in order to engage in friendly
conversation about religious and worldly affairs, about local and foreign
politics and so on."[179] Peretz used similar terminology in describing his
first experience in the municipal library of Zamość: "There was a fair in
the library! It was full of people like in the market. Full of people from all
classes and from all walks of life."[180] Jewish youth made similar observations about libraries wherever in the world they found them. One Jewish
reader in the Whitechapel Public Library of London characterized it as
"not only a place where one could just about get an hour's homework done
in four hours, but a meeting place for boys and girls."[181] For these library
users, collections of books stimulated conversation and spaces reserved for
reading were combined with sociability.

Aside from legal impediments, the primary obstacle to the organization
and maintenance of independent libraries was the challenge of enticing
readers to come. Readers complained that stand-alone libraries lacked the
warmth and community feel of libraries associated with clubs and societies to which they already belonged. The same was true of the numerous
networks of clandestine Zionist and Bundist libraries that dotted the shtetls

of the Pale. Party activists believed that nonpartisan Jewish libraries had no character or life and were therefore incapable of becoming national centers. Zionist and Bundist libraries, they contended, not only served the real masses in their own languages, they also became lively community centers. The nonpartisan libraries formed by registered social institutions, on the other hand, were cold, dead, and institutional. As soon as a library ended its subscriptions to Zionist journals in the name of nonpartisanship, they argued, it became a "deserted place" and its warmth froze over. They became archival storehouses of books rather than lively centers that reflected the dreams, lives, thoughts, and tastes of their readers. "There is no shame," wrote one proponent of Zionist libraries, "in establishing a Russian, German, Armenian or Polish library, which reflects the will of its proprietor and continuously preserves its essential physiognomy. But Jewish libraries in order to prove their 'non-partisanship' often go too far; they lose their essential look and put on a foreign mask."[182]

The need for community involvement held true as much at the turn of the twentieth century as it does at the turn of the twenty-first. In a collection of essays published in 1924 as *The Library and the Community,* Joseph L. Wheeler, the librarian of the Youngstown Public Library in Youngstown, Ohio, argued that to be successful, libraries needed to transform themselves from collections of books into dynamic organizations by responding and catering to the community outside the library building.[183] The book represented what was becoming the dominant viewpoint among American librarians. The need to take into account local characteristics and provide a comfortable environment for the population being served worked against large impersonal organizations such as the OPE. This image of the library characterized local libraries in interwar Poland, which often functioned as political and social clubs.[184] Particularly in larger cities, where anonymity breeds alienation, readers longed for intimacy not only in the books they read but also in the places they read them. The most popular libraries tended to be those attached to a lively club or active society. Clerks attending a professional or educational meeting, for instance, were more likely to stop by the library if it was located adjacent to their meeting place. Readers also wanted to feel comfortable and at home in the library. Although a brave few ventured into the larger municipal libraries where their anonymity allowed them to blend into the surroundings, the common reader preferred to be among friends.

Reading:
From Sacred Duty to Leisure Time

In his seminal work *The English Common Reader,* Richard Altick suggested new approaches to studying reading habits. In addition to compiling statistical data on book publishing, Altick encouraged historians to uncover the stories of how common readers selected their reading material, how they accessed that material, and what they gleaned from it.[1] In the half-century since the publication of Altick's work, numerous historians have taken up his methodology, providing the tools needed to (in the words of Guglielmo Cavallo and Roger Chartier) "identify the specific distinctive traits of communities of readers, reading traditions and ways of reading."[2] A study of reading habits is particularly relevant to an understanding of Jewish public culture. As Yuri Slezkine noted of the early-twentieth-century Russian Jewish adaptation to modernity, "A true conversion to modern nationalism—and thus world citizenship—could be accomplished only through reading. . . . The Jewish tradition of emancipation through reading had been extended to the emancipation from the Jewish tradition."[3]

The study of reading habits began before Altick's scholarship. Writing in the 1920s, Yiddish literary critic and public activist Shmuel Niger noted that changing reading habits are reflected in the linguistic transformation of the words used to describe reading. Niger noted that until modern times the Yiddish term *leynen* (to read) had meant primarily "the recitation of Torah in synagogue during the course of prayer." It could also be used to refer to reading secular literature, he added, but only in reference to the type of books women were expected to read: "The mother *read* (hot geleyent) the *Tsene-rene* [biblical storybook]; the sister *read* (hot geleyent) *One Thousand and One Nights,* or some other storybook. But the father *studied* (hot gelernt) Talmud." In traditional usage, Niger noted, men *studied* books as a form of religious duty, whereas women *read* for pleasure.[4] More recently, Daniel Boyarin has argued in a similar vein that reading in traditional Jewish practice was a social and public act rather than a private contemplative act. Commenting on the biblical understanding of the root *qr'* (to read), Boyarin writes: "In all of the Hebrew Bible, there is no unequivocal usage of *qr'* in the sense of 'to read to oneself,' no place where someone is described as silently (or even orally) consuming a text alone and/or without immediate public consequences."[5] "Reading in that culture," he continues "is a public, oral, and illocutionary speech act, an act, moreover, which when successful always has perlocutionary effect."[6] This type of reading, Boyarin notes, is distinctly different from the private reading of European Christendom associated with the silence and isolation of the monastic cell or the scholar's study. Further, the notion of reading for pleasure as advocated by Aristotle in his *Poetics* and continuing as a trope through European literary history is largely absent in pre-modern European Jewish thought. Instead, reading in Jewish texts is portrayed as the fulfillment of a commandment, an activity to be pursued in ritual settings.

Insofar as the act of reading fulfills a religious obligation, the benefits of reading are often regarded as being independent of actual comprehension of the text. As the *Kitser Shulkhan Arukh* put it, "a man should take care that whatever he studies he should pronounce it with his lips, make it audible to his ears, and concentrate his mind upon it. . . . The one who pronounces it with his lips, although he does not understand what he is saying, nevertheless fulfills the precept of 'And ye shall study them.'" It further assures readers that "whoever is engaged in the study of the Torah and is unable to understand it because of lack of knowledge, he will merit to understand it in the world to come."[7] It is not surprising then, that in many traditional settings, such as the Eastern European *kheyder*s of the nineteenth century, students were taught to read texts in Hebrew without being taught to comprehend the words they read. They learned through rote memorization or at most through direct translation from the biblical Hebrew to Yiddish without any contextual criticism to aid in understanding. This radical separation between comprehension and reading of the Hebrew text led to what Robert Bonfil has called the "persistence of medieval modes" in Jewish reading, specifically "memorization as one of the basic mechanisms for acquiring knowledge, a stereotyped repertory of expressions, and a complex dialectic between writing and orality."[8] Seen within this context, the establishment of libraries and reading rooms as public spaces for personal enlightenment, leisure, and social interaction represents a fundamental break not only with traditional Jewish reading habits but also with Jewish society's relationships to the written word as a whole.

Traditional Jewish societies looked upon books with reverence. The *Kitser Shulkhan Arukh* warned readers that "sacred writings should not be thrown around, even books containing Laws and Aggada [that is, religious books of secondary importance]; nor is it permitted to place them with the wrong end up." It is forbidden to use a book "as a screen against the sun, or that people may not see what [one] is doing" and, of course, "it is forbidden to urinate in the presence of sacred books, but in cases of extreme emergency they [must] at least be placed ten hand-breadths high."[9] Sacred texts instructed Jews to allow somebody carrying a book to enter or exit a room first and in case of fire or water to save books before any other valuables.[10] The twelfth-century *Seyfer khsidim* warned readers against carrying an inkwell together with a book lest the ink spill on the book and similarly warned against hiding a pen inside a book.[11] Some regarded books as too valuable even to be read. A. I. Paperna cynically recalled of the 1840s:

> Jewish residents considered complete sets of the Talmud in red leather bindings to be the most luxurious items, much like pearls and diamonds, or earrings for their wives. Both books and necklaces lent importance to the home and gave it an aristocratic coloring. In case of need, this real capital could easily be liquidated and pawned. Like diamonds, books had real value and could find buyers; at the very least they could be added to the dowry for one's daughter.[12]

Since ancient times Jews have kept books for their monetary value and prestige. Medieval and early modern responsa literature is rife with queries about pawned books. The question of whether Judaic law permitted a pawnbroker to lend out books he was holding to those who wished to read them vexed authorities.[13] Whereas some devoured books with zeal, paying little attention to the value of their bindings, others regarded books as articles of beauty, fretting if the binding was broken or the pages cut.

There was a visible and marked difference between a holy book and secular literature. The Yiddish language even distinguishes between the two semantically; *seyfer,* derived from the Hebrew, refers to a holy book, whereas the Germanic stock word *bukh* is used to refer to secular writings. When Paperna first discovered secular books, it was not just their content that surprised him: "Their exterior amazed me: all of them were of a small format, in octavo; the pages were designated not with Hebrew letters but with Arabic or Roman numerals and there were punctuation marks—strikingly unusual for Hebrew writings."[14] The physical differences between a *seyfer* and a *bukh* were crucial for the young yeshiva student, "who would hide various profane books under the Talmud on his stand."[15] The size difference—the Talmud was typically printed in folio format, making it half the size of a printer's sheet, whereas modern books were printed in octavo, or an eighth of a printer's sheet—allowed students to use the Talmud to conceal what lay beneath. Reuven Brainin recalled how "some of these unhappy students hid under their large Talmud folios little Hebrew enlightened books. They used to steal a peek at them and, terrified, they would close up the little books when they thought that someone noticed."[16] In An-sky's memoir, a would-be *maskil* read Lilienblum's *Sins of Youth* in the study house "under the cover of a Talmud."[17] When the student fell asleep, leaving his book on the lectern, it was immediately recognized as a profane book because of its appearance. Indeed, based on the reading biographies available to us, it seems that under virtually every Talmud folio was a modern Hebrew novel.

The autobiographies of the first generation to read modern *maskilic* literature reflect how individuals transplanted reverential forms of reading they had learned from talmudic study onto secular literature, including memorization and ecstatic reading. Books were studied rather than read. In the modern period, as well, observers noted the passions with which Eastern European Jews approached their books. German-Jewish writer Arnold Zweig, who traveled through Lithuania in the aftermath of World War I searching for the "authentic" Ashkenazic Jew, wrote of his subject:

> The book is everything to him, for in glorious myths, the creation of words out of the fire of the divine throne is placed at the beginning of all creation. For him, the world regulates itself in the book: that which has been adopted from it in books, that alone is worthwhile and important; all other manifestations come second to [the] book. . . . Because of this attitude, the Hebrew poet and the Yiddish poet alike are shown splendor and love that only simple people are capable of giving to their artists. . . . It is the poor and the ordinary, not the extremely erudite with the highest education, who love their poets: Mendele and Sholem Aleichem, Asch and Agnon, and, above all, the magnificent Yitzhak Leyb Peretz. They are sons of the people, and an entire people is their enthusiastic, grateful, passionate readership. The Jew who holds a book in his hand, that is the armed and consoled Jew; he lives in landscapes which are devoid of sorrow and sin.[18]

Many reported reading the same book over and over again, striving even for complete memorization of the text, much as yeshiva students memorized extensive passages from the Talmud. Those new to secular reading likely took the written word for truth, just as they had been taught to understand

FIGURE 1. "The book is everything to him," wrote Arnold Zweig of Eastern European Jews. "The Jew who holds a book in his hand, that is the armed and consoled Jew; he lives in landscapes which are devoid of sorrow and sin." This drawing by Hermann Struck illustrated Zweig's 1922 book *The Face of Eastern European Jewry*.

the biblical texts with which they were most familiar. Brainin told of a classmate with whom he began to read the literature of the enlightenment: "When he quietly read through a poem or a song he would enter the highest ecstasy; he learned it by heart. If the poem was sad he would shed tears as he read. . . . If the poem was a love poem, my friend would fall madly in love with the woman the poet was describing."[19] L. Bernstein commented on the reading habits of his acquaintance, Moisei the bookbinder, who read for spiritual and intellectual enrichment:

> Moisei's passion was to read and learn. . . . He read all that came into his hands, but in time he developed a taste for good books. Among the books he acquired for binding, he used to select only those that would spiritually enrich him, satisfy his passion to learn. He liked belletristic works and had a special interest in the classics. The works of the great satirist [Mikhail] Saltykov-Shchedrin, of [Ivan] Turgenev and [Leo] Tolstoy, of [Émile] Zola and [Charles] Dickens were his favorites. Together with other members of our circle, he would also use the books in our library.[20]

By the time he finished binding a book, he would have read through it.

> Silently, calmly he would formulate his thoughts and provide a well-thought out evaluation. The objective or subjective approach of the author interested him intensely. He was a self-taught adherent of the objective method. He thought like a committed and conscious social democratic Marxist. He studied *Wage-Labor and Capital. The Civil War in France*, the famous forward to Marx's *Critique of Political Economy*, he knew by heart.[21]

Similarly, the brother of the would-be *maskil* in An-sky's memoir read *Sins of Youth* "several times and memorized several passages."[22] Zweig commented as well on the similarities between Eastern European Jewish ways of prayer and reading: "Is this Jew praying?" he wrote, "One could swear he is. Between his face and the book in his hand there is an unrestrained magnetic connection. . . . His mouth, opened as in prayer, speaks silently the words that resonate in his heart. His hand, which holds the book, is placed like a mirror under his face, as if reflected in the white water of his beard were his concentrated spirituality; and like a little animal, expressive, adept, and composed, the other hand, still vulnerable and shy, ventures out of the hole, the cuff in his ragged, broad sleeve. However, this person with the appearance of rapt contemplation is not praying, he's reading."[23] Nineteenth-century *maskilim* brought with them the didactic methods of *pilpul* learned in the *kheyders* and yeshivas to the literature they read. Memoirs describe readers summarizing the arguments of books they had just absorbed, challenging minute points in those works, and seeking some type of dialectical resolution before moving on to the next book.

Maskilic books were sacralized on the model of rabbinic texts, often treated as relics of adoration rather than instruments of communication.[24]

Post-*maskilic* modern reading habits, though, were different. Rather than meditating upon books, poring over them and memorizing word for word, the modern reader devoured books. The Yiddish *geshlungen,* rendered as "devoured," implies more accurately eating without having chewed, gulping down. Applied to reading, the use of the term indicates that individuals read books without fully absorbing their content. To be sure, there is no chronological turning point at which old reading habits gave way to newer reading habits. In fact, the two methods coexisted for at least the last quarter of the nineteenth century. But over the course of the late nineteenth and early twentieth centuries, it became clear that the modern reader was reading extensively rather than intensively and eventually would come to do so with a nonchalance abhorrent to those accustomed to the reading of rabbinical literature. The idea of "reading everything that came into our hands" recurs throughout biographies of the period. Brainin "devoured book after book, journal after journal."[25] When he finally managed to acquire a copy of the forbidden works of Dmitri Pisarev, he "devoured every word . . . with great eagerness and with great pleasure."[26] Moyshe Shmuel Shklarsky "used to devour like hotcakes" the Hebrew novels he acquired in the 1890s.[27] "All the free time that was left to us from gymnasium," wrote Avrom Kotik, "we used to spend reading. As they used to say, we devoured books."[28]

Vladimir Medem, in his words, "had a terrible habit. Instead of reading books, I used to devour them. I would flip through the pages, give each a glance, capture the essence of an entire page, and then after a few seconds flip further. Thus I could read a lot but I remembered very little. It was not really reading, but more of a superficial nibble."[29] Only later, after reading an instructional book on good reading habits, did he come to the realization that he must read each book carefully three times: once for content, next for ideas, and finally for form. In this manner, Medem read Vissarion Belinsky's criticisms, Theodore Draper's histories, and the Russian classics: "With these," he writes of the latter, "I no longer nibbled. I would read them with earnestness and attention. From time to time I would formulate my impression in the form of a diary. For the first time, I began to look upon belletristic literature as a serious thing and not just a diversion."[30]

The new terminology and the reading habits it reflected were so new to the common reader that in Zastavye, when one of the founders of the recently formed Jewish library put a placard on the door of the *besmedresh* urging "whoever is thirsty and yearns to drink from the fountain of wisdom and understanding, must come to our library . . . come one, come all, young and old, man and woman to drink from the fountain of life," one could hear the perplexed locals in the courtyard muttering: "What do they take us for? Animals? That we should go drink from the trough?"[31] But soon enough, Falek Zolf related, "The youth threw themselves into the books with life and soul and they devoured them just like hotcakes. Every book went from hand to hand."[32] Biographies tell of a "thirst" for books that could be quenched only with the rapid intake of the written word.

The Talmud recommends that "when a person come[s] from the field in the evening, he should go directly and enter the synagogue, where if he is accustomed to read scripture he should read scripture, and if he is accustomed to study Mishnah he should study Mishnah."[33] The rabbis regarded the twilight period between the end of work and the time for evening prayer as the ideal time for reading and study. The scene Zolf described of the Zastavyer *besmedresh* at twilight was probably typical: "At one long table sat Rabbi Israel Luskeler, the Talmud teacher, with a long white beard, studying a page of Talmud with a couple dozen Jews between afternoon and evening prayers; at a second table sat the god-fearing Rabbi Nyokhke the butcher, with a long black beard and with curly earlocks studying forever a chapter of [the popular biblical storybook] *Eyn yankev;* at a third table sat Moyshe the caretaker and a tall Jew with a white-silver beard, studying a chapter of Mishnah."[34] No doubt the reading habits of the "common reader" in Eastern European Jewish society resembled Peretz's fictional Bryna's Mendl, who "was not a great scholar, but did read psalms before praying, the *Eyn yankev* after praying, and a chapter from the Mishnah in the evening."[35]

Increased access to the new public libraries formed after 1905 transformed Jewish reading habits. Aside from being much larger than the traditional libraries of the *besemedresh,* Jewish public libraries offered an altogether different collection of books. Traditional libraries associated with the synagogue contained only a very circumscribed collection of canonical works. As Paperna wrote of Kopyl: "In order to satisfy the demands of so many inquisitive minds and so many different tastes, the study hall had a rich library. Together with the Talmud, the codices and rabbinical responsa, in the library could be found kabbalistic books, philosophy (*Guide to the Perplexed*), theology (*Kuzari, Principles*), moral literature (*Duties of the Heart ; The Path of the Upright*), history (*The Order of Generations;* Book of Jossipon; and *The Chain of Tradition* and others).[36] The library lacked only the works of the New European, so-called Berlin literature that emerged in the mid-eighteenth century in Berlin, continued in Galicia, and in those times could be found as well in Russia. This new secular literature and biblical criticism was considered harmful and forbidden, but writings of this type soon appeared in Kopyl through secret contraband paths."[37] Rabbinical authorities acted as gatekeepers, limiting and guiding the reading of the community. Even the study of the Pentateuch was carefully constrained and mediated by medieval rabbinical commentaries. Critical philological editions of the Bible, on the other hand, such the *New Commentaries* by A. D. Levinsohn or Hebrew grammars, were kept away from the masses. Even the times when books and passages of books should be read were regulated: the Pentateuch and the Prophets were apportioned into weekly readings to be repeated across a calendar year. Rabbinical ordinances dictated the time not only of ritual chanting but also of meditative readings and study.

On the opposite side of the spectrum was the literature of clandestine and semi-clandestine workers' libraries. Many of these libraries skirted the law by holding books that were legal to own but could not legally circulate in public libraries. L. Bernstein recalled of the workers' library in Vilna: "The library was comprised for the most part of legally published books, which in accordance with a declaration by the authorities had been removed from circulation and could not be obtained in an open library. Among these forbidden books could be found the writings of [Alexander] Herzen, [Nikolai] Chernyshevsky, [Nikolai] Dobroliubov, [Dmitri] Pisarev, [Petr] Lavrov, [Nikolai] Shelgunov, [Fyodor] Reshetnikov, [Innokenti] Omulevsky's novel *Shag za shagom* [Step by Step], various works by other Russian writers, whose names I no longer recall, [Ferdinand] Lasalle's speeches, [Karl] Marx's *Capital,* books about the history of social movements, about social sciences, political economy, as well as about the workers in Russia and other lands." Although the clandestine nature of the library freed it of governmental control, its ideology limited its potential to develop into an expansive collection of literature. Even when the library ventured into legal literature, it retained its ideological focus: among its holdings of books that were legal to own, Bernstein mentioned Georgi Plekhanov, Vladimir Lenin's *Development of Capitalism in Russia,* and Petr Struve, among other legal works of Marxism.[38] Libraries formed by political movements, such as the Bund or the Zionist movement, ordered their books from lists compiled by their parties or were sent books from larger centers. It is doubtful that workers could find in such a library novels for leisure and entertainment or texts for personal tutelage in eccentric topics of interest. In the words of Avrom Kotik, who, like so many others of his generation, began his political readings with Chernyshevsky before advancing in step to Dobroliubov and Pisarev, "When we founded a revolutionary circle, we devoted our entire lives to the goals of the circle, and the period of free reading, of reading according to natural inclinations, ended for me."[39] Despite its claims to breadth, the clandestine library was by its very nature limited to the ideology it espoused.

Both the clandestine Bundist libraries and the libraries of the *besmedresh* limited reading to a prescribed canon of texts that was usually read in a specific order, and readers were expected to understand them within a fixed paradigm. The established order of the Talmudic tractates was simply replaced with a canon of radical literature in which Chernyshevsky took the place of the Talmudic tractate *Baba metsia*. In fact, the system of workers' education may very well have developed on the model of the yeshiva with its strictly regulated order and methods of reading. Certainly the prominent role former yeshiva students played in establishing the workers' education system lends credence to this hypothesis.

Between the extremes of the *besemedresh* and workers' libraries lay the Jewish public libraries, which, although they were subject to laws about which books could circulate, were constrained neither by the religious strictures of rabbinical authorities nor the political circumscriptions of radical ideologues. Despite the efforts of library proponents to publicize suggested reading lists and circulate catalogs of books, readers in public libraries were more likely to meander, following their own personal inclinations and interests, glancing through one book while studying another in great detail. They read out of order and took from each book their own interpretation. Their reading became what Michel de Certeau has characterized as "reading as poaching"; that is, a modern form of reading in which one's understanding of the text is not constrained by the intended meaning of the author or other mediating authorities.[40] The size of libraries and the ratio of staff members to patrons prevented the librarian from acting as an omnipresent authority. Librarians in the smaller workers' libraries were still able to guide their patrons, even testing them on every book they returned before allowing them to receive the next, but in the larger public libraries, the exercise of this type of authority conflicted with the ideology of self-enlightenment and was impractical given the available resources. Without an omnipresent authority, whether rabbinical or radical, readers in the public library were free to choose books on the basis of whim and to interpret their readings within the framework of their own experiences, fears, desires, and emotions.

According to the law, public libraries were permitted to carry all books published in Russia in any language, so long as the book was not expressly prohibited. Lists of prohibited books were periodically published by the censor, and it was the library's responsibility to ensure it did not hold any banned books. Determining whether foreign books were permitted was far more complicated. Libraries were expected to consult with local authorities or to purchase books from dealers who were aware of the rules. The holdings of most Jewish libraries were determined in large part by chance, particularly in their early years. Libraries acquired books by donation, and uninformed and untrained librarians chose books based on their own, often haphazard, criteria.

As librarians became more professional, though, they used several systematic methods to acquire books. Often each member of the library had the right to request that the library purchase certain books by writing the title in a notebook that was kept in a prominent location. Once a month, the committee in charge of the library was responsible for perusing the notebook and either ordering requested books or providing a reason for rejecting a book. Although this method seemed to satisfy popular demand, readers were unable to make informed choices without access to reliable catalogs, and the acquisition of books remained largely haphazard. These notebooks worked best as a supplement to informed choices by trained librarians rather than as the primary means of acquisition. Libraries could also rely on catalogs of books that were available through professional journals and circulars. Catalogs compiled by professional librarians listed legally available books on a specific topic, such as children's literature, Judaica, or the natural sciences, usually categorized and ranked according to the importance the librarian ascribed to them. Each catalog included the price of each book and the total price of all the books in the catalog. Complete catalogs were sometimes offered for sale as a package.

Reading in Tongues

One of the challenges of Jewish libraries was choosing a linguistic orientation. Jewish society in the Russian Empire was polylingual.[41] Although 97 percent of the Jewish population identified Yiddish as its mother tongue in the 1897 census, for many Jewish men, particularly those of enlightened inclinations or pretensions, Yiddish was primarily a spoken language whereas Hebrew was the language of the written word. Throughout the nineteenth century, however, the Russian language challenged Hebrew as the language of knowledge, authority, and status. Whereas the Nikolaevan generation of *maskilim* in the early years of the nineteenth century had written their protest pamphlets, political satires, and literary novels in Hebrew, new generations were increasingly turning to the Russian tongue.[42] Even the more assimilated activists who had previously seen the Polish language as a path to integration gradually abandoned the western Slavic language for its eastern cousin. It was this new linguistic orientation to Russian that allowed writers like Semen Frug to emerge; Frug became a Jewish national poet writing in the Russian language. As American Yiddish newspaper publisher and novelist Abraham Cahan described it, once he discovered Russian literature, "my interest in Hebrew evaporated. My burning ambition became to learn Russian and thus to become an educated person."[43]

For Jewish intellectuals seeking to partake in the cultural, social, and political movements of the nineteenth century, there was no choice but to turn to the Russian language. Avrom Kotik recalled of his gymnasium days in the 1880s, "We read a lot, and only in Russian."[44] Many intellectuals believed that within the Russian language lay the path toward Jewish civilization and normalization. For most aspiring middle-class Jews, education was synonymous with Russian-language skills. Brainin recalled, "Those who had learned to speak Russian—sometimes well, mostly poorly—looked down on those who spoke only 'jargon' [Yiddish]."[45] Leisure activities and cultural associations also took place within a predominantly Russian linguistic milieu. This is evidenced by the intrusion of Russian-language words, such as *vechernik* (evening event) and *zasedaniia* (meeting) in Yiddish writings to describe public gatherings. The Russian *liubiteli* was also used alongside the Yiddish *libhober* to describe amateur participation in cultural activities. Even the various Yiddish words for circle, as in a group of intellectuals—"*redl*," "*ringl*," "*tsirkl*," and eventually the most commonly used variant, the Germanic "*krayzl*"—were constructed as calques from the Russian "*kruzhok*."[46]

The history of the Jewish press in Russia also illustrates the growing dominance of the Russian language. Whereas the most influential Jewish periodicals in the early years of the Jewish press were the Hebrew-language weeklies *Ha-melits* (The Advocate; Odessa, St. Petersburg, 1871–1904) and *Ha-tsefirah* (Dawn; Warsaw, 1862–1896), by the turn of the century the Russian-language *Voskhod* (Dawn; St. Petersburg, 1881–1906), which had a circulation of 5,000, was unmatched in influence.[47]

Women, who were for the most part not given access to Hebrew texts and not taught to read the sacred tongue, were an adoring public for the new Yiddish secular literature that emerged in the last half of the nineteenth century. Without a female reading public, it is unlikely that best-selling authors Ayzik Meyer Dik and later Nokhem Meyer Shaykevitch (Shomer) would have been successful. Although their writing is generally regarded as lowbrow, they set the stage for the subsequent emergence of high culture in Yiddish. Reading habits of women in the early twentieth century are illustrated in the questionnaire An-sky composed for his 1912–1914 ethnographic expedition, which attempted to ascertain the national character of Jewish folklife.[48] He asked women whether they read Yiddish literature, such as the works of Mendele Moykher Sforim, Sholem Aleichem, Y. L. Peretz and Sholem Asch, and, in a separate question, whether they read "interesting novels" like those of Shomer. This question relegated the mass fiction of Shomer to a separate category of writing that An-sky believed could not be lumped together with the great literary figures of Yiddish fiction.[49] An-sky's assumption, which came after years of studying the daily habits and customs of shtetl Jews and the popular reading habits of Russians, was that Yiddish literature was the domain of women. When he asked about the secular reading habits of men, he prompted respondents instead with the names of *maskilic* social reformers and novelists who wrote predominantly in Hebrew: Moses Mendelssohn, Isaac Baer Levinsohn, Reuven Asher Braudes, Hayim Zelig Slonimsky, Peretz Smolenskin, Abraham Mapu, and Mosheh Leib Lilienblum.[50] As Sholem Aleichem wrote—only half in jest— of his reaction to the suggestion that he write in Yiddish: "Jargon! Judeo-German! That's for women! A man was ashamed to hold a Yiddish book in his hand—people would say 'what an uncouth lad!'"[51]

Although Hebrew writings in general were kept hidden from the female gaze, some women may have been given greater leniency than men in reading the secular works of the new Yiddish writers and European literature. Women were often permitted to study foreign languages, including the languages of the surrounding populations, so they could tend the family store or conduct other business with non-Jews while the men studied. This greater knowledge of the outside world combined with their liminal role in society may have provided women with less-fettered access to contemporary European literatures, what Iris Parush calls the "benefit of marginality." Wealthy parents with intellectual leanings often provided Russian tutors for their daughters. Others, like Sonya Ayerov from Ivye (Vilna Province), provided hot meals in exchange for Russian lessons with the new Russian tutor who moved to town. Young women, however, would have had great difficulty reading at home; domestic demands were undoubtedly interminable, leaving little time to sit alone and indulge oneself with a book, and in the small houses of the shtetl it would have been difficult to find a niche where one would not be disturbed by the prying eyes of suspicious parents or siblings. The library reading room was an indispensable place of refuge for young women.

The intrusion of the outside world into the minds of young women created great angst within the Jewish community. Along with Russian-language lessons came an introduction to a world beyond the shtetl. As Ayerov explained, her tutor gave her the Russian classics to read: Turgenev, Nekrasov, Goncharov, and Dostoevsky:

> After reading the books, we used to discuss and critique the works with him. He also brought from Vilna important basic texts on history and human civilization. . . . He did not agree with my orthodox way of life and said that it was interfering with my studies. After study-ing a series of books on sociology, I came to the conclusion that God is a product of primitive thinking and that the more educated people become, the less of a need they have for God. Soon I became a heretic and ceased my religious way of life. Our religious parents, understand-ably, were against our activity. (What does a Jewish daughter need education for? Only to stray from the proper path.) We were forced to study with the Karaites [a non-rabbinical sect of Jews] in a little house in the courtyard where nobody would notice us.[52]

In Yiddish fiction of the period, families and communities were torn asunder, often with tragic consequences, as young women began to read Russian literature for leisure. Peretz's Chana, the outcast, flees her family home and disappears into the world after "sitting with a novel by the win-dow" all day, while her mother grumbles, "books, shmooks. What does she know of holy days?"[53] In Sholem Aleichem's tale, Tevye's daughter Chava elopes with the non-Jewish Chvedka: "He is the second Gorky," she assures her father, leaving Tevye to wonder "and who, pray tell, was the first?"[54] In the most tragic episode of Sholem Aleichem's railroad stories, a father tells of how his daughter killed herself in a suicide pact after reading Mikhail Artsybashev's *Sanin*.[55] Whether or not young women were actually com-mitting suicide or fleeing their homes under the influence of contemporary fiction, the recurrence of this theme in the literature of the time reflects the anxiety and tension that emerged within the Jewish community when women read Russian literature.[56]

The holdings of public libraries also illustrate the predominance of Russian literature. Of the thirty libraries for which the most detailed statistics are available, 50 percent of the holdings of all but three were in

TABLE 3.1.

Language of Books in Selected Russian Jewish Libraries, 1911

	TOTAL	RUSSIAN	HEBREW	YIDDISH
Aleksandriia[1]	1,344	667	497	180
Armiansk	750	750	0	0
Baranovichi	635	405	0	230
Berezino	2,200	2,200	0	0
Bobruisk	7,119	4,090	1,455	1,574
Gomel	7,430	5,019	1,344	1,077
Gorky	2,268	2,056	150	82
Belynichi	346	346	0	0
Kopys	891	687	185	19
Liubavich	1,557	1,288	185	84
Lukoml	301	218	47	36
Liady	2,615	2,035	256	324
Liozno	906	906	0	0
Orsha	2,990	2,500	235	255
Orgeev	3,242	2,500	432	300
Odessa Clerks Library	38,507	34,128	4,379	
Odessa OPE Library	11,290	8,516	517	
Kiev OPE Library	8,238	1,921	4,332	410
Rogachev	1,834	1,455	143	236
Propoisk	1,170	1,000	70	100
Tiraspol	1,742	1,278	172	292
Tatarsk	600	582	0	18
Tolochin	3,170	2,358	595	217
Orel	1,192	612	375	205
Khislavich	3,151	2,437	450	264
Shklov	1,360	1,360	0	0
Zakharino	400	400	0	0
Mistislavl	214	41	134	53
Vilna OPE Library[2]	8,488	4,402	2,044[3]	2,042
Melitopol[4]	10,434	7,265	707	861

Source: Unless otherwise indicated, data on this table is from A. D. Kirzhnits, "Bibliotechnoe delo u evreev i zadachi Obshchestva Prosveshcheniia (Vnutrenniaia organizatsiia evreiskitch bibliotek)," *VOPE* 13 (March 12): 6.

Notes: 1. "Bibliotechnaia khronika," *VOPE* 14 (April 1912): 121–122.

　　　2. "Bibliotechnaia khronika," *VOPE* 13 (March 1912): 129.

　　　3. Hebrew and German.

　　　4. "Bibliotechnaia khronika," *VOPE* 7 (September 1911): 122–123; "Bibliotechnaia khronika," *VOPE* 6 (April 1911): 130.

the Russian language. Six had only Russian-language titles, and at least three-quarters of the holdings of an additional twelve were in the Russian language. These figures correspond to other surveys taken during the same period.[57] There are several reasons for the primacy of Russian-language books among library collections. Contemporary Yiddish proponents of libraries usually assigned blame primarily to the tsarist censorship regime for restricting the acquisition of books by free libraries to a catalog published by the Ministry of Education, which contained no Yiddish titles. While this was certainly an impediment, it applied only to free legal libraries, which were a small minority among the total number of libraries Jews used. A greater limitation on the acquisition of Yiddish language books was the condescending attitude many librarians shared toward "jargon," as Yiddish was termed even by many of its adherents during much of the nineteenth century. Librarians, most of whom came from the intelligentsia, were often immersed in Russian culture and sought to use the library as a means of russifying the masses. They continued to resist the acquisition of books in Jewish languages for fear of parochializing the library and catering to the "backwardness" of their clientele. Many librarians believed the library should be a temple of enlightenment, opening up the shtetl Jews to new worlds, rather than a *besmedresh* where traditional superstitions and habits would be reinforced.

Yiddish, on the other hand, was the language of the masses and increasingly becoming a language of world literature and written usage. Those who sought to reach the common reader realized that the most effective means of doing so was through their own language. "After intense deliberation," wrote Moyshe Shmuel Shklarsky of the library he founded, "I decided to purchase books in Yiddish because I figured the poor can't read in Hebrew and the rich children can purchase whatever books they want by themselves."[58] Using the same logic, even Cahan, whose memoirs recalled his total absorption into Russian culture, established *Forverts* (Forward) in New York City in Yiddish and used Yiddish as his language of political activity. Despite his own personal inclinations, he realized that if he wanted to attain a mass readership and popular influence he needed to revert to Yiddish. The Russian and Polish Yiddish presses as well were founded not by Yiddishist ideologues but rather by intellectuals acculturated into Russian milieus who made conscious choices to achieve mass appeal through the use of the Yiddish vernacular.[59]

Many library activists established Yiddish libraries in the hope of using them to educate the masses. At first, the library would purchase popular fiction to attract readers, and then it would gradually introduce more sophisticated highbrow works. Dvoyre Kutnik described her father's private library: "He decided to open a library for the common people, for his people. My father ordered and received from Warsaw and Vilna various transports of books in Yiddish and Hebrew. The Hebrew books were for the most part the enlightened books of Calman Shulman, Mapu, Peretz, Sholem Aleichem, Mendele and others. In Yiddish: Peretz, Sholem Aleichem, Mendele, Jacob Dinezon, etc. The Yiddish books did not have great success at the beginning. Then my father, who understood the psychology of the small-town readers who want 'interesting' books, subscribed to Shomer and [Ozer] Bloshteyn novels. . . . With time my father got the people to read the new Yiddish classics."[60] Thus, Kutnik's father drew readers in with Shomer and popular fiction but gradually introduced them to more sophisticated literature. How well this method worked and how his patrons approached the "new Yiddish classics" we cannot determine from Kutnik's narrative.

The Yiddish language gained in legitimacy during the first decade of the twentieth century. As the worker movement grew in proportion to the Zionist movement, so too did Yiddish literature grow in popularity in proportion to Hebrew literature. As playwright Peretz Hirschbein put it in his memoirs, "Mother Yiddish spread out both her hands and all her children wanted to be led by her hand. Even the pure Hebraists reached out a hand for her. . . . Mother Yiddish tore off her ragged clothing and exhibited a lively radiant body. She showed a fresh heart and fire in her eyes. She seemed younger to us than the affluent Hebrew. She beckoned and lured us young Hebrew choristers and writers. There was a spirited revolution in her eyes, red flowers in her hands, and red poppies in her black hair. The air was full of her youth."[61]

The growth of Yiddish was visible not only in the sensual longings of Yiddishist writers but also in the sudden explosion of Yiddish publishing that took place primarily in Warsaw in the early years of the century. Previously, Yiddish works tended to be published haphazardly in duodecimo format by commercial book traders with little or no capital reserves. In the early years of the century, though, a new generation of dedicated intellectuals with publishing experience—often obtained from America—began forming publishing houses with systematic goals and professional expertise. Yakov Lidsky, for instance, returned to Warsaw from New York with the sum of 2,000 rubles and matrices of Yiddish books previously published in America. He established the Progress Publishing House on

Nalewki Street, which quickly became the premiere Yiddish publishing house in the Russian Empire.[62] "To publish an academic book or even a belletristic work was for him a type of holy work," wrote Avrom Reyzen of Lidsky.[63] Competitors quickly grew up around him, and by 1911, Nalewki Street, in the heart of Warsaw's Jewish district, was the site of nearly a dozen publishing houses.

The 1903 publication of the first Yiddish daily newspaper in Russia, *Der fraynd,* helped promote Yiddish as a "normal" written language and increase the number of Yiddish readers throughout Russia. The paper reached a circulation of 50,000 its first year of publication and was accessible to many more as papers passed from hand to hand.[64] After the relaxation of censorship in 1906, Yiddish newspaper publication proliferated throughout Poland and the Pale. The combined circulation of the five Yiddish dailies published in Warsaw alone had approached 100,000 in 1905 and would continue to grow; by 1913, the Yiddish daily *Haynt* had a circulation of 150,000.[65] Yiddish writers such as Sholem Aleichem, Peretz, and Asch were achieving international fame, helping promote the Yiddish language along the way. The 1908 Czernowitz Conference in Austrian Bukovina declared Yiddish "a national language" of the Jewish people and represented the apex of an ideological and political movement to elevate and promote the Yiddish language as the most genuine and authentic expression of Jewish national life. Between 1909 and 1910, book publishing in Jewish languages increased by 50 percent; more books were published in Jewish languages than any languages in the empire except Russian and Polish. Yiddish by itself was the eighth most published language; Hebrew—owing to the large print runs of calendars and prayer books—remained slightly ahead at seventh.[66] As Yiddish came to be more broadly accepted as a legitimate form of expression, library acquisitions of Yiddish-language books increased. The Moscow OPE in particular encouraged libraries to acquire books in Jewish languages and was a significant influence on the libraries it supported.[67]

A correspondent to *Der fraynd,* who signed his letter only "A Jewish Worker," complained that major Jewish libraries, which were ostensibly dedicated to the needs of the workers, did not contain even a single book in Yiddish: "And the Jewish worker, who doesn't know any language other than Yiddish, can't find any books to read and doesn't have the ability to purchase serious books, the cost of which are prohibitively expensive, so he must read various trash and 'market pornography' that corrupt the taste and irritate the nerves of the Jewish reader."[68] Another letter-writer complained that the library of Tolochin (Mogilev Province) had 2,000 Russian-language books and only 250 Yiddish-language books. "When you ask them to order Yiddish books, you always receive the same standard answer: nobody will read them. They don't understand: how can anybody read Yiddish literature when the library doesn't have any?"[69]

By the early 1910s, a growing number of readers and activists were calling for Jewish libraries to develop their Judaica and Hebraica collections. In the previous decades many libraries had come under the influence of russifying intellectuals who sought to promote use of the Russian language at the expense of Hebrew and Yiddish. One of the libraries most often accused of this was the Odessa Jewish Clerks' Library. Kirzhnits accused its librarians of having a "denationalizing influence on its members."[70] In 1911, it subscribed to fifty-one Russian-language journals and five journals in European languages but only three in Hebrew and one in Yiddish.[71] According to one source, the library had hired as a Judaica librarian an individual who could not even alphabetize the Hebrew letters. This librarian, it was alleged, had allowed nearly all of the library's subscriptions to Hebrew and Yiddish periodicals to lapse.[72] Similarly, members of the Minsk Jewish Library complained in 1912 that over the past decade the library had been run by a group of intelligentsia who had neglected the Judaica section. Although a Yiddish faction had since seized control of the library's administration, it lacked the funds to resolve the problem by acquiring new Judaica materials and asked the Minsk OPE to take over the administration of the library.[73]

The problem was not only one of inertia and prejudice on the part of librarians who continued to favor Russian-language works. Ideological support for Yiddish could not overcome the paucity of Yiddish-language materials in print. One of the largest Yiddish booksellers at the turn of the century, Bildung, had only 323 titles in its catalog of Yiddish books, many of which were not even available for sale. Translations of modern European literature into Yiddish were also slow to materialize. Finally, while older libraries may have acquired Yiddish books at increasingly rapid rates, their preexisting Russian-language holdings continued to dominate their collections. In newer libraries, though, the Yiddish-language holdings were generally proportionally larger.

Reading habits of library patrons were, of course, constrained by the holdings of the library they frequented. Since Russian-language books were more widely available, they were also more widely read. Statistics on book usage in eighteen libraries in Mogilev and Vitebsk provinces indicate that books in Russian and Yiddish were circulated in roughly equal proportion to their holdings in libraries; the average Russian book was read

3.9 times per year, whereas the average Yiddish book was read 4 times per year. On the other hand, most libraries had more Hebrew-language books than their circulation would merit; Hebrew books were circulated on average only 2.4 times per year.[74] The most likely reason for the low circulation rate of Hebrew-language books was the fact that they were available in the *besmedresh*. Another contributing factor was the nature of library acquisitions. People who donated large book collections in their estates at the turn of the century tended to be *maskilim* of the mid-century generation, whose language of choice was predominantly Hebrew. These book collections, which were mostly comprised of books from the *maskilic* canon of the mid-century, were going out of fashion by the fin-de-siècle, and the books were more likely to collect dust on shelves than the newer and more fashionable works in Russian and Yiddish. Even Zionists intent on reviving the Hebrew language often shunned *maskilic* works written in Hebrew because of their apologetic tone and obeisance toward the tsarist state.

The language of choice for reading was by no means universal but rather was affected in part by the occupation and gender of readers. Students were most likely to read Russian books and, in some regions, Hebrew books, whereas workers and members of the service occupations were most likely to read Yiddish books.[75] These differences are reflected in the statistics for individual libraries. The Abraham Mapu Memorial Library of Kovno, for instance, was one of few public libraries where Hebrew-language books circulated most. The percentage of Jews who were literate in Russian in the city of Kovno was comparable with that in other large towns in the Pale, at about 30 percent, but for some reason Russian books at the library were less read and those who did read Russian books did so only occasionally.[76] One reason seems to be the high proportion (41 percent) of students who used the library as well as the low proportion of women who used the library (23 percent). The library, named after a Hebrew author, was probably established with the help of a Zionist organization; Zionist literary societies zealously promoted Hebrew reading. It was likely the influence of one such group, for instance, that prompted the members of the Russian-Jewish library in Berezovka (Kherson Province) to demand at its annual assembly that the library develop its Hebraica collection.[77]

More often, though, Hebrew books were underused; Hebrew-language literature suffered from reader preferences for Yiddish and Russian, hostile librarians, and official suspicions of Zionism and its literature. A petition to establish a Lovers of the Hebrew Language society in Rogachev (Mogilev Province), for instance, was denied by the authorities on spurious grounds, and one of the founders of the Zionist Jewish library in Kishinev was sentenced to three months' imprisonment, allegedly for his role in establishing the library.[78] Despite the efforts of Hebrew advocates, the public often continued to prefer Russian and Yiddish books. When the Odessa Jewish Clerks' Library expanded its Hebrew section in 1912, use of the section did not increase.[79] In Kiev, the OPE library had over 4,000 books in Hebrew, comprising over half the library's total collection but representing only 40 percent of circulation. The average Yiddish- or Russian-language book circulated more frequently than the average Hebrew book.[80] In 1909, in response to popular demand, the library began to expand its Yiddish collection.[81] In nearby Fastov, on the other hand, the Kulisher Memorial Library was criticized by Zionists for its near-total rejection of Hebrew-language materials: "While in Kiev the number of circles of Lovers of the Hebrew Language and various nationalist institutions is increasing and progressing," wrote one of the library's critics, "among us, in the suburbs, the exact opposite can be noticed." In Fastov, "our youth still all dream of the golden age of internationalism, of equality and brotherhood of nations; nationalism in general and Zionism in particular they regard as an extremely reactionary phenomenon and completely ignore it. . . . The death of L. N. Tolstoy was bemoaned in an honorable form, and appropriate telegrams were dispatched, but the death of [Isaac Baer] Levinsohn and [Osip] Rabinovich passed completely unnoticed."[82]

In Melitopol, less than 1 percent of book requests were for Hebrew-language books and less than 4 percent were for Yiddish-language books. The vast majority of visitors to the Melitopol Jewish Library sought Russian-language books. The disproportionate circulation of Russian-language books can be attributed in part to the relatively high degree of linguistic acculturation in Melitopol: although 95 percent of the Jewish population listed Yiddish as its mother tongue in the 1897 census, over 40 percent of the Jewish population in the city claimed to be literate in the Russian language and about 7 percent had received higher education.[83] Another contributing factor was the high proportion of students (56 percent) who were members of the library combined with the low proportion of workers and artisans (2 percent and 7 percent, respectively). The most significant factor was that nearly 30 percent of the library's visitors were Russians.[84] Similarly, at the Aleksandriia library (Kherson Province), which was established by the local synagogue in 1911, only half the holdings were in Russian, but these books accounted for nearly 70 percent of circulation. Its Hebrew holdings were greatly underused.[85] Both these cities, located in the frontier of New Russia, had large contingents of individuals whose mother tongue was Yiddish but were in the process of acculturating into Russian. The library was an integral catalyst in the process of linguistic acculturation.[86]

Even in Bobruisk, where 99.6 percent of the Jewish population and 99.1 percent of the literate Jewish population listed Yiddish as their mother tongue in the 1897 census, 70 percent of the books circulated in the Jewish library between 1907 and 1909 were in Russian.[87] About 30 percent of all Jews and over 80 percent of literate Jews in the city were listed as being literate in Russian.[88] These figures suggest that those who were capable of reading in Russian preferred to do so, even though it was not their mother tongue. Perhaps they regarded Russian literature as superior in quality to Yiddish works—by no means an unreasonable supposition at the time—or they recognized Russian-language proficiency as a vital skill for effectively navigating and succeeding in Russian society. Certainly the sheer number of available books in Russian contributed to the choices readers made. However, over the course of the first decade of the new century, as the library's acquisition of Yiddish-language books increased, so did the circulation of Yiddish-language books. Most important, the number of readers who read *only* Yiddish increased dramatically between 1906 and 1909, from 107 to 153.[89] This suggests that the library was expanding its reach beyond the russified intelligentsia to Yiddish readers—women, artisans, and the working class.

As Jewish libraries began to open their doors to workers and service personnel, Yiddish-language books flew off the shelves. Of the six libraries in Bialystok in 1905, for example, six held only material in Yiddish and Yiddish-language materials accounted for over 80 percent of the circulation of two others.[90] In the Vilna OPE library, where only one-quarter of the collection was in Yiddish, nearly half of all books circulated were in Yiddish.[91] Among the reasons for the popularity of Yiddish books in Vilna was the high percentage of workers and service personnel (31 percent) who were members of the library. These readers preferred Yiddish-language books to all other languages by a ratio of three to one.[92] Similarly, in the small Jewish library of Sevastopol, Yiddish books circulated at a disproportionately high rate compared to Russian-language books.[93] In the public library of Orgeev, Yiddish-language books comprised less than 10 percent of the library's holdings but accounted for over 20 percent of the total circulation. "The demand for Yiddish books is enormous," the library reported.[94] One reason could be the high proportion of women (58 percent) who used this library.[95] In Mir in 1903, one-third of the nearly 500 members of the privately owned

lending library preferred Yiddish books, although Yiddish books constituted only 20 percent of the total collection. Similarly, in Gomel, artisans
and clerks formed the largest segment of readers at the private lending
library, and they also preferred Yiddish books in numbers disproportionate to the library's overall holdings. The thirty-nine Yiddish books in the
small private lending library of Dubno (Volhynia Province) were circulated
over 600 times in a single year. Although Yiddish books constituted only 4
percent of the library's holdings, they accounted for 20 percent of its total
circulation. The OPE was flooded with requests to supply Yiddish books to
libraries throughout the Pale.[96]

Genres of Reading

Regardless of what language they chose to read in, Jewish readers
shared many interests with their Russian neighbors.[97] Israeli author Amos
Oz described the reading habits of his parents after their departure from the
Russian Empire to Palestine: "My father liked Shakespeare, Balzac, Tolstoy,
Ibsen, and Tchernikhowsky. My mother preferred Schiller, Turgenev,
Chekhov, Strindberg, Gnessin, Bialik, and also Mr. Agnon."[98] Like their
Russian neighbors, Jews preferred belletristic to nonfiction works: fiction
accounted for over two-thirds of all circulation in the Odessa Jewish Clerks'
Library, three-quarters at the Vilna OPE library, and half at the Melitopol
and Riga Jewish libraries.[99] Periodical literature, much of which contained
belles lettres as well, was the second-largest category of circulated items,
followed by children's literature. These preferences mirrored those of
Russian readers with the exception that books on religion, morality, and
agriculture often circulated at high rates in Russian libraries but were rare
in their Jewish counterparts.[100] While Jews continued to read religious
and moralistic literature, they tended to obtain their spiritual readings
from other sources, most notably the *besmedresh,* and went to libraries to
escape homiletics. The publication rates of religious materials also suggest that Jews were more likely to purchase works of a religious nature
than borrow them. A well-established system of booksellers was in place,
and Jewish consumers had fairly good access to popular religious works.
However, even in the Russian book market, works of a spiritual and religious nature declined starkly in the first decade of the twentieth century,
while economic and political works increased, particularly in the aftermath
of 1905.[101] As an urban-based population, Jews were also considerably less
likely than Russians to read technical works on agriculture. Although few

TABLE 3.2.

Book Requests at Odessa Jewish Clerks' Library

SUBJECT	1911	1910	1909
Theology	n/a	120	n/a
Philosophy and psychology	717	671	990
History	795	452	817
Literary criticism	2,204	1,704	2,700
Art	n/a	144	207
Jurisprudence and general science	n/a	450	545
Natural sciences	n/a	644	979
Geography, ethnography, and travel	n/a	73	104
Technology	n/a	1	3
Belles-lettres	52,061	44,720	49,014
Children's literature	7,488	7,901	8,175
Educational materials and textbooks	387	326	356
Reference books	n/a	7	10
Periodical publications	7,688	6,940	8,984
Judaica	231	987	58
Hebraica	847	825	399

Source: "Biblioteka prikazchikov-evreev v Odesse (po otchetu za 1910 g)," VOPE 7
(September 1911): 126.

libraries provided statistics of reading habits by gender, it is safe to presume that women read more belletristic literature than men, whereas men read more technical literature and nonfiction. This was the statistical pattern in a survey of Russian libraries in the 1890s. In Odessa, for instance, men were eight times more likely to read general history books, twelve times more likely to read books about the natural sciences, twenty times more likely to read geography books, and over 250 times more likely to read legal works.[102]

Fiction in Jewish Life

The runaway bestsellers of the era were also the most popular books in Jewish libraries. Russian novelists, like Anastasiia Verbitskaia, Mikhail Artsybashev, and Aleksandr Kuprin, while not Jewish themselves, had enormous Jewish followings. During the apex of Anastasiia Verbitskaia's

TABLE 3.3.

Top Circulating Authors/Series at Select Russian Jewish Libraries, 1909–1910

	ODESSA 1909	BOBRUISK 1909	ORGEEV 1910	SHKLOV 1910	MELITOPOL 1910
1.	Anastasiia Verbitskaia (1,512)	Ivan Turgenev (1,420)	Anastasiia Verbitskaia (353)	Anastasiia Verbitskaia (357)	Leo Tolstoy (596)
2.	Shipovnik Series (1,280)	Aleksandr Pushkin (1,239)	Znanie Series (324)	Leo Tolstoy (255)	Znanie Series (583)
3.	Znanie Series (1,200)	Mikhail Lermontov (1,103)	Leo Tolstoy (298)	Znanie Series (250)	Anastasiia Verbitskaia (544)
4.	Leo Tolstoy (1,047)	Aleksandr Sheller-Mikhailov (1,007)	Mayne Reid (269)	Kazimierz Tetmajer (217)	Fyodor Dostoevsky (427)
5.	Aleksandr Amfiteatrov (858)	Ivan Goncharov (919)	Guy de Maupassant (220)	Aleksandr Ostrovsky (195)	Ignatii Potapenko (394)
6.	Fyodor Dostoevsky (566)	Maksim Gorky (840)	Leonid Andreev (199)	Universal'naia biblioteka Series (176)	Aleksandr Amfiteatrov (360)
7.	Ivan Turgenev (477)	Aleksandr Kuprin (831)	Stanisław Przybyszewski (195)	Ivan Turgenev (172)	n/a
8.	Vladimir Sollogub (453)	Nikolai Gogol (820)	Shipovnik Series (n/a)	Shipovnik Series (146)	n/a
9.	Aleksei Pisemsky (411)	Fyodor Dostoevsky (812)	Ivan Goncharov (n/a)	Stanisław Przybyszewski (126)	n/a
10.	Leonid Andreev (387)	Leo Tolstoy (749)	Anton Chekhov (n/a)	Stefan Żeromski (107)	n/a

Sources: "Biblioteka prikazchikov-evreev v Odesse (po otchetu za 1910 g)," VOPE 7 (September 1911): 127; "Bibliotechnaia khronika" VOPE 7 (September 1911): 123; A. Kirzhnits, "K kharakteristike sovremennogo chitatelia evreia," VOPE 1 (November 1910): 41; "Bibliotechnaia khronika," VOPE 6 (April 1911): 129; D. Svailikh, "Bibliotechnoe delo v Shklove, Mogil. gub," VOPE 5 (March 1911): 128–129.

popularity, her name topped virtually every list of the most frequently circulated authors. In Shklov, 5 percent of all books borrowed in 1910 were written by Verbitskaia, and at the Odessa Jewish Clerks' Library, her books accounted for 3 percent of circulation.[103] It is worth noting as well that Verbitskaia was the most circulated author in the three libraries with a majority of women readers (Shkov, Orgeev, and Odessa). The popularity of Verbitskaia during these three years in particular owes much to her block-buster novel *Keys to Happiness,* which appeared in six volumes published over the five years from 1909 to 1913. The volumes each reached a print run of some 35,000 and impacted the Russian metropolises and provinces like no other book of its time.[104] The novel is a titillating tale of the sexual escapes and philosophical musings of Manya, a young woman struggling to define herself in the modern age. The novel centers on Manya's unhappy relationship with the Jewish sugar magnate, Mark Steinbach, who serves as her guide to the European high culture of the fin-de-siècle. Ultimately, though, Manya longs for the love of the more crass Nelidov, asserting that she longs to be in a relationship where she is controlled rather than one where she is forced to be controlling.

The cultural impact of *Keys to Happiness,* particularly within a Jewish context, can best be understood in relation to another contemporary best-seller to which the book is often compared—Mikhail Artsybashev's *Sanin.* *Sanin* celebrated hedonism and sexual licentiousness and denigrated intellectual contemplation; this was symbolized by the suicide of the novel's antihero, the Jewish student Soloveichik. Both of these novels celebrate modern decadence, and the protagonists of both are inevitably led to suicide. Artsybashev does not appear among the list of most-circulated authors because his writings appeared serially in the journal *Sovremenyi mir* rather than as independent releases.[105] However, the popularity of the journal during the time *Sanin* was being serialized as well as repeated references to the novel in Jewish memoirs indicates that it too resonated among the Jewish population. Leon Kobrin's 1909 Yiddish translation exponentially increased the impact of *Sanin* among the broadest segments of the Jewish population. A resident of Slutsk recalled:

> After the failure of the Russian Revolution of 1905–6 there was a general decline of social activity among the youth in general and the Zionists in particular. And Slutsk did not deviate from the general stream, which came under the influence of the new tendencies in Russian literature, especially Artsybashev's *Sanin* and others. The youth gave themselves up to worldly pastimes.[106]

Similarly, as A. Almi (Elias Sheps) wrote in the chapter of his memoirs entitled "Saninism":

> After the failure of the first Russian revolution, in the years 1905–1907 Saninism spread like a plague first among the disappointed intelligentsia and then among the broad masses. From Russia the plague spread over into Poland and there it captured significant numbers of Jewish youth, even young men and women in their early teens—14, 15, and 16 year-olds. . . . Wherever one went one heard discussions about Sanin. They could be heard in homes, streets and gardens. You understand that not everyone applauded Sanin, but Saninism with its philosophy of 'free love' and consumption nevertheless wreaked havoc in all the circles of youth, which had earlier been full of discussions about the people, revolution, humanity, equality and freedom.[107]

Jewish readers were apparently moved by the same sensations as those that touched their Russian neighbors. Some embraced the hedonism and sexual promiscuity advocated by Sanin and Manya, whereas others saw the novels these protagonists appeared in as a validation of bourgeois liberalism. Jews, however, were likely also engrossed by the central Jewish character in both novels, Steinbach in *Keys to Happiness* and the student Soloveichik in *Sanin*. In both cases, the Jew represents cultured liberalism in the person of the effeminate Jew made popular in Otto Weininger's influential *Geschlecht und Charakter* (Sex and Character). Manya's rejection of Steinbach represents the failure of Jewish liberalism and European high culture in one novel, while Soloveichik's suicide signifies the failure of rational intellectualism in the other. The liberal judaicized ideal of progress is unmasked as a fiction leading only to dismal tediousness and vanity. In both novels—as well as in Russian public culture of the time—the new European culture was associated with Jews. Even the avant-garde writer Harold, Manya's onetime love interest in *Keys to Happiness,* is revealed in the novel to be a Jew. This phenomenon was also apparent in another highly successful novel of the time, Aleksandr Kuprin's *The Pit,* the popularity of which probably accounts for the fact that Kuprin was a widely circulating author in Russian Jewish libraries. The novel, whose serial publication began in 1909, includes among its main characters a Jewish pornography peddler, a figure who catered to the popular conception of Jews as pornographers and pimps. Jews were commonly accused of having brought into Russia not only pornography and prostitution but also the sexual promiscuity of the modern era. It is no surprise that Jews figured so prominently in these three bestselling novels of the era.[108]

Jewish readers, like other readers in Russia, also gravitated toward French and German sensationalist novels, such as those of Guy de Maupassant and Arthur Schnitzler. In 1913, Leon Kobrin, whose translation of *Sanin* had been such a success, began translating the complete works of Guy de Maupassant, an activity that occupied him for some six years. Maupassant ranked fifth in circulation for at least one library and figures prominently in contemporary discussions of Jewish reading habits. His portraits of torrid Parisian love affairs and the urban metropolis had appeal well beyond the faubourgs of the French capital. Similarly, Schnitzler read well in the shtetl. Portraying the decadence and sensuality of the European bourgeoisie, Schnitzler came to represent European culture, for better and for worse, to many contemporary readers. The author's well-known Jewish background probably also helped his popularity in the shtetl.

Library proponents periodically decried the popularity of these sensationalist novels among Jewish readers. The *Handbook for Jewish Libraries* warned librarians to avoid writings "by people of base instincts, all the boulevard press and crime novels, despite the demand for them on the part of the readers" and urged them "not to fear that in the absence of alluring bait in the form of sensational novels readers will flee the library." The handbook assured librarians that

> those who are interested in books will stay, and the library will retain the knowledge that it is honestly fulfilling its responsibility, that it is developing the artistic taste of its readers and teaching them to see subjects in their true light, to comprehend the soul and actions of people, to consciously be concerned with the individual person, society and the world.[109]

Many librarians and observers shared this patronizing attitude toward the literary tastes of library patrons. One writer to *Voskhod* noted "the gratifying fact that" in the Jewish library of Gomel, "demand for the boulevard press and crime novels, except in rare cases, is hardly encountered," which he attributed to the fact that "the librarian is an intelligent and educated person."[110] The Poltava Russian-Jewish library and reading room reported "with feelings of moral satisfaction" that "in this terrible period of various unhealthy tendencies in literature, not a single book that could offend the ethical feelings of the readers found its way onto the bookshelves of the library." The library's management vowed to defend the "highest ideals of the workers" from the "vacillating demands of the masses and the moment."[111]

Others, however, appreciated popular literature as a genuine reflection of the spirit of the times and urged libraries to meet the demands of their readers. Library activist A. I. Izrailitin argued that librarians should avoid pushing books that might be appropriate for the intelligentsia but were completely inaccessible to the broad masses. Writing in 1905 before Verbitskaia and Artsybashev became best-selling authors, he argued, "A library is a guide to literature for the people, and must function on a literary level that reflects the social currents of the present and the past, with the lives, sufferings, dreams and ideals of humanity in all periods of its history. A library is like literature itself, an image, a distinct echo of human life."[112] In his work on popular reading habits, An-sky as well repeatedly argued that reading lists should be tailored to specific audiences and that the tastes of intellectuals should not be forced upon those with different inclinations.[113]

Russian Jewish readers were also enamored with neorealism, particularly of the Znanie Association. The Znanie (Knowledge) Association was a cooperative of realist writers that formed in 1898. In 1904 it began publishing *Sbornik tovarishchestva Znanie* (Collection of the Znanie Association), a collection of literary writings mostly by members of the group. Each volume contained several selections of stories from leading contemporary Russian writers and sold for one ruble. The first volume was printed in an edition of 41,000 copies. The Znanie collections competed with Verbitskaia as the most circulated works in virtually all locations. One of the reasons for the popularity of *Znanie* among Jewish readers was the high Jewish content in the collections. The cooperative included among its members two Jewish writers, Semyon Yushkevich and David Aizman. Yushkevich's "V gorode" ("In the City"), "Korol'" ("King"), and "Golod" ("Hunger") were published in the collection, as were Aizman's "Krovavyi razliv" ("Bloody Deluge") and "Ledokhod" ("Ice Floe"). The collection also published Russian translations of Sholem Asch's "S volnoi" ("In Waves") and a Russian translation of his *Bog mesti* (God of Vengeance). Aside from these writers of particular interest to Jews, the collection also tended to contain heavy doses of Maksim Gorky, Ivan Bunin, and Leonid Andreev. Znanie competed in popularity with *Shipovnik: Literaturno-khudozhestvennye Al'manakhi* (Dogrose: Literary-Artistic Almanac), another collection that published many of the same authors who contributed to *Znanie,* including Yushkevich and Asch. Although both publications were regarded as being on a higher literary level than the novels of Verbitskaia, many of the stories in *Znanie* and *Shipovnik* dealt with themes of sex and crime.

Both Asch and Artsybashev featured Jewish characters involved in sexual and moral transgressions, but since Asch was a Jew who wrote in Yiddish, some Jewish critics of Artsybashev believed that by reading Asch, even in Russian translation, they were somehow fulfilling their nationalist duty and contributing to the project of constructing a Jewish public culture. As one writer from Baranovichi complained, "There exists among us a small group of intelligentsia who completely ignore Yiddish literature and discourse and desire that our Jewish Literary Society degenerate into an institution of the Russian intelligentsia where the first place will be given to the collection *Znanie* and to Artsybashev's writings. There is also in our shtetl intelligentsia of a different type: nationalists 'on paper.' These intelligentsia do not read Yiddish newspapers, but they know of Sholem Asch from reading *Shipovnik*."[114] It is interesting that despite the heavy doses of Jewish writers published in the *Znanie* collections (including Asch) and the Jewish characters in Artsybashev's work, the memoirist regarded the two as entirely non-Jewish and representative of assimilating tendencies in the community. He was less critical of the second group, which did not read Yiddish newspapers and presumably read only in Russian but at least considered themselves Jewish nationalists. Notably, even though some Yiddish readers felt that Asch's work was just as scandalous as that of Verbitskaia and Artsybashev because he wrote about the themes of sexuality and Christianity, at least some of those who read him in Russian saw themselves as more Jewish simply because they were reading books by a Jewish author. Whether it was Schnitzler, Asch, or Yushkevich, Jewish readers enjoyed reading modernist works by Jews.

One Christian writer, though, had an iconic status unmatched among contemporary writers. The Russian Jewish reading public could not get enough of the works of Leo Tolstoy.[115] The feuillitonist of "Weekly Chats" (*vokhendige shmuesen*) declared on the eve of Tolstoy's death, "Who among us intellectuals, half-intellectuals or quarter-intellectuals who have at least a little access to books have not gone through a Tolstoy period, a Tolstoy month, week or hour? Who can say: I have never in my life been a Tolstoian, not even for a moment?"[116] One indication of Tolstoy's popularity among Jewish readers is the coverage the Yiddish-language press gave to his death. *Der fraynd* covered Tolstoy's last days in extensive detail with stories about his departure from Yasnaia Polyana and daily updates on his health. On Sunday, 7 November 1910, upon hearing of the death of Tolstoy, *Der fraynd* released its only extra edition of the year, consisting of a single sheet announcing the death of the writer. The following day, it devoted its entire front page to the story. Tolstoy's death still dominated the front page the next day under the headline: "The Sorrow in Russia." The page provided a series of reports on reactions to the death around the globe. Over the next several weeks, the paper continued to publish reminisces about Tolstoy as well as selected translations from his works, including a serialized abridged version of his *Confessions* and several of his stories dealing with Jewish themes. The numerous Yiddish translations of his works that appeared during his lifetime are another indication of his popularity among Jewish readers. Most Russian Jews who read Tolstoy probably did so in the original Russian rather than in Yiddish translation, a task made easier by Tolstoy's use of relatively simple language. Tolstoy's appeal to social consciousness resonated as much with Jewish readers as it did among non-Jews, despite his heavy Christian overtones. The confluence of Tolstoy's popularity with that of Verbitskaia suggests a society torn between two opposite notions of the role of leisure and asceticism in life.

Other works of highbrow Russian literature were read mostly by students. In Bobruisk, for instance, where nearly 80 percent of the members of the library were students, the circulation of Russian classics such as the works of Ivan Turgenev, Aleksandr Pushkin, Mikhail Lermontov, Ivan Goncharov, and Nikolai Gogol far outnumbered the more modern sensationalist novels.[117]

Among Polish authors, Jewish readers enjoyed the writers of the "Young Poland" movement, particularly Kazimierz Tetmajer, Stefan Żeromski, and Stanislaw Przybyszewski. Przybyszewski was best known for his Nietzschean manifestos decrying what he regarded as the banalities of bourgeois life, which earned him the nickname "Satanist." His novels *Złote runo* (Golden Fleece, 1901) and *Śnieg* (*The Snow*, 1903) were particularly popular in Russia. Żeromski wrote of the brutality and morbidity of modern existence in short stories like "Zapomnienie" ("Oblivion") and "Mogiła" ("The Grave") as well as in novels like *Ludzkie bezdomni* (The Homeless People, 1900) and *Dzieje grzechu* (The Story of a Sin, 1906). Jewish readers also enjoyed the works of Eliza Orzeszkowa, even though she came from the Positivist movement against which the Young Poland writers were rebelling. In all likelihood she owed her popularity among Jews to her sympathetic portraits of Jewish characters in novels like *Meir Ezofowicz* (1878) and *Eli Makower* (1875). Regardless of what language they read in, Jews preferred to read books with Jewish characters.

When they borrowed Yiddish-language works from libraries, Jewish readers turned first and foremost to Sholem Aleichem. In Bobruisk, his

FIGURE 2. In a rare move, on 7 November 1910, the Warsaw-based Yiddish daily, *Der fraynd,* published an extra edition with the banner headline "Count Leo Tolstoy Dies." This was one of the first times the paper published an image on its front page. The entire paper was dedicated to the story of Tolstoy's death. No other single event during the revolutionary era garnered as much attention from the Yiddish media as Tolstoy's death, including the assassination of Prime-Minister Petr Stolypin the following year.

Yiddish-language books circulated 2,220 times in 1909. This was nearly the same rate of circulation as that of all the library's Hebrew-language books put together. His books were published mostly in modest print runs of 1,000 in the Warsaw-based "Family Library" series and sold for 5 or 10 kopeks. In one year, 1909, the total print run of all his books together was 66,500. During the same period, the next-largest Yiddish-language print run belonged to Shomer, at 28,000.

With the exception of Sholem Aleichem, however, the circulation of belletristic works originally written in Yiddish was significantly less than that of Russian fiction. The continuing social stigma of Yiddish was often sufficient to prevent many Jewish aspiring intellectuals from engaging in serious Yiddish reading. Yiddish was used for devotional reading and light reading. Few texts matched the popularity of the *Tsene-rene,* which told the biblical narrative in storybook format, ostensibly for women without access to the Hebrew of the Bible but undoubtedly read by men as well. Popular storybooks of adventure and romance continued to be published and read in Yiddish, but even more popular were the collections of humorous stories that were regularly published in paperback with print runs in the thousands. Stories about prankster Hershele Ostropoler, humorous portraits of Jewish life in America, and satires about the "wise men of Chelm" were all examples of popular Yiddish fiction.[118] The writings of The Tunkler (Yosef Tunkel, 1881–1949) had print runs of up to 10,000. His series of humorous stories for the holidays sold particularly well.[119] These works do not appear in library circulation figures, though, because they were more often purchased by individuals from local booksellers than borrowed from the public library. Their affordable price and wide distribution networks made them accessible through the growing number of kiosks emerging in urban centers.

The common reader could also obtain fiction from the newspapers. Readers of *Der fraynd,* for instance, enjoyed feuilletons of city life, such as the regular column "Weekly Chats." More localized columns such as "From Lodz Life" and "Warsaw Chronicle" also appeared regularly. These columns commented on contemporary mores and issues in a lighthearted and direct form, speaking almost conversationally to the reader.[120] The works of Yiddish writers such as Sholem Asch and Avrom Reyzen also regularly appeared in the Yiddish press.

Although the total circulation of Hebrew-language works in libraries as a whole was only marginally less than the circulation of Yiddish-language volumes, the circulation of belletristic Hebrew-language titles paled in comparison with that of comparable Yiddish-language books. The most popular original Hebrew works of non-fiction were Hayim Nahman Bialik and Y. H. Ravnitsky's *Sefer agadah* (Book of Fables), a collection of legends from the Talmud, and Mordekhai Teitelbaum's *Ha-Rav mi-Ladi* (Rabbi from Liady), a biography of the founder of Habad Hasidism. Zionist polemical literature, particularly the works of Ahad Ha-Am, Mosheh Leib Lilienblum, and Joseph Klausner, also circulated well. Readers turned to Hebrew for politics, rabbinics, and polemics but much preferred their fiction in Yiddish or Russian.

Bringing Europe to the Shtetl

Russian Jews approached most European literature of the era through translations. In Russian, they read the works of August Strindberg, Friedrich Spielhagen, Arthur Schnitzler, Guy de Maupassant, Alexandre Dumas, Knut Hamsun, Georg Ebers, Karl Emil Franzos, and Henrik Ibsen. Russian translations of works originally written in Yiddish were also popular. The Moscow-based Contemporary Problems Publishing House published the first Russian translation of the collected works of Sholem Aleichem in eight volumes from 1910 to 1913. Two reprints were subsequently released. It also published two-volume collections of the writings of Peretz and Mendele. Previously selected stories of these writers were available in pamphlet form in Russian translation, through the Odessa-based Inexpensive Jewish Library series. These editions were usually published in print runs of five to six thousand.[121] Semen Frug's translations of the works of Peretz and Asch were also popular.[122] Russian translations of Sholem Asch's works were published by the Znanie publishing house, and his short stories periodically appeared in thick journals, such as the *Shipovnik* or *Znanie* compendia.

The Jewish common reader, though, was more likely to access European literature through Yiddish translation. Among the first writers to bring world literature to Yiddish-reading audiences was Avner Tanenboym, who was the second-most-circulated Yiddish writer in the Bobruisk library after Sholem Aleichem. Tanenboym (1848–1913) was best known for the historical novels he wrote in the 1890s such as *Plevna: a historisher roman fun dem Rusish-Terkishen krieg in 1877–1878* (Plevna: A Historical Novel of the Russo-Turkish War in 1877–1878), many of which were crudely adapted from the works of other authors. Among the most popular of the authors he translated into Yiddish were Jules Verne and Anatole France, whose works

TABLE 3.4.

Top-Circulating Books in Bobruisk by Language and Author, 1909

	YIDDISH	HEBREW	RUSSIAN
1.	Sholem Aleichem (2,220)	Abraham Mapu (197)	Ivan Turgenev (1,420)
2.	Avner Tanenboym (1,552)	Peretz Smolenskin (181)	Aleksandr Pushkin (1,239)
3.	Jacob Dinezon (715)	Mendele (169)	Mikhail Lermontov (1,103)
4.	Sholem Asch (579)	Isaiah Bershadsky (152)	Aleksandr Sheller-Mikhailov (1,007)
5.	Yitskhok Leybush Peretz (525)	Hayim Nahman Bialik (138)	Ivan Goncharov (919)
6.	Jacob Gordin (465)	Mordechai Ze'ev Feierberg (121)	Maksim Gorky (840)
7.	Mendele (437)	Mordekhai David Brandstetter (109)	Aleksandr Kuprin (831)
8.	Hersh Dovid Nomberg (397)	Mikhah Yosef Berdyczewski (108)	Nikolai Gogol (820)
9.	Dovid Pinski (363)	Eliyahu Meidanek (107)	Fyodor Dostoevsky (812)
10.	Avrom Reyzen (315)	Aleksandr Ziskind Rabinovich (102)	Leo Tolstoy (749)

Source: A. D. Kirzhnits, "K kharakteristke sovremennago chitatelia-evreia," *VOPE* 2 (December 1910): 55–59.

he loosely adapted for Yiddish audiences, sometimes giving the original author credit and other times claiming the novel as his own.

More systematic attempts to introduce Yiddish readers to European classics began after the Czernowitz Conference in 1908, when a group of Yiddish activists led by Avrom Reyzen began advocating that major works of world literature be translated into Yiddish. They hoped that such translations would prove that Yiddish was capable of expressing great art and ideas and encourage the creation of highbrow literature in Yiddish.

One of the products of these discussions was Reyzen's *Eyropeyshe literatur* (European Literature) series, which Progress Publishing House began publishing in 1910 with print runs of 4,000 for each issue. The series included prose and poetry by Rudyard Kipling, Knut Hamsun, Leonid Andreev, Lord Byron, Charles Dickens, Mikhail Lermontov, and Thomas Mann. The translators included Lamed Shapiro, Zalmen Reyzen, and others. In 1911, the journal also started publishing the works of Yiddish writers such as Peretz, Nomberg, and Reyzen himself.

Similarly, in 1909, the Warsaw printing press of Binyomin Shimin announced the start of its Groyse Velt-Bibliotek (Great World Library), which was intended to bring world literature to Yiddish readers. Shimin had begun his career with the publication of radical political pamphlets in 1907. The following year he started publishing translations of European literature in paperback, making available the works of Knut Hamsun and Guy de Maupassant, among others. The Great World Library, though, was intended to be more systematic and permanent. Advertisements proclaimed:

> There was a time—and that time is not so far in the past—when all Jewish literature consisted of individual slapdash brochures and paperback collections. Those readers who wanted or needed to read Yiddish literature would not find in it anything they wanted or needed. The slapdash brochures and paperback collections that used to be distributed only on a trial basis naturally couldn't provide anything systematic. Therefore the reader could only taste everything piecemeal, and it all remained foreign to him. The complete literary form is the book, and we believe that the greater part of our public already has a sufficient need for this form.

The Great World Library promised to present the best examples of European literature in an affordable hardcover format.

The first novel in the series was Mordechai Ze'ev Feierberg's *maskilic* novel *Whither?* translated from the original Hebrew by Avrom Leyb Yakubovitch, a Polish-born writer who had studied at the yeshiva of Brisk before moving to Warsaw and studying numerous European languages. Feierberg's novel tells of a disenchanted Jew who lapses from his religious heritage, embracing instead the ideology of the Haskalah before turning to Zionism as the only solution for the Jewish people.[123] The choice of *Whither?* was fitting for the enlightenment goals of the series. The novel is one of the finest *maskilic* attacks on what was regarded as the traditional mindset of the older Jewish generation that refused to allow its children to enter the

FIGURE 3. An advertisement announces the inauguration of Shimin's Great World Library series. The first books to be released include the collected works of A. M. Weissenberg, Zalmen Shneour, Mordechai Ze'ev Feierberg, Heinrich Heine, and Arthur Schnitzler. The first non-Jewish author published was Rudyard Kipling.

modern world and to imbibe modern culture and literature. The Great World Library was designed to repudiate the insularity of traditional Judaism.

That is not to say that these lofty goals were accomplished. In fact, the series did little to introduce readers to the literary products of radically different cultures. For the most part, it stuck to Jewish writers. This could be either a result of a fear of straying too far from the demands of the Yiddish-reading market or a more complex philosophical belief that world literature *is* Jewish literature. Indeed, in a 1929 article entitled "What Is World Literature?" Shmuel Niger identified several different types of world literature, one of which was literature written in such a way that it has no roots with any one particular people, a literature that "belongs to everybody and nobody." The writers of this type of literature—Stefan Zweig, Max Nordau, George Brandes—were invariably Jews.

Even before Niger developed his theory of world literature, the Jewish publishing world acted as though most modern literature of world status was written by Jews. "The first place in the 'World Library' series," stated an advertisement, "will naturally be given to our original literature." By "our original literature," the press was referring to works written by Jews. In its first two years, the series released forty-eight volumes, of which only four were written by non-Jews. Of the eleven authors Shimin included in his Great World Library the first year, only one was not Jewish: Rudyard Kipling. The majority of the authors were Jewish writers who had already been recognized at least within certain circles as contributors to world literature: Mordechai Ze'ev Feierberg and Yehuda Steinberg in Hebrew; and Heinrich Heine,[124] Max Nordau,[125] Arthur Schnitzler[126] and Heinrich Graetz in German.[127] Others, such as I. M. Weissenberg, Anokhi (Zalmon Yitshok Aronsohn),[128] Moyshe Stavsky, and Zalman Shneour, were contemporary writers; the work of most of them would never truly reach the stature of world literature, however one chooses to define the term.

The series took great pride in offering foreign Jewish writers. Nahum Sokolov's introduction to Nordau's collected works, for instance, declared him a "titan of spirit and work," a "personality that radiates genius," and "the pride and gem of our people." "Nordau, however, is more than this," he continued. "He is the Jewish genius in modern form. . . . and for us Nordau is still more: he is Nordau the Zionist."[129] Despite his apostasy, Shimin placed Heinrich Heine in the canon of Jewish writers. Although Heine had been largely neglected by the Haskalah, in the 1890s, interest in him revived among Yiddish and Hebrew writers, who forgave his apostasy as a practical necessity and instead saw within him the embodiment of the amalgamation between European modernism and Jewish nationalism to which they aspired. Despite his continued popularity in literary circles through World War I, Heine does not seem to have had much mass appeal among Jewish readers in Eastern Europe.[130]

Shimin's Great World Library imprint lasted only three years—1909 to 1911—but Shimin continued to publish European translations under the B. Shimin Press imprint. His new books included more non-Jewish writers but still clung closely to writings on Jewish themes. It also introduced some Jewish writers, such as Israel Zangwill, who had not been included in the earlier series. With the publication of Ibsen's dramas, Victor Hugo's novels, and works by Herbert Spencer, Maurice Maeterlinck, Friedrich Nietzsche, Turgenev, and Strindberg, Shimin started to branch out.

Another important source of translations was the Yiddish press. *Der fraynd* had been serializing literature since soon after it began publishing in 1903. By 1910, at least half a page of the four-page paper was dedicated every day to a Yiddish translation of European literature. Often there were two selections, constituting one-fourth of the paper. It seems likely that many of those who read the paper regularly did so solely for the daily installment of their favorite novel, skipping over the news of the Russian Duma that usually dominated the front page. The percentage of space devoted to foreign literature increased greatly in 1910. For instance, the major serializations published in 1909 were fictional works by Sholem Aleichem and Avrom Reyzen.[131] In early 1910, the paper changed its focus. A huge banner advertisement appeared on the front page of the 20 and 21 January 1910 editions announcing the beginning of the publication of an abridged version of *Les Miserables,* "one of the finest and most significant works of world literature by the greatest French literary-artistic genius Victor Hugo," attesting to the excitement the paper expected its new serialized novel to generate. *Les Miserables,* translated as *Di giber in keytn* (The Hero in Chains), appeared in abridged form over the course of 1910. It was followed by Walter Scott's *Ivanhoe,* Charles Dickens's *Barnaby Rudge,* and Hugo's *The Man Who Laughs,* all translated by Lamed Shapiro.[132] Shorter writings by Knut Hamsun and Hans Christian Andersen were also published serially over the course of 1910 and 1911. Thus, simply by reading the daily newspaper for a year, a reader could ingest three of the greatest works of European fiction in highly abridged form and sample some of the other canonical works of the time. At the same time, the reader could obtain a good command of some of the most important events in European history. The evidence suggests that Yiddish readers were interested in reading not just for pleasure but also for cultural enrichment. The abridged versions of world literature published in the papers helped them gain literacy in European culture.

Books for Knowledge

Jewish readers also devoured works of nonfiction, particularly popular science and the histories of Jewish communities.[133] In his *Noise of Time,* Osip Mandelshtam wrote of the natural science encyclopedias he loved as a young boy, which crushed "book stands and card tables beneath their

FIGURE 4. The front page of the Warsaw-based Yiddish daily *Der fraynd* announces its upcoming serialization of Victor Hugo's *Les Miserables*. The Yiddish daily press helped introduce European literature to Yiddish readers through regular serializations in translation.

weight." "There are nowadays no encyclopedias of science and technology like those bound monsters. . . . I loved the 'miscellany' about ostrich eggs, two-headed calves, and festivals in Bombay and Calcutta, and especially the pictures, the huge, full-page pictures: Malayan swimmers bound to boards and skimming through waves the size of a three-story house; the mysterious experiment of a M. fouquéa metal sphere with an enormous pendulum skimming around it in the midst of a throng of serious gentlemen wearing neckties and pointed beards. I have a feeling that the grownups were reading the same thing as I. . . . Our interests were, in general, identical, and at the age of seven or eight I was fully abreast of the century."[134] Notably, the first book Lidsky published with his Progress Publishing House was a book about meteors entitled *Shteyner vos faln fun himl* (Rocks That Fall from the Heavens), by B. Feygenboym. "The masses were then very thirsty for science; they devoured *Rocks That Fall from the Heavens* like the hungry Jews in the desert devoured their manna, which once fell like those stones from heaven!" wrote Avrom Reyzen.[135] Reyzen himself translated the enormously popular *Duner un blits* (Thunder and Lightning) into Yiddish for Progress Publishing House.

Other publishers soon followed suit. No popular science writer matched the prolificacy of Nikolai Rubakin. Many of his writings, including *Grandfather Time, Or the Development of the World, the Earth and All That Lives on It; How do Animals Live? Pictures of their Lives;* and *Wonderful Inventions* were translated into Hebrew and Yiddish, often in numerous editions.[136] His history book *On the Threshold of the Middle Ages* was published in Hebrew translation in at least four editions from 1893 to 1902.[137] Lidsky financed and promoted many of these translations. Educational series on popular science also circulated well in Jewish libraries; readers avidly borrowed *Popular Science Library for the People* (1890–1913) and *Lives of Significant People* (1890–1915). These books helped formulate the worldview of countless young people, Jews and non-Jews alike, who used Rubakin and others like him as guides to help them understand and appreciate the natural world and the wonders of modern science.[138]

Yiddish-language books of adventure, travel, and history were also popular. The historical series *Di greste krimenal protsesen* (The Greatest Criminal Trials), for instance, had a print run of 9,000 per volume.[139] A series of travel books with volumes on Europe, Turkey, China, and Japan had print runs of 8,000 per volume.[140] The daily press also endeavored to fulfill its readers' desire for history and adventure. *Der fraynd* published popular histories of Russia such as Kazimierz Waliszewski's works on the

intimate life of Catherine II, which were translated from the French origi-
nals. Anything that promised to reveal the secrets of royal life were popular.
Avner Tanenboym, for instance, published a popular adaptation of a book
on the assassination of Alexander II entitled *Di geheymnise fun rusishen
keyzerlikhen hof* (The Secrets of the Russian Tsar's Court) as well as a translation of George Füllborn's *Izabella; oder di geheymnise fun Ishpanishen hoyf*
(Isabella, or the Secrets of the Spanish Court). Short historical fiction and
anecdotes were also popular.[141]

Jewish readers found history and travel even more interesting when
Jews were involved. The Warsaw-based *Idishes tagenblat* (Jewish Daily
Press) flooded the market with its *Hoyz-bibliotek* (Home Library) series,
which published sensationalist titles like *Idishe pogrom-protesessen* (Jewish
Pogrom Trials), *Di shreklekhste momenten in der idisher istoriye* (The Most
Terrible Moments in Jewish History), and *Di falshe meshikhim bay idn*
(Jewish False Messiahs), all of which were published in runs of eight or nine
thousand. *Di geshikhte fun iden Poyln* (The History of the Jews in Poland)
had a print run of 12,000.[142] *Di idn in khino* (Jews in China) had a print run
of 9,000.[143] The most popular works of nonfiction in the Russian language
on Jewish topics were history books by Dubnow, Graetz, and Iulii Gessen as
well as the historical journal *Perezhitoe*.[144] Countless Jewish schoolchildren
learned their history from Dubnow's three-volume *Uchebnik evreiskoi istorii
dlia shkoly i samoobrazovaniia* (Textbook on Jewish History for School and
Self-Education). By 1917, the first volume had been reprinted seventeen
times, virtually every year since its original release; a total of 76,000 copies
were published. The second and third volumes were reprinted twelve and
six times respectively with total print runs of 34,000 and 13,000.[145]

Yiddish readers also read in order to better themselves, to keep healthy,
and to learn how to succeed in modern society. *Vi darf a mentsh fargigen
zayn gezund* (How to Preserve One's Health), *Vi azoy zol zikh der mentsh
aleyn bilden* (How to Educate Yourself), and *Vi azoy kon men derkenen dem
kharakter fun a mentshn laut zayn auzegen* (How to Tell the Character of a
Person by His Outward Appearance) were all successful publications with
print runs of about 5,000 each.[146] There was also a slew of works promising get-rich-quick schemes with titles such as *Vi azoy hob ikh gevunen oyf
der loterey* (How I Won the Lottery) and *Vi azoy bin ikh gekumen tsi 500
million dolar, ertseylte fun milliarder Rokfeler alayn* (How I Acquired 500
Million Dollars as Told by the Millionaire Rockefeller Himself). A book
with the promising title *Der veg tsum glik* (The Road to Happiness) had

a print run of 9,000.[147] Many readers believed that the keys to financial, educational, emotional, and personal success could be found in 32-page Yiddish pamphlets.

Libraries helped introduce Jewish readers to contemporary continental philosophy. Jewish writers, particularly Otto Weininger and Max Nordau, earned prominent places on lists of the most-circulated works of philosophy. In 1909, Otto Weininger was the most circulated author of philosophical or scientific literature at the Odessa Jewish Clerk's Library. The following year he tied with Friedrich Nietzsche and Nikolai Kareev.[148] Arthur Schopenhauer and Auguste Forel were also popular choices.[149] These writers reinforced the image of a degenerate world that readers could find in the fiction of Artsybashev and Verbitskaia. Nordau, the best-selling author of *The Conventional Lies of Civilization* (1883) and *Degeneration* (1892), argued in *Degeneration* that the ongoing degeneration of human morality would soon bring about the total devastation of the world. After his conversion to Zionism, Nordau continued to regale Zionist conventions with his gloomy depictions of European Jewish life, which he believed was headed toward a disaster that could be forestalled only by Zionism. Weininger's *Sex and Character* (1903) provided a different critique of modernism and Jewry. The misogynistic text established a gendered hierarchy in which the only people below women were Jews, whose degeneracy Weininger believed led them to radicalism and a rejection of the world. At the age of 23 Weininger rejected the world himself when he took his own life. The work was widely available in a 1908 Russian translation by A. L. Volynsky and was issued in at least six other Russian translations within a decade. Its total print run closely rivaled that of Verbitskaia's *Keys to Happiness*. In fact, it was likely one of the inspirations for the book, and Weininger was a model for *Sanin*'s Soloveichik.[150] With the addition of Auguste Forel's *Sexual Ethics,* Russian Jewish readers of philosophy could, and did, treat themselves to a trilogy about sexual licentiousness and moral degradation.[151]

Children's Literature

The circulation of children's books was second only to circulation of belletristic works. Children's literature usually accounted for between 15 to 20 percent of a library's circulation. The popularity of this literature is hardly surprising given the high proportion of children who frequented libraries. As we have seen, not only did children under 12 constitute about

15 percent of the typical library's readership, but they also borrowed books in greater numbers than adults. Further, it is also likely that Russian-language children's literature was read by adults as well, who used it as a language-learning tool. Like children around the world, Jewish children in Russia were captivated by fairy tales. They read collections of native Russian tales and Russian-language translations of the Brothers Grimm and Hans Christian Andersen. Older children tended to be enamored of Russian translations of Jules Verne, Charles Dickens, Mark Twain, and Captain Mayne Reid, all of whom ranked among the most popular writers around the world.[152] The circulation of Reid's works was surpassed only by those of Tolstoy and Verbitskaia in the Jewish public library in Orgeev. Jewish children also devoured the cheap adventure stories that Russian publisher I. D. Sytin flooded the market with in the late nineteenth century as well as serialized translations of works by H. G. Wells and Arthur Conan Doyle that appeared in the illustrated weeklies of the era.

All of these works were intended primarily for an audience of young boys. Children's authors who wrote primarily for girls, such as E. P. Roe, Miss Braddon, and Mrs. Henry Wood of England or Lidiia Charskaia of Russia, do not appear on the lists. Unfortunately, most libraries did not divide their membership figures for children by gender, making it difficult to explain the lack of literature for girls. Perhaps boys were simply more likely to use libraries than girls at an early age; certainly they would have been given greater freedom to wander through town without super-vision. It is also possible that the reading predilections of girls were better satisfied by the traveling book peddlers who sold cheap Yiddish chapbooks "for women." Or perhaps young women were bypassing literature geared toward pre-teens and jumping directly into the racy potboilers of Verbitskaia. In any case, Jewish children (or at least Jewish boys), like their non-Jewish counterparts, enjoyed fictional works of adventure and travel. Many librarians protested the inclusion of what they regarded as lowbrow children's fiction in a public library. After all, the library was intended to enlighten children and teach them useful information, not to encourage idle daydreaming. However, other modern librarians were coming to the conclusion that such books had a positive influence on their readers. As one report on a Russian free library noted of children's adventure novels, "Captains Patterson and Nemo produce in the youth positive feelings—justice, manhood, and bravery—and arouse interest in geographic information and in each case distract from the banality of everyday life."[153]

A significant children's literature in Yiddish had not yet developed. According to one cultural critic, "Among no people in the world is so little attention paid to children's leisure as among us, the Jews. The life of the Jewish child is one of boredom, without joy, without leisure."[154] In order to satisfy the reading demands of children, both the Jewish Literary Society and the Library Commission of the OPE began to encourage authors to write Yiddish children's literature. The Jewish Literary Society began actively promoting Yiddish children's literature in 1911 after it was criticized for its lackadaisical approach to developing children's literature at its general assembly in January of that year.[155] A few translations of the stories of the Brothers Grimm and Andersen by people like L. Bromberg and Chaim-Mordechai Rabinovich (Ben-Ami) did appear in Yiddish, often as newspaper supplements. These translations usually adapted the stories into a Jewish milieu, replacing christenings with circumcisions, Sundays with Sabbaths, and churches with synagogues.[156] An original Yiddish children's literature did not fully develop until the interwar period.

Periodicals and Newspapers

Numerous scholars have noted the tremendous impact that newspapers and journals had in Russia in general and in the Jewish community in particular.[157] The Yiddish press was able to attract readers with the sensationalist stories and melodrama they desired, interspersed with didactic items on health, hygiene, and public affairs. Although readers may have picked up the paper for sensationalist stories, the health column could catch their eye and impart helpful information. Indeed, this was and remains one of the advantages of the newspaper: its ability to parcel together varying forms of information and entertainment, tempting readers to notice articles that they would not have otherwise sought out. The format of a library, in which books are arranged on shelves according to topic, did not lend itself to this kind of reading.

Most libraries had reading rooms where current periodicals were available to be read on site, and many allowed older periodicals to circulate as well. Since periodicals in the reading room did not need to be signed out, it is difficult to determine their rate of circulation. However, we can estimate the popularity of individual journals based on the number of libraries that subscribed to them. With this information, we can surmise that the most popular periodicals in Jewish libraries were the Russian journals

Russkoe bogatsvo (Russian Wealth) and *Sovremennyi mir* (Contemporary World). The illustrated weekly *Niva,* which combined serialized reprints of Russian classics, contemporary highbrow fiction, and short essays on topics ranging from science to ethnography, was also popular among Jews and non-Jews—its circulation reached 200,000 in the early twentieth century. *Priroda i liudi* (Nature and People), which serialized Russian translations of Arthur Conan Doyle, Jack London and H. G. Wells, was also popular.[158] The leading Russian-language journals of Jewish affairs were the Zionist-leaning *Razsvet* (Dawn) and the liberal *Novyi voskhod* (New Dawn). Although its circulation did not meet the level of its more popular Russian cousins, the Yiddish scientific journal *Lebn un visenshaft* (Life and Knowledge) is also commonly mentioned. The Vilna-based *Literarishe monatsshriften* (Literary Monthly), established in 1908, was the first Yiddish journal to focus exclusively on cultural rather than political issues.[159] None of these, however, matched the popularity of the new Yiddish dailies, the Warsaw-based *Haynt* (Today), founded in 1908, and *Moment* (Moment), founded in 1910, which reached circulations of over 150,000 by World War I. They succeeded largely by publishing articles of broad cultural interest in addition to political news. The transformative role that the press played in Jewish public culture cannot be overstated.

Jewish Reading and Public Spaces

The Jewish public library movement profoundly affected the reading habits of Jews in the Russian Empire. In contrast to readers in the clandestine Bundist reading circles and *maskilic* private libraries of the nineteenth century, readers in Jewish public libraries tended to have a greater selection of reading material at hand. In the better libraries, which were managed by professional librarians and administered according to democratic principles, readers had access to the best and the worst of contemporary literature. Readers in Jewish libraries before World War I were truly the children of the fin-de-siècle. Those who were too young to remember the tumult of 1905 read to escape into a world of adventure, fantasy, and travel, much as their mothers—and perhaps their fathers—had done before them. Those whose formative years were traumatized by the violence and disturbances that followed Bloody Sunday devoured a diet of Weininger, Nordau, Franzos, Artsybashev, and Tetmajer—hardly a well-balanced meal. One can only imagine the aches and angst the pessimism, degradation, and decadence of these writers produced. The relative liberties that allowed public libraries to be opened and provide access to free reading did not cultivate cultured citizens better suited to contribute to society as many library activists had hoped but rather created a generation of Jews who escaped the trauma of their own lives with the decadence of the modernist movement.

Jewish reading was hardly a new phenomenon in the post-1905 era. What was new, however, was the way Jews read. Public libraries offered common public spaces beyond the confines of traditional authorities, be they rabbinical or radical. Whereas both authorities had carefully limited the types of reading and books permissible, the public library opened new vistas of books and new ways of approaching them. At the same time, the proliferation of Yiddish publishing presses, mostly in Warsaw, made both pulp fiction and high literature easily accessible to a wide public. The reading habits of those who frequented the public libraries and purchased books from the new urban book kiosks represented a shift away from Hebrew *maskilic* literature and the canon of the Russian intelligentsia to the popular books of the new commercial age. Like their Russian counterparts, Jews were drawn to the Russian popular press and romance novels as well as to the vexing psychological explorations of the modernist movement. Whereas the traditional study house promised guidebooks to the next world, the "this-worldniks" who wiled away their leisure time in the new public libraries used modern literature as a key for understanding *this* world instead.

Libraries, intended to function as ideal public spaces where members could share in the common pursuit of knowledge, often became one of the central battlegrounds in the war between Jewish and non-Jewish learning. The facts that Jewish organizations regularly founded libraries whose collection consisted of mostly Russian literature and that the most commonly circulated books were from the Russian literary canon provide concrete evidence of the close relationship between Jews and Russian culture. Even after the tumult of 1905 and general disenchantment with the promise of assimilation, Jewish readers continued to prefer the Russian canon to the Yiddish one. The Jewish reading public was in many ways indistinguishable from the Russian reading public. However, the fact that the Jewish reading public preferred to read Russian books in Jewish libraries also stands as a testament to the degree to which the two communities stood apart. Jews were enamored of Russian literature and approached it as though it was their own, but they preferred to do so in the company of other Jews.

Literary Societies: The Culture of Language and the Language of Culture

L iterary societies were the foremost means by which Jews in the early-twentieth-century Russian Empire organized for cultural activity in the public arena. They provided forums for community discussions, defined and delimited the terms of public debate, and displayed and acclaimed new elites whose status derived from their intellectual prowess and possession of knowledge the community deemed useful. Like Polish, Romanian, Latvian, Lithuanian, Estonian, Ukrainian, and Slovak literary societies, Jewish literary societies had broad national goals of asserting collective identities through cultural expression. They were visible and tangible confirmations of the national value of a language. The formation of a literary society was an assertion that one's language and its associated culture was not just a conduit for vernacular communication, a literary anomaly, or a vehicle for belletristic expression but rather was part of a living and vibrant national community active in *this* world.

The modern literary society emerged out of Herderian notions of language. Johann Gottfried Herder had famously argued that since all thought is bound by symbols, a community's culture is contained within the symbols, or language, it uses to express thought. "Has a nation anything more precious than the language of its fathers?" he asked in his *Reflections*. "In it dwell its entire world of tradition, history, religion, principles of existence; its whole heart and soul."[1] For the Jews of the Russian Empire, Herderian veneration of language generated both possibility and conflict. Herder's ideas about language divorced national identity from territorial possession and political life and provided people without territorial sovereignty, like the Jews, the means of asserting nationhood. Many Jewish nationalists seized upon the implications of this argument to legitimize their notions of Jewish nationhood. However, by elevating language to the linchpin of national identity, Herderian thought also transformed language from a casual and practical instrument of communication into the most privileged symbolic expression of identity and belonging. In the age of nationalism, it became increasingly difficult to use language on a daily basis as an apolitical and unconscious tool of communication, socialization, and education. Instead, linguistic usage was ascribed spiritual, cultural, and national significance that rendered every utterance susceptible to meaning and interpretation beyond the bare content. Time and time again, Jewish writers, speakers, and thinkers were criticized, heckled, and judged not for what they were communicating but rather for the language in which they chose to do so. Eastern European Jews, who had previously used Hebrew, Yiddish, Russian, Polish, and other languages, each for its own purpose, were now being asked by the nationalist intelligentsia to choose a single language.

In the last decades of the nineteenth century, acculturated Jews of the Russian Empire had been known to join existing Russian and Polish literary societies in large numbers, sometimes even playing dominant roles as leaders. On the eve of the 1905 Revolution, Jews constituted over 50 percent of the Kiev Literary Society, for instance, and the wealthiest members of the Jewish community were among the society's largest benefactors.[2] In the post-1905 decade, however, Jews increasingly chose to establish their own separate societies. There are several explanations for this shift. First, the new laws regarding associations made it easier to establish new societies. Second, the wave of pogroms that accompanied the 1905 revolution complicated assimilation, making Jews feel less welcome in the Christian public sphere. Finally, increased Jewish national awareness, which was in part a product of the other two factors, led to demands from within the Jewish community to segregate itself and affirm its cultural distinctness.

It is only within such an ideologically charged climate that so many could have chosen to establish, join, and participate in societies dedicating to promoting usage of Hebrew, a language nobody spoke. However, as the development of Lovers of the Hebrew Language shows, this was not always a deliberate decision. Forced out of other forums for the expression of public culture, many Jews in the Russian Empire found temporary refuge in literary societies. The coincidence of an ideological emphasis on language and the relatively benign attitudes of Russian officials toward literary societies helped facilitate the emergence of these societies in the aftermath of the 1905 Revolution.

Zionist Societies

Zionist clubs and societies were among the first Jewish organizations to seek to take advantage of the March 1906 laws regarding voluntary associations. Since the last years of the nineteenth century, Zionists in the

Russian Empire had successfully organized clandestine clubs, tea and coffeehouses, libraries, and congresses. The Russian government, for the most
part, had little interest in cracking down on Zionist activity, as it believed
the Zionist movement would divert restless young Jews away from the
greater threat of socialism. The Zionist promise of facilitating the emigration of Russia's Jewish population also appealed to government officials,
most of whom saw no reason to obstruct such a development. Until 1906,
the Zionist movement expressed little interest in interfering with Jewish
life within the borders of the tsarist empire, directing all of its attention
toward emigration. Thus, although local officials were suspicious of Zionist
activity, their fears were mostly about potentialities rather than realities:
the potential of a fusion between Zionism and socialism and the potential
that Zionism would stimulate demands for Jewish rights within the Russian
Empire. The government allowed 500 delegates to attend a Zionist conference in Minsk in August 1902, for example. It is estimated that over 1,000
Zionist organizations were established in the Russian Empire and Austria
prior to 1900. Five Zionists even sat in the First Duma. Four were members
of the Kadets and one was a Trudovik, but all of them ran as part of the
slate put forward by the Union for the Attainment of Equal Rights for the
Jews of Russia.[3] Since they were often already functioning clandestinely
(but with tacit state tolerance), Zionist organizations were well situated to
be among the first to take advantage of the laws of 1906.[4]

Nowhere was the Zionist organization stronger than in the southwest-
ern provinces. In Kamenets-Podolsk (Podolia Province), for instance, there
were six separate Zionist circles by 1905. The local movement was led by a
former member of the Kharkov-based BILU, generally recognized as the first
Zionist society.[5] As with many modern associations, these movements were
often started by students who were returning home from their studies for
the summer or who had been inspired at a recent conference. Farther north,
due west of Minsk in Ivenets, students returning home from the yeshivas
helped revitalize the Zionist movement. According to one memoirist from
the town, "first in the year 1907 with the return of young men who were
studying in the Mir or Lida yeshivas the Zionist movement was revived."[6]
Zionist clubs and societies in larger urban centers took smaller satellite
towns under their wings, organizing educational programs and traveling
libraries to introduce Zionist ideas to the towns. The Zionist movement in
Novograd Volynsky (Zvhil; Volhynia Province), for instance, held regular
programs in neighboring Gorodnitsa.[7]

In Odessa, the local Zionist chapter reacted quickly to the promulgation of the March 1906 laws permitting voluntary associations to register. On 8 June, a group of Zionists wrote to the city's town governor with a request to register a Zionist Club under the name Kadimah (Forward). The society they proposed would have the goal of gathering Zionist Jews in Odessa for pleasure and enlightenment and sponsoring activities such as discussions on Zionist topics, lectures on Jewish history and literature, and a library and reading room. The governor was unsure of how to handle the request, still being unaccustomed to the new laws and being suspicious of the society's goals and the individuals it would attract. He wrote to the Ministry of Internal Affairs and the local secret police, alerting both to the fact that several of the petitioners were already known to him and the police. However, the Ministry of Internal Affairs convinced him that under the March laws, there was no legal basis for turning down the request. Over the next year, under close police scrutiny, the society sponsored talks on a variety of topics dealing with Jewish history and literature as well as contemporary Jewish affairs from a Zionist perspective. The talks frequently attracted audiences of between two and three hundred people. However, after the Senate's decree of June 1907 prohibiting "all organizations of Zionists and consortia," the governor had the opportunity he needed to shut down the club, and the city's Zionists had to turn elsewhere for cultural enrichment.[8]

Zionist societies blossomed in the aftermath of March 1906, only to be closed or forced underground in the spring and summer of 1907. The Jewish National Club of Warsaw, which had sponsored regular talks on political topics relevant to Jewish national interests, was also closed by official order in the spring of 1907, a few weeks before the decree against Zionism, on the grounds that it was becoming a center of Jewish national activity, as if the Jewish National Club could have any other purpose. The closure came soon after the club sponsored a talk on the effects of Polish autonomy on the Jewish population. It is possible that the increased discussion of modern political issues of national relevance provided further impetus for the 1 June decree.[9]

The June 1907 crackdown was in part a reaction to the Helsingfors Program that was adopted at the third conference of Russian Zionists held in Helsingfors in December 1906. The program endorsed Gegenwartsarbeit, which called for the establishment of Jewish cultural and educational institutions with Zionist curricula and for the active participation of Jewry in the political and cultural life of the countries where they lived, including the Russian Empire. By redirecting the movement away from an elite diplomatic endeavor designed to promote the emigration of Russia's Jews to a populist movement with broad reform goals in Russia, the Helsingfors Program rendered Zionism unacceptable to tsarist officials. Ironically, while it was the new laws of 1906 that made it possible for Russian Zionists to think about organizing an institutional framework with broad cultural goals in Russia, it was their embrace of this notion that led to the 1907 decree prohibiting Zionism.

The 1907 decree, however, only encouraged Zionists to become more involved in promoting Jewish national culture by further directing their attention away from Palestine and the other world and toward Russia, in particular toward the development and promotion of Hebrew-language cultural activities. While the authorities were adamant in refusing to register societies that called themselves Zionist, they were more tolerant toward societies that said they sought to promote the Hebrew language, particularly when the petitioners learned to identify the Hebrew language as "biblical language." After all, how could local officials ban a society whose goal was to study and promote the language of the Bible? Since the promotion of the Hebrew language was regarded as an essential aspect of the Zionist project, which included the cultural reawakening of the Jewish people through language, Zionist activity was able to continue under the guise of promoting the Hebrew language.

Lovers of the Hebrew Language

Lovers of the Hebrew Language (Hovevei Sfas Eyver) was the most prominent society that sought to promote the Hebrew language. This society's goals, according to its official charter, were "to aid in the spread of knowledge of the Hebrew language among Jews, and the development of Hebrew literature." In order to achieve these goals, the society would promote the teaching of Hebrew in Jewish educational establishments; provide opportunities for Jewish children to attend such establishments; establish new Hebrew-language schools, libraries, and courses; sponsor "periodic readings and conversation" for its members; and, if resources permitted, publish a periodical in Hebrew. Notably, the statute did not specify the language in which the periodic readings and conversations would be presented.[10] The Ministry of Internal Affairs permitted the society to function only under the condition that any "periodic readings and conversations" in the Hebrew language take place "strictly for didactic purposes and only in closed sessions of the society." Public gatherings in Hebrew were expressly prohibited.[11] The St. Petersburg branch of the society was legally established in April 1907. Its first meeting, on Sunday, 6 December of that year, was attended by about 200 men and women, who listened to bombastic speeches glorifying the Hebrew language in Russian.[12] The St. Petersburg society retained the right to establish branches throughout the empire and worked conscientiously to spread its activities to regions with large Jewish populations who would be sympathetic to Zionism. By late 1910, the society boasted forty-eight branches throughout the empire.[13]

The society's charter deemphasized its Zionist sympathies and goals and instead touted Hebrew as one of the means by which the Jewish people had been able to flourish in the Diaspora: "The Jewish language, the language of the Torah and the prophets has always been dear and sacred to the Jewish people. . . . The national language occupies a primary place among the major factors contributing to the maintenance of Jewish life in the long period of the Diaspora."[14] The society repeatedly evoked the past rather than the future in its proclamations and presented itself more along the lines of an antiquarian society or a learned society with the purely academic goal of learning to decipher ancient texts rather than one dedicated to establishing a new future for the Jewish people. This presented a stark contrast with the type of messianic rhetoric that was becoming characteristic of Zionist propaganda emanating from Western and Central Europe. When the society sought permission to hold spoken-word events or theatrical productions in Hebrew, it often found it necessary to remind local officials that Hebrew is the language of the Bible. Officials permitted Lovers of the Hebrew Language to function legally in part due to its evocation of the past, particularly the biblical past, and its not entirely false claim that it was an elite society.

Although the society's formal charter made no reference to Palestine or to Jewish national interests, its discussions tended to be dominated by issues related to Palestine. Talks were sponsored on a wide array of issues dealing with emigration to Palestine and life in the Yishuv (Jewish settlement in Palestine). Speakers regularly connected the Hebrew language to the Zionist project and presented the study of Hebrew as a means of bringing about Jewish colonization of Palestine. On 23 December 1912, for instance, the members of Lovers of the Hebrew Language in St. Petersburg heard a talk by Z. N. Epstein on "The Development of the Hebrew Language and Its Relation to the Colonization of Palestine."[15] Many local branches also conducted fund-raising activities on behalf of Palestine, such as arranging collections for the Jewish National Fund.[16] Sometimes the association between the Hebrew language and the land of Palestine was made explicit. On 13 November 1911, A. A. Borukhov gave a talk on the development of the Hebrew language in which he argued that "the Hebrew language is the only repository of the Jewish spirit, which is one of two national values—language and land—preserved by the Jewish people, even if only in idea."[17] Borukhov explicitly linked the Hebrew language with the goal of establishing a Jewish presence in Palestine. In many respects, Lovers of the Hebrew Language used language as a metonym for the entire Zionist project.

Even evenings of Hebrew-language entertainment were explicitly linked to the broader Zionist goal of encouraging Jewish emigration to Palestine. The Bialystok branch of the society, for instance, sponsored several Hebrew-language plays and outdoor performances in the summer of 1909. One evening featured a rendition of the Zionist anthem "Hatikvah" performed by a children's choir, followed by a procession of children carrying blue and white flags (the colors of the future Israeli flag) led by a military orchestra. The hall itself was decorated with scenes of life in Palestine and a large portrait of Theodor Herzl, the founder of political Zionism.[18] In Rovno, "practically all the Zionists of Rovno were listed as members of the branch of the Lovers of the Hebrew Language," and the branch was led by the leader of the local Zionist chapter.[19]

Not all activities, though, made the link between Hebrew and the political movement of Zionism explicit. In 1912, nearly 100 members of the Kovno branch attended its first meeting in a Jewish school building, which was decorated for the occasion with banners bearing slogans like "Speak Hebrew" and "Read Hebrew Books and Newspapers." The main event of the evening was a talk, in Hebrew, about the national significance of the Hebrew language. The event was attended by ninety-seven men and women, most of them young people.[20] The Ananev (Kherson Province) branch spent much of its efforts on establishing a library.[21]

The need to promote knowledge of the Hebrew language was broadly recognized. In fact, Lovers of the Hebrew Language was plagued throughout its existence with the issue that despite their love of the language, few of the society's members were capable of speaking or even understanding spoken Hebrew. As a result, the society frequently touted the merits of Hebrew in the Russian language. Even the founding meeting of the society in St. Petersburg was conducted in Russian. When it held an evening in celebration of the birthday of the Hebrew novelist Abraham Mapu in November 1908, it accompanied Hebrew-language talks with a talk in Russian so that

people would understand the significance of the event.[22] The situation in
the provinces was the same. In Elizavetgrad (Kherson Province), a Russian-
language talk could be expected to attract over 100 people, but a Hebrew-
language talk by the same speaker barely attracted thirty. As one correspondent noted, "As can be seen, there are very few people among us who can
listen to a lecture in Hebrew."[23] Even in Bessarabia, where Hebrew cultural
activity was relatively well developed, the Soroki (Bessarabia Province)
branch held its meetings in Russian because, as one speaker put it, "Jargon
[Yiddish] isn't a language, and nobody understands Hebrew. So we are left
with Russian."[24]

Like Lovers of the Hebrew Language, the Ivriah Society worked to
promote knowledge of the Hebrew language. It encouraged its members
to speak Hebrew not only in the formal settings of the society's meetings
but also in public and informal gatherings. In Kielce, an Ivriah Society was
formally established in 1906 from a preexisting Zionist circle. According
to one memoirist from the town, speaking Hebrew in public spaces was
regarded as an integral activity:

> Every Sabbath afternoon, all the members would go to the town park
> for a stroll. They would stroll in pairs, each choosing a topic about
> which to converse. If during the conversation a difficulty in express-
> ing a concept arose, they would turn to a neighboring couple with
> a question. They would quickly resolve the problem and continue
> the conversation. The conversations, the questions, and answers were
> conducted loudly, so that others would hear and so that the idea of
> learning and knowing Hebrew speech would be awakened in them
> as well. The Hebrew speech of the strollers truly did make an impact
> on the elderly and the youth, the men and the women, who were
> accustomed to strolling in the town park on Sabbath afternoons. Even
> Christian strollers stopped in their tracks when the sounds of a lan-
> guage they were not used to hearing reached their ears, and they asked
> about it. They received a comprehensive explanation about Zionism,
> its purpose and aspirations and about the training of the generation
> to prepare for the task before them: the renewal of the people in its
> homeland, in the Holy Land, and the restoration of the Hebrew lan-
> guage to fluency among the youth, the language of our prophets, the
> holy language to Christians as well.[25]

The Ivriah Society of Riga included a subcommittee called the Hebrew
Speakers that met twice a month to hear talks and have discussions exclusively in Hebrew.[26] Similarly, the Zionist club in Lutsk (Volhynia Province),

which in 1912 was reorganized as a branch of Lovers of the Hebrew Language, encouraged its members to speak Hebrew openly in the street.[27]

As branches of Lovers of the Hebrew Language continued to be formed, the organization expanded by merging with the Ivriah Society. Simultaneously an effort was made to consolidate the movement. At its December 1911 conference, Lovers of the Hebrew Language committed itself to regular conferences and to establishing common goals and plans that would encompass not only the Russian branches but also branches in Romania, Turkey, Hungary, Austria, Germany, England, America, and South Africa. An international central committee would dispatch instructions to national committees, which would in turn be responsible for implementing them on the national and local level. As long-term goals, the society sought to concentrate on the issues of educating the public, publishing Hebrew-language materials, conducting research on the Hebrew language, and strengthening relations between the Jewish communities of the Diaspora and Palestine.[28]

Other Zionist societies sponsored other forms of cultural displays, including art exhibits, theatrical performances, spoken-word events, and dancing. Zionist circles, in particular, adopted the stage as a source of propaganda. Whereas Hebrew could not easily be spoken in social clubs, since many there lacked the active language skills needed for spontaneous fluent discussions, it was easier to perform a scripted play in Hebrew, in which actors could memorize their lines. Actors could even work off scripts transliterated with Cyrillic characters. Although audiences were unlikely to understand every word uttered on stage, it provided an artificial environment in which they could marvel at how well the trained actors were able to pronounce the biblical language. At such events, playwrights and propagandists could prove that Hebrew was a language capable of expressing modern thoughts and anxieties.

The Jewish Literary Society

Just as the Helsingfors Conference served as a stimulus for the establishment of Lovers of the Hebrew Language, the Czernowitz Conference helped motivate the establishment of the Jewish Literary Society. The conference, held in Czernowitz, Bukovina, in August and September 1908, famously called for the promotion of "Yiddish as a national language of the Jewish people." In addition to making platitudinous declarations, the society also sought to establish an institutional framework for supporting the

Yiddish language. In his speech on the second day of the Congress, Peretz called for the founding of a Jewish society that would coordinate cultural activity by establishing libraries, schools, theaters, and publications and by sponsoring regular conferences on Jewish culture. The conference failed to establish any type of permanent institution on this model because of internal disagreements among the delegates about which language, or languages, to use to develop Jewish culture and about the best structure for an organization that would oversee cultural development. Chaim Zhitlowsky's suggestion of a joint-stock structure, for instance, was criticized by Esther Frumkin and others for privileging the bourgeois over Jewish working people. Although the conference ended with a vote endorsing Yiddish as a national Jewish language and leaving attitudes toward Hebrew as a personal matter, it did so only after a passionate dispute that took most of the conference's fourth day.

Ultimately, the type of organizing work that would have been necessary to establish a permanent institutional body to continue the work of the conference could not take place. The delegates from within the Russian Empire, who made up a large number of the attendees, had received only short-term permits to attend the conference in the Austro-Hungarian Empire and needed to return before their visas expired. Had they been able to obtain permission to hold the conference in one of the major Jewish centers of Vilna, Warsaw, or Odessa rather than across the border in Czernowitz, perhaps this type of organizing could have taken place. But, as happened in so many other cases, it was on the other side of the Russian border that one of the major transformations within Jewish culture would have to take place. As *Der fraynd* complained, "The true Yiddish writers must travel to a strange land, go into exile, and bring their learning, their Torah, with them. An old Jewish force of habit."[29] Although conceived independently of the Czernowitz Conference and with a very different ideological agenda, the formation of the Jewish Literary Society was influenced by the same instinct to organize to promote cultural development as the conference.

Several months after the conference, in November 1908, the Jewish Literary Society was founded in St. Petersburg. As preexisting literary societies such as the Zionist clubs were closed in the crackdowns following the anti-Zionist decree of June 1907, several St. Petersburg cultural activists initiated the idea of establishing a society that would eschew all politically sensitive topics in order to retain legal legitimacy and the ability to operate publicly and openly. Among these were Simon Dubnow, Shaul Ginzburg, S. An-sky, and Izrail Tsinberg. This group of intellectuals sought out established businessmen to sign their petition and garner the trust of the government. The society's goals, as stated in the charter, were to promote the spread and development of Jewish knowledge and literature in Hebrew, Yiddish, and other languages. In order to reach this goal, the society's charter stated that it would:

- Organize for the benefit of its members discussions and readings in Russian, Hebrew and Yiddish on subjects relating to the activities of the society;
- Organize on the same subjects with the appropriate permissions in Russian, Hebrew and Yiddish public meetings, reports and lectures, performances, concerts and literary evenings;
- Publish and distribute journals, newspapers, books, brochures and other literary works; on the same subjects that interest the society, according to existing rules and regulations;
- Organize libraries, museums, exhibits, etc.; and
- Publish and support Jewish writers and artists.[30]

The charter expressly reserved the right to establish branches throughout all the territories of the Russian Empire. Its founders recognized that if the society was to help change cultural mores outside the largely assimilated imperial capital, it would need to have a sphere of activity of significant geographic scope.

Dubnow wrote of the formation of the society:

> At that time, after the political disappointment and what several of us circles of youth were calling rotten decadence, the healthy segments of Jewish society felt a strong demand for broad national-cultural work. The growth of literature in both Jewish languages as well as in the state language was next. In order to raise social energy, it was necessary to utilize the only achievement left intact from the recent revolution: the relative freedom of the press and public readings. The new law made it easier to form societies and unions with cultural goals. Thus it was decided to establish in St. Petersburg a Jewish literary society with the right to open branches in the provinces.[31]

At the address he delivered at the society's opening, he echoed the themes that had permeated his writings for years—the idea that societies living under political repression had to turn to cultural development to develop and maintain their national spirit. In such situations, he said, literature becomes the guardian of society and bears a responsibility to oversee the strengthening of this national culture.

The rapid growth of the society in St. Petersburg and beyond was unmatched among cultural associations. By the end of 1909, the society had expanded to forty branches. Within two years of its founding, the St. Petersburg branch alone had over 800 members. In 1910, an additional fifty-one branches were established. When it was closed only three years after its founding, on 1 July 1911, it had grown to a remarkable 122 branches, including twenty-four that were in the process of being registered.[32] In the last two months of 1910, applications were submitted to establish branches in Ianov (Kovno Province), Tomashpol (Podolia Province), Grodisk (Warsaw Province), Novyi Bug (Kherson Province), Enakievo (Ekaterinoslav Province), and Genichesk (Taurida Province).[33]

In order to maintain contact with the provincial branches and stimulate the formation of new branches, the St. Petersburg society regularly dispatched lecturers to the provinces for nominal fees and answered queries about issues ranging from how to organize a new branch to recommendations for reading materials. Dovid Roykhl, for instance, recalled writing a letter to the Jewish Literary Society of St. Petersburg from the town of Kremenets to ask for recommendations on Yiddish-language journals for the library he was establishing.[34] Nevertheless, the St. Petersburg branch was repeatedly criticized for failing to pay sufficient attention to outreach programs and instead catering to the St. Petersburg elite.

Many of the provincial branches emerged into large-scale societies in their own rights. In 1910, the Kiev branch boasted over 656 members, the Berdichev branch 615, the Vitebsk branch over 400, and the Grodno branch over 300. Smaller locales also had significant memberships. The Rossieny (Kovno Province) branch had 186 members, Orsha had 127, Bausk (Kurliand Province) had 124, and Bakhmut (Ekaterinoslav Province) had 100.[35] The provincial branches were often very active, sometimes even more so than the St. Petersburg society. In Vitebsk, for instance, there were eighteen spoken-word events over the course of 1910. In Smorgon (Vilna Province), the literary society sponsored fifteen discussions, three performances in Yiddish, six public lectures, and one concert in a single year. The Rossieny branch sponsored three spoken-word events, two dramatic performances, and one literary-musical evening. In Bausk, the society sponsored three talks and two literary-musical evenings. In Częstochowa, the society sponsored evenings of entertainment in beer gardens as well as formal talks and included a dramatic section and a choir that sang Jewish folk songs in Hebrew and Yiddish.[36] Even in small towns, members could expect about one event (even if it was only a spoken-word event) a month. In Baranovichi, according to one resident, who wrote in 1911, "Hardly a week goes by without a Jewish performance of some type, a literary reading or an evening with a national program."[37] Yet the frequency of events was irregular and subject to regional differentiation. A resident of Pinsk complained that

> it seems at times that you are living here in some type of neglected village rather than a city with a population of forty thousand of whom there are many people with solid, general knowledge. Here, there is not a single cultural institution in which one could gather from time to time for literary or scientific discussions. There is a branch of the Society for the Spread of Enlightenment among the Jews of Russia, but since last winter there has not been a meeting.[38]

Local branches of the Jewish Literary Society were active in establishing other institutional foundations to spread Jewish culture. In 1910, for instance, branches in Bausk, Gorodok, Kutno, Niezhin, Praga (Warsaw Province), Sokolka (Grodno Province), and Częstochowa opened libraries and reading rooms.[39] The society worked in conjunction with the OPE to promote the establishment of Jewish libraries throughout Russia and sent a contingent to the first All-Russian Librarians' Conference in St. Petersburg in the summer of 1911. The society also fostered the publication of children's literature in Yiddish, announcing a contest offering a prize of 200 rubles for the best children's book in that language.[40]

In the major centers of Jewish culture, the local branch of the Jewish Literary Society often included among its members and executive committees many of the most illustrious members of the Jewish literary community. In Odessa, for instance, the executive committee included Bialik, Frug, and Klausner.[41] The Warsaw branch was led by Y. L. Peretz and included A. Mukdoyni and Jacob Dinezon on its executive committee. Not surprisingly, the Warsaw branch was one of the most active branches of the society, meeting on an almost weekly basis to hear lectures. "The chief lecturer was Peretz himself," wrote Dubnova-Erlikh. "He had the biggest audience. Often [his lectures] dealt with social problems. . . . The lectures on literature and theaters were very popular."[42] Local intelligentsia also regularly served on the executive committees of their town's branch.

In many towns, students took upon themselves leadership roles in the formation of literary societies. Students formed societies both within the university environment and in their hometowns during summer breaks. In Moscow in 1908 a group of students at Moscow University established a Jewish Scientific-Literary Circle for the study of Jewish literature, history, economics, and philosophy.[43] Similarly, in the small university town of Iurev, where Jewish students were for the most part highly assimilated and, one would think, uninterested in Jewish affairs, an Academic Union for the Study of Jewish History and Literature existed as well as a Jewish Students' Mutual Aid Fund. The latter was not only a mutual aid society but also sponsored social events such as masquerade balls.[44] Other small-town societies were established by gymnasium students. A group of well-to-do young Jewish men, all of whom knew a little Russian and secular knowledge and had studied with private tutors or in the Russian gymnasium in town, established a literary society in Biała Podlaska (Siedlce Province) in 1909, which met regularly in a small room for group discussion and reading.[45]

The Language Question in the Jewish Literary Society

Whether in the capital or the provinces, the Jewish Literary Society often became a battleground for the broader ideological wars being waged within the secular Jewish community. Some saw the society as an opportunity to further the goals of the OPE by promoting Russian-language acculturation among Jews and exposing them to broader international literary and cultural trends taking place throughout Europe. Others hoped the Jewish Literary Society would finally give an aura of legitimacy to Yiddish, elevating it to the status of a genuine national language suitable for discussion, deliberation, and other forms of communication and cultural expression in the public sphere. Still others saw within the Jewish Literary Society the opportunity to revive the Hebrew language as a contemporary spoken dialect, capable of expressing the thoughts and desires of a modern and modernizing Jewish civilization. Although these debates often reflected profound disagreements about the future (and past) of the Jewish community, these disagreements were expressed using the issue of language.

In a feulliton "From the Jewish Street," one writer portrayed the language debates that accompanied the founding of numerous literary societies and libraries around the country:

> In Druya (Vilna Province) several young people had the idea to establish a literary society. In no time politics stuck its nose in.

FIGURE 5. Sholem Asch, Yitskhok Leybush Peretz, and Hersh Dovid Nomberg pose for a photograph with Peretz's son (lying in front). Prominent Yiddish writers and literary critics worked together to help forge a new Jewish public culture. *Photo courtesy of YIVO Institute for Jewish Research.*

- Don't rush children. You must first know what and who
  you are, you must first of all know if you are Hebraists or
  Yiddishists.

One quickly exclaimed:

- I am a Hebraist, therefore in the society we will speak the
  language of our prophets and poets, the language of Isaiah,
  Jeremiah, Ezekiel, Hosea, Joel, Amos, Obadiah.

The second stood up and solemnly declared:

- I am a Yiddishist, therefore I think that in the society we
  should speak the language of the grandfather Mendele and
  of the grandsons Sholem Aleichem, Peretz, Dinezon, Asch,
  Yehoyesh, Nomberg. Yes, they speak, yes they have an
  authentic speech.

A young woman stood up and said with great humility:

- I . . . say that Gorky and Artsybashev are the greatest writers in the eyes of the Jews.

Until late in the night they talked about the language question. In the
morning they awoke with clear heads. Each saw that in one literary
society one cannot have as members Isaiah the Prophet, Mendele and
Artsybashev. In the end three societies had to be founded, each of the
three writers needed their own society.[46]

At the founding meeting of the St. Petersburg Jewish Literary Society,
the language of business was Russian, but not without substantial objections from Yiddishist and Hebraist contingents. In his opening remarks,
Dubnow spoke about the multilingual nature of Jewish literatures and urged
the society to respect and celebrate Jewish literature in all its languages.
Shaul Ginzburg, who formally presented the society's goals to the audience, also underlined its commitment to fostering Jewish literatures in all
languages, and called for the society to speak with a united voice in promotion of all Jewish literatures. Yiddish literary critic Nokhem Shtif however,
spoke out in opposition to the founders' principles, arguing instead that
only literature in what he considered to be Jewish languages should be
counted as Jewish literature.[47] The debate continued throughout the society's existence.

The first public event the Jewish Literary Society sponsored was a
lecture by An-sky on the topic of Jewish languages, which was preceded
by Sholem Asch's reading of segments from his stories. An-sky, who wrote
in both Russian and Yiddish, drew upon the multilingual history of Jewish
literature to argue that the society should give equal rights to all languages.

The speech was followed by stormy debate among the audience members. About ten people spoke of the 200 who attended. Asch, who felt attacked for his participation in the Czernowitz Conference, defended the conference's resolution that Yiddish is a national language of the Jewish people, pointing out that such a resolution did not deny the importance of Hebrew. Indeed, Asch had been one of the most prominent defenders of multilingualism at the conference. Nokhem Shtif argued that only two languages should be given rights: Hebrew for its national (*natsional'nyi*) significance and Yiddish for its popular (*narodnyi*) significance. Dubnow acknowledged the importance of both Hebrew and Yiddish but expressed opposition to the negation of Russian, echoing his polemics against Jewish nationalists he accused of negating the Diaspora.[48] Dubnow was probably also aware, more than many of the other members, that the society's legal existence depended in part on its use of Russian. The tsarist police were always more suspicious of Jewish organizations that functioned in Hebrew and Yiddish, which they regarded as the languages of Zionism and socialism, respectively, than those that functioned in Russian. The meeting, however, can be counted as a great success in that it openly aired the major divisions within the Jewish cultural community.

Shtif presented a paper at the society's next meeting, in November 1908. Once again, he argued against the society's commitment to developing Jewish literature in all languages. Following Herderian notions of language and national identity, he proposed that Jewish literature is not simply literature written by or even for Jews but rather is an organic element of the Jewish national spirit as reflected in its language. National languages, he continued, are characterized by exclusivity and continuity: they must be used exclusively by one national group and that usage must have a continual historical basis. In the Jewish context, the only languages that meet these requirements, and therefore that reflect the Jewish national spirit, are Hebrew and Yiddish. Russian-language literature written by Jews, he continued, was merely a product of a particular group of assimilationist intellectuals who sought to validate their choice through recognition by the Jewish masses. "Russian Jewish literature has given us nothing. It gave birth to only two 'great ideas': the war against Jewish languages and the spread of farming among Russian Jews," declared Shtif sarcastically, apparently speaking in Russian.[49]

The society's insistence on maintaining a delicate balance in the language wars seemed absurd at times.[50] For instance, when the society held its first evening to honor great Jewish writers, it decided to choose three writers: Sholem Aleichem, Ben Ami (Mordecai Rabinowitch), and Nikolai Pruzhansky, the latter two of whom apparently wrote primarily in Russian.[51] However, the timing coincided with the widely celebrated 25th anniversary of Sholem Aleichem's work in Yiddish-language literature, for which Jewish communities across the country were putting together celebratory evenings. As a result of the widespread celebration of Sholem Aleichem and the relative obscurity of Pruzhansky and Ben Ami, the tripartite celebration of the three literary figures seemed to many to be an unnecessary concession and even an insult to Sholem Aleichem and the Yiddish language. The complexities of the language issue are also apparent in the way that many branches of the Jewish Literary Society celebrated the Sholem Aleichem jubilee; most conducted their activities in Russian rather than in Sholem Aleichem's own Yiddish, owing primarily to difficulties with securing permission to hold large public events in Yiddish.

In the end, the St. Petersburg branch of the society sponsored spoken-word events primarily in Russian and only sporadically in Yiddish. In 1910, for instance it sponsored nine public events in Russian and four in Yiddish. Many of the events it sponsored dealt directly with the language issue and the need to develop cultural products and performances in Jewish national languages. Yiddish literary critic Noyekh Prylucki's talk on Yiddish theater, delivered in Yiddish, for instance, was followed by B. Mosinzon's talk on the revival of Hebrew in Palestine, delivered in Russian. Aside from the difficulties in obtaining official permission to stage events in Hebrew, few prospective audiences in St. Petersburg (or anywhere else in the empire, for that matter) could understand a spoken lecture in Hebrew. Zionist-leaning speakers capable of giving an address in Hebrew were given the choice of speaking in Russian, in which case they would be accused of being traitors to the national cause by audiences who would nevertheless have heard what they had to say, or speaking in Hebrew and being heralded as national spokespeople by audiences who would have little idea of what they were actually saying. Yiddishists, though, were eager to point out that by speaking in Yiddish, lecturers could both assert their national identity and be understood—not just by the Russian-speaking Jewish elites but even by the common Jewish folk. Yet this solution was anathema to the Hebraists, who sought to do away with what they considered an uncouth jargon. They preferred to speak in their own stilted Russian, often acquired as adolescents in gymnasia, than their native Yiddish. When one lecturer, speaking in Russian, extolled Hebrew as the only Jewish national language, Yiddish activist A. Vayter, who was in the audience, angrily interrupted him, declaring that if Yiddish is to be considered solely an "exilic rag," as the lecturer had proclaimed, then the same must be said for "Russian with a Berdichev accent."[52] The entire audience recognized Berdichev as a common euphemism for Jewish.

Meanwhile, in Berdichev itself, several hundred people showed up to debate the question of which language the Jewish Literary Society should use when a new branch was formed there. Ultimately, it was decided that any language spoken by the Jews of Berdichev would be given equal status.[53] Nevertheless, within a few years, Zionist critics of the Berdichev Jewish Literary Society were accusing its leaders of being "pseudo-nationalists," "Yiddishist-inquisitors," and, "sworn enemies of our national language."[54] Clearly, the society's earlier concession had not calmed the language controversy. In 1908, a literary society was established in Częstochowa that functioned primarily in Polish but also included a Hebrew-language choir. The society was called Lira (Lyre), but only after extensive debate among its founders about whether it should adopt the Polish name Lira or the Hebraic Hazomir (Nightingale). According to one memoirist, "Yiddish was foreign to the Lira society." This society, however, never reached members beyond a rather narrow circle of proponents of enlightenment. Only after a branch of the Jewish Literary Society was established in Częstochowa did it attract "the greater part of the Jewish youth and Jewish democratic intelligentsia."[55] The language question was also complicated by legal restrictions on the use of Yiddish, the interpretation of which varied by locality and the whims of local officials. For example, in Siedlce, the Jewish Literary Society was not permitted to establish a branch in 1910. The local administration cited a five-year-old police circular forbidding the use of Yiddish in public gatherings.[56]

Literary societies, even those geared toward promoting Yiddish or Hebrew, often provided a medium for spreading Russian culture. In Baranovichi, for instance, the literary society was popularly known by its Russian name, *Literaturnoe obshchestvo,* and its regulars by the Russian *liubitel'es.* The society sponsored theatrical events, including a performance of *The Kreutzer Sonata* in Russian.[57] When the Jewish Literary Society of Kremenets was established, its leaders assumed that the society would function in Russian, only to discover that the locals lacked the necessary linguistic skills. The leaders were surprised to learn that enlightened ideas were being expressed in Yiddish: "The idea that there exists a journal with the name *Lebn un visnshaft* (sounding so close to the name *vestnik znania*) was met by us as though it were a bomb," recalled one member.[58] Many provincial literary societies were established by young students who had been educated in Russian-language institutions and saw it as their task to spread Jewish national awareness within a Russian linguistic milieu.

In the Kingdom of Poland, language debates were further complicated by the addition of Polish into the mix. Here, although mixed Jewish and non-Jewish societies had been declining in the post-1905 decade, Jews were still more likely to join non-Jewish societies than in many other regions of the Russian Empire. Jews continued to play an active role in the Society for the Spread of Enlightenment (Towarzystwo Krzewenia Oswjaty) in Lodz, which was established in 1905 with the goal of promoting the spread of Polish culture. But language debates were by no means absent here. Although the society was 95 percent Jewish, the OPE accused it of having developed a "Polish chauvinist character" in 1910. When the Jewish Section of the society sought permission from the society's governing board to send a telegram of greetings to the Yiddish writer Mendele Moykher Sforim on his birthday, the board responded provocatively that such a request would be the equivalent of sending greetings to V. M. Purishkevich, one of the leaders of the anti-Semitic Union of the Russian People—both, it implied, roused the national sentiments of those who did not belong to the Polish nation. The board then turned on the Yiddishists, eventually closing the Jewish Section.[59]

Although the Jewish Literary Society and Lovers of the Hebrew Language were in competition with each other and espoused apparently conflicting doctrines—one that Hebrew be given a privileged status within the Jewish community, the other that all languages be treated equally—the two organizations shared members and even had overlapping executive committees. Dubnow and Abraham Zevi Idelsohn, for instance, sat on the first executive committees of both societies. Many members of one organization could be found in the audience of public talks held at the other, sometimes even on the other's podium. Jubilee celebrations such as the 50th anniversary of the historian Avraham Harkavy's scholarly activity held in 1911 in the great hall of the St. Petersburg synagogue brought together representatives from many societies, including several that competed directly with each other on different fronts: the OPE, the Jewish Historical and Ethnographic Society, the Jewish Folk Music Society, Lovers of the Hebrew Language, and the Committee of the Jewish Encyclopedia all sent representatives. Celebrities such as Mendele were also lionized by those on both sides of the debate, adding further evidence of the interrelated nature of Jewish cultural activity.

Hebrew-language societies sought to transform what was a sacred written language, a language free of vulgarisms and the taint of mundane usage, a language that had never been used for baby talk (or, as Herzl famously declared, to order a railway ticket) into a spoken language that would celebrate its vitality with all these impurities. Proponents of Yiddish sought to do just the opposite: to transform a vulgar pigeon language commonly associated with gossip and marketplace bartering into a respectable medium of literary expression. Supporters of Russian (or Polish, for that matter) had no ambitions to transform a language; they hoped to transform a people. They imagined that by speaking the dominant language of the host community, a language already established as a distinguished conduit for verbalizing complex concepts and articulating inspired culture, the Jews would be welcomed into that culture and be capable of contributing to its efflorescence. The language battle then was a fight over the very future of Jewish society and public culture.

Literary Societies in the Era of Reaction

Jewish literary societies, like all voluntary associations in the Russian Empire, were forever at the mercy of the authorities. The most common reason the authorities cited for refusing a society permission to establish itself was the profile of its members. For instance, in March 1908, a group of Odessa Jews that included well-known Zionist activists Joseph Klausner, Mosheh Leib Lilienblum, and Menachem Ussishkin submitted a request to establish a Jewish social club in Odessa with the goal of "providing its members and their families with the opportunity to spend their free time with leisure, comfort and useful activity." The group proposed that it sponsor "musical and dramatic presentations, balls, masquerades, dances, literary evenings, lectures for the dissemination of useful information to its members, various legal games such as dominoes, lotteries, chess, and checkers, and a library with books, newspapers and periodical publications."[60] Although the request sounded innocuous and numerous similar requests from around the country had been approved, the names of the signatories set off alarms within the office of Odessa's town governor. The office sought input from the local secret police department, which responded with the information that Klausner and Ussishkin were members of the Society for the Aid of Jewish Farmers and Artisans in Syria and Palestine and that Klausner had recently delivered a talk on the Jewish poet Hayim Nahman Bialik. This evidence was enough to confirm the town governor's

suspicion that the organization was Zionist; he denied its request.[61] Yet
the group was not dissuaded. They appealed to their colleagues at the
St. Petersburg branch of Lovers of the Hebrew Language for assistance.
Klausner submitted a new petition, this time to establish an Odessa branch
of the St. Petersburg society. The town governor accepted the petition, and
the Odessa branch of Lovers of the Hebrew Language had its first meeting in December 1908. By latching onto a preexisting legal society with a
relatively high profile in the capital, the new society was able to assuage
the concerns of local officials.

Police harassment was a regular part of public life. When Joseph
Klausner spoke about Bialik in Odessa, the police interrupted his talk in the
middle, forbidding him to talk about the theme of exile in Bialik's poetry.[62]
At another talk Klausner gave in Odessa, the manager of the theater was
forced to announce that by order of the town governor, secondary-school
students were forbidden from hearing the talk without permission from the
authorities. The hall emptied as some 100 students left, seeking reimburse-
ment for their ticket prices.[63] In Bobruisk, a correspondent for the paper
Razsvet complained that new regulations demanding that public lectures
and other evening events be approved by the governor rather than the
municipal police had made it much more difficult to secure approval. The
town governor was turning down petitions that would have been approved
under the earlier arrangements.[64]

The first signs of a more sustained and systematic crackdown on
Jewish cultural associations came in early 1911. At this time, the press
began reporting more frequently on petitions that had been denied than
on those that had been approved. Typical was a report from January 1911
at which the Office for Affairs on Societies of Mogilev Province met to
consider petitions for the founding of a literary-dramatic circle in the city
of Staryi Bykhov (Mogilev Province) and a petition for the establishment
of a Lovers of the Hebrew Language society in Kopys (Mogilev). The Staryi
Bykhov petition was approved and the Kopys petition was not considered
on "formal grounds."[65]

The most blatant act of state harassment, though, was the closure of
the Jewish Literary Society on 1 July 1911 without any prior warning. The
St. Petersburg town governor closed it when it was accused of violating the
1906 Temporary Regulations on Societies and Union on the ground that
it "threatens public security and peace or has taken a manifestly immoral
direction." When the society sent a delegation of distinguished members
to the city office responsible for unions and societies, the office noted that

several local branches were violating the society's charter and conducting political activities. The delegation responded that no warnings had been issued and that many local branches had recently been given permission to establish libraries, indicating that the society was in good legal standing. Despite the delegation's pleas and promises to ensure that the provincial branches cease any illegal political activity, the office was unrelenting. The society had recently been ordered to turn over a list of its members to the St. Petersburg town governor, and several members of the Warsaw and Berdichev branches had been arrested in the months prior to the society's closure, suggesting that the closure had more to do with the society's members than with its activities.[66] At the same time, other literary societies were being closed across the empire, indicating that although the details may have varied and additional suspicion may have fallen upon individuals within the society, the closure of the Jewish Literary Society was part of a much larger crackdown on voluntary associations throughout the empire. This repression was primarily directed against national minorities. As early as January 1910, the Ministry of Internal Affairs had issued a secret circular warning that national minorities were taking advantage of the Temporary Regulations on Societies and Unions to "awaken narrow-minded national-political awareness" and to establish a "unification of foreign elements on the basis of their exclusive national interests." The circular counseled local officials to beware of granting petitions to establish societies from national minorities, "including Ukrainians and Jews, regardless of the goals they pursue." Local officials were urged to "examine in minute detail whether the society aspires toward the aforementioned goals and in an affirmative condition to strictly deny the registration of its statute."[67]

Soon after the closure of the Jewish Literary Society, a group of activists that included Shaul Ginzburg succeeded in registering a new society, the Jewish Literary-Scientific Society, which replicated many of the functions of the Jewish Literary Society. The addition of the term "scientific" in the title was intended to indicate that the new society would cater to more of an elite audience, thereby easing government fears that the group would incite the masses. This new society, in stark contrast to its predecessor, was not permitted to establish provincial branches, preventing it from influencing the Jewish masses beyond those living in the largely assimilated imperial capital. However, it was clearly an heir to the Jewish Literary Society. Not only did its leaders and members overlap to a significant degree, but much of the property and resources of the St. Petersburg branch of the former Jewish Literary Society was turned over to the Jewish Literary-Scientific Society and the society became the clearinghouse for excess funds from local branches. Books and library materials that were not shipped to St. Petersburg were transferred to the nearest branch of the OPE. In both public announcements and internal structure, the new Jewish Literary-Scientific Society presented itself as the heir to the Jewish Literary Society.[68]

However, its formation was clouded in a controversy surrounding the election of the society's first executive committee. Proponents of Yiddish complained that the electoral system, which elected those with a plurality of votes, favored the small number of candidates who were opposed to Yiddish over the larger number of Yiddishist candidates, whose support was split among the large but divided Yiddishist electorate. Instead, they proposed a system that required majority support. The debate over this issue lasted for several meetings, finally coming to a head on 30 January, when, in a session that lasted until eleven at night, the society voted on changing its statutes to allow for greater representation by Yiddishists. Although the motion won a decisive majority, it fell short of the two-thirds majority required to enact the change. It was emblematic of the complexity of the language issue that this heated meeting about the linguistic orientation of Jewish literature and culture ended with a presentation about Polish literary influences on Jewish writers.[69]

The Jewish Literary-Scientific Society was not entirely free of political bias and sometimes extended beyond the purview of purely literary endeavors. For instance, in a March 1913 talk on Jewish freethinking, a Mr. Berthold argued that with the loss of their political sovereignty, Jews had retreated into religious and spiritual isolationism and had come to reject enlightened ideologies. Jewish proponents of enlightenment were shunned and expelled from the community. This phenomenon, he argued, had continued to that day and could be resolved only if Jews become a free and sovereign people in their own territory, regardless of where that territory might be. The talk was attacked by B. G. Stolpner, who argued that there were three general tendencies in Judaism: Zionism, which was thousands of years old; socialism, which had begun about fifteen years earlier; and the ideas of Berthold, which nobody had ever uttered before and began only with this presentation. The discussion lasted until midnight but clearly went well beyond the realm of literature and academics to a discussion about the future of the Jewish nation.[70]

The same pattern of replacing the Jewish Literary Society with a society directed toward a more elite and specialized clientele was followed in Odessa, where an independent Jewish Literary-Scientific Society was registered in March 1913. According to its charter, the goal of the society was "facilitating the study and development of scientific and belletristic Jewish literature in Hebrew, Yiddish and other languages." The society's planned activities included sponsoring conversations and readings for its members as well as public gatherings, readings, lectures, performances, concerts, and literary evenings in Russian, Hebrew, and Yiddish. The statute acknowledged explicitly that any public gathering would require advance official approval. The society also wanted to publish and disseminate journals, newspapers, brochures, and books; establish libraries, readings rooms, museums, and exhibitions; sponsor competitions for literary and scientific works; and even establish courses for the study of Jewish literature, history, and languages.[71] The society's first elected executive committee included Bialik, Joseph Klausner, and several others who had been on the committee of the Jewish Literary Society and were well-known Zionists.[72] The society listed 706 members by March 1914.[73] Thus, the members of the Jewish Literary Society of Odessa also reacted to the closure of the Jewish Literary Society by simply reorganizing under a new banner. Similarly, in Częstochowa, the Jewish Literary Society held a liquidation meeting at which it decided to unite with the Lira society, which was oriented toward the Polish language. Although the two societies had been competing with each other for years, the local branch of the Jewish Literary Society had little choice but to unite with its erstwhile competitor, creating an uneasy alliance among the warring political positions.[74]

The closure of the Jewish Literary Society in the summer of 1911 was only the beginning of a period of reaction that intensified with the assassination of Stolypin in September that year. From this date onward, it became more difficult to establish Jewish cultural organizations. Numerous examples could be given. A request to establish a Lovers of Jewish Literature and Folk Music society was denied in Irkustk in December 1911 because the local authorities believed it would promote national separateness and would pose a "threat to peace and order"[75] A request to establish a branch of Lovers of the Hebrew Language in Rogachev (Mogilev Province) was denied in March 1912.[76] The governor of Podolia Province turned down a petition to establish a branch in Mogilev–Podolsk on the grounds that it sought to promote nationalism among the population and oppose integration.[77] In 1913, the Moscow Society of Jewish Literature and the Moscow Jewish Education Society were both refused registration.[78] Lovers of the Hebrew Language in Odessa also faced harassment in the spring and summer of 1912. In May 1912, Ussishkin's Odessa apartment was searched on order from the St. Petersburg gendarme. Thus it is not surprising that when Ussishkin submitted a request on behalf of the society to hold a banquet in honor of Hebrew-language teachers at his dacha in July, the Odessa town governor refused to grant permission. The police chief had warned the town governor to treat the petition with "extreme circumspection in view of the fact that the aforementioned will be a gathering exclusively of Jews and among them the conversation will take place in Hebrew."[79] Several months later, the town governor requested a list of members of the society, which he passed on to the Odessa gendarme. Of the nearly 250 members, the gendarme found eleven individuals who had come to its attention previously. Most had not been convicted of any crime. For instance, Bialik's house had been searched in May 1907 but no incriminating materials had been found. The investigation determined that Klausner and Ussishkin had attended the Ninth Zionist Congress and the conference of Russian Zionists in Hamburg in December 1909. It also reported the results of the May search of Ussishkin's home, which concluded that Ussishkin belonged to a Zionist organization and was participating in illegal Zionist activities in Russia.[80] Arrests of individuals accused of Zionist activity intensified over the course of the year.[81] Thus, by late 1912, even the Hebrew-language societies were feeling the impact of the changing political climate and official hostility toward literary societies and voluntary associations.

Literary Societies and Social Networking

The transmogrification of Jewish literary societies occurred as they adapted to the changing legal environment by modifying their outward structure while struggling to maintain ideological and personnel consistency. These changes ensured the maintenance of what sociologists of knowledge have termed an intellectual field. The language of intellectual fields encourages us to view the dissemination and creation of knowledge through networks rather than through atomized individuals and small groups and urges historians to take into account the influence of institutions on the production of knowledge. Intellectual fields, according to Pierre Bourdieu, developed historically as intellectuals and creative artists "began to liberate themselves economically and socially from the patronage of the aristocracy and the Church and from their ethical and aesthetic values; and also as there began to appear *specific authorities of selection and consecration* that were intellectual in the proper sense. . . . These authorities, such as academies, salons, publishing houses, theatres, and cultural and scientific associations, derived their legitimacy not from external patronage but rather from internal approbation."[82] Literary societies can thus be seen as a subculture of a larger intellectual field. They shared certain assumptions in common even while they debated and disagreed about the nature of these assumptions. Jewish literary societies that debated among themselves about the respective merits of Hebrew or Yiddish, for instance, shared the assumption that language is an integral component of national identity and that it was their duty to promote this identity through public culture. They also shared the assumption that the language question could be resolved through intellectual discussion in public forums and that there was a language question in the first place. Jewish literary societies thus helped set the terms of public debate by bringing latent political and ideological issues into open arenas.

Literary societies also functioned as networks for individuals who came to be regarded as public intellectuals and thereby provided institutional legitimization for Jewish thinkers whose ideologies may not have been welcome in traditional preexisting forums. At the same time, literary societies taught the educated classes to regard themselves as intellectuals, as members of an elite group with social standing in the local community that had connections to a wider group of like-minded individuals beyond the borders of their own town. The branch structure of these societies mediated the influence of any one individual by connecting each individual and each organization to a web of similar organizations both locally and across the empire. Individuals balanced their own participation in a broader discourse of the educated classes with diverse interests shaped by personal inclination and local needs and idiosyncrasies. Their new status endowed them with a sense of responsibility for articulating popular sentiments and encapsulating the popular mood within a public culture. Literary societies demonstrated both to their participants and observers the relevance of formal institutions in the project of constructing a public culture.

Cultural Performance:
The People of the Book and the Spoken Word

When in 1972 the anthropologist Milton Singer recalled his earlier travels through India in search of the "ethos" or "world view" of the people of Madras as they adapted to the modernization of India, he noticed "the centrality and recurrence of certain types of things. I shall call these things 'cultural performances,' because they include what we in the West usually call by that name—for example plays, concerts, and lectures." These forms of interaction, to which Singer added religious rituals, ceremonies, and festivals, served as appropriate units of study for his project because, he noted, "it seemed to me that my Indian friends—and perhaps all peoples—thought of their culture as encapsulated in these discrete performances, which they could exhibit to visitors and themselves."[1]

Similarly, cultural performances provided a visible and audible way for many Jews to assert their national presence and value in late imperial Russia. Cultural performances can be understood as events with "a definitely limited time span, or at least a beginning and an end, an organized program of activity, a set of performers, an audience, and a place and occasion of performance."[2] In other words, they are events marked by various recognizable frames such as location and time in order to differentiate them from everyday discourse. They suggest, as others have observed, "an aesthetically marked and heightened mode of communication, framed in a special way and put on display for an audience."[3]

Because of the continued difficulties of arranging large-scale performance events, which required numerous performers, set crews, designers, and coordination, the most common form of performance in early-twentieth-century Russian Jewish communities was the spoken-word event —poetry readings, lectures, debates, public discussions, symposia, and conventions.

In the annals of performing arts, the spoken-word event has received relatively little attention, dwarfed by its more extravagant cousins of theater and opera. Yet for most aspiring middling-class youth and even enlightened elders, the spoken-word event was a far more common route to participation in cultural activities, not to mention a more common way to spend an evening out. The most daring, ambitious, and loquacious learned from the best orators and would sometimes use these skills to experiment with the form themselves. The early intellectual socialization that attendance at spoken-word events instilled in young Jewish men and women helped situate them in a structure that regarded the public expression of culture through performance as a prime criterion of national identity.

Sponsoring such activities was still a complex endeavor, requiring not only talent, organization, and funds but also official permits. The limited freedom of assembly granted by the 1905 October Manifesto and the subsequent March 1906 Temporary Regulations on Societies and Unions made the large-scale presentation of secular Jewish cultural performances possible for the first time in the Russian Empire. Nevertheless, remaining restrictions on public gatherings required every cultural performance to be preceded by a large degree of coordinated organization and planning. Planning a cultural performance became in itself a communal event and was best conducted by a voluntary association or society rather than an individual.

Officially registered societies, such as the literary societies discussed in the previous chapter, were the primary presenters of cultural performances. Typically, the charters of literary societies contained a statute that included presenting cultural performances on a list of activities the society indicated it would support in pursuit of its official stated goal. The charter of the Jewish Literary Society of St. Petersburg, which had branches throughout the empire, included among its goals organizing readings, lectures, and discussions in Russian, Hebrew, and Yiddish for both its members and the general public.[4] In order for a society to receive legal status, its charter had to be approved by local authorities, usually the office of the town or provincial governor. A legal distinction was always maintained between events planned for the sole benefit of members of the society and events that were open to the general public. The former were regarded with far less suspicion and could be held as part of the society's regular functioning, as every individual in attendance was required to have their name included in the society's annual report, which was made available to the authorities. In order to stage public events, on the other hand, societies needed advance permission from the authorities. The letter requesting such permission had to include information about the date, time, and venue; the expected audience; the ticket prices; the name of the speaker; the language of the talk; the title of the talk; and a detailed abstract of the talk. Normally, these requests had to be submitted seventy-two hours before the event if it was to take place in the society's permanent dwelling and seven days if it was to take place elsewhere. There was no guarantee that permission would be forthcoming in this time period, so requests were better submitted two weeks before the planned event. The governor usually sent a request to his secret police asking for information on the performer from the police files. Assuming that the speaker was not on the police's list of politically suspect individuals, the governor could approve the performance, reject the performance, or request some type of clarification, such as a more detailed abstract. Once the performance was approved, it was incumbent upon the governor to send an inspector to ensure that the talk was carried out as planned. The society was also required to send a report to the governor after the event. The entire process was characterized by perceptions of arbitrariness, often based on the personality of the officials concerned. Residents of Bobruisk, for instance, complained that when they were required to submit requests to the city gendarme for permission to hold spoken-word events, they normally received permission, but when they were required to submit requests to the governor, their requests were refused.[5] The bureaucratic process ensured that private individuals would have a great deal of difficulty organizing events on their own. Instead, individuals who wished to present a public event usually did so as a group, allying themselves with respected members of the community to secure permits and dividing up the preparatory work.

Avrom Reyzen, for instance, who spent much of 1907 visiting his family in Minsk, recalls that a small group of intelligentsia began to meet regularly at the home of a wealthy local publisher for literary readings and discussions. Over the course of the winter, they decided to hold a public literary reading at a local wedding hall. They enlisted some of the city's most respected Jews to petition the authorities for permission on their behalf. With this intervention, they were able to obtain a permit to hold the reading, provided that advertisements were in Russian rather than Yiddish. The authorities likely hoped that Russian-language advertisements would attract a less troublesome audience, even if the event itself was permitted to take place in Yiddish. The first literary evening the society sponsored featured Reyzen himself as the speaker. Buoyed by the success of this first event, the society decided to invite the most famous of all public intellectuals, Yitskhok Leybush Peretz, to Minsk. Reyzen hoped that this would attract a large audience and establish the society as a mass organization.

Reyzen's story may seem mundane—and by the end of the first decade of the century, such events were becoming increasingly common—but to the Jewish community of Minsk, a community of nearly 50,000 by the early twentieth century that accounted for over half the population of the city, such an event was virtually unprecedented.

The custom of attending lectures, hearing talks, and participating in symposia was new to most Jews in the Pale of Jewish Settlement and the Kingdom of Poland. Prior to the blossoming of formal literary societies, Eastern European Jews were most likely to encounter cultural performances of spoken words outside formal prayer rituals only when itinerant preachers (*magidim*) would come to town, usually in the summer months. Rabbis would occasionally deliver sermons as well, particularly on special occasions, such as the Sabbath before Passover (*shabes ha-godl*) and the Sabbath between Rosh Hashanah and Yom Kippur (*shabes tshuve,* or *shabes shuve*). Preachers would preach at dusk, in the period between the afternoon and evening prayers, from inside the synagogue or the *besmedresh* or outside in the synagogue courtyard. After the talk, they would invite donations, from which they earned their livelihood. Some larger towns had resident preachers as well, who gave more regular presentations. Overall, though, Eastern European modes of Jewish preaching were less developed than elsewhere. German and American Jewish sermonizing, for instance, had come under the influence of Protestantism and Christian homiletics and adopted edificatory practices to replace the traditional explicatory sermon. German *maskilim* and reformers sought to emulate what they saw as the rationality and simplicity of Protestant models, which they believed contrasted starkly with complex Jewish modes of exegesis. In Eastern Europe, where reform had not made significant inroads, older, more prescribed and exegetical forms of preaching still predominated. Jewish preaching in Eastern Europe never reached the level of popularity that it achieved among Sephardic and Italian Jewish communities, where it proliferated as an influential genre, providing the preacher with a great deal of latitude on which to sermonize.

In Eastern European practice, the *droshe* (sermon) and the *hesped* (funeral oration) were the most common rhetorical forms employed by preachers. A *droshe* is actually more of an oral explication or expository recitation of the weekly readings from the Torah. The delivery of a *droshe* was constrained by the need to refer to the particular portion of the Torah being read that week in the synagogue and the requirement that all argumentation return to the portion as a proof text. Nevertheless, many itinerant preachers were probably like the Old Preacher in Avrom Reyzen's fictional short story of the same name, who had memorized a repertoire of six speeches that he delivered in town after town, time and time again, regardless of occasion.[6] The *hesped* allowed for a little more leniency in delivery but was still heavily dependent upon conventions and the need to refer to the deceased. Despite these constraints, talented preachers were able to operate within the expository framework to insert their own agendas. Moses Isaac, for instance, used the pulpit to spread the Mussar (homiletics) movement through Russia, often departing from the exegetical tradition in order to moralize about contemporary affairs. Others, like H. Z. Maccoby (the Maggid of Kremenits), used the genre of preaching to promote Zionism and encourage the establishment of Zionist circles. These "new preachers" became increasingly common and popular in the latter years of the nineteenth century. Because they used humor, inserted fables, and incorporated elaborate gestures and movements, talented preachers were also valued as great entertainers.[7]

All these forms of speech depended heavily on written texts. The *droshe,* in particular, could not be fully understood without reference to the written text and assumed that its audience was engaged with these texts on a written basis as well. As such, it can be more accurately regarded as oral commentary on written texts rather than an autonomous oral creation. As Barbara Kirshenblatt-Gimblett notes, Eastern European Jewish culture differentiated between two distinct modes of speech: the secular and the sacred. The distinction is reflected semantically in the Yiddish language, which uses the term *droshe* (a derivate of the Hebrew root signifying interpretation) to refer to a sacred oral presentation and commonly refers to a secular talk as a *rede* (derived from the Germanic stock word for speech). This distinction mirrored that between the Hebraic *seyfer,* signifying in Yiddish a sacred book, and the Germanic *bukh,* signifying a secular book. This distinction is reflected in the expression a *droshe* is a *rede* with a yarmulke (*a droshe iz a rede mit a yarmulke*).[8] In other words, a *droshe* is a religious *rede*.

We can surmise what these oratories may have sounded like from descriptions left to us by those who witnessed them. Zalman Shazar (Shneur Zalman Rubashov), for instance, the third president of the state of Israel, wrote in 1950 of an early memory he had of the famous Maggid of Minsk, Binyomin Shakovitzki, whom he had heard deliver a *hesped* some time in the late 1890s, when he was a young boy:

> The particular details now seem to me like they are coming out of the
> fog. But the melody still lives in my heart like the day it happened. As

I think of it, it rises and hums and awakens and resurrects an entire world. . . . The synagogue was completely full. A man of about forty years stood at the *bime*. He appeared elderly and was wrapped in a tallis. His voice was the voice of a lion, and rivulets of water came from his eyes. "Esteemed guests," the voice trembled, and instilled oppressive mourning. One story linked to the next, and one parable to another. The language was folksy and colorful, accented with many Russian words, popular sayings, and expressions culled from life and circulated among the people of the town for many years thereafter. . . . With convincing drama, he presented to the excited congregation a dialogue between the spiritual rabbi of Israel and the grieving community. With a prosecutor's paternalism, the Maggid beseeched the congregation in the name of the departed to abandon their evil ways, to rectify their deeds and to purify their thoughts to enable the soul of the departed to pray on behalf of this community before the Heavenly Throne.[9]

The institutionalized performance of secular spoken-word events was relatively new to the Jewish community and provided a novel means of acquiring and sharing information. The spoken word, at least as cultural performance, was not the usual form of Jewish education. Traditional modes of Jewish education consisted more commonly of engagement with and interrogation of talmudic texts through dialogic discourse, usually enacted through studying in pairs. Talking was a highly valued skill, but listening was underrated. The format in which individuals were expected to sit quietly for an hour or two and absorb knowledge imparted to them from an authority figure was unusual. Certainly students in some yeshivas would be exposed to occasional addresses by the head of the yeshiva, but these were reserved for special occasions. Audiences at Jewish preaching performances were also expected to behave differently than those at secular events. For one, these audiences commonly stood and were often "excited," in Shazar's words. Unaccustomed to sitting quietly while knowledge was imparted to them from a podium, Jewish audiences famously (and perhaps apocryphally) reacted to early Yiddish cultural performances raucously and actively, embarrassing many critics who chastised them for their lack of dignity, poise, and decorum. There were few opportunities for the entire Jewish community to sit together and listen to a single speaker as their non-Jewish neighbors were apt to do at a Sunday church service. Literary societies and the lectures, symposia, and conferences they introduced taught their members important organizational skills and helped them adapt to a modern bureaucratic world. One participant recalled his involvement with the Zionist movement, one of the leading forces in the establishment of literary societies and promoters of spoken-word presentations:

> From meeting to meeting, the number of those raising their hands to request the right to speak grew. Soon the members became accustomed to speaking in this manner, everyone tried to make a public impression in his manner of speech, his knowledge, and in his victory over his rival. Everyone already knew the parliamentary rules and would demand his right to verbally express an opinion. Sometimes, the chairman had to cut off the list of speakers because the meeting had gone on for too long. At the meetings and sessions, over time, people learned to listen patiently to the speech of their opponents and not to stop or interrupt them. In the beginning it was difficult for many of the members to unlearn their habit of speaking over others. In the *besmedresh* during elections for the officers, they used to speak publicly; nobody could stop talking when others were expressing themselves. The speeches would get crossed and confused. Among the muddle of voices it was impossible to hear the opinion of everyone. Here in the Zionist movement, though, everyone behaved with proper manners. From this point of view, the Zionists played a large role in the cultural education of the adults.[10]

For centuries, Jewish readers had been distanced from the authors whose texts they read because the most popular works were medieval and antique rabbinical writings. Rarely did common people have the opportunity to interact in any way with the authors of the texts they read, nor did they expect to do so. Even the most famous of writers were largely anonymous. Yiddish writers, in particular, hid behind pseudonyms, originally probably because they were ashamed to be writing in "jargon" but by the early twentieth century simply because it had become an endearing custom. Even the most famous Yiddish and Hebrew authors were rarely recognized in public. Although well acquainted with Bialik's writings, Sholem Aleichem claimed that when he first met the Hebrew writer at the 1907 Zionist Congress in The Hague, he assumed when he first heard him speak that Bialik was some small-town freethinker.[11] Literary societies, spoken-word events, and in particular touring authors provided a rare opportunity for readers to have direct contact with, or at least to be in close proximity to, the writers of the texts they read. Literary societies, then, helped reconcile the divorce between reader and author by establishing a new relationship—that between audience and speaker. On a local level, these efforts helped individuals, who were no longer held in sway by a dominant religious authority, to coalesce into relatively cohesive communities.

The Celebrity Lecture Circuit

By the early twentieth century, a select group of Jewish speakers could attract enormous crowds and publicity wherever they spoke in the Jewish-inhabited parts of the empire. For those who lectured and spoke in public as part of their professional development, the act of public speaking articulated not only their own status as learned individuals, providing platforms for the exhibition of their knowledge, but also legitimized the act of learning and the subject itself. Spoken-word events reinforced and worked in conjunction with the press to create a shared experience, introduce a common language, and open communal debates among geographically disparate Jewish communities within the Russian Empire. The speaking tour was an important medium for expressing public debate in the era before mass communication made its way into people's living rooms.

By all accounts, a public appearance of a star like Peretz was more than a forum in which to hear an oral text; it was a communal happening, an event to be remembered. When Peretz spoke at the Warsaw Philharmonic Hall, his colleague A. Mukdoyni wrote, "It is difficult to describe what happened in the hall when Peretz finished speaking. It seemed to me simply like mass hysteria among the multitude."[12] When Peretz toured the cities of the Pale and Poland, enormous crowds came out to greet him at the railway station. When he arrived in Częstochowa at the invitation of the Lira Society, tickets were sold out a week in advance.[13] Some 300 people attended a talk he delivered in Vilna in 1912.[14] On the Friday of Peretz's arrival in Minsk in 1907, "the entire town was topsy-turvy—Peretz is coming to Minsk!"[15] By 8:00 PM, the Paris Hall in Minsk—a large hall normally reserved for weddings and other activities—was "so packed that one could hardly breathe. . . . College students, the labor force and the radical intelligentsia had come." Peretz Hirschbein described Peretz's first visit to Vilna in biblical terms, likening the image of Peretz to the face of God: "The Vilna youth greeted him like the pillar of fire. It was as though the youth would be blinded by looking at Peretz's image."[16]

In the summer and fall of 1909, S. Y. Abramovitsh (Mendele Moykher Sforim) also toured the western provinces of the Pale and Poland, visiting Vilna, Bialystok, Brest-Litovsk, Lodz, and Warsaw to much acclaim. According to writer Dovid Frishman,

FIGURE 6. Hebrew poet Hayim Nahman Bialik meets with Yiddish writer Sholem Aleichem at the 1907 Zionist Congress in The Hague. This was the first time these two Ukrainian-born writer-celebrities had met.

> Thousands of people waited at every train station, thousands of people pushed and shoved to get closer to him, and were joyful. . . . I remember in Lodz there were tens of thousands of people, gathering on the street and waiting in front of the hotel where S. Y. Abramovitsh was staying. Women were standing in their fine clothing with flowers in their hands. From time to time one could hear cries of "Mendele Lives! The Zeyde [Grandfather] lives!" And when the writer would show himself for a minute at the window or on the balcony, the screams were virtually endless.

When he visited Warsaw, according to one observer, he broke down all barriers between high and low cultural divisions:

> Here we saw the most striking thing: the same masses that threw themselves with fervor on desolate junk novels received the grandfather of Yiddish literature with the greatest and most spirited enthusiasm. All Jewish Warsaw came out for the elderly writer. The worker put down his work, the shopkeeper his shop, and the merchant his wares. The normally active Jewish community of Warsaw turned a weekday into a holiday. In my life I have never seen such a large enthusiastic and celebratory Jewish crowd.[17]

The Zionist weekly *Razsvet* agreed:

> The visit of S. Y. Abramovitsh to Warsaw will remain in the memory of the local population for a long time. The Jewish street has not seen such a sincere delight for a long time. . . . Already at the station on the day of the guest's arrival from Vilna, a large mass of admirers had gathered, the majority of whom came from the national and democratic Jewish youth, who arranged a stormy ovation for the "Grandfather."[18]

The highlight of Mendele's Warsaw visit was a banquet in his honor sponsored by the Hazomir Society. The festivities and speeches lasted until six o'clock in the morning.

Other speakers were also received with great acclaim. Sholem Aleichem was shocked when crowds met him at the Lubava (Courland Province) train station at two in morning after his train was delayed: "There were many women there, one of whom seemed to be seven months pregnant." After only a few hours' sleep, he was awakened again by crowds demanding that he make an appearance: "In order to pacify the public, I am to be displayed publicly in the marketplace today so that people can be convinced that Sholem Aleichem is not a myth, not a phantasm, but a reality," he wrote that morning to his daughter.[19] Huge crowds came out to see Sholem Aleichem

FIGURE 7. Sholem Yankev Abramovitsh (Mendele Moykher Sforim), tall and bearded in center, visits the Jaroczinski Trade School in Lodz during his 1909 tour. The students peering out the window and the fans standing on the windowsill give an indication of the crowds that followed Abramovitsh during his regular speaking tours. *Photo courtesy of YIVO Institute for Jewish Research.*

when he visited Częstochowa. They greeted him in the pouring rain at the train station and followed him through town to his hotel.[20] When Bialik visited St. Petersburg in 1908, he too was greeted with enthusiastic crowds. Even the Yiddish-language *Der fraynd* celebrated the Hebrew national poet: "A bright warm sun, which is so rare here, greeted him. He brought brightness and warmth with him to Jewish Petersburg. In those Jewish circles that know Bialik, a holiday spirit prevailed." Some thousand people showed up at the concert-ball given in his honor. When Bialik took the stage, "the word 'Bialik' thundered through the entire large hall, and the large stage filled up with roses and flowers." When he finished his poetry reading, "the entire hall as one person answered him with stormy applause and spirited enthusiasm."[21] When he visited Vilna a few days later, estimates of the number of people who came to see him ranged from three to four thousand. A correspondent for *Der fraynd* declared, "Nobody among us had ever before seen such a large public audience for a Jewish national event."[22] Eight hundred people even showed up in Odessa to hear a talk *about* Bialik delivered by the literary critic Joseph Klausner—and even with this turnout, *Der fraynd* chastised the Jewish public of Odessa for failing to show up in large numbers and attending instead a dance show that competed with Klausner's talk that evening.[23] And at the same time, Bialik was having difficulty finding a publisher for his poetry. Clearly the word was of lesser significance than the flesh of Bialik, or at least than the image of Bialik.

Nothing brought out the crowds, though, like a star-studded benefit that included several Yiddish writers speaking on the same bill. In a large Odessa concert hall, Sholem Aleichem, Abramovitsh, Semen Frug, Sholem Asch, Bialik, and Peretz Hirschbein spoke together at a benefit for the family of the recently deceased poet Yehuda Shteynberg. Despite the high price of tickets—the evening was, after all, a benefit—the 2,000-seat concert hall was sold out weeks before the show. The unfortunate who could not get tickets went begging for extra seats. Hirschbein, who was staying at Bialik's home at the time, recalls one individual who came to Bialik the day before the show to say that he was ill and would soon be undergoing surgery from which he might not recover. His last wish, he explained, was to hear the writers speak, if only Bialik could spare a ticket. Bialik apologized that, alas, he himself had no tickets but that the unfortunate patient-to-be could come in and join Bialik and Hirschbein for tea right then and there. But the visitor was apparently less interested in speaking with the writers than in simply being a part of the event. Tea with Bialik and Hirschbein probably felt a little too much like tea with any other two Odessa Jews. Unless they were on stage and he in an audience of thousands, he could be talking to just about anyone.

On the day of the event, the streets in front of the theater were filled with people, 20,000 by Hirschbein's estimate, who prevented traffic from proceeding and threw the police into confusion. The inside of the theater was packed as well; Hirschbein estimated that 5,000 people were crammed into the aisles and balconies. Abramovitsh, who took the stage at midnight and delivered the longest recitation, recited for well over an hour before being interrupted by a loud crash as one of the audience members whose appreciation for Yiddish prose was tempered by the late hour dozed off and fell out of his chair. In the confusion that followed, it was suggested to Abramovitsh that those who wished to hear more could read the rest of the work in its published form. Clearly not everybody understood the important distinction between the aural experience of hearing the story recited in public and the solitary experience of reading the story. In all likelihood, few members of the audience chose to find out what happened at the end of the story. Abramovitsh thanked the audience and retreated

FIGURE 8. Sholem Aleichem on a riverboat in Grodno during a 1914 speaking tour. Popular authors routinely toured through the Pale of Jewish Settlement and the Kingdom of Poland, delivering talks and readings in large cities and small towns. These tours helped unite disparate communities around public celebrities.

from the stage. Despite the late hour, the audience remained in their seats as Sholem Aleichem took the stage for his reading. The crowd finally dispersed at dawn.[24]

As the episode with the young man who sought tickets illustrates, spoken-word events and celebrity visits were as much symbolic moments of national unity as they were opportunities to learn from the words spoken. The communal act of gathering together to witness and be in close proximity to a celebrity often overshadowed anything the celebrity actually had to say. An-sky commented about the audience at a talk Peretz delivered in St. Petersburg: "The hall was full, you understand, but a large part of the audience was composed of those who came to see Peretz rather than to hear him. There were not a few among them who could not understand, or barely understood, Yiddish."[25] *Razsvet* speculated, as well, that Abramovitsh's popularity was not a result of acquaintance with his writings but rather a result of his reputation and the ideas he represented. His writings, the paper argued, were too sophisticated for the broad masses, and therefore many who came out to welcome him at the train station had probably never read his works and knew of him by reputation alone. Since only two publications of his were published in the Russian Empire over the course of the year, both with modest print runs of 1,000, it seems likely that this assumption was accurate.[26] Indeed, if it is true that many among those who came out to welcome Abramovitsh had not read his works—and could not even stay awake to listen to them being recited—then one must assume that they came out to be a part of something, to express their solidarity with the crowd, and to acclaim Mendele—that is, Abramovitsh's literary persona—as a national figure. Mendele, who had written in both Yiddish and Hebrew, could conveniently be embraced as a symbol by Jews of all ideological stripes. In the best of circumstances, less erudite audience members could be moved to purchase or borrow a book after hearing its writer speak, thereby beginning to join the ranks of the cultured and well read. Lecture tours and public readings boosted book sales.[27]

The emergence of celebrities also was a unifying force across the community. Individual celebrities not only molded cultural attitudes through the force of their intellectual positions but also gave rise to cultural meaning as iconic figures. These figures were constructed and interpreted by a growing public that imprinted its own yearnings for self-culture, companionship, and community on the individual being elevated to the status of celebrity. As Mary Kupiec Cayton notes of nineteenth-century American audiences, "Cultural meanings emerge as specific audiences interpret the utterances of those individuals in society who function as intellectuals. The intellectual discourse that emerges from a given culture is made not by 'great men' who transcend the conditions of their age but by communities of listeners who define 'discourse conventions' and by the intellectuals to whom they choose to listen."[28] This type of public image-making transferred easily to the Eastern European shtetl.

Audiences were far more enthusiastic about the idea of hearing Peretz speak than about actually listening to him recite his less-accessible poetry. Although the masses were eager to greet and cheer Peretz at the railway station in Minsk, their boredom and restlessness set in very quickly at the poetry recital. According to Reyzen, when Peretz finally took the stage at his first appearance,

> A stormy, long, lingering ovation . . . cheery cries of Peretz! Peretz!
> All kinds of exclamations: *Zol lebn hoykh* [Yiddish: Long live] and
> even *'heydad'* [Hebrew: hurrah] could be heard. . . . And then Peretz
> is standing on the stage, inwardly nervous, outwardly cool, with a
> subdued, clever smile radiating on his face, and with the sparkles in
> his big eyes, he barely noticeably bows . . . and it is silent in the hall.
> . . . Peretz begins to read. . . . He reads in a Polish-Yiddish dialect . . .

the hall exchanges glances . . . a murmur . . . soon the murmur turns
into a faint noise. . . . Some insolent person shouts out *"Gromche!"*
[Russian: Louder!] and Peretz answers *Oboidetes'!* [Russian: Make do!]
. . . The tumult becomes greater. . . . Some in the last rows can no longer hear. . . . People start to talk among themselves. . . . Peretz reads
"Love," his poem in prose. The words make no impression. It ends. A
weak noise of applause—from the most devout followers, from those
who are standing closest.

But, Reyzen continues, when Peretz left the stage and the audience started
to call his name again, he reemerged as a different man.

Ascending the stage with his clever smile the hall now sees Peretz in
his grandeur. . . . Peretz comes into himself. . . . He warms us. . . . And
he has now in this short time caught on to the local audience. . . . Why
would he read a difficult rhetorical piece like "Love" for an audience
of revolutionaries? Something livelier would be better. Peretz begins
to read his "Monish" and the crowd comes to life.

After reading "Monish," Peretz continued with a reading of his short
story "Bontshe the Silent" and a few poems. "The evening ended as a
success."[29]

Reyzen's account underlined the diversity of Peretz's audience. Among
those cheering and yelling were the common folk yelling their Yiddish *"zol
lebn hoykh,"* Hebraists cheering *"heydad,"* and Russian-speakers shouting
"gromche." Three different languages were used in the same auditorium
as a multitude of linguistic groups came together in solidarity around a
single unifying figure, who read in Yiddish and answered his hecklers
in Russian. But at the same time, Peretz's own "Polish-Yiddish dialect" is
incomprehensible to his Minsk audience, who would have spoken in more
of a Lithuanian-Yiddish dialect and respond by exchanging glances and
murmuring at their inability to understand his accent. The coming together
of these diverse groups is, then, in part, artificial. Although they all share
in a multilingual culture, at the same time they have trouble understanding
each other even while speaking the same Yiddish language.

If individuals in a single audience could respond so differently and
if a single audience could vacillate in its response as Reyzen described,
certainly speakers and performers could elicit vastly different responses in
different venues and locales. An-sky commented that when Peretz spoke
in St. Petersburg to a large assimilated audience, for instance, his style
was "too intimate, too genteel, too peculiar; his craft of reading was more

suited to a small intimate circle. For a large public, his voice was too weak and his intonation not strong enough. Therefore, his Polish-Yiddish accent sounded strange to the Lithuanian Jewish public."[30] But when he spoke at the Czernowitz Yiddish conference, another witness wrote of his performance: "He did not disappoint. We received strong, powerful words from his mouth."[31]

Celebrities at spoken-word events were routinely interrupted by hecklers. A common complaint from rowdy audiences was that the speaker was not speaking in a politically appropriate language. When Bialik spoke in St. Petersburg, some members of the audience called for him to recite some poetry in "simple Yiddish" for those unable to understand Hebrew, but Bialik did not oblige them. "Does he not have a poem, a word, a single word, for the simple Jews? Does he feel nothing of the two thousand years of tears in which the Jews cried in languages other than Hebrew?" asked the sympathetic Yiddishist paper *Der fraynd*.[32] One is left to wonder why this audience came out to see a Hebrew writer if they did not understand Hebrew. Either they, like many other educated Jews, were capable of reading Hebrew but did not understand it spoken or they had never read Bialik in the first place, admiring him only as a national figure. On the other hand, when Sholem Aleichem delivered readings during his 1908 tour, he not only read from his own Yiddish works but also recited from the Hebrew poetry of Bialik. At least once, however, in Minsk, Sholem Aleichem was interrupted by a heckler who shouted "No Hebrew! Only Yiddish! Nobody understands Hebrew!" Sholem Aleichem silenced the heckler, presumably in Yiddish, and continued his recitation in both languages.[33] When Bundist activist Vladimir Medem came to Ponevezh (Kovno Province) in 1906 to deliver a talk, he too was initially met with "an ovation, cheers and claps" until he started his talk in Russian. He was quickly interrupted when someone from the audience shouted "Jews, he should speak Yiddish!" and others began chanting "Yiddish, Yiddish." Medem apologized with a smile that he would love to speak Yiddish but had only just begun to learn the language. The now-sympathetic audience allowed him to continue in Russian.[34] Clearly Jewish audiences were still unaccustomed to the practice of sitting in silence and deferring to the speaker at the podium.

On the other hand, celebrity speakers were only beginning to develop the art of public oratory. It became clear to audiences that many of the greatest writers were not necessarily gifted orators. Sholem Asch, for instance, was well recognized as one of the best Yiddish authors of the period but was routinely dismissed as a boring speaker. Those who took the podium needed to learn that spoken-word events were indeed performances and entailed, in the words of one of the leading scholars of performance, "the assumption of responsibility to an audience for a display of communicative competence."[35]

Shtetl Talks

It was not just celebrities, though, who participated as lecturers on the spoken-word circuit. Many local branches of the Jewish Literary Society filled their schedules with talks given by local intellectuals, often exclusively for the benefit of members. These talks were often participatory and were sometimes even advertised as "discussions," "debates," or "literary chats." In many small towns, such talks took place on a monthly basis, usually in Yiddish. Public lectures were less common, limited to perhaps once a year at the time of the society's general assembly and main membership drive. A number of branches held weekly readings of works by Jewish writers. When possible, these events were supplemented with other activities. In Smorgon in 1910, the local branch of the Jewish Literary Society sponsored fifteen discussions, six public lectures, three theatrical productions in Yiddish, and one concert of Jewish folk music. The Semiatichi (Grodno Province) branch held weekly readings of the works of Jewish writers but sponsored only four lectures during the same period. Praga held a regular series of eight Yiddish-language public lectures as well as a theatrical production, two concerts of Jewish folk music, and three "literary-musical evenings."[36] Jewish Literary Societies also regularly sponsored activities to celebrate the jubilees of prominent members of the Jewish community. Such events would also usually feature a talk about the honored individual's activities.

These gatherings gave members an opportunity to fraternize with the intelligentsia of a city or locale; most were open only to members of the society, but some were open to the general public as well. Many of the regulars would also see each other at events sponsored by competing societies and numerous other groups to which they belonged, particularly in larger towns. Further, the discussions that followed presentations were usually dominated by the same figures. Not surprisingly, the same people always seemed to ask questions and contribute to the discussion, while the majority of the audience remained silent, carefully absorbing the information being presented, daydreaming, or simply contemplating the hat of the person sitting in front of them.

The most common topics for discussion and presentation were Jewish literature, Jewish history, and contemporary Jewish life. Talks often focused on themes in the writing of a particular Jewish writer, such as L. Ia. Yoffe's talk "The Poetry of Semen Frug" or M. S. Rivesman's "Children in the Work of Sholem Aleichem." Rivesman's talk included extensive quotations from the works of Sholem Aleichem and ended with a challenge for other writers to write works for children.[37] Presentations often looked at a popular non-Jewish writer's depictions of Jews, such as Hersh Dovid Nomberg's "Stanislaw Wyspanski and the Jews" or the numerous talks that dealt with Tolstoy's complex portrayals of Jews. Other presenters directly addressed some of the most vexing and divisive issues in the Jewish community of the day. Zionist intellectual Vladimir Jabotinsky, for instance, went on a major speaking tour in 1911, delivering his pro-Hebrew lecture "The Language of Jewish Culture" to dozens of locales throughout the Russian Empire. In the interwar period, Jabotinsky emerged as one of the most sought-after public speakers in the Jewish world. On a similar topic, M. Shalit spoke around the country on "The Character of Jewish Literature." Other discussions focused on contemporary political issues, such as I. A. Kleinman's 1912 talk "Polish-Jewish Relations at the Current Moment" or B. A. Goldberg's "The Problems of Jewish Life in the West." Another popular topic was ancient and biblical Judaism, particularly when it could be related to contemporary affairs, as in S. I. Ayzenstadt's talk "Biblical Studies and Its Significance for the National Cultural Development of Jewry" or S. Ia. Rozenbaum's "The Study of Jewish Law According to the Bible and Talmud." Speakers often used the podium to present some of the latest economic or sociological findings of relevance to the Jewish community, as in L. Kantor's "The Economic Role of Jews According to Sombart's Studies" and B. G. Stolpner's "Jewish Psycho-Historical Traits."[38]

The 1912–1913 season at the Vitebsk Society of Jewish Literature and Music, for example, included talks on ritual murder, art and its meaning in the life of the nation, medieval poet and philosopher Judah Halevy, Semen Yushkevich's portrayals of the Jewish ghetto and the Jewish intelligentsia, Judaism and its relationship to contemporary world powers, anti-Semitism, modern Hebrew, representations of Jews in the writings of Eliza Orzeszkowa, the Jewish intelligentsia in contemporary literature, and fifty years of Jewish publicists. The talks were delivered for the most part by writers and Jewish public activists, many of whom, like Lazar Motylev or Grigorii Landau, had received some legal training, but most of whom made a living as freelance writers, contributors to the Jewish-oriented press, and public speakers.[39]

Talks were also designed to instruct the audience about effective rhe-torical skills by providing examples and learning opportunities. The best speakers trained themselves on the art of communication and followed basic rules of public speaking: they began with humorous anecdotes, filled their talks with illustrations and examples, repeated their main points, and concluded with an appeal for action. By the beginning of World War I, a new custom was becoming popular, where audience members would write down a suggested topic of discussion and place the paper in a box at the front of a room. A speaker would then randomly draw from the box and present an impromptu talk on the topic he or she picked. These events, which became increasingly popular in the interwar era, were known as *kestl ovntn* (box nights). Topics could be political, social, literary, or cul-tural and ranged from issues of local concern to world events. These events helped orators hone their skills before an audience and increase their self-confidence. It was hoped that *kestl ovntn* would help prepare individuals for life in a public realm.[40]

It seems that the reasons Jews attended these lectures were similar to those that historian Donald Scott has observed about mid-nineteenth century Americans: "The lecture-going public was . . . made up of people who perceived themselves in motion, in a state of preparation or expecta-tion."[41] They were people in a state of "continuing self-construction" who believed that useful knowledge obtained from experts would help them realize their personal and professional goals. But evidence also suggests that many talks cut across traditional communal divides, uniting segments of the population that would not normally socialize together. When Hillel Zeitlin came to Lodz to speak about the founder of Hasidism, the Baal Shem Tov (Rabbi Israel ben Eliezer), for instance, the audience was packed with diverse segments of the population, some of whom were unaccustomed to socializing together. According to *Der fraynd,* the event was attended by "Hasids with long capotes, elements that are coming for the first time to a Jewish reading."[42]

Memoirs also commonly refer to the novelty of young men and women sitting together in the audiences of secular events and of young women braving the wrath of their parents in order to socialize in public with pro-gressive young men. One participant of a reading group in Biała Podlaska drew attention to the common perception that Jews who attended secular public events were forswearing their Jewishness and likening themselves to non-Jews. The idea of women joining such heretical circles was some-times regarded as even more shameful than men: "For the women the idea was even more perilous than for the men because of what awaited them at home with their mother and father if they found out they were with men, and gymnasium men at that, who are surely already *goyim* [non-Jews]."[43] In some towns, where many had already become accustomed to the idea that young Jewish men were being led astray by the appeal of worldly pursuits, the idea of losing women to the "this-worldniks" was still anathema. The world of the spoken word was still heavily gendered. Women were beginning to participate, but they could be found mostly in the audience. Women's access to the podium was still heavily restricted.

Extensive press coverage of spoken-word events, particularly in the nascent Yiddish- and Hebrew-language presses, attracted the community to events and summarized their content afterward for those who missed the live performance. Most major papers contained a section on happenings around town and around the country. The Russian-language newsletter of the Society for the Spread of Enlightenment among the Jews of Russia entitled its section "Cultural-Educational Chronicle"; The Hebrew-language *Hamelits* called its section "In Our Country." *Razsvet* had sections on "Jewish Life" and "From Life in the Provinces." These sections summarized local happenings around the empire, sometimes in a sentence or two, sometimes in a few paragraphs. Larger events were also regularly covered as separate articles in the press. Needless to say, the same event could be summarized in contrasting ways by two newspapers of different ideological inclinations. Nevertheless, the content of what was being said in public halls, libraries, fire halls, and auditoriums around the country was disseminated to audiences well beyond the auditorium itself, thereby furthering the reach of the speaker's words and bringing a greater number of individuals into the new community that was forming. Street chatter and workplace murmurings about these events also created a sense of a public culture that was shared by the community at large. Residents of small towns and large cities alike could be proud of the eminent personages their community attracted, whether or not they themselves attended. The commonality of the experiences of Jewish communities in geographically disparate regions of the empire, whether in villages, small towns, or large urban centers, makes it possible to speak of a common public culture that embraced the Jewish community of the entire empire.

The most prominent writers toured through the provinces, delivering the same speech in Tomashpol and Częstochowa that they had delivered in St. Petersburg and Warsaw. When A. Vayter sought to establish a professional Yiddish theater, for instance, he raised money for the event by traveling along the Jewish Literary Society lecture circuit, delivering his

FIGURE 9. A typical listing of cultural events taking place one weekend in Warsaw in 1909 includes a Yiddish-language lecture on "religious themes in general and Jewish literature," several Yiddish theatrical performances and a "musical-dramatic concert."

talk on Jewish theater in several towns in the Pale. Literary societies also set up lecture circuits for less-prominent speakers, asking small towns and other cities to book one of the speakers they were currently promoting. Lovers of the Hebrew Language issued a notice in the Zionist paper *Razsvet* stating that "noted expert on ancient Jewish law, Dr. S. Aizenstadt," was willing to speak at any branch on the topic of "Ancient Jewish Law and Its Development."[44] Local branches of the society were encouraged to contact the Central Committee to book Dr. Aizenstadt. Similarly, the Jewish Literary Society of St. Petersburg dispatched five lecturers to deliver lectures in selected locales around the Pale.[45]

In order to extend its reach beyond the most traveled routes, the society also had a special lecture bureau that mailed the written texts of prepared speeches to provincial branches for a fee of ten rubles per speech. Provincial branches could then have a local member read the prepared speech to its members. If a provincial branch wanted to sponsor a public lecture, as opposed to one exclusively for members of the society, the St. Petersburg Society would provide a written lecture for two additional rubles that had been approved by the theatrical censors for public delivery.[46] In 1910, the year the society started this practice, they sent prepared lectures to ninety-five locations.[47] This system enabled information and opinion to be distributed even to those who did not subscribe to newspapers or spend their leisure time reading.

Jewish Modes of Orality

Anthropologist Milton Singer observed of towns and the countryside in India during its period of rapid modernization that "it is because they perform and know the same stories that we can say that villager and urbanite belong to the same culture and civilization."[48] Donald Scott made similar observations in his study of mid-nineteenth-century America: "The popular lecture was a ceremony, which in form and content brought the public into self-conscious existence. It was a collective ritual that invoked the values thought to define and sustain the community as a whole."[49] The Jewish community of early-twentieth-century Eastern Europe benefited in similar ways from the public lecture, as traveling lecturers who spoke the same words introduced the same ideas to disparate Jewish groups around the vast empire.

It was not just new ideas though that infiltrated provincial Jewish communities; new modes of cultural presentation also impacted the community, supplementing and altering the ways that Jews accessed information. Formal secular speech introduced new forms of orality into a literary culture, enticing individuals to supplement their reading and talking habits with listening skills. Traditional Jewish modes of literacy were supplemented with newer forms of orality and aurality, reversing the trajectory imagined by Marshall McLuhan and others of a linear progression from oral tradition to written text. This new orality was similar to what Walter Ong termed "secondary orality," the introduction of modern media, such as radio and television, into predominantly oral cultural traditions. In these cases, an oral medium is used to disseminate written texts, which are recited over the radio or enacted on the television. "Secondary orality," he wrote, "is founded on—though it departs from—the individualized introversion of the age of writing, print, and rationalism which intervened between it and primary orality and which remains as part of us."[50]

Touring speakers and the distribution of prepared written speeches shared many of the characteristics of secondary orality outlined by Ong, but they did so in advance of the age of mass media. In the Jewish community of Eastern Europe, oral forms of performance were introduced into an overwhelmingly literate community. That is not to say that orality in general was novel to the Jewish community or that Jewish interactions had not previously been mediated through speech. As Daniel Boyarin, Martin Jaffee, and others have emphasized, Jewish textual interpretation has always been articulated orally as well literarily. Normative rabbinical Judaism is premised on the existence of an oral Torah, or a "Torah in the mouth," in Jaffee's more literal translation.[51] Nevertheless, ever since the oral Torah was set in writing some 1,500 years ago, the dominant form of transmission of knowledge within the Jewish community has been through written texts. Even when the words were read aloud, as in the ritual recitation of the Torah in the synagogue or the daily recitation of Talmud in the yeshiva, they were understood literarily. This fact is reflected in Yiddish-language usage, which still used the term *leynen* (reading) to refer to the oral recitation of sacred texts.

Literary societies embraced the communal aspects of spoken-word events and moved them to the forefront of Jewish public culture. These societies, originally conceived as organizations to promote textual literacy, actually functioned in the Jewish community as promoters of the spoken word, encouraging Jewish audiences to question their tendency to privilege the written word over the spoken utterance. In their efforts to use the March 1906 regulations to establish a cohesive community around a national idea, literary societies recognized the vital role of socialization in community formation. While one could certainly read the words of a lecture in the privacy of one's own home, attending a communal event— hearing the same words spoken in public—had a radically different effect. As Ong observes, "sound always tends to socialize," and more specifically, "oral communication unites people in groups. Writing and reading are solitary activities that throw the psyche back on itself."[52] This is why, Ong says, the English language has no collective noun for readers that corresponds to the word "audience" to refer to listeners. "When a speaker is addressing an audience, the members of the audience normally become a unity, with themselves and the speaker."[53] Indeed, any individual who has watched even the greatest of orators deliver a lecture both on television and in person can attest to the difference physical proximity can make. Today television watchers channel-surf past speakers they would wait in line for hours to see in person at their local university campus. Similarly, when a celebrity author came to town, it was a memorable event for town residents in the early twentieth century, worth waiting in line to see even if one had not read his writings. Jewish communal solidarity, though, needed to overcome a fundamental hurdle to the large-scale establishment of an imagined community. Without a single language they could collectively hear as an audience, it was difficult to maintain a national unity.[54] This is why the language question became such a critical component of identity at this juncture.

Communication became dependent on many of the attributes associated with the transmission of oral texts—personal performance, audience response, flexibility, and immediacy. These attributes of speech contrast with the abstract meditation often associated with the act of reading, in which the author is remote, the reader is frequently isolated, and the text is stable.[55] However, performers whose cultural education stemmed from written texts would have been more prone to incorporate characteristics of literary-based thought and expression into their oral performances, particularly when these performances were delivered to audiences who were also likely to be members of a literate culture.

The tendency to combine oral and written modes of communication was reinforced by the juxtaposition of two very different linguistic cultures: Hebrew, which was used as a literary language, and Yiddish, which was used as an oral language. Sholem Aleichem famously parodied the convergence of different speech modes in the dialogue he attributed to Tevye and numerous other characters in his works. Tevye's speech combines the excessive analytical philosophizing and intertextual allusions of rabbinic writings with a folksy idiom and lenient attitude toward authoritative texts. The fictional Tevye represented the way Sholem Aleichem imagined the common reader processed the written text and formulated an oral response. The oral presentation of written materials combined the conservative characteristics associated with oral cultures, which tend to attribute knowledge to tradition, and the emphasis on originality more common to literary culture. This form made it possible for speakers to offer abstract impersonal knowledge and elaborate analytic categories culled from written texts in a form that presented them as "close to the human lifeworld."[56] The type of public gathering literary societies offered worked against the trend toward individuality and personal isolation that private reading and meditation promoted and instead proposed a more social model of communication and personal relations. In other words, they led to action in this world as opposed to meditation on the other world and helped create a public that was prepared to consume the secular culture they proffered.

Theater:
The Professionalization of Performance

E ven before theater activists of the early twentieth century began to see the theater as a mystical conduit to another world, the role of theater on the path to cultural refinement and sophistication was well established in this world. As Russian theater critic Ivan Ivanov declared in 1899: "For us, plays and theatres are what parliamentary affairs and political speeches are for Western Europe."[1] For the Jews of the Russian Empire, who for the most part lacked access to even the few forums of public expression available to the Russian majority, theater was even more than a surrogate parliament; it was a temple of art and the actors its priests. In his post–World War I observations of Eastern European Jews, Arnold Zweig identified two types of Jewish folk artists: the theater and its actors, he wrote, "rest next to the religious service and its representatives, next to the second folk artist, the chazan, the cantor."[2] It is no coincidence that the Yiddish word for stage, *bime,* is the same word used to denote the synagogue pulpit.

The performing arts in Western Europe became increasingly specialized over the course of the nineteenth and early twentieth centuries. In the early modern period, European performance artists were expected to combine oratory with dance, song, and other genres (often as dilettantes), but the advent of modernity and the accompanying culture of celebrity required artists to become virtuosos in a single genre. When modern performances combined genres such as music and dance, they did so simultaneously, as in opera or ballet, rather than serially, as in circus or vaudeville. Although audiences continued to enjoy vaudeville in America, cabaret in Europe, and *estrada* in Russia, the intellectuals who regarded themselves—and were regarded by others—as the guardians of legitimate culture often decried the failure of both audiences and performers to renounce the dilettantism of variety acts in favor of professional specialization. As Jewish public culture became more institutionalized and professional over the course of the first two decades of the century, performance genres became more independent and differentiated, as well as more accepted across the community. Nevertheless, the distinction between professional and amateur theater remained porous in Jewish culture. As Zweig noted, "The step from being an amateur to being a professional actor, and that from being an actor to being a person without theater, is taken with a kind of ease that is inconceivable in the West."[3]

Since it combines numerous artistic genres, such as literature, visual arts, dance, acting, and music, theater requires an advanced level of coordination and institutionalization. In addition to the acting that takes place on stage, the production of theater requires a great deal of backstage activity, including securing space, permits, props, and funds. Most important, theater, like all performing arts, requires a public. When a preexisting audience is unavailable, theater must create its own public. Because of the interactions of individuals on stage, behind the stage, and in the audience, theater truly represents what anthropologist Victor Turner has called a "collaborative social performative system."[4]

Theater shares many commonalities with spoken-word events; both are fundamentally the recitation of texts on stage. The primary distinction is that in the theater, these texts are enacted in a mise-en-scène. Theatrical texts combine verbal and nonverbal elements to varying degrees. There are exceptions to this rule—in mime, for instance, verbal communication is absent—and by the early twentieth century, new modes of theater were already deemphasizing the verbal element in favor of dance and costume. But in general it is the interplay between the verbal and nonverbal, the aural and the visual, that defines theater.

Theater can be related to ritual and often evolves out of ritual performances; many cultures include elaborate staged and masked performances that enact scriptural narratives as part of their sacred ritual. This is often the primary means of transmitting knowledge of scripture to largely illiterate populations. Indian performances of the Ramayana or Christian passion plays are examples of this type of performance. The core of the Jewish Sabbath and holy day prayer ritual is also the recitation of scripture, but despite the highly ritualized recitation, which includes an elevated stage (*bime*), specific attire (prayer shawl), and a procession, the story is not enacted and therefore is distinct from normative theater.

Jewish theater may have evolved more out of the ritual tradition of the *purimshpil,* a form of folk theater that was common throughout the Ashkenazic world from early modern times, in which yeshiva students would celebrate the festival of Purim by parading through the streets and town squares dressed in costume and performing skits and plays on biblical themes in public squares and private homes. These performances, which probably originated on the model of medieval Christian mystery plays, folk carnivals, and German Fastnachtspielers, were traditionally restricted to a single day of the year—Purim—and to a few biblical themes. The story of Esther, which Purim celebrates, was the most common subject of performance, but plays about the near-sacrifice of Isaac, the sale of Joseph into slavery, the battle between David and Goliath, and other popular biblical stories were also common. Like the early modern commedia dell'arte, these performances were improvised along strict conventions that dictated the play's frame but allowed the performers to express their artistic individuality within the established plot and stylistic guidelines. As is common in such traditions, catchphrases and mnemonic devices served as cues to both performers and audiences and helped standardize repertoires. Typically, the *purimshpil* performance was framed by a prologue that introduced the characters and the play and an epilogue in which the performers asked for a reward for their performance. Larger performances—those that took place in town squares and in front of the synagogues rather than in private homes—were often accompanied by instrumental music, particularly trumpets and violins.

Through the course of the nineteenth century, the *purimshpil* began to take on some attributes of bourgeois theater while retaining most of its carnival and folk qualities. The constituency of the performers, for instance, expanded beyond yeshiva students into the mercantile classes. In the last decades of the century, plays on secular themes also seem to have been occasionally presented as *purimshpils*. However, *purimshpilers* themselves repeatedly emphasized the distinction between their activities and theater. Even at the turn of the century, they always called their productions plays (*shpiln*) or performances (*forshteln*), never theater (*teater*). While the continuities between these folk festivals and modern theater was not direct, when Jewish actors and playwrights—who were influenced by bourgeois European theatrical traditions—sought to construct a national Jewish theater, the idiom of the *purimshpil* was a logical source of inspiration, if not actual influence.[5]

Other styles of cultural performance arose out of Austrian Galicia and Bukovina in the mid to late nineteenth century.[6] The Broder singers, the most famous of whom were Berl Broder (ca. 1817–1886) and Velvl Zbarzher (Binyomin Wolf Ehrenkrantz; d. 1883), were itinerant entertainers from Brody who traveled around Austrian Galicia performing shtick with music, dance, and monologues pertaining to daily life and current events. Like both the *purimshpilers* and the peasant actors who sometimes performed in Russian manors, they originally performed in private homes for closed audiences. Over the course of the century, however, they began performing

FIGURE 10. A group of *purimshpilers* poses in 1890s Leczyca. Purim plays are often recalled as an early influence on amateur and professional Jewish theater. *Photo courtesy of YIVO Institute for Jewish Research.*

for public audiences in coffeehouses, beer gardens, and restaurants, setting up small stages in a corner of these establishments, eventually playing to packed houses on Saturday nights after the Sabbath. Their ditties reached beyond their own audiences. Avrom Goldfadn (1840–1908), who is usually credited with establishing the first professional Yiddish theater, first encountered the tunes of the Broder singers in his Volhynian hometown of Starokonstantinov when a Galician teenager came to work as an assistant in his father's watch-making shop. While he worked he would sing songs from the canons of both the Jewish liturgy and the Broder singers.[7] It is little surprise, then, that Goldfadn's initial successes in Odessa and Bucharest in the 1870s were based on performances modeled on those of the Broder singers. Some of these singers performed in costume and would periodically invite a local youngster to perform on stage with them as a straight man to sing one part of a duet earnestly while they performed the other in mockery or satire.[8] Many of these local performers likely received their musical training as choristers (*meshoyrerim*) in the synagogue. They performed under the assumption—or at least the fervent hope—that the cantor under whom they were studying was unlikely to find his way into the tavern where they were performing secular shtick to drunken audiences.

Goldfadn's success as the founder of the first professional Yiddish theater and as a prolific playwright who wrote some of the most enduring works of Yiddish theater was in large part due to his ability to integrate a variety of performance genres and textual traditions into his works. Plays like his anti-Hasidic satire *Tsvey kuni-lemls* (Two Kuni-Lemls), his biblical adventure-romance *Shulamis,* or his melodramatic operetta *Di kishuf-makherin* (The Sorceress) incorporated catchy upbeat tunes, poignant tear-jerking ballads, comic episodes of disguise and mistaken identity, and exotic fantasies, combining motifs familiar to Jewish audiences with tropes universal to early modern European spectacle. But the venues for Goldfadn's initial performances during his early career differed little from those of the Broder singers; his theatrical stages were restaurants, taverns, and coffeehouses and his casts consisted of only two or three male performers, each of whom sometimes took on numerous roles in a single play. It was arguably the combination of his business acumen and the opportunities created by the presence of numerous soldiers in need of entertainment during the Russo-Turkish Wars that made it possible for him to turn a profit and eventually establish, in Iasi, Romania, what is widely regarded as the first professional Yiddish theater in 1876. For the next three years, the theater, which came to include a larger cast of musicians, singers, and actors of both sexes, functioned in Romania with wide success. In 1879, Goldfadn and his troupe moved to Odessa to great acclaim, where he performed in local clubs before graduating to larger theaters.

These early manifestations of Jewish theater share a geographical commonality. It is not by chance that the Broder singers are associated with the town of Brody, located on the Austrian side of the border between Austrian Galicia and Russian Volhynia, and that Goldfadn is associated with the city of Iasi, in Romanian Moldavia, just across the Prut River from Russian-controlled Bessarabia. As border towns, Brody and Iasi were located just outside the reach of Russian imperial authorities but well within the reach of traveling Jewish merchants and performers. It was in the coffeehouses and wine cellars of Romanian Moldavia and Austrian Galicia and Bukovina that Russian Jews first encountered the cultural styles and aesthetics of Central Europe. Itinerant performers played a significant role in transporting cultural styles and products across imperial boundaries.

On the Russian Side of the Border

The development of theater in Russia was hindered by legal restrictions and inadequate copyright protections. Modern commercial theater in the Russian Empire began in the late eighteenth century with the development of the Imperial Theater monopoly. Although the theaters were based in the capitals of St. Petersburg and Moscow far from the masses of the Jewish population, summer tours to the provinces, which became increasingly popular throughout the nineteenth century, exposed wider audiences to the stars. Traveling performers also sometimes set up shop at local taverns, entertaining travelers and locals alike. In the Pale of Jewish Settlement, where there were some 50,000 taverns—five times the number in the rest of Russia—Jewish travelers and tavern owners came into contact with touring actors from the Imperial Theaters and itinerant troupes of performers.[9] These traveling performers were as much an influence on the development of the Jewish theater as the folkish *purimshpils,* which, after all, were restricted to a single day of the year. The association of theater with taverns and drinking, though, inhibited public support for the art.

The provinces were not bound by the imperial theater monopoly, but until 1865 they were subjected to a system of censorship that legally limited theatrical performances to plays that had been performed by the imperial theaters. Despite this restriction, the provinces abounded in private manorial theaters, commercial theaters, and the occasional people's theater. Even with censorship constraints these theaters managed to provide a wide repertoire of performances and styles. One scholar has noted an "astonishing variety and richness of the repertoire presented to virtually every social class among the non-serf (and sometimes serf) population of the provinces," which included "tragedies, historical works, comedies, melodramas, operas, ballets, and vaudevilles—works by Shakespeare, Schiller, Hugo, Mozart, Meyerbeer, Ozerov, Griboedov, Gogol, Kukolnik, and Glinka."[10] After the 1865 censorship reforms, which created the Main Administration for Press Affairs, part of the Ministry of Internal Affairs, authors were required to submit their work to the censors for approval prior to publication or performance. The censor then published a periodic circular that listed all plays submitted for preliminary censorship and the censor's verdict—rejection, approval, or approval with excisions. Plays intended for performance were submitted to a special theatrical censor, whereas plays intended only for publication were submitted to the regular censor responsible for published materials. Plays approved for publication were not necessarily approved for performance.

Government authorities regarded the performance of a play as significantly more dangerous than its publication: not only did the unpredict-
ability of a live performance naturally pose a greater threat than a static
published text (Who could predict how a performer would alter the meaning of his or her lines with gestures and intonation or even stray from the
published script altogether?) but the stage was also accessible to wider
and less literate audiences. Censors always allowed greater leniency for
material that would be restricted to the more trusted upper classes than
material accessible to the feared illiterate masses. The censorship regime
also established legal distinctions on the basis of language; it was more
lenient toward Russian-language materials than toward materials written
in minority languages. Once a Russian-language play was approved by the
Main Administration of Press Affairs, its approval was universal and the
play could be performed anywhere in the empire. Plays in languages other
than Russian, however, required the approval of both the central authorities and local officials.

A growing leisure class and new attitudes toward culture stimulated
the emergence of widespread amateur theaters in Russia in the late nineteenth century. The appearance of journals that published plays intended
for amateur performances in homes and public spaces around the country
made it possible for local groups to obtain dramatic texts for performance.
A movement to establish Russian popular theater geared toward the lower
classes began soon after the imperial theater monopoly was rescinded in
1882. Although the government of Alexander III saw how desirable it was
to use theater to enlighten the masses, it was also wary of the potential
of theater to create unrest. Imperial censors viewed amateur and popular
theater with great suspicion. Their fears of corrupting the lower classes
led them to institute a two-tiered system of theatrical censorship in 1888
with separate guidelines for professional theaters and popular theaters, an
elusive distinction that depended primarily upon ticket prices. These new
regulations prohibited theaters intended for lower-class audiences from
performing many plays that had already been approved for elite audiences. Popular theaters were restricted to a separate list of plays explicitly
approved for the lower classes. Since these lists were sometimes difficult to
obtain, particularly in the provinces, and not all officials or theater entre-
preneurs even knew of their existence, enforcement was haphazard at best
and often subject to the whims of individual local officials. Because of the
socioeconomic status of Russia's Jewish population, Jewish theatergoers
were usually subject to the more restrictive laws.

The government was unwilling for the most part to allocate large sums to construct entertainment facilities for the masses, and private funding was needed to establish popular theaters. Thus, popular theater became primarily a commercial venture that proliferated in beer gardens, fairgrounds, teahouses, and factories. However, commercial theaters were widely criticized for failing to educate and enlighten the masses. Once it became subject to the vagaries of the marketplace, theater shed its enlightened inclinations in favor of attracting audiences through crass entertainment. Although these theaters rarely viewed education as their raison d'être, some observers were quick to notice, or at least argue, that theater had a positive effect on social behavior, particularly with regard to promoting sobriety. Thus, in the 1890s, the Ministry of Finance began to sponsor popular theaters, often in the context of temperance movements. The Guardianship of Popular Temperance, for instance, was created in 1894 in part to subsidize the establishment of teahouses and People's Houses as substitutes for taverns. Its efforts were backed by local governments, amateur associations, and educators.

By the early twentieth century, Russian popular theater was flourishing. Government supervision, however, was intense. The Ministry of Interior permitted and even encouraged popular theater as a means of entertainment and amusement. It was always careful to ensure that theater did not overstep its bounds and enter the realm of the political. In 1901, new measures were put in place to ensure that performances were monitored for political or offensive references even in cases where the text had already been approved. Inspectors were instructed to investigate the intentions of the producer and watch for audience reactions . Only after 1905 did the social and political context become more lenient toward theatrical performance. But preliminary censorship remained in force for materials intended for performance even after it had been lifted for materials intended solely for publication.[11]

The Jewish Encounter with Russian Theater

Many Jews in the Russian Empire received their first introduction to professional theater through Russian-language theater. In his monumental *Lexicon of Yiddish Theater,* Zalmen Zylbercweig notes that as young men and women, many actors "often visited the Russian theater, to which he [or, as the case may be, she] felt a deep love" and several were even "personally acquainted with many Russian writers and theater directors."[12] Mendl Elkin (1873–1962), who would become a prominent theater activist, had his first foray into theater in the mid-1890s, when he was in his early twenties, as part of a Russian-language theatrical production to raise funds for Bessarabian Jews affected by a famine that had hit the region. The local Russian amateur theatrical society was impressed with his performance and invited him to join. Over the next several years, Elkin became a true theater fan, regularly attending the local theater to watch the traveling troupes that visited Bobruisk during summer tours. "These troupes were my theater-school and [Grigorii] Motkovskii and [Olga] Rakhmanova were my teachers," he recalled of the famous Russian actors.[13] He eventually became the leader of the local Russian-language dramatic circle, performing from the contemporary European repertoire. Elkin's path to cultural performance could not be more archetypal. Like many upwardly mobile Jews of his generation, he had left the local yeshiva to seek work. He had pursued dentistry as a profession that could enable him to obtain a permit to leave the Pale, but his professional training only increased his thirst for cultural enlightenment. In 1902, when he found himself stationed as a dentist outside Moscow, he spent more of his time directing the local amateur theater group than capping molars.

The impact of Russian-language theater is a recurring motif in Jewish memoir literature of the period. L. Berman recalled going to the Russian theater on Friday evenings after dinner. The crowds in the gallery and the military orchestra that would play prior to the performance left an imprint on his memory, but ultimately his experiences were about cultural enrichment and political education—he recalls in particular Hamlet and George du Maurier's *Trilby*. His experiences, in his interpretation, instilled in him a commitment to socialism and eventually to the revolutionary movement. His attendance at the theater on Friday evenings, though, indicates he was already predisposed to reject traditional Jewish life. Even though as a Yiddish speaker he did not understand every word spoken on the Russian stage, "the acting alone had meaning and a definite meaning at that: we used to see a hint of the struggle against backwardness, against a lack of cultural refinement, a sign and symbol to unite for a new culture—a culture that was entirely different in custom and direction from our own surroundings."[14] As he went to see the same play week after week, he and his friends came to understand the gist of the story. As for the specific content of the plays, Berman remembered that "one felt in them a protest against the world of falsehoods and hypocrisy, scorn and mockery toward high society, the deception of the powerful—in a word, all that we had begun to see in the social body."[15] Vladimir Medem, whose Jewish parents baptized him at birth and brought him up in a Russian-speaking environment, was more impressed with the histrionics of the theater than the dramatic content:

The first time I was in a theater was when I was a child of about six. I was brought with my mother and sister for several weeks in Moscow and there they took me to a matinee at the Bolshoi Theater. A ballet called *Pharoah's Daughter* [by Maurius Petipa and Cesare Pugni] was playing, it was a fantastical thing with thousands of effects, and the impression it made was forceful. There was a lion on the stage and I can still vividly see today how they shot him and he fell off the bridge. I can see even more clearly a scene in which a prisoner was led to a big basket of flowers, from which sprang a snake that bit him in the chest, and he fell down dead. And there was also a monkey and a black knight, and a maiden who threw herself into the river Nile, and other similar things. It was a delight.[16]

Prominent Yiddish writer, playwright, and sometime actor and theatrical entrepreneur Peretz Hirschbein also recalled that as a child:

whenever I had enough money for a ticket, I loved to go to the Russian theatre. Visiting companies and guest performers from the world theatre used to come through Vilna, performing plays by Chekhov, Hauptmann, Ibsen, Shakespeare, and Maeterlinck. The language onstage sounded clear and musical. Sitting in the theatre, I learned from the actors how to speak Russian beautifully.[17]

Jews flocked to Russian-language theater especially when the play was about Jewish life. Performances of Evgenii Chirikov's pogrom-inspired play *Evrei* (Jews) and Osip Dimov's *Slushai, izrail* (Hear, O Israel) and Russian translations of plays with Jewish themes, such as Hermann Heijermans's *Ghetto* and Karl Gutzkow's *Uriel Acosta* always attracted large Jewish audiences.[18] Russian translations of plays written by Jews were also popular. Sholem Asch's Yiddish-language drama *Got fun nekome* (God of Vengeance) was staged in Russian at St. Petersburg's Korf Theater in 1907 to great acclaim. The following year the theater staged Max Nordau's *Doktor Kohn*. Both plays touched upon some of the most controversial issues of the time: the former was about a Jewish brothel owner and the latter about Jewish-Christian intermarriage. Jacob Gordin's *Got, mentsh un tayvl* (God, Man, and Devil) was performed throughout the empire in Russian translation under the title *Satan*. According to *Der fraynd,* when *Satan* was performed in Moscow in 1910 after successful runs in Odessa and Petersburg, "the theater was packed—with Jews."[19] Even in Moscow, with its relatively assimilated Jewish population, Jewish audiences filled theaters if the play was on a Jewish theme. Regardless of how hard they may have tried to integrate into Christian society in their daily lives, Jews continued to come out in droves for the performance of a play on a Jewish theme.

Avrom Reyzen's 1904 two-act comedy *Di repetitsie* (The Rehearsal) was one of the earliest of many attempts to dramatize and parody the central role theater was beginning to play in the life of Jewish youth. Boris, a 25-year-old clerk, promises Berte a life of pleasure and happiness if she will agree to be his wife. But Berte, her mind on the performance of *Aida* she hopes to attend that evening, responds with an analogy to theater. In theater she explains,

> Looks and talent are not enough. . . . One must also have practical skills. This is the most important thing. The actors do not go directly onto the stage before the public; rather they spend several days rehearsing, you understand? They are not so rash as to go on stage before the public without rehearsals. . . . I am saying that marriage is a serious drama, you understand, and a drama not for one evening, but for one's entire life. And you want to jump straight into performing without a single rehearsal?![20]

In Reyzen's comedy, life itself became theater for the young middling class, who aspired to a life of cultural refinement and leisure, symbolized by the evening's performance of *Aida*.

Even those with little interest in patronizing the performing arts found it useful to see the theater, or perhaps more precisely to be seen at the theater. The theater was not just a place of entertainment, it was also a site of sociability. In the words of one memoirist, "In the slight light that fell over the gallery one recognized friends that one had previously not seen in the dark. One called over, sending greetings to one another, sharing good tidings brought from home, regaling one another with gossip and other cultural delights."[21] In his 1933 play *Trupe Tanentsap: a Goldfaden-shpil in a Galitsish shtetl* (The Tanentsap Troupe: A Goldfadn Play in a Galician Shtetl), theater director and critic Mikhl Weichert savagely mocked pretentious middle-class audiences who attended theater solely to be seen in public. In one scene, a flashily dressed woman wearing a high feathered hat storms out of the theater when she is asked to remove her hat so that those behind her can see. The only reason she came to the theater in the first place, she declares as she jumps up from her seat, was to show off her new hat. And if she can't be seen with her new hat, there is no point in remaining in the theater at all.[22]

Others complained about how audiences flocked to the buffet and chatted animatedly during the intermission of Chirikov's *Jews*, apparently feeling nothing of the savage pogrom they had just seen unfold on stage.[23] Perhaps by their lighthearted banter the bourgeois Jewish audience members who attended this Russian-language theatrical production were trying to demonstrate to themselves and each other their distance from the poor shtetl Jews being victimized on the stage. If so, their choice to attend *Jews* rather than any of the other entertainments that competed for their attention that evening betrayed their intentions.

Theaters were transformed into central meeting places for all types of legal and illegal activities, often of a political nature. At times, political activists in the audience would even throw political proclamations and protest notes into the gallery. For many, the theater was a school of political radicalism. It was during the turbulent days of October 1905 that Vladimir Medem gave his first public address in Russia, at a revolutionary rally being held at the Vilna circus. He claims to have come to the realization that the revolution had genuine momentum that very evening. He spent the evening at the theater, where he saw Gorky's *Deti solntsa* (Children of the Sun). But before the play began, members of the audience started calling on the orchestra to play "The Marseillaise." When the orchestra obliged, the crowd erupted into enormous applause, and Medem thought to himself "the Revolution lives."[24] Whereas for some a trip to the theater provided confirmation of their bourgeois status, for others it represented the moment of the start of their revolutionary activity. Official suspicions about the revolutionary potential of the theater were not always off the mark.

Yiddish Theater

The enlightenment plays that inaugurated the modern age of Yiddish letters were written for private readings by friends and peers or at most for reading aloud in private salons. Shloyme Etinger's *Serkele* (1825 or 1826), for instance, which is regarded as one of the first modern Yiddish plays, was not performed until almost four decades after its composition. The text, which the censors forbid Etinger to publish in his lifetime, was known only in small *maskilic* circles through the transmission of manuscript copies. The play tells of a woman who mistakenly assumes that her brother is dead and forges his will in order to obtain his fortune. It was first performed at the Zhitomir rabbinical academy, where the audience was mostly young *maskilim*. The lead role in this production was famously played by Avrom Goldfadn himself.

The influence of *maskilic* texts on Jewish theatrical performance, then, was limited to the elite of *maskilic* playwrights. Goldfadn's early experience playing *Serkele* on the stage of the Zhitomir rabbinical academy clearly established a direct lineage between his own popular plays, which became ubiquitous on Yiddish stages around the world, and those of his *maskilic* forerunners. However, most participants in Jewish theater—actors, musicians, set designers, and audiences—had little contact with the satirical plays of the Yiddish enlightenment and little interest in them. Their influence stemmed from performance traditions independent of dramatic composition.

Although theatrical productions that were at least partially in Yiddish seem to have taken place in Warsaw as early as the 1830s, the first stable ensembles were not established until later in the century.[25] For the most part, Yiddish theatrical performances emerged out of the artisanal circles in the 1870s and usually took place in the cellars of cafeterias in remote corners of the city. In larger metropolitan centers, such as Odessa and Kishinev, theater companies began renting performance spaces in larger auditoriums and theater halls. These companies usually performed evenings of literary and musical performance rather than fully scripted theater. In 1879, the imperial censor in St. Petersburg began to receive applications for Yiddish theatrical performances and approved numerous scripts over the next four years. Even though groups that wanted to perform these plays still needed to obtain permission from local authorities, Jewish theatrical activity flourished briefly in the early 1880s as itinerant troupes traveled around southern Ukraine and Bessarabia performing works of Yiddish theater.

Even during this period of relative freedom, troupes routinely encountered difficulties. When Nokhem Meyer Shaykevitch took a troupe performing his plays to the shtetls of Bessarabia, many towns refused to allow him to perform. Shaykevitch complained to the town governor of Odessa, asking him to intervene on his behalf. The governor obliged by writing a letter to the governor of Bessarabia informing him that there was no legal basis for forbidding Shaykevitch's troupe from performing plays that had been approved by the censor. In the correspondence, though, Shaykevitch expressly sought permission to perform "both during the week and on the Sabbath" and indicated that it was actually performances on the Sabbath that were arousing the ire of local authorities. The Odessa town governor had stated in his letter that "there is no legal basis on which to forbid Jewish shows over the Sabbath." It seems, therefore, that Shaykevitch was not being refused permission to perform in general but that he was being refused permission to violate the Sabbath with theatrical entertainment. Since the governor of Bessarabia had little independent reason to forbid Sabbath performances, it seems probable that the opposition to Shaykevitch came not from state authorities but rather from the Jewish community, which likely appealed to the Bessarabian governor to forbid the performances on Sabbath.[26] This episode and others like it indicate that opposition to Yiddish theater emerged as much from within the Jewish community as from non-Jewish authorities.

The situation grew more complex in the summer of 1883, when the minister of internal affairs issued a circular prohibiting the performance of theater in Yiddish.[27] The overall effect of this ban was mixed. Although it hindered the development of professional Yiddish theater in the Russian Empire, local police authorities sometimes granted permission for select performances throughout the period of the ban. Other performances took place clandestinely when the participants disguised themselves as German-language troupes.

Among the more popular of the professional Yiddish theatrical troupes that performed during the period of the ban were those of the director Avrom Fishzon (1843/48–1922) and Yankev Spivakovskii (1852–1919), Fishzon's business partner turned rival. Spivakovskii was born in Bucharest and became acquainted with Goldfadn's theater while serving as a Romanian war correspondent for an Odessa newspaper. He joined the Goldfadn troupe in 1877 but left soon after to form his own theater in Odessa, where he performed vaudeville and couplets and eventually selections from the growing Goldfadn repertoire. Soon thereafter Spivakovskii took his troupe on the road, performing around Poland and the Pale. Fishzon was a devoted actor and shrewd businessman. According to Mukdoyni, he was able to use his humor, optimism, and confidence to operate within the Russian bureaucracy, securing permission to perform even "in the most fortified cities with the strictest governors and the most sinister and stubborn bureaucrats," an achievement he accomplished "not like an intercessor, not like a lawyer, but like an actor; with theatrics, melodramas and operettas he could overcome all obstacles."[28] The troupes that operated during the ban were forced to travel from town to town as permits expired, and the casts were highly unstable. Actors came and went and troupes merged and split up only to merge again at the next town. Actors included people such as Mordukh Rybalskii, who had been born in Fastov into a petty merchant family. He received his vocal training as a cantor's assistant and began a professional career as a singer, performing in various productions in western Ukraine in the hope of making enough money to pay for vocal training at one of the growing number of musical academies. Instead, he turned to Yiddish theater, establishing a reputation performing from the Goldfadn repertoire with various troupes that were active in the region in the early 1890s. Other early stars of Spivakovskii's troupe, such as Nadezhda Neroslavskaia, came from more middle-class homes and had received formal vocal train-

FIGURE 11. A horse and carriage advertises a Yiddish theater troupe in early-twentieth-century Warsaw. In the early years of the century, Yiddish theater became a hallmark of the Warsaw Jewish cultural scene, earning the city the title of the "cradle of Yiddish theater." *Photo courtesy of YIVO Institute for Jewish Research.*

ing. The response to Goldfadn's *Doctor Almasada* at the Great Theater of Lodz in 1902, in which Fishzon performed, was typical. According to *Ha-melits:* "Through the entire presentation of the play, calls of hurrah did not cease."[29] Indeed, Yiddish theater audiences cheered throughout the play at the appearance of the hero and his exploits.[30]

During the period of the ban, much of the theatrical action took place in Warsaw. Avrom Goldfadn's troupe arrived there in 1885. In the two years Goldfadn stayed in Warsaw, he revolutionized Polish Yiddish theater with his style and his repertoire. By this time, Goldfadn, who had begun his career as a playwright as a proponent of enlightenment ideals, had turned to the melodramas, operettas, and burlesques that produced commercial success. His influence on Polish Yiddish theater, and indeed world Yiddish theater, was immeasurable. In the words of Yiddish poet and playwright Itzik Manger, "He was and remained the inspiration for many successful experiments on the Yiddish stage. . . . He remained a great inspiration to Yiddish theater whether he was played authentically, whether he was modernized or whether the Goldfadn style was applied [to other productions]."[31] Goldfadn achieved enormous success in Warsaw and attracted young people from the provinces who abandoned their own professions to come to the capital to try their luck on the stage. Among these new stars was Ester-Rokhl Kaminska (1870–1925), who arrived in Warsaw as the working-class daughter of a small-town cantor and became the matron of a dynasty of high-quality professional Yiddish actors, includ- ing her daughter Ida Kaminska and Ida's first husband and stage partner, Zygmunt Turkow. When Goldfadn left for New York in 1903, the Goldfadn era in Eastern European Yiddish theater came to an end.

Jewish Theater and the Jewish Intelligentsia after 1905

The enforcement of the ban on Yiddish theater was relaxed after 1905, although it continued to be enforced in some provinces as late as 1909. During this period the number of Yiddish plays that were submitted to the theatrical censor increased enormously.[32] But even in the period after the ban was relaxed, bureaucratic and censorial impediments restricted theatrical performances. The lingering impact of the ban has commonly been blamed for the relatively late development of Yiddish theater in the Russian Empire, where it emerged in force decades after the theaters of New York's Second Avenue blossomed. Harassment of playwrights and performers continued through World War I. In order to perform a play in public, theater troupes needed permission from both the theatrical censor in St. Petersburg and local authorities. This often required extensive travel back and forth from the capital to the provinces as well as large outlays of money to cover travel and bribes. The trouble of obtaining permits from the censor for each new play also restricted the repertoire of theaters, forc- ing them to perform the same play for long runs when introducing newer works would have held audiences longer. As a result, theater troupes were forced to travel often, as individual cities and towns could not sustain the limited repertoire for extended periods of time.

Misunderstandings and the whims of local officials sometimes pre- vented troupes from performing plays that had already been approved by the censors and that contained little to offend local sensibilities. When Sam Adler's troupe was playing in Mogilev in 1908, for instance, the local police allegedly shut the theater down for a week in the mistaken belief that the popular theater song "Chava" was a revolutionary song. Apparently, the police could not imagine that an audience would applaud a song with such vigor and enthusiasm unless it was for revolutionary reasons.[33] In 1907, Kiev's prominent Solovtsov Theater was denied permission to perform Lessing's enlightenment drama of religious tolerance, *Nathan the Wise*, on the grounds that the performance was "untimely."[34] Hirschbein was forbidden from performing Asch's *Mit'n shtrom* (With the Stream) on the grounds that the title was revolutionary, despite Hirschbein's objections that if it were revolutionary, it would be entitled *Against the Stream* rather than *With the Stream*. In Siedlce, in 1908, the local authorities cited an outdated 1904 circular prohibiting the public use of Yiddish as the reason for denying an application to form a local Hazomir Society that would perform on stage.[35] The Vilna Musical-Dramatic Society was also temporarily prohibited from performing in Yiddish during the summer of 1908 on the basis of a state instruction prohibiting public performances in local languages in most of the northwestern provinces.[36] These measures were not always without basis. In the turbulent revolutionary years of 1905–1907, working-class audiences were prone to respond with revolutionary cries to any pathos or mistreatment of the working class on stage. In Rovno, workers from the local brewery erupted into chants of "long live freedom" and "down with the oppressors" during Ester-Rokhl Kaminska's portrayal of a poor suffering woman on stage. In response, the troupe—not wishing to cause any trouble or threaten the newly relaxed ban—dropped the curtain and fled to their hotel to grab their suitcases and get out of town in advance of the police as the theater audience made its way into the street, still chanting revolutionary slogans.[37]

Although some local authorities welcomed the idea of a literary Yiddish theater as a means of raising the general level of culture among the Jews or as a curiosity worth checking out, others remained suspicious of Yiddish altogether. The debut of Kaminska's theater in St. Petersburg was delayed half an hour as the troupe sorted out matters with the local police, who were still refusing to allow a theater to perform in Yiddish.[38] In 1908, local police prevented Avrom Fishzon's troupe from performing openly in Yiddish in Kiev despite the fact that his Yiddish repertoire had been approved by the censor and he had earlier received permission from the previous governor.[39] A request to establish a Yiddish theater in Bialystok was dismissed out of hand in December 1908.[40] Continued residency restrictions made travel difficult for itinerant troupes and touring groups. Sholem Asch was expelled from St. Petersburg in April 1907 for failing to have a proper residency permit.[41] Peretz Hirschbein's troupe received permission to perform in Poltava, outside the Pale, but was forced to travel beyond the city limits each night to sleep in an area where Jewish residency was permitted.

Contemporary writers were as quick to blame the Jewish intelligentsia for the slow growth of Yiddish theater as they were the tsarist ban.

According to historian of Yiddish theater Bernhard Gorin, "The trouble with the [Jewish] intelligentsia in Russia was that when they had a need to go to the theater, they would go to the Russian or Polish theater and would never allow themselves to be found patronizing the Yiddish theater."[42] The Jewish intelligentsia, he continued, belittled any alternative to the Russian-language art theaters of Moscow and mocked attempts to stage melodramas in the Yiddish language. If a native Jewish theatrical art form was to be established and gain the support of the intelligentsia, he believed, it would have to emulate Russian high theater rather than use distinct Jewish styles. It was not just supporters of Russian and Polish theater who blocked attempts to establish Yiddish theater, though: Peretz encountered difficulties from Hebraists in Odessa, who refused to use their influence to help him obtain permission for Yiddish performances.[43]

Others faulted the intelligentsia for treating Yiddish theater as quaint folk entertainment rather than as serious art capable of expressing Jewish national sentiments. One letter from the provinces to *Der fraynd* complained about "a doctor of ours, an intellectual," who had hired Fishzon's troupe to perform for a fund-raiser for the children's hospital. Rather than allow the troupe to perform a literary drama that Fishzon hoped would appeal to an upper-middle-class audience attending a fund-raiser, this doctor insisted that the troupe perform a light musical of Jewish folk theater. "Our intelligentsia," complained the writer, "ought to start considering our national theater seriously instead of seeing it as simple fairground entertainment."[44] Already some were ascribing to Yiddish theater the role of a national theater. Another letter-writer seconded this complaint, noting a similar episode in which a Yiddish theater was asked to perform light-hearted entertainment for a fund-raiser: "Where is the true Jewish intelligentsia, who we can hope will truly bring about a revival on the Yiddish stage?"[45] Another writer complained in the fall of 1911 about the recent summer season of Yiddish theater in Odessa. Only in the summer, when the Russian-language theaters were closed, would "many representatives of the Jewish intelligentsia gladly visit a Yiddish theater." Yet the theaters were neglecting the new literary repertoire, performing instead "vulgar melodramas."[46] According to a report in *Razsvet* from Kishinev, although the Genfer family theater was playing in town and performing several Yiddish plays a week, such as *In nets fun zind* (In a Web of Sin) and *A mentsh zol men zayn* (Be a Decent Person) with some success, "a portion of the Jewish intelligentsia has lost interest in Jewish theater: the troupe does not attract them with its cast and even less with its repertoire. The Jewish public goes to the circus, watches French fights, and isn't interested in anything more productive."[47]

Jewish Theater Critics

These sentiments were echoed by the growing cadre of professional Yiddish theater critics, many of whom directed the bulk of their criticism toward the audience in the gallery rather than the actors on stage. Typical of this attitude was that expressed by Y. Sanin in his review of a performance by the Kaminska troupe during its St. Petersburg tour. Sounding like a mother scolding her son on report card day for not having done as well as the next-door neighbor, he writes, "Not long ago in the very same Komisarzhevskii Theater a Polish troupe performed that was no better than Kaminska's Yiddish troupe and the theater was full every evening." Why can't you Jews be more like the Poles down the street? he implored. To belabor the point, he heaped guilt on the Jewish community of St. Petersburg for ruining his enjoyment of the tour by their indifference. "These last few evenings," he wrote, "were really festive for me. The St. Petersburg Jews, though, marred my celebration."[48] In a speech on the history of theater that Mukdoyni delivered in Warsaw, he rhapsodized about the role of theater when it was regarded as a religious event and actors were venerated as priests. Although he noted that this attitude declined during the middle ages, when actors were shunned from society, once again the stage had become a temple of art in European society. Only Jewish audiences had failed to entrust to theater this mystical and religious significance: "The god of art is still not their god." Jewish theater, he continued, could only succeed when society embraced it and recognized its national, and even sacred, significance.[49]

Other critics complained of a gap between the performance of theater, which was still largely relegated to improvisational performances at teahouses and beer gardens, and the composition of literary plays. Although some writers were turning one by one to the dramatic form as a literary experiment, few did so with the intention of actually having their creative output performed, and even fewer sought in any way to make a performance happen. Many Jewish writers saw themselves as successors to the enlightenment tradition of using the dramatic genre as a form of parody and as a means of attacking their ideological adversaries through the voice of invented characters. Dramatic texts were more likely to be read by the author at a literary evening than to be performed in a mise-en-scène by costumed actors on a stage. The performance of dramatic texts as theater required an attitudinal shift among the intelligentsia. This shift began to take place along with the cultural turn among Jewish activities that followed popular disillusionment with the politics of the post-1905 Duma.

Since at least 1908, a few self-styled theater critics began making demands in the press for a model Yiddish theater that would bring together the best actors, directors, and playwrights and educate them in professional theatrical techniques. A. Yarkhi dreamed of uniting the most talented itinerant performers who went from town to town in search of audiences and providing them with the resources to form a professional literary theater. Their repertoire, he suggested, could be drawn from the works of Jacob Gordin, Sholem Aleichem, Dovid Pinski, Y. L. Peretz, and Sholem Asch. Each of these writers could be counted among the new Yiddish literary elite who chose to write in Yiddish in order to introduce sophisticated literary works with psychological depth and realism to the emerging audiences of Yiddish readers with a taste for complex and challenging material. Gordin (1853–1909), for instance, wrote for the provincial Russian-language press before he turned to Yiddish theater after his 1891 immigration to New York. There he became one of the leading Yiddish playwrights of the 1890s and 1900s, writing a series of plays that shunned the bombast and predictability of popular Yiddish theater in favor of moralistic plays with borrowed plots and adapted themes from the contemporary European literary repertoire. Pinski (1872–1959) was also well versed in the European literary scene and has even been compared to Gerhart Hauptmann. Although born in Mogilev, he had lived in Vienna, Berlin, and Warsaw before settling in New York and later in Haifa. His plays often reflected his socialist activism with their realist portrayals of the struggles of the working class. In other works, he depicted different types of love and was critically lauded for his complex portraits of modern Jewish women who were full of energy and psychological depth. He would become one of the leading Yiddish writers of his generation. Since there were not enough plays for a permanent theater to fill a season, Yarkhi suggested that his model theater be a touring troupe that would perform in each town for a maximum of two or three weeks. The theater, he suggested, could even be funded by stocks. Anticipating the objection that the Jewish community should not be subsidizing a theater during times of such intense suffering, hunger, and poverty, Yarkhi argued that "in addition to the hunger of the stomach there is a hunger of the spirit. . . . All work done with the goal of satisfying the spiritual hunger of the people with a fresh and healthy diet must be regarded at all times as great and useful national work."[50] Just as advocates of public libraries had spoken of devouring books, theater advocates saw the stage as an integral part of the Jewish diet. Yarkhi believed that as a serious Yiddish repertoire developed, professional Yiddish art theaters should stage the new plays. In contrast to the earlier itinerant troupes, the groups who performed in these theaters would not rely exclusively upon star power and commercial tastes but would also use ensemble work and a commitment to the aesthetic value of the production as a whole. The director would replace the lead actor as the heart of the production, on the model of Konstantin Stanislavsky's famed Moscow Art Theater.

Sholem Asch largely agreed, lending his voice in an opinion piece published in *Der fraynd*. "There are Yiddish actors, a Yiddish public, the beginning of a Yiddish repertoire, but there are no Yiddish theaters," he wrote. "The reason is clear," he continued, "there are Yiddish troupes but there is not a Yiddish theater." Asch criticized the Russian Yiddish tradition in which each talented actor would form his own troupe in competition with other skilled actors rather than cooperate to form a first-rate theater. In addition to preventing any type of collective of talented actors from forming, this system discouraged troupes from performing from modern literary repertoires, which often did not allow stars to show off as much as they would like. Many performers preferred to interpret well-known and well-recognized stock roles in order to demonstrate that they could do it best. Literary theater and ensemble work required individual actors to repress their exceptionality and refrain from grandstanding in order to blend into the cast as a whole. Like Yarkhi, Asch called for actors to unite in a single ensemble. "This," he wrote, "would be a Yiddish theater."[51] There was widespread agreement that in theory this would be a desirable goal, but the practical, technical and financial problems, as Avrom Kaminski pointed out in a rebuttal, were significant.[52]

Yiddish writer, publicist, and critic Hersh Dovid Nomberg, on the other hand, saw the primary problem as one of repertoire rather than ensemble. Speaking in 1910, he complained that Jewish theater had not only failed to progress since the Goldfadn years a generation ago but had actually regressed. Whereas Goldfadn had taken folk types and developed them into well-developed Jewish national heroes, current playwrights were reverting to street humor and shtick.[53] As Avrom Reyzen noted, though, audiences were devouring this type of theater. When he first visited the Jardin d'Hiver in Warsaw in 1905, he wrote: "Notwithstanding the fact that the first time I went some type of operetta was playing with poor acting, a poor choir and a poor orchestra, I felt like I was refreshed in a stream of pure water. The audience, which was full of common people and even some of the 'good boys' of Warsaw with their fun-loving friends, greeted me in high spirits."[54]

Yiddish Literary Theaters

While some members of the intelligentsia were writing articles in the press calling for a literary theater, others were establishing model theaters on the ground. One of these was Sam Adler, whose literary skills in Yiddish were limited to writing Yiddish with Latin characters. Adler (1868–1925) had been born in Poltava Province in 1868 and had spent much of his youth as an itinerant performer wandering around the shtetls of Galicia with actor-singer-hatmaker Khayim-Shmuel Lukatsher before heading for New York in the late 1880s, where he performed in Yiddish and English theaters and even toured North and South America. He returned to Odessa in 1900, bringing newer American styles. Adler first attempted to form a Jewish literary art theater in 1905. He gathered first-rate actors and established a firm entitled Sam Adler from America. Adler brought to Yiddish theater a level of professionalism he had gained from America and made sure that his actors received regular wages. He also sought to elevate the level of theater by performing a repertoire of written texts and drafted Sholem Aleichem to help mold the repertoire. However, according to Zylbercweig, the authorities denied the troupe permission to perform, fearing its revolutionary potential. Adler moved to the freer grounds of Warsaw, where he performed in a Yiddish translation of Schiller's *Robbers*. Eventually he succeeded in touring the Pale and even had access to cities beyond the Pale, such as Kiev and Petersburg.[55] Adler's introduction of a regular repertoire of literary texts helped stimulate interest in theater among both shtetl and urban Jews.

Among the most successful of the new literary troupes was that established by Peretz Hirschbein, who was already emerging as a talented playwright in 1906. He visited Peretz in Warsaw that year and credited Peretz with convincing him that the performance of Yiddish plays need not be restricted to private readings in the apartments of the intelligentsia but could actually be staged enactments in a community auditorium before the general public. "At that visit to Warsaw, living with Peretz at his home, I had the pleasure of seeing from afar a new world that grew up around Peretz—a world of theater," wrote Hirschbein.[56] Hirschbein's opportunity to make the transition from writing drama to performing theater came in 1908 when, while living in Odessa, he received an invitation from David Herman, who had studied at the Warsaw Theatrical School and would later become artistic director of the famed Vilner Trupe, to act in a production of his play *Tkies kef* (The Handshake), which Herman was producing in Lodz. Buoyed by the success of this production, the two decided to form a Yiddish theater that would seek to provide a theater of national significance. In Hirschbein's words, the theater was "not a private whim" but rather was formed "as a type of national creation." The two placed advertisements in Yiddish newspapers, declaring, "Jews, come help us establish a Jewish art theater. Help us raise the theater arts to a higher level."[57] Over the course of the year, Hirschbein gathered several talented young actors. Some had completed a course of study at the Odessa Drama School and were on their way to careers in Russian-language theater before they decided to work instead for the benefit of their own Jewish community. Others were recruited from among the most recognized and capable actors of existing Yiddish theaters. According to Mukdoyni, who first met the troupe in 1910 when it came to Warsaw,

> Most of them belonged to the genteel and cultivated autodidactic Jewish intelligentsia. The women were all more or less cultured and educated; all had gone though some type of school, sometimes a Russian middle school. All were well-read in Russian literature. There were a few who even knew Hebrew well. All came from a higher Jewish class, all came from good Jewish homes, devoted to the upbringing of the children.[58]

Hirschbein's success, though, was restricted by the limited repertoire available to his troupe; after several months of performing in Odessa, he had exhausted it. That is not to say that there was a lack of good-quality plays in Yiddish; the problem was that only a few had been approved by the censors. So Hirschbein's troupe took to the road, touring southern Russia, first in larger centers such as Akkerman (Bessarabia Province), Nikolaev (Kherson Province), Elizavetgrad (Kherson Province), and Ekaterinoslav and then in smaller shtetls. They eventually developed a repertoire of fourteen plays: Sholem Asch's *With the Stream, Yikhes* (Pedigree), and *God of Vengeance;* Pinski's *Yankl der shmid* (Yankl the Blacksmith) and *Isaac Sheftel;* Berl Shafir's *Avrom'l der shuster* (Avom the Cobbler); Heijermans' *Ghetto;* Yushkevich's *In shtot* (In the City); Gordin's *God, Man, and Devil;* Sholem Aleichem's *Mentshn* (Men) and *Tsezeyt un tseshpreyt* (Scattered and Dispersed); and the three plays by Hirschbein: *The Handshake, Yoel,* and *Di neyvole* (Infamy). Hirschbein and Jacob Ben-Ami, who had performed in Russian-language theater in Minsk and later achieved fame in Yiddish American film in the 1930s before embarking upon a career on Broadway, directed most of the theater's productions. According to one report, the

FIGURE 12. The Hirschbein Troupe, posing here in Odessa, was one of the first groups to create a Yiddish literary theater. Although the troupe was short lived, Peretz Hirschbein became a prolific writer for the Yiddish theater. *Photo courtesy of YIVO Institute for Jewish Research.*

Hirschbein troupe gave 200 performances in seventeen towns over the course of 1909.

However, when the troupe returned to Odessa, Hirschbein discovered that his theater had come to the attention of the governor, who refused to grant it permission to continue performing. As Goldfadn had done a generation before, Hirschbein reluctantly abandoned Odessa and made his way to Warsaw, where he rented the Muranover Theater from his rival, Yiddish theater producer Aba Kompaneyets, for a week. Unable to secure a venue for longer, he was forced once again to take his troupe on the road. After a planned month-long stay at the invitation of Mendl Elkin in Bobruisk was cut short, Hirschbein sent the troupe on to Kovno without him. He returned to his writing desk, and the troupe soon disbanded.

Ester-Rokhl Kaminska made an even greater impact on professional Yiddish literary theater. Like Hirschbein, Kaminska was seeking to break away from the performance of the Goldfadn melodramas that had been favored by the itinerant performers of the last two decades. She wanted to introduce a literary repertoire and complex ensemble work to Yiddish theater. Like Hirschbein, her theater drew from the newer repertoire of plays by writers such as Dovid Pinski and Jacob Gordin. Kaminska's theater began on the model of other Yiddish theaters, performing from a repertoire of operettas and melodramas billed as Judeo-German works in order to circumvent the ban on Yiddish theater. After the relaxation of the ban in 1905, it began transforming itself into a dramatic and literary theater. Soon after the Russian-language press began writing about "Yiddish theater" instead of about "Judeo-German theater," a group of Odessa philanthropists saw indications that the political climate may be more hospitable to genuine Yiddish theater and began raising funds to establish one. They appointed Spivakovskii director and promptly asked Kaminska to be their star. Kaminska, however, decided to return to Warsaw, where she teamed up with Fishzon at the Jardin d'Hiver. They began performing operettas from the American repertoire of Joseph Lateiner and other melodramatic pieces but soon decided to try staging some of the newer literary material being made available. Their first attempt in the months after October 1905, performances of Pinski's *Di muter* (Mother) and Peretz's *Shvester* (Sisters), achieved only moderate success. Their next attempt, in April 1906, to stage Peretz's *Nisoyen* (Temptation) provided further evidence that any attempt to perform literary theater would be an uphill battle. With the departure of Fishzon, whose business sense could not tolerate the financial consequences of performing literary theater on the Yiddish stage, Kaminska turned to the repertoire of Jacob Gordin, performing his *Kreytser sonata* (Kreutzer Sonata), *Mirele Efros,* and *Di shkhite* (The Slaughter) and Pinski's *Familiye tsvi* (Family Zvi) and *Yankl the Cobbler.* The theater gradually created a public in its new home, Warsaw's Elysium Theater, and gained a reputation predominantly among the growing middle class of Warsaw Jewry. The Literary Theater, as it was now called, also regularly toured the small towns and larger cities of the Kingdom of Poland and made occasional forays into St. Petersburg. It soon added the works of lesser-known playwrights to its repertoire, such as Zalmen Libin's *Tsubrokhene hertser* (Broken Hearts), about the difficulties a young Russian Jewish woman has adjusting to American life, and Rakhov's *Talmid hokhem* (The Clever Student), a romantic comedy about a yeshiva student who finds himself bored with traditional Jewish learning.[59]

Soon numerous theaters throughout the empire began adopting literary repertoires. As one critic wrote, "All the troupes one after another began to become 'literary': first Kaminska, then Liberts (formerly Rapels), then Zandberg (in Lodz), then Kompaneyets, even Fishzon's theater also became 'literary.' All of the 'soldiers' started to look the same. Today they played *Sore-Sheyndl from Yehupets* (*Sore-sheyndl fun Yehupetz*), tomorrow *Scattered and Dispersed,* and the next day *The Slaughter.*"[60]

The new actors, who had talent and a professional commitment to bringing literature to life, worked in a symbiotic relationship with contemporary Yiddish playwrights, particularly those who had emigrated to America and whose repertoire had begun to reach the Russian Empire, seeping in through the porous borders with Austria and Romania. The plays of Jacob Gordin, in particular, had an enormous impact on Russian Jewish theater. By the end of the first decade of the century, Gordin's repertoire was becoming popular not only in the major metropolises but even in the provincial shtetls. Between 1906 and 1908 alone, the theatrical censor receiver over 150 submissions of eighteen different plays by Gordin.[61] The emerging cadre of theatrical critics agreed that Gordin's repertoire was a significant improvement upon the type of ad hoc performance common during the period of the ban. Avrom Reyzen recalls that when he first saw one of Gordin's plays performed, it appeared to him "as a miracle."[62] Critic Noyekh Prylucki agreed, arguing that if Goldfadn was the father of Yiddish theater, Gordin should be the father of Yiddish drama.[63] Ester-Rokhl Kaminska helped make Gordin famous throughout the Russian Empire and in Warsaw in particular. Even those who questioned Gordin's aesthetic judgments conceded that with Kaminska performing his plays, they were first-rate art.[64]

The Jewish Literary Society and the New Repertoire

Further synergy was created with the participation of the Jewish Literary Society, which took a leadership role in promoting Yiddish theater and helped forge a union between stage performance and dramatic literature. At its very first meeting in the fall of 1909, the Warsaw branch included on its agenda a discussion of theater. Similarly, in September 1909, one of the first general gatherings of the St. Petersburg Jewish Literary Society featured Noyekh Prylucki's talk on Jacob Gordin.[65] Several months later the St. Petersburg Jewish Literary Society adopted a resolution declaring the creation of "artistic plays from Jewish life" to be the "most important goal of the moment."[66]

The general public was also very interested in theater. According to Mukdoyni, who led a regular series of lectures on theater at the Warsaw branch of the society, the hall was so crowded when he presented his first lecture that "people were standing cheek to cheek in the little hall."[67] But the society's support for highbrow theater over popular melodramas and operettas earned it a mixed reputation among the masses. The society was unrelenting in its insistence that Yiddish theater be uprooted from the marketplace and resettled in the concert hall. When the society decided to hold a public discussion on Yiddish theater in January 1910, Peretz insisted that the event be held in the Warsaw Philharmonic Hall rather than in a Yiddish workers' club or synagogue, where the common folk would feel more comfortable. The biggest opposition to the choice of the location came from those who feared that a group of Jews renting out this bastion of the Polish aristocracy would provoke an anti-Semitic reaction. Few argued that Warsaw's Jews would be more comfortable on their own turf.

Nevertheless, when the speakers—Mukdoyni, Nomberg, Peretz, and Yiddish theater activist A. Vayter—arrived for the event on the afternoon of Saturday, 9 January 1910, they found "the entire street was completely black with people. The broad entryway was overcrowded. We just stood there and could not make a path to the entrance. But soon a few dozen excited youth, students, workers, and young men in long frock coats appeared, and they split the sea of people and made a pathway for us."[68] The metaphor of splitting the sea was not accidental; Vayter saw his mission in biblical terms as though he were leading the people of Israel to a new place of culture and refinement. According to the front-page article that appeared in *Der fraynd*, "It has been a long time since Warsaw has seen a gathering as impressive as yesterday's gathering that the Jewish Literary Society organized in the Philharmonic Hall. The great hall, which holds up to 2,400 people, was packed from corner to corner. The galleries and balconies were also packed. An hour before the gathering the tickets sold out, and many thundering people pressed up against the ticket booth uncertainly."[69]

For two hours Mukdoyni, Vayter, Nomberg, and Peretz, all seemingly oblivious of the size of the crowd, lambasted the Jewish intelligentsia and Jewish theater audiences for failing to demonstrate any type of interest in the development of Jewish theater and thereby preventing the Jewish nation from emerging into the modern age. "The public is to blame," declared Nomberg, "Our able class is dead to Jewish theater." At the conclusion of the day, the audience responded with "thunderous applause." It seems that they—along with the hundreds of others who were denied entry to the sold-out hall—agreed with the speakers that there was a general lack of interest in theater among Jewish society despite the abundant evidence to the contrary. Even *Der fraynd's* coverage of the meeting and accompanying advertisements for Yiddish theater performances taking place at the Hermitage Theater and Alexanderplatz that evening failed to convince the Jewish public that Yiddish theater was alive and well in Warsaw. One solitary worker, though, mustered the courage to write a letter to *Der fraynd* protesting the characterization that the Jewish masses were uninterested in serious theater.[70] If any others among the thousands of people who attended either Yiddish theater or speeches on Yiddish theater that Saturday objected to the characterization of the Jewish theater public as being dead, their objections were not recorded.

Each of the speakers that day touted an elitist view of theater and denigrated the type of Yiddish theater that was attracting audiences. As Mukdoyni wrote a few days later, "Dilettante artists think that they are performing, dilettante critics think they are critiquing, and the naïve public thinks it is going to the theater."[71] Mukdoyni's criticisms of the overall state of Jewish theater were always severe. Elsewhere he criticized the theater for failing to specialize: "Every theater plays for everyone or for no-one, every artist must be able to accommodate the demands of all types of theater audiences; he sings couplets, performs drama and dances. The blind public wanders; they go to see a drama performed by dancers and dances performed by dramatic actors." The most blatant exhibition of this lack of specialization, he continued, was the phenomenon of performances of several one-act plays in a single evening.[72] It was not just in Warsaw that critics complained of the lowbrow tastes of the Jewish theater-going public. An-sky echoed Mukdoyni's critique, complaining that "Jewish troupes hardly know any artistic type other than the universal. The Jewish dramatic artist is also an opera singer. He is tragic and comic, plays the elderly and the young, the first lover and the elderly uncle."[73] Others complained that the theater refused to pay attention to sets and costumes. Revelskii complained of one production, in particular, set in medieval Spain in which the streets on the set were lit with electric lights.[74]

Among the most ambitious attempts to elevate the status of Yiddish theater was the formation in late 1910 of a joint-stock venture that was intended to unite the artistic world with the business community in order to establish a Jewish theater in Warsaw. The venture was initiated by many of the same individuals who had been active in the Jewish Literary Society and was headed by A. Vayter. He and his associates were committed to combating what they regarded as the low artistic level of Yiddish theater by creating a "genuine Jewish and artistic dramatic theater in Russia."[75] The venture sought to form a cooperative theater that would unite the most talented actors and directors from Eastern Europe with a repertoire of highbrow plays, including original plays written by the Yiddish literati

FIGURE 13. In this photo, published in the New York *Forverts,* young boys scale a fence around the Muranover Theater in an effort to sneak into a Yiddish theater performance. Although critics derided the Jewish public for its failure to patronize the theater, theater was a popular pastime among the youth. *Photo courtesy of YIVO Institute for Jewish Research.*

and Yiddish translations of the European repertoire. They realized that in order to gain momentum and establish contact with key luminaries, they would need the support of Y. L. Peretz, Warsaw's most well-known Jewish cultural figure. Peretz suggested that they establish the society as a joint-stock venture and hired a lawyer to help them draft the statute and terms of incorporation. The statute established two managing boards—a financial board and an artistic board. Peretz and Vayter then set up meetings with potential board members around the city. They eventually persuaded writers Sholem Asch, Jacob Dinezon, Hersh Dovid Nomberg, and Avrom Reyzen as well as other prominent patrons and financiers to support the project. Shares sold for ten rubles.

Vayter left Warsaw to travel around the country to establish local branches that would then form a large organizational network and bring in enough funds to establish a viable theater with a first-rate company. Within months he had collected over 10,000 rubles and established the first provincial branch in Kiev.[76] Most of his support came from local Jewish literary societies. In Kiev, for instance, it was the Jewish Literary Society that sponsored Vayter's visit and provided him with the opportunity to address its members. Similarly, the Jewish Literary Society of St. Petersburg took an interest in the project, inviting Peretz to address its members and encouraging them to support the venture.[77]

Although on paper the venture appears to have attracted broad segments of the Jewish intelligentsia of Warsaw, the participation of most shareholders and members of the board ended when they attached their signatures to the statute. In Mukdoyni's own estimation, "The entire theater society was A. Vayter and me. I was the silent secretary and A. Vayter was the sole practical activist. All the other names that are remembered in connection with the theater society were only names and nothing more."[78] Although Mukdoyni probably overemphasized his role in the affair to the detriment of others—various sources mention Sholem Asch's involvement, for instance—it is probably true that the financial backers and signatories played little role in the day-to-day affairs of the society, which were left largely in the hands of the few artistic members.

Whereas most of these projects were geared toward high art, other projects were designed to broaden the appeal of theater to the Jewish masses. For instance, in Minsk, theater entrepreneur Solomon Genfer found that lowering ticket prices not only increased audiences but also changed the composition of the audience. As one correspondent explained, "It enticed to the theater those elements that had previously never even dreamed of theater. The theater became a place of rest and enjoyment for residents of poorer neighborhoods, for the Jewish underprivileged, who are deprived of every cultural pleasure."[79] In order to attract crowds the theater largely abandoned the literary repertoires of plays by Asch and Gordin and instead performed popular melodramas and comedies. Despite rebukes from the press and critics, the troupe succeeded in attracting some 40,000 people to its theater through the summer of 1909. Within a year, Genfer's influence contributed to the establishment of a new inexpensive troupe that performed Yiddish theater on a nearly daily basis in Minsk with heavily reduced ticket prices.[80]

In the last quarter of the nineteenth and the first quarter of the twentieth centuries, Jewish theater became more professional and more specialized and began adapting literary texts for stage presentation. Although amateur theater and vaudeville-style shows remained popular, by the 1910s many artists began to eschew basement stages and private readings in favor of public performances in legitimate theaters. Following the example of their Russian neighbors, Jewish intellectuals embraced the newfound freedoms of the post-1905 era to establish joint-stock theater ventures and perform dramatic works from the growing Yiddish literary repertoires. In the process they introduced theater as a legitimate form of expression and as a reflection of life to new audiences. As Arnold Zweig noted during his travels after World War I:

> The Eastern Jewish audience, which is easily excited about anything Jewish, greets even bad acting troupes with sold-out houses overflowing with applause. Yet the special role of the theater is indicated by the participation of the otherwise critical Jew; it is still an expression of national hope, for the rhythm of the people and their feelings are intensified and exhilarated by the performance of the actor. The Jew feels represented, elevated, secured, and celebrated by the figures on the stage, who appear in various guises of himself.[81]

7

Musical and Dramatic Societies: Amateur Performers and Audiences

In the shtetls that dotted the Pale of Jewish Settlement and the Kingdom of Poland, it often seemed as though every young Jewish man and woman was striving to become cultured and modern. "My shtetl longed for beauty," wrote Moyshe Olgin in his nostalgic portrait of an anonymous Ukrainian town. "It was a dark life with filthy roads, damp houses, earthen floors, smoky ovens, shoes without rubber, pillows without covers, a dinner of bread with a bit of herring . . . but in the midst of this bleak life, people thirsted after beauty, refinement and elegance. We envied the wealthy not for their fortunes, but for their education, for the good life."[1] Their image of what this meant was rooted in an imagined urban milieu often derived largely from newspaper accounts and novels. For Olgin, this image was derived from stories of famous and fictional cantors and klezmer musicians—Nisi Belzer, the Vilner Balebesl, Yosele Solovey, and Stempenyu (the latter two the subjects of Sholem Aleichem novellas)—as well as painters, singers, and performers. Upwardly mobile Jews often looked beyond Ukraine and Belarus to the Russian metropolises in the east or to the Polish, German, French, and American capitals in the west for inspiration about what it meant to be cultured. In the vision of modernity they received from popular culture, leisure and performing arts loomed large. No respectable young Jewish man or woman could expect to be perceived as modern unless they had mastered some basic cultural performance skills: dance, music, or theater. Those who did not feel they had the natural talent could enroll in classes with local tutors. In the last decade of the nineteenth century in Bobruisk, for instance, a local Jewish drama circle organized dance classes for young men and women. According to *Hamelits,* "They danced even on the Ninth of Av fast, and not only young Jewish women, but women and men together."[2] In fact, the practice of hiring dance teachers was so popular by the early twentieth century that *Der fraynd* published a warning about "a dance teacher, a Jew" who was traveling around towns signing up people for dance classes, taking their money, and then fleeing town without providing the lessons. He had picked up 400 rubles in Aleksandrovsk (Kovno Province) alone. "The community must beware," warned the paper.[3]

Others sought a route to modernity through musical performance. Sholem Aleichem recalled his desire as a young man to become a *kener,* an expert in all things:

> To learn to play the fiddle was in those days part of the program of knowledge. It was equal to other things, and belonged with other studies, such as French and German, that a father would teach his child. It had no practical purpose, but a father who wanted his child to be accomplished needed to have him learn everything. Almost all the fine boys in town studied the fiddle.[4]

As it became more possible to form groups to present theatrical and musical performances, groups of young people got together in the shtetl and formed amateur drama circles. In Taurage (Kovno Province) a correspondent for *Der fraynd* wrote, "Our shtetl is in the midst of a major competition. The competition is not in the market, though, but on the stage." Three competing groups of amateur performers were trying to perform three different plays.[5] Amateur drama circles were, in the words of *Der fraynd*, "very much in style" in 1908. Throughout Poland and the Pale, local small-town intellectuals were emulating the big city professionals by establishing their own dance groups, orchestras, choirs, and theaters.

Amateur theater was not new to the Eastern European Jewish world. Since the last quarter of the nineteenth century, performance of theatrical pieces had been a popular form of entertainment and leisure in many Jewish communities. Even during the period of the ban on Yiddish theater, amateurs continued to perform in small shtetls throughout the Pale. Unfortunately, few sources about these theaters have survived as they tended to avoid public advertising and were rarely mentioned in the national press. Many probably followed the example of Mordukhe Rybalskii, whose troupe performed Goldfadn's *Sorceress* in Bialystok "in a private lodging without any advertisements and without the approval of the local authorities. Announcements about the performance were spread only in the synagogue and tickets distributed by hand."[6] One colorful description of how a group of theater lovers managed to perform a play in Dubossary (Kherson Province) during the period of the ban can be found in the town's memorial book. As Isaac Hurwitz recalled, over the summer of 1901 a young man named Calman Beilis arrived in town from Gorodok (Podolia Province) to visit his brother. Beilis told the local youth about a theater group in his shtetl and inspired the locals to establish their own.

> It was late summertime and the swimming area at the Dniester soon became a meeting place for us, Calman Beilis and a young group of

friends. We saw in him a force that would push the backwards and provincial Dubossary young men and women forward. After a few meetings with Calman Beilis, it was clear to us, the more progressive Dubossary youth, that we must also do something. With his initiative and help, we got together a group of around ten friends [to put on plays].[7]

The amateur troupe began with a performance based on Mark Varshavsky's "Dos lid fun broyt" ("Song of Bread"), a popular Yiddish poem about farming one's own land. Buoyed by initial success, the theater group became more and more serious as the summer progressed and continued through the fall with rehearsals in a local *kheyder* for their next production, *Zerubavel,* written by *maskil* and Zionist activist Mosheh Leib Lilienblum. The play, which Lilienblum had written in Yiddish in 1888, was a historical drama about the return of the Babylonian exiles to the Land of Israel. Beilis had earlier performed the play in Gorodok. The two plays suggest that this particular theatrical group had a Zionist orientation. Eventually, in a move rich with symbolic importance, the group succeeded in renting the town theater hall by promising that they would be performing only in Judeo-German and not in Yiddish. A small bribe helped as well. They thereby moved out of the *kheyder* and its parochial connotations and into the public sphere. Hurwitz describes this process in colorful detail, worth quoting at length:

> A hunt began as we all ran around trying to find out how and through whom we could approach the police officer in order to obtain the required permit. I was given this difficult job. Fortunately, a friend of mine came to help. Shmelke Melamed was close to the government; he was practically a member of the police officer's household. Shmelke undertook the role of emissary, but only under the condition that I would go with him to the police officer. We both left one morning, taking with us, on Shmelke's suggestion, the booklet *Zerubavel* and a three-ruble note, which Shmelke placed between the cover and the first page. To put us at ease, he joked that it was because this was where the censor had put the stamp stating "permitted by the censor." When we arrived in the office, Shmelke asked to see the police officer and we were permitted to enter. We went into the reception room and Shmelke in a few words let the police officer know what our business was. At the same time, he handed over the book, saying "this book is permitted by the censor." The police officer opened the book, skillfully rolled the three-ruble note into his hand, closed his hand into a fist and wrinkled his brow. He made some type of noise, handed the

book back and said, in a half contrived, half commanding voice, "Yes, it's been approved." He advised us to send a telegram under his name to the supervisor in Tiraspol with the following content: "I request permission for a free private performance of a Judeo-German play." When he received an answer, he would let us know.

I did as he suggested, and in three days a policeman came to call me to the police office. I went to get Shmelke and we went over the same game: the book, a three-ruble note where required, and together we went to his lordship. And he, the lord, looking at us with the book in our hands, received us with a bit too much sweetness and in a contrived joyous tone declared "it is permitted." Shmelke handed the book over to him. The officer, while rolling the money, read the reply for us: "Notify Isaac Hurwitz that a free and private performance of the Judeo-German play is permitted."[8]

These troupes performed from a repertoire that relied heavily on the works of Goldfadn, which they often had to re-title in order to fool local officials into believing that they were performing in Judeo-German rather than Yiddish. Occasionally plays by Goldfadn's competitors would enter the repertoire, along with a few productions based on the popular Yiddish novels of Shomer or the plays of the American Joseph Lateiner. In addition, these troupes relied heavily on hastily written productions on biblical themes, often inspired by and derived from popular *purim-shpils*. Performances with titles like *Mekhires Yoysef* (The Sale of Joseph), *Shloyme ha-meylekh* (King Solomon) and *Ahashverush* were well-known as Purim plays and often were only moderately adapted to fit the nonfestival stage. Playwrights such as Lateiner and Moyshe Hurwitz also made careers for themselves writing melodramas and romantic musicals on biblical and historical themes. In America, Lateiner's biblical compositions such as his *Ester un Homen* (Esther and Haman) and *Yoysef un zayne brider* (Joseph and His Brothers), which were also based on Purim plays, flooded the New York Yiddish stage in the late 1880s and early 1890s and gradually made their way to Eastern European markets as well. Moyshe Hurwitz competed with Lateiner, writing over fifty operettas on biblical and historical themes or on contemporary events. These included *Shloyme ha-meylekh* (King Solomon, 1887), *Yeshua ben-nun, oder der fall fun yerikho* (Joshua ben Nun, or the Fall of Jericho, 1898), *Don Yoysef Abravanel* (Don Joseph Abravanel), and *Kapitan Dreyfus, oder geheymnise fun pariz* (Captain Dreyfus, or the Mystery from Paris, 1898).[9]

All these plays relied on romance, adventure, melodrama, and song to entice audiences. Performances retold well-known stories with recognizable characters, which meant that the actors did not need to concern themselves with the burden of character development and setting the plot. Instead, they could simply perform and entertain, singing, dancing, and acting out the adventures and escapades of their characters to the delight of the audience. Audiences as well were free to socialize during the production and to come and go as they pleased. They could allow their attention to lapse periodically, turning their attention back to the stage when something exciting was happening or when a pleasant song was being sung. Audiences enjoyed watching the gallant feats of biblical heroes and medieval chivalry acted out on stage.

In the early stages of its development, amateur theater was rarely differentiated from other genres of performing arts. Only over the course of the first two decades of the century, as Yiddish literary theatrical repertoires developed and spread, did theater emerge as a distinct genre in smaller communities. Throughout most of the period under discussion, theatrical presentations were usually part of an evening of entertainment that combined public lectures, dances, concerts, art displays, competitions, and other celebrations with dramatic performances. These events were typically sponsored by dramatic-musical societies, literary societies, or political associations, chiefly of a Zionist or Bundist persuasion. Theater had not yet gained an adequate level of legitimacy in either the Jewish community or the community at large to warrant a full evening of public attention and commitment.

It was only after the March 1906 laws that eased restrictions on voluntary associations that dramatic societies proliferated, often in conjunction with literary or musical societies. Yitshak Katzenelson (1885–1944), for instance, who was becoming a recognized writer in Hebrew and Yiddish literary circles and had recently been released from military service, formed a dramatic circle in the Hazomir Society in Lodz, where he and a group of amateur actors performed works from the repertoires of Sholem Aleichem, Peretz, and Hirschbein as well as some of his own original pieces.[10] In nearby Częstochowa, the local branch of the Jewish Literary Society also included a dramatic section of some thirty men and women who regularly sang in the society's auditorium on Friday evenings. Its first dramatic productions took place in the spring of 1911, when it presented two one-act plays in a local garden theater: Yitzhak Katzenelson's *Di bokhurim* (Boys), and Mark Arnshteyn's *Eybike lid* (Eternal Song), both realist portraits of everyday Jewish life in contemporary Poland.[11] In Baranovichi, the Jewish

Literary Society made its headquarters on the second floor of a private home and included in addition to a library and reading room a "long theater hall and stage, which was small and uncomfortable. . . . The amateur circle was composed of a big group of talented men and women who acquired a reputation not only among the local Jewish population, but also in theater circles throughout the entire region."[12] In Zabludov, as well, a small dramatic circle emerged out of the group of youth who frequented the library. In a private home, they performed Avrom Reyzen's *Di fir gute brider* (The Four Good Brothers), complete with a choir. Later the group tackled two one-act plays of Anton Chekhov in Russian.[13]

Hebrew-language societies also commonly included musical-dramatic sections. The Riga branch of Ivriah, for instance, had a choir and orchestra under its direction and sponsored dramatic presentations in Hebrew. Other Hebrew literary societies, like the Ha-Karmel Musical, Dramatic and Literary Society of Riga, were established with the express goal of combining spoken-word performances with other forms of performing arts. This society, which was founded in 1910, had 342 members by 1911 and organized fifteen musical-dramatic events over the course of the year as well as a regular series of lectures on literary themes.[14]

The bylaws of the Hazomir Society, which had branches throughout the Pale and Poland, declared its goal of "developing and promoting the spread of music, song, history and literature among its members and acquainting them with the best musical and literary works" through the sponsoring of "public concerts, readings, recitals, talks, lectures and conversations on musical, historical and literary themes."[15] Theaters, libraries, fire brigades, literary societies, and musical societies all interacted with each other on a regular basis, sharing resources (including human resources), raising funds for each other, serving similar constituencies, and even performing together at a single evening of entertainment. All shared in the fundamental project of constructing a modern Jewish public culture.

Numerous other literary or cultural societies listed the "putting on of plays" as one of many methods to be used in promoting their goals, along with publishing a newsletter, sponsoring lectures, and establishing a library. In this sense, the theatrical production was presented as a means of propagating a society's ideology rather than as a goal in and of itself. Those who supported theater as an end in itself also saw establishing a formal society whose statute included a clause specifically permitting the production of plays as an effective way to override capricious police officials, who, despite their corruption, were reluctant to refuse permission for activities expressly sanctioned by a written statute. Like spoken-word events, theatrical performances required 72-hour prior notification and permission from the local authorities if the event was taking place in the society's permanent dwelling and seven days if it was taking place elsewhere. The best of these societies focused on promoting literary theater, adopting the new repertoire becoming popular in the big cities.

Theater as Fund-Raiser

Theatrical performances in the provinces often first gained legitimacy as fund-raisers for other societies. In Korelichi, a theater group raised money for the fire brigade.[16] In Zhvanets (Podolia Province), a group of amateurs performed a play as a benefit to purchase wood for the poor folk in town, while in Shavli local amateurs performed Sholem Asch's *With the Stream* to benefit the town's religious school.[17] An amateur theater group in Liubcha (Minsk Province) performed *Der yeshive bokher* (The Yeshiva Student) and *Golit ha-filishti* (Goliath the Philistine) to raise funds for the local library, while in Ungeni (Bessarabia Province) a group of amateur actors performed Sholem Aleichem's *Scattered and Dispersed* for the same purpose. In Ungeni, the show was such a success—it raised over 100 rubles—that the troupe organized a second benefit several months later, this time performing Gordin's *God, Man, and Devil* and Sholem Aleichem's *Mazl tov*.[18]

In Kurenets (Vilna Province), theater was used as a means of raising funds for the community library. According to one native of the town who had been living in Vilna and had been a member of the Vilna branch of the Hazomir Society, "One summer when I returned home for vacation, the gang came to me with the request that I, and only I as the sole person with the know-how, set up and prepare a play for the benefit of the library that was being enlarged." He suggested that they perform one of the works of Peretz Hirschbein, but others suggested instead one of Gordin's plays. In the end, the group decided upon a Gordin play because "it would be understood better and liked better by the community." The group rented a barn, cleaned it out, poured sand over the floor, decorated the walls with tree branches, borrowed benches from private houses, and constructed a stage. By converting the barn into a theater, they imagined themselves making the leap from a rural agrarian-based economy to a modern, urban, and cultured society: "From here on in, we were no longer an out-of-the-way shtetl; we began to resemble the large cultured world."[19] Many of these troupes, ostensibly formed for one-time efforts to raise money for a particular cause, enjoyed the experience so much that they continued to perform together even after the fund-raising objectives had been met.

Although most theaters could operate as fund-raisers, a few sought to make a profit as well. As their level of institutionalization increased, members of drama circles started to think in financial terms. As one amateur actor from Novogrudok (Minsk Province) recalled:

> For the first plays we the actors (or as we were called by the locals, the comedians) would walk from house to house in order to sell tickets. We succeeded mostly by appealing to people's charity and support. After a little time, though, our treasury was supported completely by ticket sales and I recall many plays for which it was hard to obtain tickets. We became a true theater, but we remained amateurs and kept our day jobs.[20]

Many amateur theater groups performed without the resources and leadership serious professional theater requires. Often the only guidance an amateur troupe received was what it could learn from observing traveling troupes that visited during summer tours. A visit from one of the leading itinerant troupes commonly inspired students, still excited by what they had just seen, to decide on their own to emulate the performance by establishing a local drama club. Locals remembered that soon after the Fishzon troupe came to Luninets in 1909, for instance, they formed their own drama circle, emulating his repertoire. The theater group of Międzyrzec (Siedlce Province) was inspired by the Kampaneyets troupe, which often visited the shtetl.[21] When a group of workers and intelligentsia formed a Yiddish theater in the town of Biała Podlaska, they trained themselves by watching a visiting troupe perform Gordin's *Hasia the Orphan* before beginning rehearsals of the same play. They even traveled together to neighboring towns to see different variants of the play's performance in order to perfect their own interpretation.[22]

Preexisting amateur troupes also were inspired by professional performers who visited the provinces, sometimes gracing the local community stage with cameo appearances. According to one observer, when Ester-Rokhl Kaminska came to Nikolaev, "'all Nikolaev, and by 'all' is understood to be the Jewish part" came out to see her. Kaminska even gave an unrehearsed performance with the local Lovers of Jewish Dramatic Arts.[23] When famous literary figures visited a small town, it was customary for the community to greet them by showing off its best talent. The great writer, for instance, would often be expected to endure a theatrical performance by the town's

FIGURE 14. A children's dramatic group in the town of Bragin poses in their costumes. In the early twentieth century, amateur theatrical performance, which had long been taboo in Jewish society, became a regular part of children's upbringing. *Photo courtesy of YIVO Institute for Jewish Research.*

amateur theater group or listen to a recital by the amateur choir before beginning his own talk. If a famous Yiddish actor chanced to come through town, she or he would be expected to perform on stage with the local theater group.

Small-town drama circles learned both technique and repertoire from the theaters of the metropoles and traveling troupes. However, without adequate libraries and access to published scripts, many amateur theaters improvised, simply repeating or duplicating as best as they could remember productions they had seen before. In Briansk (Grodno Province), for instance, the drama circle performed *Shmendrikune,* a combination of two of Goldfadn's more famous plays, *Two Kuni-Lemls* and *Shmendrik, oder di komishe Chaseneh* (Shmendrik, or the Comic Wedding). In what was surely an amateur production in all senses of the word, the lead actors each played five different roles. It is not surprising that for the most part, *purimshpils* "were enough for Briansk."[24] The Kielce amateur dramatic section of the Hazomir Society was similarly amateur:

> Of course, it was formed without a teacher or leader. Lacking training in dramatic arts, they would do everything from their intuition alone

or by copying something they saw once in the Jewish or Polish theater that would from time to time visit Kielce. Despite the faults that were apparent in their plays, the audience received them with acclaim because its demands were also not very high.[25]

Mikhl Weichert satirized this type of ad hoc performance in *The Tanentsap Troupe,* a play within a play about an amateur performance of Goldfadn's *Two Kuni-Lemls.* In other cases, local amateur writers would write plays for the local drama society. The play that the newly established Jewish Art Society of Bialystok performed to benefit the society was composed by a local writer.[26] Members of the local intelligentsia supported the theater and often wrote plays to perform on their hometown stage.

Few provincial theater companies had the resources to perform in permanent theater halls. Some performed in stables, as in Weichert's fictional depiction, or used the wooden platforms of unfinished houses as a stage. Others set up stages in grain stores, which they decorated with colorful banners. Sometimes amateur theater groups performed in a private home of one of the actors or a local intellectual. In a private home in Rokishki (Kovno Province), "admission was free, and we always had a full house. The doors were always open to everyone, and those who could not come into the house would stand by the windows, near the door."[27] Sometimes the local fire hall was transformed into a theatrical space. It was there that the *purimshpil The Sale of Joseph* was performed in Luninets in 1908, as were the first theater productions of Rokishki.[28] In Lenin, they would take the water pump and fire equipment outside so the fire hall could be used as a performance space. Audiences contributed in the days before the performance by providing chairs to help convert the fire hall into an auditorium. It served as a playhouse for *purimshpils* such as *The Sale of Joseph* and *David and Goliath* and later for modern plays such as Moliere's *Misanthrope.*[29]

The fire hall served as a cultural space in other contexts as well. In Bobruisk, there were public readings of the poetry of Frug and Bialik in the fire hall as well as various plays and public lectures.[30] Some communities were fortunate to have a permanent theater hall. Not all were welcome spaces for Jewish theater, though. In Baranovichi, the theater, which had been built in the first years of the century by a local nobleman, was so close to the Jewish cemetery that few Jews wanted to visit it. Instead, Yiddish theater was more often performed in the town hall, where Jewish and non-Jewish cultural events were regularly scheduled.[31] Civic buildings such as fire halls, dance halls, wedding halls, or meeting halls were ideal spaces for theater. Not only could they be easily emptied and transformed into auditoriums, but they also represented civic secular space that was unassociated with partisan ideology. The fire hall, and by extension theatrical performances in it, represented the entire community, cutting across the numerous political and ideological associations that claimed much of the physical space of the shtetl.

Not all small-town drama circles, though, were tools for fund-raising or childish fun. Societies and groups of individuals with enlightenment goals also used theater as a didactic tool. In Chelm (Lublin Province) in 1910, according to one testimony, the amateur Yiddish theater troupe had little theatrical talent; theater was only a tool for propagating ideology. According to one memoirist: "Inasmuch as the amateur ensemble at first was composed for the most part of those elements who were captivated by assimilationist tendencies and who spoke more Russian than Yiddish at home, the first performances were very weak. They were amateurs who didn't even understand the text of the plays well. Later this amateur circle was enlarged with simple folk and workers."[32] The troupe performed in a theater hall in Chelm and later toured neighboring shtetls. The theater group of Lenin was established by an outsider with enlightened goals. When the old synagogue needed to hire a bookbinder to repair some prayer books, it hired a specialist from Pinsk, "an intellectual young man who was full of life" and who also enjoyed theater. During his time in Lenin, he befriended a group of choristers from the synagogue and set them up to perform Goldfadn's *Sorceress*. They rehearsed three times a week in the cantor's home. They performed once to a small audience but disbanded when the bookbinder finished his work and returned to Pinsk for Passover.[33]

In some towns, there were individuals who took the dramatic arts very seriously and saw theater as a path to modern culture. Some drama circles were led by individuals with knowledge of the theater who hoped to instill a love of theater among audiences and actors alike. The Habimah theater of Lipkany was formed "not simply by young men and women who did not know exactly what theater was, but rather by the very Jewish intelligentsia who knew their goal and what they wanted to accomplish with Yiddish theater."[34] One of its directors was Jacob Sternberg, who went on to become director of the Vilner Trupe in Bucharest. This theater even had its own orchestra and toured the region. It was usually these intelligentsia theaters that introduced literary repertoires into smaller towns. Sometimes literary productions were combined with melodramas and other performances. The drama group in Rokishki performed Sholem Asch's *With the Stream,* several one-act plays by Sholem Aleichem, and evenings of cabaret-style entertainment that mixed song with dance and short skits. Theaters established specifically by literary societies generally had a greater interest in promoting literary theater than ad hoc drama circles.

Theater, even more than most other forms of cultural performance, demanded a wide array of resources and commitment. Whereas it takes only one individual to establish a library or deliver a public lecture—although certainly both these activities rely upon the community to attend the lecture and read the books in the library—theater requires a much larger group and a more intensive commitment of human and material resources. According to one participant in theater activities in World War I–era Luboml (Volhynia Province):

> The putting on of plays involved great effort not only for the actors, who had to overcome the opposition of their parents, memorize their parts, prepare the appropriate costumes, etc., but also for the devoted helpers, the "technical corps" who had difficult tasks: getting censorship permits from officials, which required traveling to the big city (Lublin or Warsaw); finding somebody to use his "pull" to get that permit; preparing the hall and stage; bringing in benches from the synagogue (mostly by stealing) and chairs from private homes; finding large lamps to light the hall (also taken from the synagogue); borrowing stage props, such as furniture; bringing a make-up specialist from the big city; engaging musicians to play before and during the intermission as well as for the dances that followed the performances and lasted well after midnight.[35]

Drama circles brought together new social groups that were united by taste and interest. The stage could become an equalizing force in the town on which even someone from the bottom of the social ladder, like Feyge Pomerantz, the daughter of the Luboml water-carrier, could become a local celebrity, admired by her peers and desired by the local boys.[36] Undoubtedly many young girls and boys came into their own on the stage, performing against their parents' will for the benefit of new peer groups.

The intermingling of boys and girls on stage and in audiences is a constant refrain in memoirs. In contrast to spoken-word events, where women were rarely at the podium, drama circles allowed women to perform on stage. This development, which broke a long-standing Jewish taboo against women appearing on stage (women's roles had traditionally been performed by men dressed as women), led to women's widespread interest in the theater. Although it is difficult to determine the gender breakdown of theater enthusiasts in the prewar period, pictures and memoirs of the amateur drama circles that proliferated in independent Poland and throughout Eastern Europe indicate that young women were flocking to the stage. The prominence and visibility of female role models, particularly Ester-Rokhl Kaminska, the mother of Yiddish theater, helped stimulate female enthusiasm for theater. Finally, the new Yiddish theater repertoire with its bourgeois sensibilities often dealt with women's issues, family life, and questions of courtship. Hirschbein, Gordin, Asch, Pinski, and Sholem Aleichem all wrote plays with complex leading roles for women who were struggling to become modern and engage actively in this world. Yet the conflicts between fathers and daughters and suffering mothers that permeated the Yiddish stage alluded to the degree to which conceptions of modernity were gendered and the gendered ways in which access to this world was understood.

The Repertoire of the Yiddish Stage

Although it is not possible to compile a statistical analysis of amateur repertoires, anecdotal evidence suggests that theater enthusiasts in provincial towns closely emulated the repertoire of professional theaters in the cities. Small-town provincial drama circles eagerly awaited news of the latest production to be staged in the big city and quickly staged their own version. Crudely published scripts of popular American operettas and historical dramas could be acquired from Warsaw brokers like Kompaneyets's Warsaw Yiddish Theater (Varshaver idisher teatr) publishing house or could be read in serials like *Di yidishe bihne* (The Jewish Stage). More highbrow dramatic literature was regularly published in serial publications or in book form.

Most often these plays were literary manifestations of the encounter with modernity, often portrayed as a youthful rebellion against the morals of the elder generation. This generational conflict was a version of the battle between the asceticism of traditional Jewish life and an appreciation of modern culture, which included, of course, theater. Often, theatrical portrayals of the aspiration to become modern were heavily gendered, as the conflict between enjoyment of this world and anticipation of the next interfered with romance and expected gender roles. On stages throughout the empire, young Jewish men neglected their Torah studies and familial obligations in favor of music and theater, while young Jewish women rejected nuptial obligations arranged by their parents in favor of the true love depicted in modern romance novels or a chance at becoming cultured. Plays mirrored the angst many Jews felt about enjoying the riches and

pleasures of this world. It is difficult to determine how deeply these conflicts resonated among audiences, but they likely expressed the mood of
upwardly mobile actors and local theater enthusiasts who chose to express
themselves on stage. Since amateur troupes were not constrained by commercial demands to the same degree as professional theaters, they had
greater latitude to perform plays that expressed their own longings and
dealt with themes their members may have been grappling with off stage.

One of the most popular plays of the period, Gordin's *God, Man, and
Devil*, deals in part with this issue. When the Devil in disguise helps the
pious Hershele win the lottery, Hershele is torn about what to do with his
newfound spare time and money. He ultimately chooses pleasure, following the advice offered by the devil in disguise. "God created great joy and
happiness in man's life. Man need only do one thing: live and enjoy. We
live only once in this world," the devil exhorts. Hershele initially responds
with shock: "What are you saying? This is not Jewish talk! These are not
Jewish thoughts! Leave me alone! Leave me alone! You want to poison me
with your heretical thoughts!"[37] But as the play progresses, Hershele succumbs and embraces the materialistic life at the expense of his family, his
friends, his ideals, and his religion. But he abandons the one material item
that truly gives him pleasure: his violin, which he associates with the life
he is leaving behind. Only at the play's tragic end does Hershele return
again to his violin as he realizes that he has allowed money to destroy his
life and those he loves. The devil realizes that although he can destroy a
man's life, he cannot destroy his soul. Hershele's return to his violin demonstrates that a Jew can embrace culture and the arts while rejecting the
excesses of modern materialism and hedonism.

Similarly, in Hirschbein's 1904 play *Barg arop* (Downhill), Miriam, a
young orphan employed as a shoemaker in the home of a loving Jewish
family, falls for a worldly and debonair older wealthy man. In pursuit of a
life of pleasure, she leaves her secure home, enticed by her lover's promises
to show her the broader world outside her sheltered environment. The final
act finds Miriam in a Russian whorehouse, pregnant and abandoned by
her lover.[38] The playwright exhorts his audience to enjoy the new cultural
opportunities the modern world offers in moderation, without abandoning
what is most meaningful. It is possible to live in this world, he argues, as
a cultured Jew without forsaking one's identity.

Both Gordin and Hirschbein, like their Russian literary counterparts
Artsybashev and Verbitskaia, wrote about how young Jewish men and
women were unprepared to confront modern urban leisure culture. These
Yiddish literary plays self-consciously spoke about contemporary Russian

cultural mores, bringing Russian theatrical realism into the Yiddish theater and Russian literary tropes and issues of public concern into Jewish
homes.

Most of these plays viewed the struggle for a life of leisure through
familial conflict, sometimes portrayed as a conflict between generations and
sometimes as a conflict between husband and wife. Sholem Asch's *With the
Storm,* for instance, tells of a young man who abandons his wife, his child,
and his faith in pursuit of a modern life. As he explains to his wife before
leaving her,

> Do you see the holy books (*sforim*) here, the big and the small, every
> holy book (*seyfer*) is a chain on my hand and I want to free myself of
> the chains! You understand, here there are dead people, wintry people,
> they were born in winter, they lived in winter and they died in winter.
> And a long dead winter continues from generation to generation.

He wants instead to live "the life that looks in from outside the window."
"What kind of hope are our young generations given?" he continues.

> I want to go into the world and search for a path for my child so that
> the younger generation can grow up to have a new life. . . . I don't
> want my child to be a gloomy child of the Diaspora. Listen, I am also
> a man, I have a heart, and my heart wants to have something to live
> for, something to hope for."[39]

Although the play was set in the 1870s, the themes it addressed were even
more relevant to Asch's own time, when the world "outside the window"
offered so much more to those who were willing to leave the *besmedresh*
behind in order to discover where the river flows. The play was enormously popular among amateur drama circles. The subject matter resonated
with many young would-be actors in the provinces. The play reflected the
struggles these actors were undergoing as they stepped onto a theatrical
stage and recited a text so different from that which their forefathers had
recited from pulpits for centuries before. It gave voice to the struggles the
youth of the 1900s faced as they sought to reconcile the faith of their parents with the cultural and leisure opportunities the world boldly promised.
The fact that the play was widely available and had extensive scene directions made it a relatively easy choice on technical grounds as well.[40]

Peretz Hirschbein's *Oyf yener zayt taykh* (On the Other Side of the River)
also used running water as a symbol for modernity. In this terrifying tragedy, Mirl and her blind grandfather, Menashe, are overcome by a flood from
the same river that took the lives of Mirl's parents. The two seek safety

as the freezing water rises to their knees, but in the middle of the night Menashe succumbs to the cold. Mirl is saved by an anonymous man from the other side of the river who urges her to let go of her dead grandfather and seize life instead. In the last act, Mirl has survived the deluge but has gone insane, dreaming of the golden palaces she believes lie on the other side of the river. As the play ends on a stormy night much like the night on which the play began, Mirl throws herself into the raging river in order to reach the other side. Like the young protagonists of so many other plays of the era, Mirl dreams of a new life outside the claustrophobic Jewish community of the older generation, a generation often portrayed as blind. Her dreams, though, are outrageously unrealistic—there are no golden palaces on the other side of the river and the river is much harder to ford than it seems from the banks. Ultimately she will be drowned by the fast-flowing river just as her father and grandfather were before her. The fast-paced movement of modernity is really nothing new but is simply the same river that had flowed for generations before.

Hermann Heijermans's *Ghetto,* another popular play performed by the Hirschbein troupe, dealt with similar themes and bears a marked resemblance to *On the Other Side of the River.* The story takes place inside the Amsterdam ghetto, where Raphael, an ambitious young man, cares for his greedy, business-minded, and blind father, Sachel. As in Hirschbein's play, the older generation is presented as blind, both metaphorically and literally. Sachel does not know, however, that Raphael is secretly married to the family's Christian servant Rosa. The secret marriage comes out into the open only when Sachel tries to arrange a marriage for Raphael. The marriage and Sachel's interests in it are portrayed as a strictly business deal, and the haggling over the price of the dowry is intertwined with haggling over the sale of a piece of wool, equating the two. Raphael will have none of it. He seeks a life beyond the ghetto, where he will be free to continue with his music career as a composer. As in numerous other plays of the era, the new life beyond the ghetto that the younger generation craves is represented by European culture, especially music. The community conspires against Raphael, convincing Rosa that her husband has left her. The play ends with a distraught Rosa throwing herself into the canal.

One of the most common theatrical devices of the period was the family dispute, which provided the frame for debates about a variety of philosophical and political positions raging in contemporary society. Each member of the family typically represented a different position. The family patriarch, either a father or grandfather, would cling to an imagined traditional life, full of piety, while sons and daughters would debate among

themselves the merits of a life of hedonistic pursuit of wealth and pleasure, the Zionist idea of establishing a Jewish homeland in Palestine, or the
socialist dream of the international liberation of the working class. Often
the play was set against the backdrop of a pogrom that forces these debates
to the foreground, as the community must quickly decide whether it will
act alone in self-defense, seek the support of non-Jewish sympathizers, or
prepare itself for martyrdom. The most famous example of this model is
probably Sholem Aleichem's *Tevye the Dairyman,* in which each of Tevye's
daughters represents a different dimension of the new social norms while
Tevye struggles to come to terms with it all. The play, however, was not
composed until 1915—although the first of the short stories that constitute
the Tevye cycle was written in 1894—and therefore was first performed
only late in the interrevolutionary era.

Evgenii Chirikov's 1904 Russian-language play *The Jews* was an early
prototype of this model. In Chirikov's version, the watchmaker Leyzer represents the Zionist viewpoint, while his children, Borukh and Leah, reject
any utopia that does not include the emancipation of the international
working class. Leah's cosmopolitanism, which is characteristic of portrayals of younger Jewish women and is symbolized by her love of the Christian
Beresin, is tempered by her fear of becoming too close to her lover and her
memories of an accusation of ritual murder made against the Jewish community by the Christians of her childhood village. It is this anti-Jewish hatred
expressed by the Christian masses to which the family ultimately succumbs,
as a pogrom breaks out leaving all, including the Christian Beresin, dead.
The play was an inspiration for Yiddish-language imitations and was commonly performed in Yiddish translation (and in Ukrainian).

Dovid Pinski's *Family Zvi,* written in the aftermath of the 1903 pogrom
in Kishinev, similarly traced the different responses of individuals in a
single family to the threat of violence. As word spreads of an upcoming
pogrom, Reb Meyshe, the family patriarch and town preacher, runs to the
synagogue to defend the sacred Torah scrolls. He expects to be greeted by
the entire Jewish community, which collective memory says had always
gathered together in the synagogue in historical times of stress, willing
to face martyrdom rather than allow the holy books to be profaned. But
instead he finds the synagogue empty. In this generation, he is the last Jew.
Meyshe realizes at once that the Judaism he knows, in which faith in the
world to come takes precedence over life in this world, has been destroyed
even before the pogrom perpetrators reach the sanctity of the synagogue.
Meyshe's son Yekef, on the other hand, thinks little of the danger posed to

the synagogue; his thoughts are on his store, whose prime location in the center of town is suddenly in the center of the path of destruction. Yekef, the middle generation, represents the materialist "this-worldniks" who measure the value of life in monetary terms. Yekef's three sons, Meyshe's grandchildren, also each respond to the threat of violence with their own ideologies. Lipman and Reuben run off to join underground fighters who will respond to the enemy with force. But they will not fight together; Lipman joins the Zionist faction, fighting to protect Jews against anti-Semites, whereas Reuben joins the socialist faction, battling for the liberation of the downtrodden and oppressed. Leon, the third son, chooses to go into hiding, still convinced that civilized Russian society will not allow atrocities to be committed against Jews. If only the Jews adopt local customs and assimilate, he argues, Russians will welcome them as brothers. Only a cousin, Eda, is completely safe from the pogrom. She has followed Leon's teaching to the extreme by taking the ultimate and only logical step in merging Jews into Russian society: she has converted. As for Minye, Yekef's wife, she thinks only of the safety of her children. The play ends with the death of Meyshe, "the last Jew," as Leon watches, horrified.

Sholem Aleichem's *Scattered and Dispersed,* written in 1905, was another commonly performed play that followed the model of a political dispute within a family. Mayer Cholent, the patriarch of the family, is identified as a "Jewish merchant, recently having become a rich man, a simple man of the street, who aspires to become an aristocrat." His daughter, Flora, is a *"fin-de-siècle* divorcée," while his sons are identified respectively as "a dandy" (Motvey), "a Zionist" (Khayim), a "scamp" (Volody), and a "spoiled child" (Sasha). Mayer seeks a path for himself and his family within the nouveau riche while his children each seek earthly salvation in their own way. Sasha seeks to amass material objects and commodities; Motvey finds solace in hedonistic pastimes such as playing cards and smoking; Khayim sees salvation in his attachment to the land of his forefathers; and Volody finds answers in the revolutionary books that eventually lead to his arrest. Malke, Mayer's wife, is convinced that all the strife the family faces can be traced to the impact of wealth and the family's move from the shtetl to the city—in other words, from the traditional past to the modern. "If only we hadn't thrown away our old livelihood," she complains.

> If only I hadn't lusted after easy street, counts, and estates, and not moved here, to this accursed city, living among scoundrels who only know how to spend, throwing away rubles on the devil knows what—

on mirrors and dish displays, on theaters, gymnasia, meetings, and pleasure grounds—tfu! . . . I was better off without money. If there were no money, the children could be children. Now the children aren't children at all, and the mother isn't any mother either. Everyone goes wherever he pleases—one this way, one that way. Scattered and dispersed over the seven seas.[41]

The family distress increases when the aristocratic parents of Khane's fiancé drop by for a visit to complain that Khane wants to delay the wedding so that she can "be free and continue studying."[42] Flora, the divorcée, has fallen in love with a dentist, a connoisseur of the arts who takes her to the theater and opera and writes her letters in Russian but looks down on her brothers, who attend demonstrations and meetings, and on Khane "with her short hair," a reference to her feminist ways. Mayer, for his part, can't seem to understand what Khayim sees in Zionism and why he would want to go to Palestine to dig the earth and plant trees. For Khayim, though, "we are all obligated because we are all children of the poor Jewish folk, who have already suffered for two thousand years, and who have only recently begun to awake from their deep frightful sleep, only recently opened up their eyes and seen where in the world they stand."[43] When Motvey disappears for three days, presumably out partying with his friends, and Khane rejoices at the end of her engagement and reveals her plans to study in Berne, Mayer can no longer take it. Confusing the name of the strange city in which his daughter seeks to study, Mayer bursts out: "One goes to Berl, one to the Land of Israel, one sits in prison, one is gone for no good reason for three days, and this one wants to go out into the world."[44] When Mayer worries about what will become of the family inheritance, Khane is ready with her reply: "As long as one lives, one should worry about life and not death."[45] The play tackles the dilemmas of Jewish youth head on.

By the second decade of the century, light operettas from New York stages had begun to supplement the Yiddish literary repertoire. In 1911, for instance, much to the annoyance of theatrical critics and promoters of literary theater, three different versions of Anshl Shor's *Be a Decent Person* ran in Warsaw. This play tells of a bookkeeper who elopes and runs off to America with the daughter of his wealthy boss. The boss loses his fortune and emigrates to America himself, arriving as an impoverished greenhorn. According to Mukdoyni, the play was popular primarily because of its light music, humorous couplets, and a scene featuring women in bathing suits.[46] Its loose structure and lack of extensive dialogue made possible a variety of interpretations around the basic plot, making it an easy production for amateurs and the type of professional performance one could see numerous times. Similarly, the loose plot of *Dos pintele yid* (The Jewish Spark), by American Yiddish theater star Boris Thomashevsky, connected melodramatic scenes from Jewish life and was popular for its humor, dance, and music. These plays were among the first to link the appeal of melodrama with the problems of contemporary life.

The new repertoire centered on familial relations, emulating the shift in theatrical production that had occurred in European theater in the early modern period. Whereas early modern plays, particularly those of the commedia dell'arte and even Shakespearean productions, relied overwhelmingly on plots highlighting conflict between the lower and upper classes or on situations of disguise and misunderstanding, European theater shifted away from these topics in the late seventeenth century toward plays about the family. This shift mirrored changing attributes of the audience. In the early modern period, audiences represented a large cross-section of society and could include both royalty and members of the lower classes who crowded town squares and fairgrounds to watch the theater. As theater moved out of the fairground and into enclosed theater halls that charged admission, audiences became more homogenous and middle class. Whereas poking fun of class antagonisms eased real tensions among the heterogeneous audiences in the early modern plays, interfamilial conflict was more likely within a middle-class audience of the modern period. Thus, early Yiddish plays—*Two Kuni Lemls, Serkele,* and *Silliness and Sanctimony,* for instance—all followed the early modern model, whereas the new repertoire used as its model more contemporary bourgeois European theater, emulating the embourgeoisement of the Jewish audiences they attracted and mirroring real life in this world.

Musical Performance

The theme of pious Jewish children discovering their God-given vocal talents only to leave the synagogue and their families behind in order to run off and join the opera permeates Jewish theater. It was an adaptation of this theme that became the first "talkie" film: Warner Brothers' 1927 *The Jazz Singer,* starring Al Jolson. An earlier version, Mark Arnshteyn's 1902 Polish-language play *Pieśniarze* (The Bard), told of a Vilna cantor who joined the Warsaw opera. Arnshteyn's play *The Vilna Gentleman,* in its Yiddish translation as *Der vilner balebesl,* was a standard in the Yiddish literary repertoire. Although musical interest could be a means of bridging ideological and political cleavages within the shtetl—it was with the express goal of providing an apolitical meeting ground for socialists and Zionists alike that the Hazomir Society in Kielce was established—music was just as often a source of strife.[47] Stories about musical societies from memorial books echo the themes in Arnshteyn's play. When Berish Perlmutter established a Hazomir Musical-Literary Society in Mlavy (Plock Province) in 1909, for instance, it caused extensive turmoil in the town. According to one source, after the windows of the house that housed the society were broken by Hasidim,

> the rabbi sent emissaries to Berish Perlmutter and then he came in his glory . . . and pleaded with them to stop destroying the town and to stop boys and girls from dancing and singing together. Delegates from the Alexandrover prayer house came and warned Berish that he must knock it off or else he would be thrown out of the prayer house. They closed the Alexandrover prayer house for weeks so that Berish could not come to pray there. But none of this helped. Berish left the prayer house and put on a stiff white collar—among the Hasidism a greater sin than shaving one's beard: "A beard grows back, but a stiff collar is forever."[48]

In this case, the clash of modernity and tradition is portrayed through fashion as a conflict between the stiff collar of contemporary style and the traditional Jewish beard.

Musical societies such as Hazomir were able to draw on new repertoires made available in sheet music. One newspaper ad, for instance, promoted "original Jewish music for piano, violin or voice" and combined a variety of forms of Jewish music under a single rubric. The holiest of music, like the "Kol Nidre," was advertised alongside songs from the Yiddish theater and Zionist songs, including the "Jewish national song" "Hatikvah," the future anthem of the state of Israel. Sheet music was advertised to the public as a way to recover authentic cultural and national traditions. "Kol Nidre," sung on the eve of the Day of Atonement, for instance, was advertised as a "historically authentic orthodox melody," and a series of Hebrew melodies was advertised as "a musical fantasia utilizing entirely old traditional melodies."[49]

Professional adaptations of Jewish folk songs were also published by the branches of the Jewish Folk Music Society in St. Petersburg and Moscow. The St. Petersburg branch was established in 1908 in order to "spread and develop Jewish music (liturgical and secular); collect and artistically adapt examples of Jewish folk music to be disseminated within the Society; and provide moral and financial support for young Jewish composers."[50] In order to reach these goals, the society sponsored ethnomusicological expeditions to transcribe folk songs, promoted the publication of popular articles on Jewish music, published Jewish sheet music, and sponsored concerts, recitals, operas, and lectures on Jewish music around the country. In 1913, the society began discussing the possibility of producing gramophone recordings of its music for more widespread distribution, which it did the following year. In 1909, musicians acting under its auspices began touring the provinces with repertoires of classically arranged pieces inspired by Yiddish folk songs, Hasidic melodies, and liturgical tunes. Others put the works of popular Jewish writers to music, presenting musical monologues of Sholem Aleichem or the poetry of Semen Frug. Holiday-themed music, such as selections of Purim songs, Hanukkah songs, or Lag Ba'omer songs, was particularly popular for performances during holiday seasons.[51] Often these performances were mixed with the occasional Schubert chorale, Mozart quartet, Mendelssohn canon, or other classical piece. A program performed on 24 January 1909 included selections from Haydn's *The Creation,* two monologues by Sholem Aleichem (*S'align* [A Lie] and *Yoysef* [Joseph]), Luigi Boccherini's "Minuet in A Major," and a Mendelssohn canon.[52] Over the next few years, the society successfully adapted enough Jewish material to fill entire evenings. A 1910 concert included a dozen compositions by classically trained conservatory graduates, such as Yulii Engel, Lazare Saminsky, Efraim Shkliar, and Aleksandr Zhitomirskii, all of whom became active in the Jewish Folk Music Society after becoming convinced that Jewish musical motifs could inspire a national music, much as Rimsky-Korsakov and others had been inspired by Russian idioms. The Jewish Folk Music Society's first publications of sheet music drew from the works of these composers; it included works like *Hatikwo* (The Hope) for four a capella voices by Shkliar, *Dem rebens nigun* (The Rabbi's Tune) for string quartet by Zhitomirskii, and *Chsidesch* (Hasidic) for violin and piano by Saminsky. This music was distributed by the society around the empire and formed the nucleus of the repertoire of Jewish Folk Music Society branches in Odessa, Kharkov, Kiev, Ekaterinoslav, Rostov, Simferopol, Moscow, and elsewhere.[53] This sheet music appealed to a new generation of Jewish musicians who had studied musical notation in the new music schools in major urban centers throughout Poland and the Russian Pale or one of the conservatories. Others obtained their musical literacy by serving as choristers to one of the new breed of cantors who had received formal professional musical training.

While professional dramatic acting was new to the shtetl, professional

FIGURE 15. An advertisement for "Jewish music for piano, violin or
voice" mixes different styles of music for performance at home or in
amateur settings. This advertisement includes sheet music for "Kol
Nidre," touted as "a historically authentic orthodox melody"; the
Zionist anthem "Hatikvah"; and "a musical fantasia utilizing entirely
old traditional melodies." Jewish sheet music helped middle-class Jews
retain cultural ties with their traditions.

klezmorim (musicians) were not. Although most Jewish musicians still came
from families of *klezmorim*—many of whom also worked part-time as barbers
or as other skilled service workers—a growing number of young people
from middle-class families were seeking musical training and sometimes
excelling to the point of pursuing professional careers in music. By the late
nineteenth century, Jews were visible minorities in the newly established
conservatories and music schools throughout the empire. Jews constituted
nearly half the students of the St. Petersburg conservatory and about a
quarter of the students enrolled in the more than twenty schools established

FIGURE 16. A group of Jewish musicians in Ostrowiec at the turn of the century. During the first decade of the century, as increasing numbers of Jewish musicians received conservatory educations, the status of Jewish musicians within the community improved. As evidenced by their European dress, these musicians regarded themselves as professionals. *Photo courtesy of YIVO Institute for Jewish Research.*

by the Russian Musical Society. Nearly two-thirds of the 200 students who attended the Odessa Music School were Jewish. The high level of Jewish enrollment in music schools and conservatories can be attributed both to the traditionally high level of Jewish participation in musical life in Eastern Europe and to the tangible legal, economic, and social benefits for Jews who were enrolled in these institutions. As private institutions, the conservatories were not subject to the numerus clausus that hindered Jewish access to public institutions of higher learning in the Russian Empire. Graduates of the conservatories were granted the status of "free artists," releasing them from many of the legal restrictions imposed upon Jews, including the residency restrictions of the Pale of Jewish Settlement. Thus, music school provided a path to greater civil rights.[54]

The prominence of Jews in formal musical educational institutions began to impact Jewish liturgical music in the early twentieth century, as some cantors adopted Western harmonization and counterpoint to the modal embellishments and improvisation styles of traditional Eastern European cantorial music. Others sought to introduce institutionalized professional schools and organizations to replace the apprentice model of cantorial education. Abraham Baer Birnbaum (1864–1922) of Częstochowa, for instance, published textbooks on cantorial music and founded a cantorial school in 1907. Choristers were well situated to make the move from the pulpit to the stage. Some, who received training from the newer breed of cantors who promoted formal musical training, found the transition easy. Others found that once they crossed this chasm, they were unable to return. In the late 1890s, when the head of the yeshiva of Vasilishki (Vilna Province) discovered that young chorister Matisyahu Kovalsky had secretly taken part in a performance of Goldfadn's *Shulamis,* he kicked him out of the yeshiva, propelling him into a lifelong career in the Yiddish and Hebrew theater.[55]

A typical example of the progression from chorister to secular musician can be found in Kovno, a town that had been recognized as a center of music in the nineteenth century. Around the time of the 1905 revolution, the eldest son of the well-known cantor from the Tailor's Synagogue opened his home to a group of young men and women to sing songs and talk about music. Initially they stayed away from anything they considered Jewish music, because "this was a matter for the lower classes, not for intellectuals," which they considered themselves to be. Only after a group of singers from the Hazomir Society in St. Petersburg gave a concert in Kovno did the group become interested in Jewish music. They began singing songs from the Goldfadn repertoire and soon decided to mount a full-fledged performance of Goldfadn's *Shulamis.* They assembled an orchestra, a choir, stage decorations, and actors, some of whom they recruited from neighboring towns. The production was so successful that the group formally incorporated itself as the Kovno Jewish Dramatic-Musical Society and successfully applied for and received official permits. The group continued to perform other works by Goldfadn, including *Bar Kokhba* and *Doctor Almasada.* Within a few years it had several hundred members, some of whom branched off to form an orchestra associated with the society. The group was introduced to the newer repertoire of Yiddish theater by literary critic Baal-Makhshoves (Isidor Eliashev, 1873–1924), a native of Kovno, who took an interest in the group when he returned to his hometown. Under his influence, the theater started performing some of the works of Pinski (*Family Tzi* and *Mother*) and Gordin's *Der meturef* (The Insane). Eventually the society had over 500 members and began renting out a wedding hall for theatrical performances, concerts, holiday celebrations, and visiting lecturers.[56]

Other sources of inspiration for such societies were fire brigade or military orchestras, which often included Jews as members. Often musicians performed in both a family klezmer orchestra (*kapelye* or *khevrise*) and a fire brigade orchestra. Shloymele, who led the Kozienice fire brigade, for instance, also participated in a family *kapelye*. Many Jewish musicians who became community leaders in cultural affairs got their start in fire brigade orchestras or military bands. In both Kielce and Mława, the conductors of the Hazomir Society choir were formerly conductors of the military band. Fire brigades, which began to form in the last decades of the nineteenth century, were responsible not only for fire prevention but also for civil policing. They were one of the most institutionalized forms of Jewish-Christian cooperation, as Jewish firefighters often served alongside Russian, Ukrainian, and Polish colleagues. Sometimes the role Jews played in firefighting organizations aroused resentment. In Kobrin, for instance, riots took place after a tax was imposed on farmers entering the city in order to fund the firefighters. According to one account, when the farmers heard the firefighters speaking Yiddish, they became enraged and started chanting anti-Jewish slogans.[57] For the most part, though, fire brigades were peaceful points of intersection and cooperation between the numerous communities that shared the city space.

Many who joined fire brigades did so at least in part for the orchestra. Local authorities tended to be supportive of fire brigades and recognized them as essential community organizations. Therefore they were given relatively wide degrees of latitude to engage in corollary activities. The Jewish community also tended to give greater prestige to musicians performing in fire brigade orchestras than it did to klezmer musicians, who were still commonly regarded as lower-class ruffians. Fire brigade orchestras attracted talented Jewish and non-Jewish musicians searching for a forum for their musical skills. The fire brigade orchestra of Korelichi "was famous throughout the region, in all neighboring villages and towns. Korelichi used to hire the orchestra to play at weddings."[58] The Mezhirichi (Volhynia Province) fire brigade, which was composed almost entirely of Jews, had a

> fully equipped brass band. . . . Every Sunday the firefighters would do maneuvers and the orchestra would play various marches. Many times the local klezmorim would also play along. This was only when special concerts were given, such as the Hanukkah concert in the synagogue, etc. . . . Special evenings also used to be arranged in a large orchard or sometimes in the courtyard park, and the money was used to purchase equipment the firefighters needed.[59]

In Kobrin, the fire brigade orchestra was led by a Pole and included many Jews among its members. Its repertoire included a mix of Christian religious hymns, patriotic military marches, overtures, and waltzes. The band performed in clubs, carnivals, and—much to the chagrin of the Jewish players' parents—outside the church on Christian holidays. They also played to accompany a touring theater, for weddings, to welcome troops returning home from their military service, and to welcome visiting dignitaries at the train station. One Jewish memoirist in the Kobrin fire brigade orchestra told of how he was obliged to perform at the train station and in a parade to welcome a visiting bishop. While the band played and the bishop emerged from the train, he "passed by us, asked us who we were, blessed us, and sprinkled holy water over us. Since I was one of the first in line, I was graced with a full drop."[60] According to the memoirist, it was this experience that convinced his family to send him to America.

Sometimes fire brigade orchestras would perform drills to the delight of the town, which viewed the drills as both spectacle and theatrics. One memoirist, apparently writing of the interwar period, included the fire brigade in her discussion of theater and music in the town. She wrote, "When talking about the artistic forces of the town, we must remember the fire brigade, which was a faithful accompaniment to the artistic forces of the town. None among us could forget the Sunday fire drills or the parades accompanied by the musicians. The entire town took to its feet when the fire brigade appeared in the parade."[61] The mixed Jewish and non-Jewish fire brigade of Nesvizh (Minsk Province) drilled every Sunday afternoon, to the delight of the town:

> The firefighter company had an orchestra which used to play during parades. . . . Orchestra rehearsals and fire-fighting drills took place in summer time almost every Sunday. The ringing of the fire alarm on Sunday afternoon signaled that a rehearsal was going to take place. The fire-fighters in the helmets are placed in rows. In front stand the commander and the orchestra. They wait for the arrival of the commander-in-chief. Meanwhile they are doing drills. Then the commander arrives. His deputy salutes; the orchestra plays; the chief takes over the brigade. Then they bring the hoses, the kegs, and a wagon with a hook and ladder out from the depot. The brigade marches through the streets to the market, accompanied by children and other curious folk. . . . In the market opposite the town hall they perform exercises and test out the hoses. With the hydro-pump, they get the water from the well in order to fill up the tap. With the hoses they spurt water into the air until it reaches the roof of the town hall. . . . After the rehearsal finishes,

FIGURE 17. A fire brigade orchestra in Lubcza poses for a photograph. Jewish musicians often joined the fire brigade orchestra, which provided an important point of intersection between Jews and non-Jews. Fire brigade orchestras also played vital roles in the musical life of smaller communities.

the brigade returns to the depot, marching through the streets to the music of the orchestra.[62]

Many members of the fire brigade hoped to use the musical training, experience, and pay they received as a stepping-stone to a career in the performing arts. The prominence fire brigade orchestras have in numerous memorial books is striking, as is the degree to which they were regarded as cultural actors rather than public safety officials. Rarely can a photograph be found of a fire brigade posing in front of its hoses, kegs, or wagons. Instead, photographs of the fire brigade typically show a group of young men holding French horns, coronets, and tubas, as though these were naturally the instruments and tools of firefighting rather than of music-making.

Aaron Shuster recalls that the fire brigade of Lipkany so enjoyed its drills that one fine Purim afternoon soon after the group was founded, the entire fire brigade went for a hike into the fields adjoining the shtetl, where they spent an afternoon practicing their drills. They had strayed so far from the shtetl that they failed to see the smoke or hear the screams as Moyshe Bodner's house burned to the ground. Alter Zeldes, a member of the Lipkany sentry, gave up his guard duties to become a *badkhn,* a wedding entertainer.[63] Sometimes the reverse was true as well, at least if we are to believe Naftoli Gross's famous poem, "Yosl Klezmer (Saves the Town from a Fire)," in which Yosl's music guides the flames licking at the rooftops away from the houses.[64] Fire and music were clearly intertwined in popular imagination.

Gala Evenings of Entertainment

Performing arts in the shtetl, then, could take on a variety of forms, ranging from musical performances and concerts to fire brigade drills. Often different genres of entertainment were combined in a single evening. In 1912, the local Jewish intelligentsia in the shtetl of Dunaevtsy (Podolia Province) sponsored a ball in the fire hall with a program that included a show, dancing, party games, and a performer who recited racy couplets. The evening ended on a sour note, though, when the Jewish couplet performer apparently went overboard in his self-mockery, offending many in the audience.[65] In Baranovichi, the Jewish Literary Society included a group of amateur performers who not only performed plays but also gave concerts, held evening celebrations of Jewish holidays, sponsored jubilee celebrations, and organized spoken-word events and literary evenings.[66]

Gala evenings typically combined a variety of musical and dramatic performances with spoken-word events and evening balls. Theater performances routinely ended with a dance that often "lasted well after midnight," as one Luboml resident recalled. "The custom of dancing after the performance was common," recalled a former resident of Rokishki.[67] Sholem Aleichem's June 1908 reading in Bialystok was accompanied by an amateur theatrical performance of two of his one-act plays, *Mazl tov* and *Der get* (The Divorce Paper).[68] Several months later, the Jewish Literary Society sponsored an evening of Russian-language readings by a number of well-known Jewish writers. The readings were followed by performances of selections from the works of Anton Rubinstein and Adrian-Francois Servais's "Souvenir de Spa."[69] When Bialik spoke in Lodz on Hebrew and its role in Jewish life, the event was accompanied by a choir singing Hebrew songs.[70] When Max Nordau's *Doctor Kohn* was performed in Odessa in 1909, it was accompanied by an exhibit of Jewish art "in the national style," including works from the Betsalel school. A military orchestra played the Zionist anthem "Hatikvah" during the exhibition, and the play was followed by an evening of dancing.[71] Masquerade balls, one-act plays, buffets, raffles, musical performances, and, toward the beginning of the war, short motion-picture shows filled the social calendars of cultured Jews.

The tendency of amateur groups to favor one-act plays or even short monologues, both of which were easy to perform because they involved little preparation and memorization, made it difficult to fill a two-hour evening program of entertainment. Even the most ambitious theater circles would have had difficulty finding four-act Yiddish plays, as the repertoire of modern literary Yiddish theater was still limited and was characterized by shorter works. Therefore, theater groups and dramatic societies used a variety of performance genres. The genre of "living pictures" (*lebedike bilder*), in which short scenes, usually of a historical or documentary nature, were enacted, often on an improvisational basis, was popular among amateur performers and audiences alike, particularly when they supplemented the spoken-word part of a literary evening. In February 1910, the Hazomir Society of Warsaw presented an evening of entertainment featuring a choir, orchestra, and dramatic performance. An advertisement for the event promised that in addition "the stage will be illustrated with various living national and historical pictures."[72] When Peretz decided to raise money for his literary circle, he organized a masquerade ball that featured "living pictures" as well as dancing, a buffet, and a raffle.[73]

The Zionist movement, in particular, championed this art style. It was especially appropriate for audiences who could not understand the spoken word. Few potential audience members would have been able to understand a play in Hebrew, so Zionists resorted to portraying staged scenes from an idyllic imagined life in Zion—whether in the biblical land of Israel or contemporary Palestine. This was a popular way to celebrate the festival of Hanukkah, which commemorates the Maccabean conquest of the land of Israel. Since normal activity is permitted during the holiday, its celebration need not interfere with *halakhic* (Jewish legal) restrictions on activities on holy days. Thus the Zionist movement elevated the festival of Hanukkah to one of the most important Jewish holidays of the year, not for its religious significance but rather for its national potential. Enactments of the Maccabean military victory could be easily portrayed in a living picture with harrowing battle scenes between easily identifiable Seleucid villains and heroic Hasmonean victors. The Bund also embraced Hanukkah as an ideal opportunity to lionize the lower classes who, in its interpretation, led a rebellion against the imperialist Seleucids. Regardless of the political message being imparted, Hanukkah performances were usually followed by a dance, a buffet, and games of chance.[74]

Living pictures also accompanied spoken-word events and celebrity visits. When in 1908 the Society for the Aid of Jewish Farmers and Artisans in Syria and Palestine sponsored a concert-ball in St. Petersburg, it featured speeches by Bialik and others as well as a series of "living pictures." Advertisements also promised that the "hall will be decorated in an Oriental style."[75] A few days later in Vilna, when Bialik appeared again, this time with Sholem Asch, the evening also featured "living pictures" entitled "By the Rivers of Babylon" and "Wanderers," both of which depicted Jewish suffering in exile, and another, "The Revival," which showed Jews returning to Palestine. The hall was also decorated with Oriental (Mediterranean/Middle Eastern) and Palestinian motifs.[76] The display of "Oriental" images was an important component of Zionist iconography.

Local branches of Lovers of the Hebrew Language also sponsored Hebrew-language plays as a way to promote the use of Hebrew. Yaakov Levin recalls a Zionist play he saw in Kobrin in 1909:

> It seems like a fairy tale, the first play, *Hebrew Farmers in the Holy Land* (*'Ikarim 'ivriim be-'erets ha-kadosh*), which was performed in the Zionist hall in our town. Less than three dozen participated, all of whom were invited by their friends and acquaintances, the few Zionists in town, to see a Zionist play about the Land of Israel. I recall the tension and fear that prevailed . . . before and during the play. The doors were closed, the window shutters were locked, even the cracks between the shutters were covered with chalk . . . all for fear of the Russian police. . . . The goal of the play was to show Hebrew farmers in their land working their soil, plowing, planting and harvesting.[77]

Hebrew-language plays like *Hebrew Farmers in the Holy Land* as well as living pictures served functions similar to that of propaganda newsreels, bringing an imagined reality from distant places to the small towns of Eastern Europe.

Later, as theatrical performances became more common, Hebrew-language societies started performing Hebrew translations of plays and sometimes even plays originally written in Hebrew. The repertoire of available Hebrew-language plays, however, was even more limited that that of Yiddish plays. Most Hebrew plays were composed as part of the enlightenment project to purify the Hebrew language and were either allegorical or biblical in content, hardly suited to the tastes of audiences desperate to see the modern world portrayed on stage. Middle-class audiences went to the theater to escape from the biblical world of the synagogue.[78]

Audiences, critics, and the press greeted these productions for the most part as novelty items or curiosities. In the summer of 1912 in Gomel, for instance, a visiting troupe of actors performed a Hebrew translation of Karl Gutzkow's *Uriel Acosta*. According to a correspondent for *Razsvet,* the show attracted a large audience that was composed not only of locals but also of many individuals from neighboring villages. Although the audience could not have understood every word, they listened with rapt attention to the sound of the language. The performance was followed by a brief talk given by a member of the local Lovers of the Hebrew Language society, who explained the importance of Hebrew-language theater in the spiritual development of the Jewish nation.[79] Apparently audiences could sit through a theatrical performance in a language they did not understand just as they regularly sat without comprehension through sacred rituals in Hebrew. In this manner, the Hebrew stage served as a surrogate synagogue, where the language was recited as though it were sacred rather than quotidian. The correspondent who wrote about the theatrical performance in Gomel, for instance, found it necessary to note that although there were several errors in "both the acting and the language, the Hebrew language flowed freely and beautifully from the lips of the majority of participants."[80] Similarly, when Lovers of the Hebrew Language sponsored a performance of *Samson and Delilah* in Hebrew translation at the St. Petersburg Conservatory the same year, *Razsvet* promoted the performance by noting how "interesting [it] will be to see an opera on a biblical topic performed in the same language in which the protagonists actually spoke."[81] In both cases, *Razsvet,* along with the actors and much of the audience, viewed the fact that the play was being performed in Hebrew as far more important than the content of what was actually being performed.

The Stage and the Public

Theater presupposes a public, constructing one out of an apparently diverse group of individuals in an auditorium. Jewish and non-Jewish theater activists were acutely aware of the possibilities of theater as an instrument of community unification. In an article entitled "The Stage and the Public," Mikhl Weichert described how the theater constructs its public:

> Some time ago the following story occurred in Warsaw: on a Friday evening at a dramatic presentation someone in the public coughed. Soon one could hear another cough, and a little bit later a significant portion

of the audience was coughing. It turned into a racket, a commotion, and the actor, a certain older artist, lost his patience. He stopped the production and turned to the public with the words "I can't perform any more. I will not perform any more." . . . What does this cough mean? It is one of those forms through which the masses who by chance meet each other in the theater—one calls this a public—react *collectively* to that which is being done on the stage. The clapping of the hands, the stamping of the feet, the shouting and the whistling express in a different form the satisfaction or lack of satisfaction with the production.[82]

Theater, argued Weichert in another article, must always be an overtly public act.

[Theater] stands and falls with the social community, with the masses, with the public. Other forms of artistic production are not dependent upon the masses, upon the public. One can write books even if nobody reads them or paint pictures even if nobody buys them. One can even perform theater without possessing plays, as the history of theater up to the eighteenth century teaches us. One can even perform theater without actors, as it was performed in old times and as can still be found today in certain theaters. But nobody has ever performed theater without a public. *The public, broadly interpreted, has always been and will always remain the decisive factor, the father of its theater.*[83]

As Weichert noted, theater audiences can be diverse, including men and women, young and old, and a variety of ethnic and religious groupings. Once they enter the theater hall, though, this diverse group of individuals is expected to act as a cohesive collective, laughing and applauding in unison. The theater audience is qualitatively different than the distant and inaccessible person to whom a literary work is directed. It is a visible collective composed of individuals who are in close proximity not only to the performer but also to the other individuals who together constitute the public. The audience is compelled to react as a collective and to respond to each other's reactions, just as they respond to the action emanating from the stage. Even the actors on the stage respond not just to the written script they are reciting but also to the response of the live audience. In this sense, the actions and reactions of every individual in the hall, whether they are on stage or off, are registered publicly and are intended to produce a public effect. The theater, by which is meant not only the text of the play but the experience of theater-going as a whole, becomes a mirror of society, an encapsulation of public culture as experienced in the world outside the auditorium.

The Jewish Historical and Ethnographic Society: Collecting the Jewish Past

Recent scholarship has acknowledged the dominant role that remembrance of the past and evocation of history plays in public culture and the formation of national identity. Nineteenth- and early-twentieth-century historians have often been credited with creating a "usable past" that then becomes the basis for nation-building. This trend has been particularly noticeable in Jewish history, a discipline that has always been acutely aware of the authority of memory and its connection to communal awareness.[1] In the words of Ismar Schorsch, historical thinking has become "the dominant universe of discourse in Jewish life and historians its major intellectual figures."[2] Historical thinking, he argues, defines Jewish modernity itself.

Because of the role of history in Jewish public culture, the Jewish Historical and Ethnographic Society (JHES) came to represent the pinnacle of the Jewish voluntary association movement in Russia. The learned society was designed more explicitly than most to establish a public sphere on the model of Western and Central European voluntary associations. The membership roster of the society and the list of contributors to its journal read like a who's who of Jewish public life in late tsarist Russia. Its membership included not only historians—in fact, very few were professionally trained practitioners of history—but also a diverse group of political activists, scholars, writers, and lawyers. Among those who found a place within the society are historians as diverse as Simon Dubnow, Iulii Gessen (1871–1939), Majer Balaban (1877–1943), and Ignacy Schipper (1884–1943), the latter two of whom contributed from Galicia; Kadet leader Maksim Vinaver; writer and folklorist S. An-sky; racial anthropologist Samuel Weissenberg (1867–1928); liberal jurist Genrikh Sliozberg (1863–1937); and ethnographer Lev Shternberg (1861–1927). The story of how this disparate group of individuals from around the Russian Empire came together in St. Petersburg to advance the scholarly study of Jewish history provides a case study of social networks and voluntary association formation in action. It also elucidates the role of elites in stimulating broad public initiatives and identity formation and demonstrates the role history played as a cultural marker and rallying point for people of diverse political and ideological backgrounds.[3]

The JHES was part of a broad movement in Russian middle-class and intellectual circles to use private initiatives to disseminate higher education to adults, both to advance science and to cultivate morality and a sense of civic obligation. The predominantly liberal educators who served as its organizers believed that liberalization, civic emancipation, and a civil society were impossible without the spread of education. With government permission they set out to disseminate education to those excluded from universities on academic grounds and on the basis of their socioeconomic and religious status. They believed that only education could turn subjects into citizens.[4]

The preponderance of Jewish academic societies in Russia and through-out Europe can be at least partially attributed to the difficulties Jews faced in gaining access to universities. Unable to establish themselves in for-malized academic environments, many Jews throughout Europe turned to informal journals and societies as surrogates for the ivory tower. Many institutions whose charters did not discriminate on the basis of religion were pressured throughout the nineteenth century into preventing Jews from receiving academic appointments. Even after they opened their doors to Jewish instructors in the second half of the century, these individuals were limited in how far they could advance professionally in certain fields, including history.[5] Among the Jewish students who could be found in disproportionate numbers in German universities were many from Eastern Europe, where access to universities under Russian control was limited even further.[6]

History was one of the primary fields of academic and educational enrichment for Eastern European Jews, although the founding of mod-ern historical societies among Jews began in Western and Central Europe. The prototype of all Jewish historical societies was the Society for Jewish Culture and Learning, which was founded in 1819 by a group of German Jewish intellectuals that included Eduard Gans, Heinrich Heine, Isaac Jost, and Leopold Zunz. The society's tremendous success in modern-izing Jewish scholarship by introducing textual criticism, epigraphy, and a synthetic approach to historical sources cannot be overlooked. Its achievements culminated in the publication of the *Monatschrift fur die Geschichte und Wissenschaft des Judentums* (Monthly Journal of the History and Science of Judaism, 1851–1939) and the establishment of the Jewish

Theological Seminary of Breslau in 1854, the first to integrate secular subjects in a seminary environment and to teach reform Judaism along the
lines of that preached by Zacharias Frankel. Its success was soon followed
by imitators and innovators. In 1880 in Paris, the Society of Jewish Studies
was founded, whose mouthpiece, the *Revue des études juives* (Review of
Jewish Studies) sought to combat the Germanocentrism of the German
Wissenschaft movement. In 1892, the American Jewish Historical Society
was established to research early Jewish settlement in America, the role
of Jews in the discovery of the continent, and other topics relating to the
community. In England, the *Jewish Quarterly Review* was founded in 1888,
followed by the Jewish Historical Society of England in 1893. The fin-de-
siècle also saw a resurgence and popularization of historical scholarship in
Germany, where in 1891 Gustav Karpeles founded the Society for Jewish
History and Literature in Berlin, which rapidly emerged as a model for
other local organizations. New Jewish historical societies continued to form
into the twentieth century. In 1919, Eugen Täubler founded the Academy
of the Science of Judaism, and in 1924 and 1925, two of the longest-lasting
institutions for the study of Jewish history were established: the Institute
of Jewish Studies in Jerusalem and the YIVO Jewish Scientific Society.[7]

Jewish History and the Law

Through much of the nineteenth century, most of the Jews of Russia
continued to learn a version of history that was shaped by a theological
worldview. *Maskilic* historians, though, endeavored to mold the minds
of the young generation, inspiring them with positive historical examples of Jewish integration into society and encouraging them to emulate
these heroes. The Russian Haskalah may not have transformed the youth
of Russia into freethinkers, but it did introduce modern methods of historical research to the leading Jewish intellectuals of the empire.[8]

A modern Russian-Jewish historiography that used archival and pri-
mary sources emerged chiefly as a means of ascertaining the legal status of
Jews in Russia. A similar process occurred in Poland, where the Four-Year
Sejm necessitated the first systematic surveys of the legal status of Polish
Jews. In his *Rozprawa o Żydach i Karaitach* (Treatise on Jews and Karaites,
1807), for instance, Tadeusz Czacki used his legal training to argue, like
Christian Wilhelm von Dohm had before him, that emancipation should
be contingent upon the Jews giving up their separate institutional struc-
tures. This proposal echoed similar offers made to the Jewish communities

of Western and Central European nations during their respective emancipation processes. The promises of emancipation offered by the French
Revolution and more distantly by Joseph II's Edicts of Tolerance, to name
two of the most celebrated examples, were both predicated on the assumption that the Jewish community would relinquish its corporate privileges,
parochial institutions, and distinct culture and language in exchange for
the promise of equal rights of citizenship in the former case and a lessening
of legal restrictions in the latter.

The juridical training of early East European historians of the Jews
led them to think in terms of individual legal rights rather than collective
cultural rights. Ludwik Gumplowicz, a Polish convert from Judaism, for
instance, urged assimilation in his 1867 legal history of the Jews in Poland.
Even Polish proponents of the enlightenment who looked at the economic
history of the Jews, such as W. A. Maciejowski (*Żydzi w Polsce, na Rusi i
Litwie* [Jews in Poland, Russia and Lithuania]), used legal history to argue
that Jewish dominance of trade was the result of historical conditions, not
racial predisposition. Following the Enlightenment axiom that humans are
born as a tabula rasa and are conditioned and socialized by their environments, these thinkers argued that by changing the environment, particularly the legal setting, they could reform Jewish behavior. Thus, the study
of Jewish legal history was predicated on the premise that the study of the
past could lead to future reform.

The first Russian works on Jewish legal history were written by F. I.
Leontovich, a non-Jewish lecturer in Russian law at Odessa's Imperial New
Russia University. In his "Historical Survey of Enactments on the Rights
of Lithuanian-Russian Jews," which was serialized in *Sion* in 1861–1862,
he argued that prior to Nicholas I, the Russian government had sought to
integrate the Jews into existing legal categories. Ultimately, he believed in
the European Enlightenment attitude that Jews should be given civil rights
in return for abandoning their exclusivity and separateness.[9] His work was
taken up by two of his students, Sergei Bershadskii and Ilia Orshanskii.

Bershadskii hailed from a Russian Orthodox clerical family but had
received a secular education in Kerch, where he attended primary and secondary school. In 1868, he enrolled in the Department of Law at the Imperial
New Russian University in Odessa, where he studied with Leontovich. He
later continued his studies in St. Petersburg with liberal constitutional
legal scholar A. D. Gradovskii. After Bershadskii served as an instructor
at the Military-Juridical Academy, his professional career took him to the
Department of Law at St. Petersburg University, where he was appointed

privat-dozent and later to the faculty of the famed Alexander Lycee. He continued to be interested in the field of Jewish legal history and spent much of the late 1870s and early 1880s collecting documents relating to the Jews of Lithuania in the archives of the State Senate and in the Kiev and Vilna Central Archives, which he helped publish.[10] These documents included decrees granting privileges, court decisions, and tax rolls and revisions, and were meticulously edited, copied, and indexed. He used these documents as the basis for several articles and his seminal monograph *Litovskie evrei* (Lithuanian Jews).

Orshanskii was one of the first scholars of Russian Jewish history who was himself Jewish. He had received a traditional Jewish upbringing but had also been exposed to enlightenment ideologies. Before entering the Imperial New Russian University, he studied law at Kharkov University. Although he hoped for a university lectureship within the Russian Empire, he was unable to attain such a position without first converting. Orshanskii instead left for Germany, where he conducted research on Russian law at Heidelberg University. His three-volume history of Russian inheritance and family law, much of which was researched while abroad, was published posthumously in 1875. In enlightenment tradition and following upon the arguments presented by other academics who had turned their attention to the plight of the Jews, Orshanskii sought to explain the miserable conditions of Jewish life as the result of the legal restrictions imposed upon the Jews. He believed that if these restrictions were removed, Jews would join Russian cultural and social life. For Orshanskii, the russification of Jews was contingent upon the granting of legal equality.[11] In the aftermath of the Odessa pogrom of 1871, Orshanskii led a group of lawyers in conducting a systematic survey of the damage and preparing a report they hoped to use as evidence to seek official compensation for the victims. Orshanskii also called for the study of Yiddish song as a means of studying Jewish life.[12] In this sense, Orshanskii may have been the first historian to appreciate the cultural development of Jewish life in Eastern Europe. At a time when his colleagues were preoccupied with arguing for the expansion of legal rights for Jewish residents, Orshanskii, virtually alone, investigated the daily life and leisure of the community he was defending with such ardor.

In their own ways, both Orshanskii and Bershadskii had a profound impact on the subsequent development of Jewish historiography in Russia. Many of the participants in Orshanskii's circle were young Jewish lawyers whose careers were on the rise but who were encountering the glass ceiling of imperial Russia. Aleksandr Passover (1840–1910), for instance, became one of the leading legal orators in Russia after failing to achieve an academic post. Passover was a fourth-generation member of the intelligentsia. His maternal great-grandfather, Jacob Abramson, was part of the first generation of Galician *maskilim* and received a medical degree in Lemberg before becoming the doctor for Count Potocki in Nemirov. His maternal grandfather, Bernard Abramson, had studied medicine in Berlin, Cracow, and St. Petersburg before settling in Uman and later in Odessa, where he became active in enlightened educational endeavors. Bernard's eldest daughter, Alexander's mother, married Galician doctor Jacob Passover, who served as a military physician in Uman, where Aleksandr was born. He graduated from the juridical department of Moscow University before studying abroad in England, France, and Germany in the hope of acquiring a professorship. Upon his return to Moscow, though, he found that this path had been closed to Jews. He was able to receive an appointment from the justice ministry as a deputy prosecutor in Moscow and then in Vladimir before the liberal atmosphere in the justice ministry was abandoned. He resigned his government post and settled for a private legal practice in Odessa, arriving in time to witness the pogrom of 1871 and to join the Odessa branch of the OPE.

The ultimate goal of this group of lawyers was to use the courts to air the testimonies of victims and eyewitnesses of the pogrom. Although these efforts failed to achieve justice in the courts, they had a cathartic effect among both the victims who were able to tell their stories and the many Russian Jewish intellectuals who were emboldened by this move toward action.[13] It was this group that Genrikh Sliozberg saw as the nucleus of what would become the JHES. By systematically compiling data on past events in an effort to understand and interpret them, the lawyers were introducing modern historical methods into their work. "Almost all of the participants in the circle," he wrote, "later formed a group with the goals of historical-ethnographic investigation under the authority of the Society for the Spread of Enlightenment among the Jews of Russia. . . . I could not but be glad that finally in Petersburg representatives of the Jewish intelligentsia were organizing in the interest of Jewish affairs."[14]

There were other attempts to modernize the study of Jewish history in Russia, many of which involved the OPE as well. In 1880, Avraham Harkavy, the librarian of the Oriental and Semitic Department of the Imperial Russian Library and a scholar of oriental studies, petitioned the OPE to provide financial support for historical studies, perhaps by providing grants to fund the publication of documents and materials relating to the history of the Jews in Russia.[15] On several occasions branches of the

OPE sponsored lectures relating to Jewish history and attempted to garner interest in the topic. In 1887, for instance, Mikhail Morgulis suggested that the Odessa OPE work on preparing a popular Russian-language history of the Jews. Plans included involving such luminaries as Harkavy and the renowned Orientalist and convert from Judaism, Daniil Chwolson. The effort, however, came to naught. The OPE was at the time more interested in promoting the russification of the Jews than in bolstering what it regarded as an archaic Jewish national identity.

It was not until Simon Dubnow's arrival in Odessa that the academic study of Jewish history generated genuine popular interest among the intelligentsia. Simon Dubnow was born in 1860 in the Belorussian shtetl of Mstislavl. His grandfather was a distinguished rabbi; his father was a lumber merchant who traveled frequently. As a child, Dubnow excelled in traditional Jewish learning, but in 1874 he enrolled in a state school, initiating a long period of alienation from Judaism and assimilation into the Russian intellectual milieu. When the school was closed, Dubnow bounced from school to school, never receiving the degree he needed for university admission but becoming increasingly russified in the process. He endeavored to become an autodidact and ingested all the canonical texts of the contemporary Russian intelligentsia he aspired to emulate. In 1881 he began publishing articles in Russian-language journals on Jewish affairs, often taking positions against traditional Jewish rabbinical thought.

Toward the end of the 1880s, however, Dubnow began a return to Judaism, but in its nationalist manifestations rather than as a religious faith. He was motivated by the apparent failures of the attempts of Jews to assimilate in Russia and abroad and by the influence of the members of a new Russian intelligentsia who challenged the materialism and cosmopolitanism of the 1870s generation with more nuanced approaches to the spiritual realm and a newfound appreciation of national sentiments. The most influential of his early writings was "On the Study of the History of Russian Jews and on the Founding of a Russian-Jewish Historical Society," in which he proposed that a Jewish historical society be created.[16] The article asserted that Russian Jews needed an understanding of history as a basis for a new Jewish national idea. "Essentially, *a conscious relationship to the past* can serve as an accurate measure of spiritual maturity," he wrote.[17] Lacking the material bases of nationhood—a territory and a state—Dubnow believed that Jews could reconstitute their nation only through the study of their history and that the way to do this was to found a historical society. Whereas Western European Jewry had already established societies with this goal, Russian Jewry had not yet done so. Dubnow wrote his article for the journal *Voskhod* in the spring of 1891, just as the Ministry of Internal Affairs was temporarily closing the journal, and his article did not appear until the following October when the journal was revived. The article was published not just in *Voskhod* but was spread widely in pamphlet form, appearing in Hebrew as well.[18] On 13 March 1891 Dubnow wrote in his diary of the excitement he felt after conceiving of this mission: "As I write this, I fathom an even more important idea to which I am ready to dedicate my life. The work is complicated, demanding enormous strength of mind. But all physical torments that it will cause are nothing compared to the spiritual enjoyment it will bring."[19]

Although Dubnow was not the first to propose that such an organization be established—both Harkavy and Hermann Zvi Schapira had tried in the 1880s—he was the first to elicit a resoundingly positive response. The article was written at a fateful moment in Russian Jewish history: the Jews of Moscow were being expelled, the Jews of St. Petersburg were witnessing renewed repression, and the Jews of Odessa were waiting in fear of an expected Easter pogrom. Most important, in the decade since Harkavy and Schapira's attempts, a nucleus of individuals with modern notions of enlightenment and organizational skills had emerged who had an interest in history as a source of national awareness.

Largely in response to Dubnow's call, the OPE helped establish a commission to study the history of Jewish Odessa in celebration of the hundredth anniversary of the community in 1894. The group began to meet regularly in the late 1890s as a commission of the OPE. By then it included many of Odessa's Jewish luminaries, including Morgulis, Mendele, Ahad Ha-Am, and Dubnow. It also generated interest among doctors, lawyers, and civil servants from the elite of Odessa's Jewish community.[20] This group became one of the first Jewish learned societies to reach beyond itself and resonate intellectually in the general public.

By the 1890s, organized circles of Jewish youth had also emerged in St. Petersburg with broad social goals of assisting the Jewish population. Many of these itinerant intellectuals were alienated lawyers. After1889, Jews were prohibited from being admitted to the bar without explicit authorization from the minister of justice, an authorization that was rarely given. With most of the civil service and academic positions closed to them, upwardly mobile Jewish youth who had earned law degrees were channeled into the only jobs available to them—defense work as barristers. Many still hoped for academic posts but settled for reading and discussion groups as the next best thing. These groups provided opportunities for the leading lights of Jewish society to meet regularly, discuss matters of common interest, and enjoy some of the benefits of academic life from beyond the ivory tower.

Aleksandr Passover's Circle

Aleksandr Passover formed one of the most important of these groups. Frustrated by the lack of opportunity in his native Russia, he left for England, where he was admitted to the bar. In 1874, he returned to Russia, this time to St. Petersburg, hoping once again to attain the elusive post of professor. There he was repeatedly elected a member of the governing council of the St. Petersburg bar but could not obtain a professorship. Passover decided not to let institutional impediments stand in the way of dedicating his life to academic work and Jewish public affairs.[21] He published articles on legal theory, edited the collected works of Orshanskii, was a member of the Society for the Spread of Enlightenment among the Jews of Russia, helped found numerous voluntary associations, and was a member of the delegation of Jewish dignitaries that met with Tsar Alexander III on 11 May 1881 to appeal for assistance in the aftermath of the pogroms of that year. Vinaver said of Passover, "You could take him out of the academy, but you could not take the academy out of him."[22]

Passover, an eccentric and social recluse, was an unlikely figure to play a leading role in the formation of Jewish civil life. He had few close friends and never married. "Too much knowledge and too much understanding—this will often become a source of suffering and unhappiness," wrote historian Shaul Ginzburg of Passover.[23] He was always more comfortable among antiquarian books, particularly those on jurisprudence and natural science, than he was among living people. "Passover had only one passion—books," wrote Ginzburg.[24] He had a large private book collection that he divided between his home in St. Petersburg and his second residence in Berlin. Ginzburg wrote of him that "his extraordinary sharpness, multifaceted mastery of all branches of Russian and foreign jurisprudence, his iron logic, remarkable acuity, exquisite memory, and unparalleled oratorical talent, all made him into the premier and most famous lawyer not only in Petersburg but in all of Russia."[25] He was, in Sliozberg's words, a man of "colossal talent."[26]

In 1889, when the St. Petersburg bar's governing council began to compile statistics on the religious affiliation of barristers, Passover resigned from the council, correctly surmising that this was a prelude to the establishment of a quota system that would limit the number of Jews admitted to the bar. Soon after, he formed an alternative group of young Jewish lawyers and legal assistants who met on Sunday mornings to discuss issues of common interest. This was the only social activity Passover felt fully comfortable with and truly dedicated himself to.[27] At first this group discussed literature and general academic issues, but over time it began to focus on legal and political issues.

Passover ran the meetings with a meticulous concern for protocol and formality. Many acquaintances commented on his punctuality; he could sometimes be seen pacing outside offices, waiting for the exact time when his meeting was scheduled so as not to arrive a minute late or a minute early. He ran his own meetings in a similar fashion:

> At exactly 11 o' clock Passover sat down at the head of the table and invited the "colleague" in charge of keeping minutes to read the minutes from the previous meeting. This term "colleague" was somewhat artificial. Passover knew this person very well—in fact, he was one of his closest co-workers and helpers, but in the meetings he was to him an anonymous "colleague": "colleague on the right," "colleague on the left," "colleague in the middle," "colleague third from the edge." And this was not just some Ivan Ivanovich, although he spoke with him as though he were Ivan Ivanovich. Moreover, there were among us at that time established people who were well known in literary circles. . . . But even they were transformed into "colleague on the left" and "colleague on the right.[28]

The group sought to carve out an egalitarian space within the stratified society of imperial Russia; members shed their official status outside the meeting room. The myth of universal accessibility and the demand that rational debate take precedence over private interests and class distinctions are common attributes of the ideology of the public sphere. Passover's insistence on maintaining these fictions to an absurd degree demonstrated his consciousness of the public role he believed his study group was serving.

The heart of the meetings was a formal presentation by a regular member or a visitor on a topic of common interest. Passover preferred to have the presenters deliver their reports without a prepared text; indeed, Passover himself was known for making formal appearances in court without any notes or files and for delivering addresses to the court completely by heart or off the cuff.[29] Most presenters lacked Passover's confidence and preferred to read from a written text. The occasional presenter who dared to say "as illustrated above" or "as I will show below" during the course of his talk could always expect to be heckled by Passover, who would stare up at the ceiling or crouch down under the table, yelling "Where?" The formal presentation would be followed by a ten- to fifteen-minute break, after which the participants would return for a question-and-answer session. During the break and as members lingered after the meeting for informal conversation, lifelong friendships were made and informal and formal networks were constructed. The bourgeois formality that Passover introduced remained a consistent part of Russian Jewish intellectual life in the capital and informed the voluntary associations that proliferated there in the first decade of the twentieth century. The almost comical formalities Passover insisted upon forced old friends to distance themselves from their personal lives and to come to the table as professional discussants and members of the society rather than as the network of "old boys" they were. This professionalism ultimately created greater institutional flexibility, transparency, and inclusiveness. In contrast to the "old boys'" networks, these formal meetings allowed anybody who learned the rules to join.

Mikhail Kulisher (1847–1919) was an important member of Passover's group; he had been active since its early days in Odessa. The son of a Volhynian agriculturalist and grandson of a *maskil,* Kulisher had attended gymnasium in Kamenets-Podolsk and the rabbinical academy of Zhitomir before pursuing legal studies. In the late 1860s, Kulisher contributed articles to various Russian journals and liberal papers. After completing his law degree in St. Petersburg, he traveled to Europe, spending time in Paris and Berlin, where he studied with the philosophers and founders of racial psychology, Hermann Heymann Steinthal and Moritz Lazarus. Under Steinthal's influence, Kulisher developed an interest in Jewish antiquity, publishing a book questioning the historicity of the story of Jesus as told in the Gospels.[30] When he returned to Kiev in the late 1870s, he helped found the journal *Zaria* (Dawn). The journal adopted a liberal perspective that was far removed from the radical populism that was becoming the ideology of choice among most intellectuals. Kulisher's journal had an enormous influence on Ukrainian youth of the time. In the words of Vinaver, "I would hardly be mistaken if I were to say that in the history of the Russian periodical press there was no provincial paper with such success and such influence as Kulisher's *Zaria.*"[31] Here Kulisher demonstrated his encyclopedic knowledge and profound moral conscience. At the same time, Kulisher was a correspondent for the journal *Novyi vremeni* (New Times) before the journal changed owners and moved toward the political right. Referring to his insatiable crusade for social moral justice, Sliozberg described Kulisher as the "prophetic type."[32] Unfortunately, this personality type did not mesh well with the working world, and Kulisher had a great deal of difficulty finding material sustenance wherever he lived. Unable to support himself writing, Kulisher sought legal work but was blocked from admission to the bar because of the 1889 numerus clausus. Unable to open his own practice, he became Passover's assistant. Although he shied away from public appearances in court, Kulisher became a highly respected legal writer who specialized in appellate briefs. In 1896 he published his influential and encyclopedic *Razvod i polozhenie zhenshchiny* (Divorce and the Status of Women).[33] Soon after his arrival in Petersburg, Kulisher became a member of the Executive Committee of the OPE, where he pushed the organization toward more populist policies.

Passover invited Kulisher to join his circle and present papers on sociology and jurisprudence. Kulisher became a standing member of all the conferences Passover organized, including the one that would become the Jewish Historical and Ethnographic Society. Despite his near-total rejection of the Jewish religion, Kulisher retained a strong Jewish identity. In Vinaver's words, "The bond Kulisher had with Judaism was so strong and inescapable. He felt this bond. He did not deny it; he was proud of it."[34] In contrast to those who fought for Jewish rights on the grounds that the Jews should be considered only "citizens of the Mosaic Faith," Kulisher refused to relinquish a Jewish national identity, arguing that the Jews are not only a religious group but also a cultural and historical group. Thus, in addition to sympathizing with the Kadets following 1905, Kulisher also counted himself a member of the Jewish Peoples Group (Evreiskaia narodnaia gruppa), which stood for recognition of the Jewish nation as a corporate collective in Russia.[35]

Passover's group also included Maksim Vinaver. Vinaver was born in Warsaw in 1862, where he remained through his university studies. He moved to Petersburg in 1888 after studying in Warsaw University. In Petersburg he worked as an assistant to the preeminent lawyer Vladimir Spasovich. By the late 1890s, Vinaver had become one of the leading lawyers of Petersburg and one of the leaders of the Jewish community of the capital. His presence in the emerging Jewish civil society was ubiquitous; wherever Jewish voluntary associations were being formed in the imperial capital, Vinaver was among them. His signature can be found on countless statutes and appeals, attesting to his dominant role within the liberal Jewish community of St. Petersburg. He helped establish and lead the

Kadet Party, in which capacity he served in the First Russian Duma. He was a talented organizer and a particularly effective mediator, able to find a common interest among competing groups. With his outstanding organizational and people skills, it was inevitable that he would eventually take over leadership from the reticent and reserved Passover.

The only Zionist among Passover's circle was Vasilli Berman (1863–1896). Berman was at the center of Jewish university activities; he had been instrumental in the creation of a "student commission" under the auspices of the OPE and later became involved in the Jewish Colonization Association. Early in his short career, he became a highly visible lawyer in St. Petersburg as an assistant to the renowned criminal lawyer Prince Urusov. His career was cut short by illness, forcing him to leave Russia. He perished in Egypt at the tender age of thirty-three. Berman is usually credited with having brought to the attention of Passover's circle Dubnow's 1891 article "On the Study of the History of Russian Jews and on the Founding of a Russian-Jewish Historical Society."

The Historical and Ethnographic Commission of the OPE

With the consent of Passover and his circle, Vinaver responded to Dubnow's call by sending a letter to Odessa asking how the St. Petersburg group could help. Dubnow suggested that the St. Petersburg lawyers continue their work on Jewish legal status in Russia by compiling collections of legal and historical documents relating to the Jews.[36] As Sliozberg noted, "Knowledge on the laws relating to Jews was so weakly disseminated, even among professional lawyers who occupied themselves with Jewish communal affairs. I know that even to the end [of the tsarist regime] many of them did not know what regions belonged to the Pale of Jewish Settlement."[37] Thus, the circle, under Vinaver's leadership, began combing archives for antiquated edicts relating to the Jews.[38]

Unable to receive permission from the Ministry of Internal Affairs to start a new society, the group became a commission of the Society for the Spread of Enlightenment among the Jews of Russia with the stated goal of collecting and publishing important documents that illustrated the facts of Jewish legal existence in Russia. The circle managed to collect enough material to release a compilation of laws relating to the Jews. The 536-page volume included 1,111 documents dating from 80 CE to 1800 that were derived from 212 sources. The nature of the documents ranged from medieval gravestone inscriptions from the Crimea and medieval Arabic-language travel accounts to privileges, contracts, legal enactments, complaints, and guild statutes from the Polish-Lithuanian Commonwealth.[39]

At the same time, a group of youth in Moscow led by Leon Bramson (1869–1941) and Iulii Brutzkus (1870–1951) was working on a guide to Russian-language literature on the Jews.[40] This group also wrote Dubnow and received his blessing. The following year, Bramson and some members of his group left Moscow for St. Petersburg to join Vinaver's commission. Bramson arrived in Petersburg after studying law at Moscow University. He came to the capital as a young activist committed to Jewish causes in general and to the goal of reviving Jewish land-ownership and handicrafts in particular. He became involved with the Society for the Spread of Enlightenment among the Jews of Russia, especially its efforts to develop Jewish primary education, and became its inspector of schools. He was a member of a commission that collected material for a textbook for Jewish primary schools.[41] In 1906, he was elected to the Duma as a representative from his home Kovno district, where he fought for Jewish rights, a fight he continued later under the Bolsheviks. Iulii Brutzkus had studied medicine at the University of Moscow before becoming active in Zionist circles. After arriving in St. Petersburg he served first on the editorial board of *Voskhod* and later on the board of the Zionist *Razsvet*. He was elected to the Constituent Assembly following the Russian Revolution of February 1917 and was later elected to the Lithuanian Parliament. Bramson and Brutzkus both continued their scholarly activities in St. Petersburg as members of the newly established Historical and Ethnographic Commission of the OPE.

The commission's meetings were held in accordance with a strict protocol and formal procedure derived from Passover's example. Meeting in Vinaver's apartment, the group decided to concentrate on seven themes and to form sections to deal with each theme: history (led by Vinaver), law, economy (led by Kulisher), literature, daily life and education, physical life and medicine, and emigration (led by Berman, whose Zionist sympathies made him an appropriate choice for the topic). The section heads were empowered to hold individual meetings of their section, and together the heads of each section were to constitute a committee, which in turn would select a central governing board. The first board consisted of Kulisher, Berman, and Vinaver. This group met as a commission of the OPE for the next seventeen years.

The commission's primary interest was in ascertaining the legal rights of Russian Jews, which they believed could best be established through the study of historical legal enactments relating to the Jews. This was the subject of numerous presentations to the commission as well as the subject of continued research. The interest in legal history was also reflected in the society's approach to other contemporary issues such as the status of Jewish women. When Rabbi Cherikover presented a paper on personal relationships between spouses according to Mosaic and talmudic law, he framed his discussion around a comparison of Jewish legal sources and those of medieval and contemporary Europe. Cherikover argued that Jewish legal precepts from talmudic and biblical sources were designed to protect the legal rights of women. These rights, he argued, were gradually eroded by medieval legal norms, which denied women independent access to the courts.[42]

The group kept abreast of the latest scholarship, which came mostly from Germany, regarding ancient Near Eastern history and Assyriology. For instance, on 26 March 1903, Isaac Dov-Ber Markon, a librarian at the Imperial Public Library of St. Petersburg and a graduate of the University of Berlin, presented a paper on the latest scholarship comparing Babylonian and ancient Israelite cultures. Markon granted that German scholarship had demonstrated many Babylonian influences on Israelite culture but argued that many of the most fundamental Israelite beliefs, such as that of the Sabbath, had developed independently.[43]

Other sessions of the society addressed matters of contemporary debate, including one of the most divisive issues facing the modernizing Jewish community—the language issue. Although the society functioned in Russian and would not have dreamed of using any lesser language for such exalted conversation, some of its members were willing to put forward the case for Yiddish. In his 15 January 1903 talk, for instance, literary historian Izrail Tsinberg (1873–1939) advocated the expansion of Yiddish literary activity among the Jews of Russia by presenting a history of the Yiddish language and literature. "Language exists for the people, not the people for the language," he asserted. The point was challenged by others present, who argued that Jews had enough knowledge of Russian and that if a new literary language was to be developed it should be Hebrew.[44]

The Jewish Historical and Ethnographic Society

It was not until the liberalization of censorship and the Temporary Regulations on Societies and Unions of 1906 that it became possible for groups to petition for official permission to break off from the OPE and form independent societies. In March 1908 the first steps were taken in this direction with the publication of the statute of the JHES.[45] The statute, signed by Kulisher and several other activists, adapted several themes from Dubnow's 1891 article into the formal language of legal statutes:

1. The goals of the JHES are a) studying and researching all realms of Jewish history and ethnography; and b) working out theoretical questions of historical and ethnographic scholarship.

2. To reach these goals the Society will a) arrange meetings of its members, with proper permission [from the authorities], for the purpose of hearing academic reports and engaging in discussions; b) arrange public lectures about Jewish history and ethnography; c) publish, in fulfillment of these articles, works in the form of books, collected volumes, and periodical publications; d) propose problems to be solved by awarding monetary prizes and rewards.[46]

A few months later, in the fall of 1908, Vinaver received official permission to establish the Jewish Historical and Ethnographic Society. He realized, though, that no Jewish historical society would be complete without the participation of the dean of Russian Jewish history, Simon Dubnow. Although the group had corresponded with Dubnow during its inauguration some seventeen years earlier, there had been little contact between them in the interim. Dubnow was anxious to return to academic work after a break in order to conduct his political activity and happily accepted the offer.

The first meeting of the constituent assembly of the JHES took place on 16 November 1908 in the Aleksandrovskii Hall of the Choral Synagogue of St. Petersburg. The society had no permanent meeting place until the winter of 1913, when wealthy entrepreneur Moisei Ginzburg allowed it to use his house on Vasilevskii Island to be shared between the society and the Course of Oriental Studies. Kulisher, with Vinaver and Dubnow sitting by his side, chaired this first meeting, which was attended by sixty-five participants. The main item of business was to elect an executive committee. Kulisher was elected chair, Dubnow and Vinaver were elected vice-chairs, and historian Iulii Gessen was elected secretary. The rest of the executive committee was comprised of representatives from the Russian-language Jewish affairs journal *Voskhod*, ethnographer Lev Shternberg (1861–1927), archaeologist Salvian Goldshteyn (1855–1926), and young historian Mark Vishnitser (1882–1955), who had recently arrived from Germany. Aleksandr Braudo (1864–1924), a literary critic for the journal *Russkoe bogatstvo* (Russian Wealth), headed the library committee.[47]

"A Historical Role in the History of Our People"

Despite the façade of academic objectivity that surrounded the society's first meeting, Dubnow delivered an opening address that clarified his thinking about the society:

> I am speaking here about history not only as a scientific discipline, but also as a vigorous factor of national culture. If we are truly to be called an "eternal people," we must clearly understand the eternal thread that connects our past, present and future into a single unity. . . . In the great struggle for our national existence, what does the energy of one generation mean when it is cut off from the great accumulation of national energy that forms thanks to the heroic strength of a hundred generations?[48]

The society did more than just passively study history; it actively played a part in making history. Dubnow argued that although Russian and Polish Jews constituted the greatest Jewish Diaspora since the 1492 expulsion of the Jews from Spain, they were now living in an era of reaction and spiritual exhaustion. The revival of Jewish historical and ethnographic studies was deliberately intended to revive Jewish life in the region. The community was clearly facing a historic challenge, and Dubnow was confident they would be able to meet it: "Do not forget, gentlemen, one historical truth: in the life of a vibrant people, epochs of political reaction always coincide with epochs of the accumulation of strength. In this dark period we are accumulating spiritual energy to spend in the future epoch of liberation." To further emphasize the historical society's role in this rejuvenation, Dubnow declared, "My warmest hope is that our new society will become authentically historical, that it will serve to play a historical role in the history of our people."[49] This passion was a far cry from the clinical detachment he had expressed in his 1893 essay "What Is Jewish History?" where he had likened history to a laboratory experiment in which "it becomes possible to arrive with mathematical precision at the share each of several cooperating causes has in the result."[50] By 1908, in contrast, Dubnow had come to believe that the role of the historian was not merely to passively observe but rather to actively influence the result.

The stakes, he argued, could not have been higher:

> I have lost faith in personal immortality, but history teaches me that
> there is a collective immortality and that the Jewish nation can be
> considered relatively eternal, for her history coincides with the entire
> course of world history; therefore the study of the past of the Jewish
> people connects me with a type of eternity. This historicism united me
> with the national collective, guided me from the circle of individual
> problems to the social expanse, less deep but more authentic. National
> sorrow is closer than universal. There the path is opened to a national
> synthesis in which the best elements of the old thesis are combined
> with the new antithesis, Jewish and universal ideals, the national and
> the humanist.[51]

Dubnow's sentiments were not unique. in his address at the society's opening, Vinaver declared: "We didn't discuss the 'national idea,' we felt it as a
more invigorating activity."[52] The members of the society clearly believed
that they were not just writing the Jewish past, they were also writing its
future. "Through an understanding of the past lies the path to the future,"
declared Vinaver.[53]

The chief activity of the society was the publication, under Dubnow's
editorship, of the quarterly journal *Evreiskaia starina* (Jewish Antiquities).
The journal was intended to supersede the existing *Perezhitoe,* a historical
journal edited by Shaul Ginzburg and several members of the JHES, including An-sky, Tsinberg, and Braudo. Dubnow criticized *Perezhitoe* for favoring memoirs and stories about the recent past over academic articles and
archival material. He petitioned *Perezhitoe* to enlarge its scope to include
a more academic orientation, but his suggestions were turned down—
in his view, solely on personal grounds.[54] In contrast, *Jewish Antiquities,*
Dubnow declared in the first edition, would have four goals: 1) publishing
new research; 2) publishing primary source material and documents; 3)
publishing reviews and bibliographies of relevant literature and 4) publishing news about the Jewish Historical and Ethnographic Society.[55] In his
attempt to carve out a distinct niche for *Jewish Antiquities,* though, Dubnow
overstated the differences between the two publications. Like Dubnow's
creation, Ginzburg's journal also included academic articles representing
new research (much of which was written by the same authors who contributed to *Jewish Antiquities*) as well as primary sources and bibliographic
material. Articles from *Perezhitoe,* such as Vishnitser's "Reform Projects of
Jewish Life in the Duchy of Warsaw and the Kingdom of Poland (on the

basis of unpublished material)" or I. E. Joffe's "From the Life of the First Jewish Community of Riga (on the basis of archival material)" would have been equally welcome in *Jewish Antiquities*. Dubnow himself supplied some of the primary source material that was published in the first volume of *Perezhitoe* under the title "from my archive." The second issue of *Perezhitoe* bore a closer relation to Dubnow's description: it did not include a bibliography section and had less of an academic apparatus, but the differences between the two journals were more of degree than of type.

Beginning in 1910, *Jewish Antiquities* was sent free to all members of the society who had paid the 5-ruble membership fee. The journal met the highest standards of academic scholarship for its time. Each article contained a full academic apparatus. All sources were properly cited in footnotes, the full text of important documents was given in the original language either in the text of the article or in a footnote, the provenance of sources was discussed either in footnotes or in the text, and articles were written as part of an ongoing conversation with existing historiography, usually in the first footnote. The authors maintained a balance between the academic apparatus of historical methodology and the polemical outlook of political activism.

Like the society as a whole, the journal had a nationalist agenda. In his editorial introduction to the first issue, for instance, Dubnow declared in language echoing his 1891 article:

> In the great process of development there are no borders between the past and the present, between the old and the new: all this is one chain of the national experience, which continues to manifest itself in us, in the various life processes of our generation, in our individuality, society, culture and spiritual creativity. . . . In our "antiquity" one can always hear the "present" not in terms of a binding tendency but in the vibration of life, which transmutes the voice of the centuries in a single chord. In *Jewish Antiquities* is found reflections only of the *living* past, that is, that through which the long chain of generations leads us to the threshold of the present.[56]

Thus despite his claims in the same introduction that the journal would strive for the systematic and academic study of Jewish history on par with Western journals, Dubnow's ulterior goals were explicitly nationalistic. The journal would not only do history, it would also become history. It would always have one eye on the past and another on the present and future. The society and the journal, Dubnow firmly believed, would usher

Еврейская Старина

ТРЕХМѢСЯЧНИКЪ

Еврейскаго Историко-Этнографическаго Общества

ИЗДАВАЕМЫЙ

подъ редакціей **С. М. ДУБНОВА**.

Томъ первый.

С.-ПЕТЕРБУРГЪ.
1909.

FIGURE 18. The title page of the first edition of *Jewish Antiquities* (*Evreiskaia starina*). The quarterly journal, which began publishing in 1909, was the chief organ of the Jewish Historical and Ethnographic Society.

in a new period of Jewish history centered on the ideals of populism, humanism, and liberal nationalism.

History as a Public Process

The JHES sought to not only act as a forum for the academic study of Jewish history but also to influence how its members and the general public thought about history. The national revival its members sought would be made possible both by disseminating their own research and by encouraging smaller endeavors throughout the Russian Empire, in essence engaging the broad population in the project of creating a usable past. In addition to telling the history of the Jews, the JHES also encouraged ordinary Jews to tell history.

The JHES realized that an academic and scholarly journal such as *Jewish Antiquities* would never achieve the type of mass appeal needed for a revival of public history, so in 1912 it embarked on activities designed to reach beyond the membership of a historical society. Chief among these was the publication of what was intended to be a two-volume textbook designed for schoolchildren and youth as well as for adults seeking to further their knowledge of Jewish history. Government-sponsored readers for Jewish secondary students that balanced Jewish history with Russian history already existed and had been used widely throughout the latter half of the nineteenth century, but these presented a *maskilic* interpretation of history that was outdated in the new age of national identities.[57] The first volume of the new textbook, entitled *Ocherki po evreiskoi istorii i kul'ture: istoricheskaia khrestomatiia* (Studies in Jewish History and Culture: A Historical Reader) covered the biblical period. It was published in 1912, was distributed free to members of the society, and was sold to nonmembers for 1 ruble and 50 kopeks. The book, which was designed to present modern biblical criticism to a popular readership, contained essays with titles such as "The Bible as a Historical Source" and "The Most Important Results of Archaeological Digs in the Lands of the Ancient East."[58] In connection with the release of the textbook, the society sponsored a series of lectures in January 1912 on the biblical epoch in Jewish history. These included presentations by Kulisher on "The Bible as a Historical Source," M. A. Soloveichik on "The Bible and Biblical Studies," and B. G. Stolpner on "The Fate of Secret Jewish Science (Kabbalah)."[59] Although plans were made for additional volumes, financial considerations and poor sales of the first volume seem to have prevented their realization.[60]

Publishing the textbook was part of a broad effort to popularize the study of Jewish history. In 1912, the Executive Committee of the OPE sponsored two prizes, one for writing a textbook on Jewish history in Yiddish and another for writing a Russian-language textbook for Jewish primary schools that would acquaint Jewish children with Jewish legends, holidays, history, literature, and Jewish life and "cultivate in children national self-awareness and a feeling of love for their people and for their past."[61]

The JHES also sought to include members of the Jewish community in the project of constructing Jewish history by engaging them in collecting historical evidence. As the committee affirmed in 1910:

> In order to reach [its] goals, the society must popularize its activity in all of the Russian Empire. . . . Only through the energetic participation of Jewish activists in the "Pale of Settlement" and outside it can the enormous and long-term goals of the society be fulfilled. This activity must manifest itself first of all in collecting and sending to the committee of the society every type of *material* (original manuscripts, copies of correspondence, memorial material, etc.), related to the history and ethnography of the Jews in Poland and Russia.
>
> The committee appeals to all individuals who are interested in Jewish history and ethnography with the urgent request: *to collect everywhere appropriate material and to send it to the committee* for permanent or temporary use. In various communal and family archives, in libraries of private individuals, and sometimes in forgotten corners or attics of houses, discarded manuscript books or separate documents that have remained intact, residues of lived culture, disappear every year from careless handling, fires, and all types of accidents. We must immediately take steps to save these residues of historical material from complete disappearance.[62]

The committee recommended in particular the collection of minute books, "manuscript protocol books of Jewish communities, unions, and brotherhoods in all cities and shtetls of Poland and Russia (the minute books of *kahals,* burial societies, *khevres,* and unions—religious, voluntary, mutual aid, etc.)"; individual manuscripts and letters of historical content; "correspondence information relating to Jewish historical material preserved in local government, church, city, and private archives"; "*local legends,* which have a historical or ethnographic characters, *popular songs, anecdotes, proverbs, riddles,* etc."; "information about *local customs,* "stories about local old folks"; etchings from old Jewish gravestones; and material objects from the past, such as domestic objects, clothing, synagogue objects, old money, portraits, publications, engravings, and prints.[63] The list echoed Dubnow's 1891 appeal, which had outlined the specific sources he regarded as most integral for the study of Russian-Jewish history; that list had included community minute books, government documents, Jewish folk sayings, and gravestone impressions.[64] Dubnow's attempt to establish a central archive of Jewish history in Russia followed the outlines of Eugen Taübler's work to create a Total Archive of German Jewry (Gesamtarchiv der deutschen Juden), which he established in 1905 as a central repository of archival material relating to Jewish life in Germany. However, in Germany, Taübler encountered hostility to his goals when people in the provinces resisted having their local historical materials moved to a central location. Like Taübler's project, Dubnow's work represented a centrist—and elitist—urge to relocate materials from their native provincial contexts to a central location, but his project does not seem to have elicited resistance.[65]

In order to bring about Dubnow's goal, the JHES began a campaign to enlarge its membership. At a 12 January 1912 meeting, the executive committee decided to allocate funds to advertise in the major Russian Jewish journals.[66] It also decided to begin conducting public activities for both members and nonmembers. In early 1912, for instance, it sponsored a concert with the Jewish Folk Music Society.[67] The membership drive had some success: membership increased from 362 in 1909 to 427 in 1910 to 774 in 1915. Membership was also expanding beyond the society's base in St. Petersburg. In 1909, 73 percent of the society's members lived in the capital; by 1915, that number had decreased to 42 percent.[68] In 1911, specific efforts were made to expand membership to other centers of Jewish life in the Russian Empire, such as Kiev, Odessa, Ekaterinoslav, and Minsk. The Executive Committee of the JHES declared:

> Let there form in every Jewish center, in every significant city, a group of members of the Jewish Historical and Ethnographic Society; let every group pick among itself a commission to unite the local members and to get to work immediately, to gather in circles of societal activities: to collect historical materials and memoirs of elders, to study Jewish history, etc. The sum total of these groups will animate the intellectual life of the provinces.[69]

To help encourage local initiatives, the St. Petersburg branch of the society provided grants to other cities to pursue projects related to historical studies.[70]

The goal of spreading historical knowledge, awareness, and curiosity did have an effect beyond St. Petersburg. Much of the material the JHES published in *Jewish Antiquities* was sent in from private individuals. The journal printed lists of donations and published the full texts of documents deemed particularly important, usually with an introduction and annotations. Donations were stored in an archive established by the society.[71] Among the donations were documentation of Jewish sites such as etchings of Jewish gravestones and photographs of synagogues; ritual objects, including amulets with purported protective powers; statistical information such as tax records; documents on the legal situation of the Jews such as official edicts and correspondence with the state; and documents from within the Jewish community such as correspondence among Jewish officials and community minute books. Of special concern to Dubnow were the minute books of Jewish communities, which he repeatedly urged his readers to send. Some responded to Dubnow's call by publishing the minute books of their own communities outside the journal. Dubnow praised these works, citing one rabbi, Hayyim Ze'eb Margalioth, for instance, as "a good example to rabbis of other historical centers" for publishing the minutes of the Dubno *kahal*.[72]

The active participation of readers and members of the society in donating objects was a significant step toward the fulfillment of Dubnow's 1891 dream, although still on a relatively small scale. The donations came overwhelmingly from intellectuals and semi-intellectuals, only some of whom were members of the society. In 1909, for example, only four of the eleven individuals who made donations to the society were listed in the JHES registry of members.

Slowly but surely, a two-way dialogue was being established between the journal and its readers. Yet correspondence suggests that in the journal's first two years, its readers understood the journal within a different conceptual rubric. In contrast to most of the articles in the journal, which presented academic interpretations of history by intellectuals who were conscious of their role in constructing a historical narrative, the donations represent the public conception of history, or collective memory. One revealing aspect, particularly among objects donated in the early years, is that most of the donated objects were directly related to religion and synagogue life. It seems that the readers of the journal still associated Jewish history with the history of Judaism. When they did address issues of secular history, it was usually in the form of martyrology. Many sent in elegies or statistical data on pogroms.

Others wrote to inform the society of items of interest or to tell anecdotes they thought would help constitute the historical past of Russian and Polish Jews. One writer told of a cemetery in a small village in Mogilev

Province, far from the nearest Jewish settlement, "that is very popular among the Jewish population. Primarily in the month of Elul pilgrims gather here for prayer, because miraculous powers to heal various ailments are attributed to this cemetery. What sort of cemetery it is, who is buried there and when they were buried nobody can say, but there are different legends about it." He explained that both Jews and local Christians believed that anyone who touched the gravestones to try to read the inscriptions would be cursed. The letter concluded, "In general this place is interesting and deserves attention. Maybe it is possible to establish the historical origins of the cemetery by investigating the inscriptions on the gravestones."[73] Other letters told of other abandoned Jewish cemeteries and former Jewish towns, the memories of which were fading.

Another issue contained a letter that Eliia-Borukh Liberant of Ianov (Grodno Province) wrote to his children about the 1863 Polish rebellion. The letter was originally written in Hebrew and translated by the local crown rabbi (a state-appointed rabbi) into Russian. The manuscript was sent to the journal by an individual from Semiatich (Grodno Province). The letter told of how Liberant was attacked by Polish brigands who broke into his house at night in January 1863 after he had voiced his opposition to the rebellion. Liberant wrote the letter to tell his descendants of how "God kept watch over me . . . so that you can tell your children and grandchildren about the mercy of God"[74] The letter is in the tradition of Jewish ethical wills (wills expressing personal values) and martyrologies.

Others contributors sent the journal more extended commentaries or observations in the hope of contributing to the goal of creating a narrative of Jewish history. For instance, one reader, who chose to remain anonymous, sent in his recollections of the pogroms of 1881 with the comment, "Issue No. 1 of the journal *Jewish Antiquities* contained information on the anti-Jewish movement of 1881–82 with an introduction by Dubnow. This article gave me the opportunity to recall that as an eyewitness to the affair, it is well known to me. Thinking that my recollections may serve as a supplement to the previously mentioned article, I decided to share them with the readers of *Antiquities*."[75] Other articles were based at least partially on "sources and family legend," such as David Kogan's account of the Odessa pogrom of 1821, during which his grandfather was killed.[76] Similarly, the nephew of an intercessor who had represented Shklov and Vitebsk during the reigns of Nicholas I and Alexander II wrote about "family recollections" of his uncle.[77] At least some people were moved to consider the importance of their historical recollections for the construction of the history of Russian Jewry. There could be no clearer affirmation of Dubnow's goal to inspire the populace with historical awareness and the realization that they, as individuals, could contribute to the historical narrative, than this type of correspondence. The academic articles in *Jewish Antiquities* were a stimulus to others to come forward with their own personal recollections and interpretations of historical events, thereby bringing broader segments of the population into the historical and national project and integrating the collective memory of the people into public history.

Daily Life

In November 1910, the executive committee of the JHES discussed ways of enlivening the journal. In an attempt to broaden the base of subscribers, Shternberg proposed that the journal dedicate more attention to issues of daily life.[78] One year later, little progress had been made and it was becoming increasingly apparent that the society could not support the burden of funding the journal unless drastic changes were made.[79] In consequence, Dubnow enlarged the space given to memoirs and ethnography, both of which appealed to broader segments of the readership than academic history. The publication of individual memoirs presented one means of telling the stories of ordinary people to supplement the traditional concentration on the histories of dignitaries and luminaries. For the Jewish people, whose modern history had no kings or noblemen and few government officials, the importance of telling the history of ordinary folk was even more obvious.

Among the ordinary folk whose stories Dubnow wanted to tell were Jewish cantonists, Jews who had been recruited into the tsarist army. Dubnow wrote, "We are prepared in the future to find a place for both archival and oral material concerning this historical tragedy, the last heroes of which are now dying out, taking with them to the grave the secret of this enormous martyrdom of young people."[80] The journal published a document showing the oaths recruits were forced to take.[81] *Jewish Antiquities* also serialized the diary of the cantonist M. Merimzon. In this autobiography, Merimzon recounted his 1852 abduction as a young boy and his subsequent experiences as a cantonist and army recruit. He told of how he managed to retain his religion despite enormous pressure to convert while he was isolated from his community. His parents, who were swayed by rumors that he and his entire group of cantonists had converted, disowned him, despite the poor child's insistences to the contrary in pleading letters to them.[82] The memoir played an important role in defining popular Jewish perceptions of the cantonist experience.

Writing from Irkutsk in Siberia, Ilia Isaevich (Izrail-Leyb) Itskovich sent his memoirs as a cantonist with the preliminary remarks that "having read in *Jewish Antiquities* the recollections of former cantonists Mr. Ermanovich and Mr. Shigel, I decided as a former cantonist (from 1853 to 1857) to share with readers my own recollections about the time of the recruitment inquisition. I will try in simple but true words to explain what my colleagues and I went through in the Archangelsk half-battalion of military cantonists."[83] He described how he was captured at the age of 7 and taken into a battalion of cantonists, where he and almost his entire battalion were forcibly converted. Only a single member of his battalion resisted forcible conversion, preferring to succumb to weekly beatings. Itskovich was able to annul his conversion after his military service concluded in 1872, when he was 26.

In 1912, the journal began a series called "Notes and Communications" (*Zametki i soobshcheniia*) in which "the editors of *Jewish Antiquities* present[ed] a series of episodes from the life of Jews" on a particular topic, "using for this letters of correspondence from various individuals and extracts from rare recent memoirs and journals of the time."[84] Although the journal had published similar segments before, such as one on Jewish life under Alexander II, its editors seemed at this point to be making a conscious decision to highlight this type of human-interest story. The first segment contained a series of four pieces on the war of 1812. The first, entitled "A Victim of the War in Belorussia," presented a letter written by one Nison Katsnelson about his father, a leaseholder who died fighting against the French in 1812. The second presented an excerpt from an 1816 publication about a Jewish townsman named Reuven Gummer who risked his own life and the life of his family (his wife was killed and his property destroyed) when he sheltered a Russian courier who was delivering important information to a general at the front. The third, "A Patriotic Speech in a Synagogue," recounted a speech given by a "learned Jew" to a group of Jewish refugees from Poland and Lithuania during the Jewish New Year in which the speaker praised the Russian tsar for protecting the Jews and for treating them fairly. The fourth, "The Jewish Quarter in the Burning of Moscow," was an extract from the memoirs of eighteenth-century French sergeant Adrien Jean Baptiste François Bourgogne, who told of the burning of the Jewish quarter of Moscow. All four examples demonstrated the loyalty Jews had shown to the Russian government during the war of

1812, providing evidence of Jews who actively defended Russian interests and Jews who suffered together with their Russian compatriots.[85] Another issue contained official correspondence about Jewish colonization in "New Russia" (southern Ukraine) from 1862 and restrictions on Jewish clothing under Alexander II.[86]

Oral History/Ethnography

According to Shternberg, an "ethnographer is also a historian. The sole difference is that historians study more or less the distant past, whereas ethnographers study the recent past and the present, both of which will become subjects of history in the future. Ethnography gives material to sociology, to the future historian, to the psychologist, and at the same time promotes national awareness and national creativity."[87] Dubnow largely agreed. He saw history as an aspect of sociology, which he believed had both static and dynamic manifestations.[88] In Dubnow's thinking, ethnographers collected data to ascertain the current state of affairs, whereas historians collected data to ascertain change over time. Before the JHES was established, some individuals had already begun to collect Jewish folklore in Central Europe. In 1896, for instance, Hamburg rabbi Max Grunwald had appealed for scholars to collect rhymes, songs, and fairy tales that illustrated aspects of Jewish life. The following year Grunwald established the Society for Jewish Folklore.[89] But it was in the Russian Empire under the aegis of the JHES that Jewish ethnography became a major discipline and an integral part of Jewish public culture.

Jewish Antiquities was interested from its inception in documenting the daily life of ordinary Jews, initially in the form of scholarly articles and later in the form of human interest stories. One of the journal's primary practitioners of ethnography was the rabbi of Irkutsk, S. Kh. Beilin. In one article, he published riddles that were used in *kheyder* in the 1860s as a way to test and strengthen children's intellect. Beilin's examples came from "those preserved in my memory from childhood . . . or heard by me later from others." Beilin regarded his own memory as an important primary source. This lack of division between the informant and the researcher was characteristic of Yiddish folklore collection, in which distinctions between "the folk" and the intelligentsia who researched the folk were often absent.[90] Many of those who regarded themselves as members of the intelligentsia had been born and raised in "folk" environments, and they saw folklore as the lore and traditions of their own communities. In an article recounting stories he heard from cantonists, Beilin provided context for each of the stories by introducing the individual who shared his or her stories: "An old resident of the city of Irkutsk, an honored parishioner of our synagogue, Iakob Gershanov (Grigorevich) Ermanovich, a discharged Nikolaevan soldier, who was born in the village of Ekimovskii near the city of Irkutsk in the year 1828 and received his discharge in the year 1869, told me the following of his cantonist life."[91] Beilin believed he could collect folklore and practice ethnography in his own synagogue because of his close proximity to the "folk."

In 1909, Beilin published a collection of anecdotes relating to Jewish discrimination in Russia. "Jews often like to laugh at their misfortunes," he wrote. "Most of the anecdotes I came to hear in Petersburg and in the provinces in the last two decades of the past century, during that period of severe persecution of the Jews . . . are ethnographic material insofar as the people's humor is reflected in them. These anecdotes are also historical documents that shed light on the people's relations with the legal restrictions imposed upon them."[92] One anecdote, for instance, told of a Jew who was stopped by a police officer outside the Pale. The Jew told the officer that he had a note from the minister of finance authorizing him to travel. When the officer asked to see the note, the Jew handed him a note from the State Bank—for twenty-five rubles.[93] In another, a Jew toasted the coronation of a new tsar who had supported pogroms and anti-Jewish discrimination with the toast: "Friends, exclaim after me: *hu ra,* hu-ra!" This joke, as Beilin explains, plays upon the Hebrew, in which *"hu ra'"* means "he is evil."[94] In his memoirs, Dubnow recalled that publishing this anecdote caused him some trouble because the censors thought the anecdote referred to Alexander III.[95] Most of the anecdotes showed tsarist officials speaking in single-sentence commands while Jews outwit them with verbal cunning and quick thinking, eventually getting the better of the officials and mocking them.

The major proponent of ethnography within the JHES was S. An-sky, who was born in Vitebsk Province in 1863. After a traditional Jewish education, An-sky broke with Jewish tradition, instead turning to the populist movement that engulfed Russian youth in the 1870s. His first literary efforts were published in the leading Russian journals, where he started using the pseudonym An-sky. In the late 1880s he earned a living by teaching and by working in the salt and coal mines near Ekaterinoslav. He drew inspiration from these experiences for his sketches of rural life and the coal industry. In 1891 he lived briefly illegally in St. Petersburg before departing for Europe in 1892, eventually settling in Paris. In the French capital he became involved with Russian émigré populist circles, becoming secretary to the leader of Russian populism, Petr Lavrov. After Lavrov's death in 1900, An-sky left for Berne, where he joined circles of Russian Jewish revolutionaries. From Switzerland he wrote his famous "Shvu'ah" (Oath), which became the Bund's anthem. He later also translated the "Internationale" into Yiddish. He returned to Russia in 1905, becoming active in the JHES, particularly in its ethnographic work. Under An-sky's directorship, the JHES engaged in its most important and productive work among the folk, the famed Baron Horace Gintsburg Expedition to Volhynia and Podolia. In 1912–1914, An-sky and his team visited over seventy sites, collected over 1,800 folk tales and 1,500 Jewish folk songs, took over 2,000 photographs, collected over 300 objects of religious and cultural significance, and made over 500 wax cylinder recordings.[96]

In several seminal articles published in the journal, An-sky laid out his vision of Jewish ethnography. In an article on Jewish folk song, he argued that "folk songs often reflect all those aspects of Jewish life that are weakly expressed in literature, which is the product of the intelligentsia's disposition. Folk song responds not only to individual feelings, but also to certain social movements. Even in those epochs, when the Jewish masses were far from active participants in social life, the folk muse responded a little to all the most important happenings and communal events."[97] An-sky called upon the people to help collect Jewish folk songs as a way of analyzing the life of the Jewish masses. In his review of Noyekh Prylucki's *Jüdische Volkslieder,* An-sky complained that many of the songs included had already been published elsewhere or were not genuine examples of folk creativity but rather were canonized prayers or songs written for the folk rather than by the folk.[98] These criticisms illustrated a fundamental divergence within Jewish ethnography: the debate over whether folk creativity should be defined as the expression of the folk masses, as An-sky believed, or whether folk music should be defined as any music sung by members of the nation regardless of social class, as Prylucki believed. In the latter case, the song was seen as a subject for scientific study rather than an expression of some type of innate spirit representing the people. In that case, it was advisable to have as many variations of the song as possible, and therefore it was of little significance whether it was a reprinted variation or an original composition.[99]

In another article, An-sky looked at popular children's songs. "When we speak about traditional Jewish upbringing," he wrote, "it is customary to speak first about the old *kheyder* with its 'stale' teachers, with its archaic methods of instruction and its unsanitary environment. This completely overlooks the fact that both before they enter the *kheyder* and outside it children receive a different upbringing."[100] Children, he continued, are gradually introduced to Jewish religious and national life by their families and the community through children's rituals associated with individual holidays and with their own life-cycle milestones. "Alongside these children's rites, celebrations, and amusements, all of which have a religious and national character, there also exists a significant oral literature that aids in children's home upbringing, provides food for their thought, and develops their imagination."[101] An-sky felt that it was essential to study informal modes of cultural transmission as well as the formal system of schooling in order to understand the development and upbringing of Jewish children.

It was this less formal mode of cultural transmission that An-sky sought to uncover and document in his ethnographic expedition. "The Jewish people," he wrote in the introduction to his *Jewish Ethnographic Program*,

> have not without reason had the honor of the highest title to which a people can aspire, the honorific title of People of the Book. The book has been and remains to this day the most important basis of Jewish life. But together with the book, with the great written Torah that we have received as an inheritance for hundreds of generations of the chosen ones—righteous and great individuals, thinkers and leaders—we possess another Torah, an Oral Torah, that the people themselves, the masses, have never ceased to create during the course of their long, difficult, and tragic historical lives. This Oral Torah, which stems from folk stories and legends, parables and aphorisms, songs and melodies, customs, mores, beliefs, etc., is also an immense important creation of the same Jewish spirit as the written Torah [and] reflects the beauty and purity of the Jewish soul, the tenderness and civility of the Jewish heart, the height and depth of Jewish thought.[102]

An-sky was adamant in his insistence that all aspects of Jewish life had to be documented, echoing Dubnow's exhortations to record everything. The *Jewish Ethnographic Program* he developed and published in 1914 was intended as a guide to Jewish ethnographers, providing them with both practical advice and a detailed questionnaire. The first volume alone included 2,087 questions. In his introduction, An-sky urged ethnographers to record all the particulars of the individual with whom they were speaking—"their first and last name, their parents, their professions, the town or city in which they live, and the time (day, month, year)"; to "write exactly as the locals speak, even if it is not grammatically correct"; to "make absolutely certain you only record answers you have heard correctly"; and to "write the answers in a dedicated notebook, preferably on one side of the paper, with clear, light, and legible writing."[103] The questions were organized according to the Jewish life cycle with sections addressing "the child," "from *kheyder* to the wedding," "the wedding," "family life," and "death." The first question asked about the nature of the soul before it enters the body and the final question asked "what type of life will there be after the resurrection of the dead." Between these two questions, An-sky and his team devised questions about beliefs, customs, and rites relative to hundreds of life events. The section on the child, for instance, had over 300 questions on pregnancy, midwifery, childbirth and labor, the first week of life, circumcision, *pidyon ha-ben* (redemption of the firstborn son), wet nurses, the suckling child, *upsherenish* (the first hair-cut), and early education. Questions ranged from the prosaic—"What do you say when a child sneezes?"—to the peculiar "Is there a custom that before you lay a child down in a cradle you should put a cat and a piece of gingerbread there? What do you whisper into the cat's ear?"

An-sky's passion for the collection of folklore was contagious. Inspired by his work, especially by the visits of his expedition, small-town intellectuals began their own campaigns to document and preserve local customs and folklore. One resident of Kremenits (Volhynia Province) recalled:

> The Yiddish language ceased to be only a national and political symbol; it also took on a spirituality and the character of the folk. All the customs and ways of life, stories, legends, expressions about the evil eye, placing garlic on gravestones, throwing a pebble when one meets a priest on the road, the hymns one sings over one's bed during childbirth, the prayers one says for the child during childbirth, the rolling of eyes over a terrified child, and so on—everything the Jews of Kremenits used to do in their lives was perceived by the youth as a higher cultural word.[104]

This impetus to find new ways of collecting folk culture and presenting it in accessible forms united An-sky's approach to ethnography with Dubnow's approach to history and defined the people's perception of their own culture. Both saw within their respective fields of study living remnants of the Jewish world as it stood. Both agreed that the Jewish people were much more than subjects of academic scholarship; they were active participants in the collection and recording of living memory. Both agreed, as well, that the institutional infrastructure the JHES made available could serve as a viable framework for the public presentation of the essence of Jewish collective memory and, in the process, the reconstruction of Jewish public life.

Public History: Imagining Russian Jews

The historians associated with the JHES regarded history as a tool for advancing their vision of the present and disseminating research about the past. Although they preferred to think of themselves as contributors to a professional field that relied on scientific values, they were equally concerned with creating a utilitarian conception of Jewish history that would advance their vision of a secular, liberal national identity. *Jewish Antiquities* sought to teach its readers how best to function as a semi-autonomous Jewish community within the structure of the modern state and how to articulate and assert a distinct public culture.

Most nineteenth-century Russian Jewish historians sought to prove the antiquity of the Jewish presence in Russia in order to justify the extension of legal rights to Russian Jews. For instance, Avraham Harkavy hoped to advance the goal of emancipation by arguing that Russian Jews were the descendants of ancient Jewish colonies in the Black Sea and the Caucasus that predated the Russian state rather than immigrants from Germany in the thirteenth century. By concentrating on the earliest Jewish settlements on the Eurasian land mass, many of the historians of Harkavy's day downplayed the impact of Russian rule and Russian state borders on the history of Russian Jewry.[1] Instead, many of those who polemicized on the topic sought to demonstrate the interconnectedness of Jews and Slavs. They hoped that by publicizing evidence linking the past of the two nations, they would provide justification for granting equal rights to Jews in the present. For later generations of Russian Jewish historians, who were more concerned with defining Russian Jewish identity than with proving the antiquity of Jewish settlements, the issue of the genesis of East European Jewry was also central, albeit for different reasons. For them, the prehistory of Jewish settlement in Russia constituted the origin myth of their people, defining their ethnicity and consequently their very nationhood.

Thus, for the first historians of Russian Jewry, the important questions of the origins of their community were debated largely on ideological grounds. Those who sought to distance Russian Jewry from the rest of European Jewry argued that the forefathers of Russian Jews had converted during the Middle Ages. The specific version of who converted, why, and when varied among these historians, but the version spread most widely was that of Sergei Bershadskii, who suggested that most Russian Jews were ethnic Slavs who fell under Khazar rule and converted to Judaism along with the Khazars. Harkavy contended that the first Jews in the Russian Empire were Caucasian Jews who arrived in the Caucasus from the ancient kingdoms of Judea and Israel during the persecutions of Nebuchadnezzar and Sargun. Others believed they were Persian Jews who had fled the Babylonian and Persian empires in the seventh century. German Jewish historian Heinrich Graetz believed that the first settlers were Byzantine Jews who arrived during the eighth and ninth centuries. Still others contended they were Greek Jews who migrated to the Bosporus Peninsula in the first century. Despite their differences, all these theories shared the assumption that Jews first arrived in the lands of Russia before the Russian state was formed.

Twentieth-century scholarship has concluded that in fact the majority of Russian Jews are descendants from Jewish immigrants who fled the Rhineland during the twelfth and thirteenth centuries, motivated to come east by the push of anti-Jewish discrimination in German lands and the pull of generous privileges granted by Polish and Lithuanian monarchs. The Jewish immigration also corresponded with a general German migration eastward into the lands of what would become the Polish-Lithuanian Commonwealth. By the early twentieth century, most scholars accepted this theory, including those based in Galicia, but specialists in Russia itself were generally slower to accept it.

The Jews in a Multinational Empire

Russian Jewish historians regarded the spoken language of medieval East European Jewry as important evidence of the ethnic origins of the first Jewish settlers in Russian imperial lands. It is little surprise, therefore, that the first article published in *Jewish Antiquities,* Dubnow's "The Spoken Language of Polish-Lithuanian Jewry," directly addressed ongoing debates about the origins of the Jewish community in Poland and its relationship with the host community. In this work, Dubnow set himself apart from the deans of East European Jewish history, Harkavy and Bershadskii, both of whom believed that Jews during the Golden Age of the Polish-Lithuanian Commonwealth generally spoke Slavic languages.[2] Harkavy believed that Ukrainian Jews did not acquire Yiddish until they fled westward into Poland during the persecutions of the seventeenth century. Dubnow, however, criticized Bershadskii and Harkavy for basing their conclusions primarily on official documents and complaints from Jews to Christian courts. Obviously, he argued, such petitions would be written in Slavic languages—Christian officials could hardly have been expected to be literate in Yiddish or Hebrew, and in any case supplicants were expected to write in the language of the authority to whom they were appealing. Using documents generated within the Jewish community such as responsa literature, biblical concordances, and other rabbinic materials, Dubnow showed that Jews in the sixteenth century actually spoke a Yiddish dialect. Whereas Bershadskii and Harkavy had been interested in placing the Jewish community of Eastern Europe within the orbit of the Slavic nation, Dubnow sought to demonstrate Jewish difference and demonstrated that historically the Jews had possessed their own language, their own system of meaning, and their own distinct culture.

Dubnow also showed that the radical difference of their language did not prevent Jews from fully partaking in the social, economic, and political life of the surrounding society. In the early modern Polish-Lithuanian Commonwealth, he argued, Jews understood local Slavic languages and functioned in a multilingual realm. In some legal cases, Jewish witnesses quoted conversations with their Slavic neighbors in Slavic dialects. Many learned men understood Hebrew, but the authors of the first printed materials of the sixteenth century found it necessary to explain difficult Hebrew passages in Yiddish. Dubnow argued that during the golden age of Polish Jewry, Jews were able to preserve their own linguistic, and hence national, identity while simultaneously acting as full participants in Polish and Lithuanian civic life.[3] This first article set the stage for the journal to advocate for a distinct Jewish public culture to be articulated within a larger multinational society thorough the medium of autonomous institutions.

The principle of polylingualism was a recurring theme in the writings of the JHES. Historian and publicist David Maggid (1862–1942), for instance, showed through an analysis of macaronic spells and incantations that Jewish folklore developed in close proximity to the folklore of the surrounding peoples. At times, it was difficult to determine if a given spell is of Jewish or non-Jewish origins. "Perhaps," wrote Maggid, "it is the collective work of Jews and non-Jews."[4] In the keynote address Mikhail Kulisher delivered to the society's 1910 general assembly, he emphasized commonalities between Jews and their neighbors, noting similarities in superstitions and political organization.[5] Samuel Weissenberg was interested in the similarity of the amulets Jews and Christians wore in southern Russia.[6] Each of these writers imagined a pluralistic society in which a distinct Jewish culture existed in tandem with neighboring cultures, each benefiting from mutual influence. Without denying the often-hostile relations that existed between individual Jews and their neighbors, each of these contributors imagined two cultures that retained distinct characteristics while developing harmoniously. When the two cultures interacted, they merged to form a new hybrid culture comprised of elements of both. The members of the JHES rejected both the assimilationist dream that minority cultures could join the dominant culture on an equal basis and the enlightenment ideal of universal human attributes. Instead, they celebrated diversity and difference.

One of the corollary effects of Jewish emancipation wherever it occurred was the loss of Jewish corporate identity. Many of the thinkers associated with the Jewish enlightenment and its offshoots were concerned with replacing this identity. The most extreme of those offshoots advocated outright assimilation, including even apostasy, as a means of permanently eradicating the mark of Judea upon the world or at least as a practical means of attaining social and occupational positions that would otherwise be closed to them. Others, including the preeminent *maskil* Judah Leib Gordon (1831–1892), famously called upon their co-religionists to be "a man in the street and a Jew in your home" in emulation of the "Germans of the Mosaic Faith" who believed that all that separated the Jews from those in whose midst they lived was personal faith. Still others, particularly in the German lands, advocated a complete reform of the Jewish religion in order to bring Jewish ritual practice into agreement with contemporary fashion and Jewish law into agreement with modern European legal norms.

The populist intelligentsia that formed around the JHES, in contrast, believed that the solution to the disintegration of the Jewish community in the aftermath of emancipation, even the limited and selective emancipation of Russia, was to strengthen Jewish communal activity within the legal structure of the imperial multinational state.

The ideology of the JHES was reflected both in its proceedings and in the writings it chose to publish in its flagship journal. The new direction the JHES took can be ascertained by comparing its concerns with the concerns of the *maskilic* generation of historians that preceded it. One issue, for instance, that concerned some of the most prominent *maskilic* historians of the Russian Empire, from Samuel Joseph Fuenn to Mordechai Aaron Guenzberg, was Jewish dress. The *maskilim* had advocated against wearing traditional Jewish dress, which they were convinced contributed to perceptions that Jews were separate and acted as a "mark on the forehead of the Jews as a sign of their religion."[7] The JHES mocked such admonitions. Writing in St. Petersburg in 1912, in circles where traditional Jewish dress was largely a historical curiosity, Dubnow published decrees forbidding traditional Jewish dress issued under Alexander II that, in his words, "sketch a tragic-comic picture of this campaign."[8] The debate over the precise size of permitted beards and the distinction between Russian and German frockcoats—the former have a length of four vershoks (approximately 18 cm) from the ground, whereas the latter go to the knees—struck some twentieth-century observers as absurd. Whereas Guenzburg and Fuenn had endorsed such decrees as impetuses toward incorporating the Jewish community into genteel and gentile society, Dubnow and the JHES saw them as examples of the forceful intrusion of the state into the internal affairs of the Jewish community. The decrees on dress were a link in the vast chain of discriminatory legislation that interfered with Jewish life and were designed to coerce the Jews into assimilation. They were, in essence, merely a less noxious variation on the forced baptisms of the medieval period. Although Dubnow certainly did not think such dress styles should be emulated in the modern world, he regarded traditional Jewish dress as a valuable ethnographic trait of the community and as an authentic expression of Jewish culture. No longer embarrassed by the strange garb of their co-religionists—at least not when represented historically in a faraway place—Dubnow was able to regard the garments as public and visible expressions of cultural difference, allowing the Jews of that age to fulfill the role assigned to them in the social structure of the time while simultaneously maintaining their difference from the larger community. Dubnow himself preferred contemporary European suits, as did most of those associated with the society.

The JHES described precedents from an idealized past in an effort to advocate for a better future. One of the primary examples of this process was the publication of the minute book of the Council of Lithuanian Lands, which was published first in installments as a supplement to *Jewish Antiquities* and later as an independent volume. The publication of these minutes was an integral project of the JHES that was forestalled only in 1914 due to wartime censorship regulations forbidding the publication of Hebrew texts.[9] Unfortunately, the minute book of the larger and more significant Council of Four Lands was not preserved. However, many of its decisions were recorded in regional minute books, some of which had previously been published,[10] and others of which appeared for the first time in *Jewish Antiquities*.[11] Dubnow regarded Jewish communal bodies as the institutional expression of Jewish public culture, which he characterized in his "Letters on Old and New Judaism" as "spiritual-historical."[12] Dubnow believed that in the halcyon pre-emancipation days, communal Jewish autonomy served as a surrogate state and the *kahal* as its governmental apparatus:

> For the Jews, communal autonomy had enormous national and cultural significance; it united and strengthened the Jewish nation among hostile peoples and at the same time civilized the Jewish masses and accustomed them to social discipline, self-rule and self-help. The Jew felt himself as a living part of an active national organism; he had his own social and spiritual center and was a complete person. . . . The Jew sacrificed his individual freedom, willingly or unwillingly, for the sake of national discipline.[13]

Dubnow's appreciation for Jewish communal records was shared by others throughout Europe, most notably by Yitzhak Fritz Baer, who drew attention to the protocols of the Jewish council of Cleve in the early modern period in order to provide historical precedents for Jewish communal autonomy.[14]

Pantheon of Historical Heroes

Like all histories, the history constructed by the members of the JHES had its "pantheon of historical heroes," figures of the past who were presented as examples of the values of the present.[15] They are harbingers who were often persecuted in their own time or were pivotal figures around whom new values emerged. For *maskilic* historians of the nineteenth century, the historical heroes most often elevated to the pantheon were Baruch Spinoza and Moses Mendelssohn. Mendelssohn in particular was praised by many (but by no means all) *maskilim* for his alleged wisdom in matters both secular and religious and for his righteousness, modesty, sense of social justice, communal activity, and engagement with the gentile world. In the pantheon of the JHES, the latter trait was elevated to a supreme role. Jewish historical heroes were extolled for actively partaking in general society while retaining their own autonomous values and culture.

One of the models for this type of relationship was the leader of Tadeusz Kościuzsko's Jewish regiment, Berek Joselewicz. Joselewicz was born in Kretinga near Kovno sometime between 1765 and 1770. He received a traditional Jewish education before becoming an agent of the bishop of Vilna. Joselewicz accompanied the liberal bishop on his frequent trips to Paris, where in the bishop's beloved salons Joselewicz acquired the French language and a familiarity with French political and philosophical affairs as they stood on the eve of the French Revolution. By the time Joselewicz left the service of the bishop to settle with his family in the Praga suburb of Warsaw, he had become a liberal freethinker. In September 1794, during the height of the Kościuszko rebellion, Joselewicz and Joseph Aronowicz applied to Kościuszko for permission to form a Jewish regiment of light cavalry volunteers to join the Polish liberation. Kościuszko agreed and appointed Joselewicz the commander of the new regiment. The regiment attracted approximately 500 volunteers in less than three weeks. On 4 November, the regiment participated in the defense of Praga, where most of the recruits "bravely met their ends" at the hands of the Russian troops. Joselewicz survived and fled through Austria to France, where he became a freemason. He served in Napoleon's Polish Legion and in 1805 participated in the Napoleonic campaigns against Austria. While in Napoleon's military service, he received the medal of the Légion d'Honneur. Three years later, after the establishment of the Duchy of Warsaw, Joselewicz's unit was incorporated into the Polish army and Joselewicz was welcomed into the lodge of United Polish Brethren. He was killed by Austrian troops in the 1809 battle of Kock while fighting for the Polish army of the newly created Grand Duchy of Warsaw.

The discussion of Joselewicz was stimulated by the 100th anniversary of his death. In 1909, the Lemberg-based Jewish journal *Jedność* (Unity) published a collection of documents dealing with his life and historian Ernest Luninski published the first account of his life based on archival materials.[16] In a speech delivered on the occasion of the anniversary and subsequently published in the Polish journal *Przegląd historyczny* (Historical Review), David Kandel portrayed Joselewicz as a proponent of Jewish assimilation who followed in the tradition of sectarians and apostates Shabbetai Zvi and Jacob Frank. The portrayal of Joselewicz as an assimilationist was vehemently rejected in numerous articles that appeared in *Jewish Antiquities*. Galician Jewish historian Majer Balaban lambasted Kandel's speech. In addition to its numerous factual errors, he argued, Kandel's interpretation was completely ahistorical and turned Joselewicz into a polemical tool devoid of real historical attributes. Balaban also challenged Kandel's assertion that the Jews lost their national attributes after the 1648 Chmielnicki rebellion, which destroyed numerous Jewish communities in Ukraine, and therefore had no choice but to assimilate with the surrounding peoples.[17]

In her review of Ernest Luninski's historical account, Sofia Dubnova, Simon's daughter, writing under the pseudonym S. Mstislavskaia, chastised polemicists for viewing Joselewicz as either a proponent of assimilation or as a nationalist, as though the two sentiments were inherently incompatible. "By simple instinct," she wrote "he cut the Gordian knot of two interlaced affections: love of one's people and love of one's motherland." She extolled the colonel as an exemplar of Jewish participation in universal society and as a reflection of the general sentiments of Polish Jewry at the time. She admired Joselewicz because his regiment functioned as a Jewish national institution within the framework of Polish society and argued that it was a concrete example of Jews participating as Jews within Polish society, expressing their distinct culture in public.[18]

Dubnow contributed to the debate several years later, following his daughter in emphasizing the fact that the regiment was a separate Jewish unit. Both Dubnow and his daughter quote at length from the appeal Joselewicz issued to attract volunteers to his regiment, which was full of biblical images and phrasings: "Hear, o sons of the tribes of Israel, all in whose hearts is implanted the image of the Lord Almighty, all who seek to help fight for the fatherland."[19] The appeal provides evidence that Joselewicz was consciously identifying as a Jew and urging his followers to do the same. Joselewicz was by no means an advocate of mass baptism or submission in the image of Shabbetai Zvi and Jacob Frank but rather proudly proclaimed his Jewish heritage and the future role of Jews in the defense of the Polish state. *Jewish Antiquities* published numerous articles giving examples of Jews who sympathized with and supported the state in which their community lived. Evidence of Jewish remembrance and commemoration of the Kościuszko insurrection was one of the most obvious examples.[20]

One of Dubnow's allies in promoting a liberal vision of Jewish public culture through the study of Jewish communal life was Galician Jewish historian Majer Balaban. In his article on Jewish participation in the Spring of Nations uprising of 1848, Balaban celebrated the role enlightened Jews played in opposing Metternich, singling out for praise Adolf Fischhoff and Gabriel Riesser. Fischhoff (1816–1893) was one of the leaders of the group that gathered in the Viennese palace courtyard on 13 March 1848 to demand the removal of Metternich. In Balaban's words, "At the head of the gathered masses stood a Jew—the great fighter for freedom, Dr. Adolf Fischhoff."[21] He was appointed head of the Committee of Public Security by the revolutionary government and was a member of its parliament. Often considered one of the intellectual forefathers of autonomism, Fischhoff advocated a federal system of government based on self-governing bodies for each of the empire's national minorities independent of territorial borders. Fischhoff's program of national autonomy anticipated not only Dubnow's autonomism but also the national program of Austro-Marxism. Riesser (1806–1863) was a Jewish statesman from Hamburg who was a member of the Temporary Parliament of Frankfurt and briefly served as the vice-president of the National Assembly. In his writings, Riesser insisted that Jewish emancipation should not depend on conversion and advocated the formation of Jewish public associations. He later played a prominent role in the formation of the Hamburg Temple, which spearheaded the reform movement in Judaism. Dubnow regarded him as "a tireless fighter for the emancipation of peoples without rights," although he criticized him for using the rhetoric of assimilation.[22] Balaban and Dubnow lionized Riesser, just as they had Joselewicz, for participating in general civic and political institutions while continuing to publicly identify as a Jew and partake in Jewish communal life.

Balaban also added local heroes to this international pantheon. Among these was the Bohemian-born preacher and district rabbi of Lemberg, Abraham Kohn, a *maskilic* advocate of educational and religious reform. He was a leader of the group that seized control of the Lemberg *kahal* in the 1840s and was appointed district rabbi of the city by the Austrian authorities. During the revolutionary period, he signed a petition by a group of Lemberg liberals that demanded full equality for all subjects, regardless of social class and religion. He also participated in the delegation to Vienna that presented the petition to the government. Balaban's history was not without its villains. Chief among these was the Ruzhin dynasty of Hasidism from whom Kohn and his followers had to wrest control of the Lemberg *kahal*. Balaban wrote of Israel Friedman, the dynasty's *tsadik*, who was implicated in the murder of two Jewish informants, that he was "a new type of *tsadik*. Being ignorant of Talmud, or knowing very little, in contrast to other Podolian and Volhynian *tsadiks*, he tried to win hearts with external splendor. He set up a magnificent palace, had many servants, traveled in a carriage harnessed with six horses, distributed money to the poor, and in this way obtained glory among his followers from who he received luxurious presents that allowed him to live in luxury."[23] For

Balaban, Israel of Ruzhin represented all the negative attributes of Jewish life in Galicia—corruption, parochialism, and ignorance. The story of Kohn, though, hardly ends well. Although he did achieve a victory over the religious radicals when he was installed as district rabbi of Lemberg, his victory was short lived. He died of poisoning in 1848, most likely the victim of a murder perpetrated by his Jewish opponents.[24]

Balaban showed that Jews participated in every stage of the uprising in Galicia. Even in the Cracow Jewish community, where the reaction to the events of 1848 was more reserved, Jews mourned the loss of the Polish victims as martyrs and Polish newspapers cited the involvement of Jews in the uprising. "The fact itself of the enrollment of Jews in the National Guard as well as their admission to the National Assembly and to the newly formed city councils gives evidence that at this time a general platform was beginning to be built for all residents of the country regardless of religion," he wrote.[25] Despite their separate cultural identities, he continued, Jews and Poles shared in a basic concern for humanistic justice: "The Jewish intelligentsia, without even knowing a single word of Polish, related to the victims of absolutism with profound sentiments."[26] All these examples demonstrated that a humanistic public culture could be articulated on a national basis.

Humanism and Nationalism

The relationship between humanism and nationalism was also the subject of the first lecture sponsored by the JHES, delivered by Dubnow. "Processes of Humanism and Nationalism in Modern Jewish History" provided a theoretical framework for the society's vision of Jewish public culture in the past, present, and future. Dubnow began his address by critiquing Jewish historiography for adhering to theological methods on one hand and teleological methods on the other:

> The old theological method, which viewed Jewish history as a chain of events regulated by providence, persists today only among orthodox believers, but contemporary science has done little to displace the tele-ological method, which measures Jewish history from the perspective of a defined religious-ethical "mission" being fulfilled by the Jewish nation. . . . The difference between theology and teleology is that the first centers historical processes around a providential force external to the nation, whereas the latter centers it around a providential force immanent to the nation itself.[27]

Both methods, in other words, regarded history as perpetually progressing toward a definite, immutable, and unalterable goal. For the proponents of theological history, that goal was the messianic age, the world to come; for teleological historians, the goal was a return to an idealized world of the past.

In contrast, Dubnow proposed a "scientific evolutionary method" that would concentrate on change through time. Following Herder, Dubnow did not believe that history progressed toward a particular goal; rather, he posited that it evolved as an organism. The evolution of nations was a product of the vacillation between universal values and parochial interests: "One leads to the development of national peculiarities and the other leads to the merging of a national community with the surrounding culture, or universality."[28] The central determinants in a nation's evolution are both the individual traits with which its people are endowed and that evolve based on their interactions with surrounding peoples and environments and universal values shared by all peoples. These two determinants can be called nationalism and humanism. "A normal historical evolution," he concluded, "consists of the harmonious development of both processes—humanism and nationalism."[29] Those cultures able to achieve this balance would become a normal healthy people. Those that allowed nationalism to overcome humanism would become xenophobic and exploitative, while those that suppressed their communal interests in favor of humanistic values would become exploited and lose their political independence. The Jews, argued Dubnow, had historically erred on the side of the latter, particularly in the modern period. "Modern Jewish history shows no manifestation of extreme nationalism, only of extreme de-nationalism. There is no centripetal tension, only centrifugal tension. . . . The contemporary Jew cloaks himself in universal culture, remakes himself into a foreign nation, and essentially loses the connection to his own nation."[30] This tendency was most evident in the path of Jewish emancipation in Western Europe, where Dubnow believed the Jews had surrendered their communal language, literature, and sovereignty in exchange for the promise of equal rights as individuals.

The members of the JHES who shared this aspect of Dubnow's vision sought to find historical examples of a balance between humanism and nationalism. They found them in Berek Joselewicz, Adolf Fischhoff, the Council of Four Lands, Jewish usage of the Yiddish language, and macaronic songs and proverbs. Jewish public culture in the Russian Empire, Dubnow insisted, needed to follow these precedents and balance national distinctness with universal ideals. In order to facilitate this vision, he advocated emancipation for Jews not just as isolated individuals but as a communal body that would retain national rights and autonomous institutions. He optimistically believed that the twentieth century would finally see a balanced resolution between humanism and nationalism.[31]

Conceptions of Russian Jewry

More complex than the relationship between Jews and Slavs, though, was the relationship between different Jewish communities within the Russian Empire. Paragraph 3 of the charter of the JHES states: "The region of activity of the society is the entire territory of the Russian Empire."[32] This clause echoed those of similar societies formed in Western Europe, such as that of the Jewish Historical Society of London, whose charter stated: "The objects of the Society shall be: a) the promotion and organisation of research into and study of, the history of the Jews of the British Empire."[33] The JHES insisted that the histories of ancient Jewish settlements in the colonies be incorporated into the imperial narrative. In Dubnow's introduction to the first issue of *Jewish Antiquities*, he articulated the goal of encompassing the entire region of imperial Russia by including in its purview the entire history of Poland, including periods that predated its incorporation into the Russian Empire: "We intend to embrace all epochs—from the development of Jewish settlements in ancient Rus and Poland to the present times; our range of interests encompass the Dark Ages of medieval times, as well as the bright prospects of modern times and the recent past, through which our generation is living."[34] Dubnow and the other St. Petersburg–based founders of the JHES sought to embrace the geographic area of the Russian Empire as it stood in their own time at the beginning of the twentieth century as a legitimate framework for envisioning the extent of Russian Jewry. In practice, they found that this was a harder vision to maintain than their rhetoric implied. For instance, despite the relative novelty of a Russian Empire that incorporated the lands of the former Polish-Lithuanian Commonwealth, the society saw fit to include the entire history of the Commonwealth under the rubric of the history of the Russian Empire. In its acceptance of the early-twentieth-century borders of imperial Russia as legitimate historical and national boundaries, the Jewish Historical and Ethnographic Society sought to form a new sense of cultural identity among its constituents. Although most JHES members recognized the vast differences among the Jewish communities within this broad rubric, the historians who constituted the leadership of the society nevertheless felt it proper to include all within a single category, regardless of the separatist tendencies of individual communities. Thus, the JHES leadership implicitly imposed Russian imperialist notions of nationality upon its subject communities.

It should be noted, however, that many of the historians of the JHES were ardent opponents not only of tsarist policies toward the Jews but also of tsarist rule in general and even belonged to opposition political parties. Thus, political opposition to the tsarist order coexisted with a cultural or intellectual endorsement of the imperial project. This is hardly unusual in the history of historiography. Many have observed before the imperialist tendencies of national histories that fold peripheral communities into a single narrative rubric. However, in this case it was not the conquerors cementing a military conquest by enforcing their own historical narratives upon their subjects. Rather, many Jews embraced imperial boundaries as both a means of solidifying awareness of Russian Jewish identity within the Jewish community and of communicating with Russian society through the recognized categories of national minorities and imperial borders. The JHES's sanction of these borders led many of its members to construct a narrative that provided a justification for greater rights for Jews and recognition of a distinct Russian Jewish national identity within the empire. These Jewish historians constructed an imagined proto-nation that embraced all Jewish groups in the Russian Empire while at the same time differentiating it from non-Jews within the same geographic area and from other Jews outside its borders.

The problem with this endeavor was that the territory of the Russian Empire did not correspond to the way the Jewish communities living within its borders traditionally defined their own communal limits. The nucleus of the community and the largest segment of the Jewish population in the Russian Empire was the Ashkenazic community of the dismembered Polish-Lithuanian Commonwealth, who despite geographic, ideological, linguistic, and other differences had since at least the eighteenth century shared many basic cultural assumptions and historical perceptions. The Jews of the Polish-Lithuanian Commonwealth constituted only a segment of an even larger bloc of world Jewry—Ashkenaz. But with the advent of the Haskalah and subsequent formation of nation-states in Western and Central Europe, Ashkenaz as a collective identity diminished in importance. It had largely failed to adapt to the new conditions of nationalism that emerged throughout Europe. Instead, Jews in the lands of Ashkenaz grafted new national identities onto preexisting Jewish notions of the self. The Ashkenazic Jews of the French Rhineland became French Jews, whereas those on the east side of the Rhine became German Jews or even "Germans of the Mosaic Faith." In the mid-nineteenth century, though, Jews living in imperial Russia had not yet adopted the identity of "Russian Jews." Instead, the Ashkenazic segments of this population, which lived in the lands of the former Polish-Lithuanian Commonwealth, were widely regarded by Jews of Western Ashkenaz as Ostjuden (Eastern Jews).

This bloc of world Jewry was united by a common language—Yiddish in one of several eastern variants—as well as several shared historical experiences, including a religious life dominated by Hasidism (either in support of or in opposition to it), similar socioeconomic roles, and living arrangements in *shtetls*. It included not only most of the former Polish-Lithuanian Commonwealth but also parts of what became neighboring Romania and Hungary.[35] However, the Polish partitions had divided this population, most evidently by excluding Galicia from the Russian Empire, annexing it instead to the Austro-Hungarian Empire. Although Galicia was the most obvious region whose Jewish population was excluded from the new category of Russian Jewry, it was not the only one. The new imperial borders of the Russian Empire cut across the territory of the Ostjuden. The new Russian Jewish identity had to take these anomalies into account.

The Russian Jewish community was innovative not only in terms of those it excluded but also in terms of those it included. The territory of the Russian Empire embraced numerous Jewish communities whose cultural identities had little in common with the Ashkenazic majority. These included Bukharan Jews of Central Asia, Tat-speaking Mountain Jews of the Caucasus, Greek Jews in the Crimea, Karaites, and even Subbotniks (Sabbath Observers). The JHES's charter obligated it to amalgamate the histories of these communities with those of the Ashkenazic Jews. The proponents of a Russian Jewish identity knew that the test of their success would be how well they would be able to incorporate these liminal groups in their rubric. As a subaltern group within the empire themselves, the leaders of the JHES were particularly sensitive to the need for inclusiveness. For this reason, *Jewish Antiquities* and the JHES spent a good deal of effort on these marginal communities. Through an analysis of the limits of Russian Jewry, those communities who are borderline by virtue of geographic location or cultural distance from the Ashkenazic Jews of the former Polish-Lithuanian Commonwealth, we can examine the process of consolidating Russian Jewry.

Karaites

The Karaites are a Jewish sect characterized primarily by their rejection of the Talmud and rabbinical tradition. Traditional Karaite histories trace their origins to ancient Israelite schisms from the reign of Jeroboam in the tenth century BCE . More likely they came into being in eighth-century Babylon under the influence of eastern Islam and the leadership of Anan ben David. The first Karaite communities in the territory of the Russian Empire emerged sometime during the Tatar conquest of the thirteenth century, when Karaite communities appeared in the Crimea, probably having emigrated from Byzantium. By the end of the fourteenth century, many Karaites had migrated to Lithuania, forming significant communities in Troki, Lutsk, and Halicz. Although Polish authorities had treated the Karaites similarly to rabbinical Jews, once they came under Russian rule, the two communities began to separate.[36]

One of the major theories of the origins of Russian Jewry, against which Dubnow and others fought, was that advanced by Abraham Firkovich, who in the 1830s claimed to have found documentation demonstrating that the Karaites had settled in the lands of Russia in antiquity and were even the first settlers of the Crimean peninsula, arriving before the time of Jesus. Firkovich used these documents to polemicize against imposing the same prohibitions on the Karaites as those the Jews suffered. The Karaites, he maintained, were a completely different group.[37] Firkovich's arguments were very successful: in 1828 Karaites were exempted from military service, and in 1863 they were given full citizenship. Although Harkavy later showed that Firkovich had falsified names and dates and even made up crucial parts of the documents, many Karaite historians and activists continued to resist identification with rabbinical Jews.[38]

Along with the refutation of Firkovich's scholarship came a reaction against his ideology and support for Karaite independence. Liberal historian Iulii Gessen, for instance, looked back upon a period when Karaites and Jews were equated in legal discourse. He showed that the privileges Grand Duke Witold of Lithuania granted to the Jews of Troki, dated 24 June 1388, probably referred to the Karaites of Troki rather than the rabbinical Jews, as did the privileges he granted to the Jews of Brest one week later. Yet both seem to have been applied to rabbinical Jews in practice. Similarly, most official documents of the next century and a half (including the privileges granted by Casimir Jagiello in 1441, Aleksander in 1492, and

Sigismund I in 1507) did not recognize the Karaites as a distinct community and presumably equated them with rabbinical Jews. Although the Jews and Karaites were continually engaged in polemics against each other, argued Gessen, they were regarded as a single legal community throughout the fifteenth century.

The first instance Gessen could find of the Karaites seeking separate status was in 1514, when Mikhail Yosefovich was appointed elder of all Lithuanian Jews, at which point the Karaites of Troki petitioned the king not to be counted as Lithuanian "Jews." Their petition was approved. The legal separation of Jews and Karaites continued in many respects from this point on and was affirmed by the Russian government after the partitions, first when Catherine freed the Karaites of the double tax and permitted them to own land and then when Nicholas I exempted them from the military draft. In 1835, the government found that the 1388 privileges of Troki did not apply to rabbinical Jews and revoked their residency rights on this basis. Gessen ended his article with an appeal to reinstate the spirit of the ancient privileges that had allowed Jews and Karaites to live side by side as a single community.[39] By including articles on the Karaites in its flagship journal, the JHES implicitly included them in their history of the Russian Jews.

Central Asian, Caucasian, and Crimean Jewry

Ethnography, which in the late nineteenth and early twentieth centuries was closely related to both racial anthropology and travel writing, was often used by expanding empires to assert authority over remote subject peoples. Colonial administrators knew that knowledge of a society could be used to possess it. It was in this context that the Imperial Russian Geographic Society conducted its work to classify and describe the numerous communities over which the Russian Empire ruled. Ethnographers working in the service of the imperial project also recognized that in order to promote the ideology of a united state, it was crucial that residents of one region feel a sense of affinity with their new neighbors in another part of the state.[40] Similarly, the JHES sought to familiarize its readers with Jewish communities in Russia from beyond St. Petersburg, the Pale of Jewish Settlement, and Poland and to create a historical narrative for these peoples when a usable one was lacking. An article on Uralic Jews, for instance, complained of the lack of information available on the history of that community.[41] In his article on eighteenth-century historian David Ben

Eliezer Lekhno, Isaak Markon called for more attention to Crimean Jewry, especially for the publication of the Russian translation of Lekhno's *Devar sefatayim,* a Hebrew chronicle of the Crimean kingdom of the Tatars of the seventeenth and eighteenth centuries.[42]

In order to help remedy the lack of information about the non-Ashkenazic Jewish communities of Russia, the society sponsored an ethnographic expedition by Jewish anthropologist Samuel Weissenberg, who in 1912 traveled from Tashkent to Eupatoria, traversing Central Asia, the Caucasus, and the Crimea. In December, Weissenberg delivered his findings to a meeting of the JHES. His report, which was subsequently published in *Jewish Antiquities,* was filled with ethnographic observations on the language, customs, education, physical appearance, and religious observances of the Jews he encountered. Weissenberg, who was probably the most prominent Jewish anthropologist in Russia at the time, had made a reputation for himself both in Russia and abroad as a physical anthropologist and cultural ethnographer.[43] He opposed theories that posited universal Jewish racial characteristics and studied the differences among world Jewish communities. "Although by religion and national-spiritual temper they constitute a single common group," he wrote, "Jews of various countries differ from one another not only ethnologically—by language, beliefs, and habits—but also anthropologically—by type."[44] Weissenberg's previous research, based on extensive travel through the Near East, Europe, and Russia, had led him to advance the theory that world Jewry is divided into two fundamental types: the dolicocephalic (long-headed) Jews of North Africa and Palestine and the brachycephalic (broad-headed) Jews of Eastern Europe and Germany. The question that interested Weissenberg was how those he regarded as the original dolicocephalic Jews had become brachycephalic. The answer, he believed, lay in the Caucasus, where the Jews were also brachycephalic. He believed that this theory gave credence to the idea that modern Russian Jewry is descended from the pre-Christian Jewish communities of the Caucasus rather than from German Jews who fled Christian persecution in the medieval period. Thus, modern Russian Jews, he believed, were the descendents of the ancient Jewish communities of the Caucasus.

Like Harkavy and other historians of the previous generation, Weissenberg connected the Jews of the Caucasus and Eastern Europe to the Jews of Central Asia and Crimea, but Weissenberg came to his conclusions on the grounds of physiognomy, arguing that both groups were brachycephalic and had arrived in the region before it was christianized.

According to Weissenberg, not only are the Jews of Central Asia ethnically analogous to Ashkenazic Jewry but they are even ethnically related to non-Jewish populations of the Russian Empire. Further, Weissenberg continued, both Crimean Jews and Karaites are related to the possible progenitors of all Russian Jewry—the Khazars. His theory of the ethnic composition of Crimean Jewry emphasized the intermingling of Crimean Jews with Ashkenazic Russian Jews, cementing the geographic proximity of the two with ethnic mixing.

Weissenberg portrayed Russian Jewry as a mosaic, to which he ascribed hierarchical values. Following anthropological practice of his time, he located his subjects on a temporal trajectory, imagining all people gravitating toward a normative culture epitomized by the West European bourgeoisie. Those people he classified as backward, he endowed with a primitiveness and exoticism toward which his "modern" readers could nostalgically yearn. He located the non-Ashkenazic Jews of the Caucasus and Central Asia at the bottom of this hierarchy. He noted:

> The rather low cultural level of Mountain Jews and of Georgian Jews is particularly striking in comparison with the Armenians and Georgians among whom they live. At the time that the Armenians and Georgians were developing independent cultures, flourishing in breadth and depth despite unfavorable conditions, and their intelligentsia was enthralling the entire Caucasus, supplanting all that is foreign, the Jews remained behind. And if there was subsequently a turn for the better, it should not be ascribed completely to their own initiative; rather it is a result of the influence of Russian Jews, whose success called forth some emulation. The complete backwardness in everything, even in religious matters, has forced the Jews of the Caucasus to search for support among their Russian brethren.[45]

Weissenberg placed Georgian Jews on an even lower level than the Mountain Jews. The latter, he argued, had a higher standard of living, claimed to be an older group (tracing their descent to the Lost Tribes), and had their own language (Judeo-Tat), which he believed would help them preserve their unique customs against the hegemony of Ashkenazic Russian Jewry. Weissenberg predicted that Crimean Jews, on the other hand, would mix easily with Ashkenazic Jews:

> The origins of the Crimean Jews have been lost for centuries. One can only say that the Turkish blood in them is less than in the Karaites, although the well-known relationship of the two peoples with the

Khazars can hardly be denied. But the Crimean Jews during the Middle
Ages and modern times constantly mixed with their European brethren.
. . . In more recent times, the opportunity to mix with Russian Jews
became more frequent.[46]

In his public lectures and the series of articles he published on his travels,
Weissenberg articulated a vision of Russian Jewry that contained disparate
groups, each of which had their own perceptions of history, origin myths,
and cultures. Yet all were intermingled and connected, ultimately forming
a single diverse community, albeit one to which Weissenberg assigned clear
hierarchical values.

Subbotniks

In its efforts to amalgamate non-Ashkenazic Jewish communities
within the rubric of Russian Jewry, the JHES expanded the category to
embrace sects and religious groups not always identified as being Jewish.
For instance, it included the Subbotniks in its narrative of the history of
Russian Jewry. The Subbotniks were converts to Judaism from Russian
Orthodoxy who originated in Inner Russia (primarily Riazin, Saratov, and
Voronezh) and spoke Russian as their mother tongue. They observed the
Sabbath and prayed as Jews (in Hebrew whenever possible and with phylacteries and prayer shawls), observed Jewish dietary restrictions and laws
regarding ritual purity, and celebrated Jewish holidays. Nevertheless, as
Weissenberg observed, "among the Bukharan Jews the opinion is widespread that the Jews of the Caucasus are not Jews at all, but are proselytes."[47] In its efforts to be inclusive and to bring as many groups as possible
within the Russian Jewish collective it was constructing, the JHES decided
to include sectarians.

In 1913, the journal published a serialized article about the Subbotnik
community in Siberia. Dubnow identified the author as "a Subbotnik from
the village of Zima, in Irkutsk region (he signs 'Moisei Zakharov Kozmin,
from the Jewish Subbotnik sect'), who used to be a farmer, but now teaches
children Hebrew literacy and Bible in a Subbotnik *kheyder*." Dubnow followed up with a call to further investigate the group: "Welcoming this
first attempt to portray the unknown life of the Subbotniks from the perspective of one of their own, the editors of *Jewish Antiquities* will gladly
give a place for similar authentic accounts of the life of Jewish sectarians
(Subbotniks and other proselytes) in various places, particularly in the
Caucasus, where their numbers are very significant."[48]

The article was a compilation of information Kozmin gathered from his 83-year-old father together with Kozmin's personal observations. "Having begun to collect information on my co-religionists a long time ago," he wrote, "I did not intend on using this for publication, and was making notes only for myself and for the memory of my descendants. But on the advice of those who are interested in daily life and Subbotnik believers, I decided to make this information available for publication."[49] In addition to a historical account, the article provides ethnographic information on the community, describing their relations with Jews and their language, prayer houses, religious practices, daily life, economic situation, demography, and social life.

Throughout the article, Kozmin differentiated between "Jews" and Subbotniks with phrases such as "in the village of Zima, amidst the settlement of our Subbotniks, there lived several Jewish families,"[50] thereby taking for granted a distinction between the two groups. Kozmin noted that tension between Jews and Subbotniks had increased in recent years, with some Jews referring to Subbotniks as "ignorant goyim," and Subbotniks countering with the epithet "*zhid*." Intermarriage between the two groups was extremely rare, and when it did occur, the marriage usually failed. The only successful marriages between the two groups came when the husband was a Siberian-born Jew rather than a migrant from the Pale. Even more rare were intermarriages in which the husband was a Subbotnik and the wife a Jew. Thus, in most respects each community recognized its own distinctness and kept separate from the other.

As with all non-Ashkenazic groups, though, Kozmin admitted that a hierarchical relationship existed between the Subbotniks and the Ashkenazic Jews living in Siberia. The Subbotniks, according to Kozmin, were always entirely reliant upon the local Jewish population for knowledge of Jewish religious practices. Kozmin displayed a great deal of reverence toward Jews and described how the Subbotniks emulated Jewish practice and learned from resident Jews:

> The names of these good and noble people, the former teachers of our ancestors, were always recalled with reverence by my father. . . . This is confirmed in many of my father's stories of their good lives. It is evident that they were not aloof observers. Recognizing the religious poverty of our ancestors, who were like children, not knowing anything about the Jewish religion, they took them into their embrace. They were both teachers and mentors for the Subbotniks, leading them in close friendship.[51]

Kozmin wrote that in contemporary times, as well, the Subbotniks followed the example set by the Jews, even when that example was not a positive one, such as the failure to observe the Sabbath.[52]

Kozmin's narrative of Subbotnik history mirrored precisely that of Russian Jewry. His story began with anti-sectarian persecutions under Nicholas I and the expulsion of the Subbotniks to Siberia. Kozmin was very reverent toward the elder Subbotniks who retained their faith in the face of such persecutions. The story ended with a sense of apprehension about the future of the community. Kozmin lamented the decline of religious observance, noted the newfound predilection of the community's young people for secular learning (freethinking) and political parties, and chastised the community for intermarriage. In a warning that could have come from countless Jewish writings of the time, Kozmin wrote: "It is not very difficult to foresee their dismal future. Scarcely three to four generations have passed and they, whose religious spirit is not being preserved by anyone or anything, scatter like sheep without a shepherd and mix with the surrounding population."[53] By adhering to established tropes in contemporary Jewish historical writing, Kozmin seems to have sought to include Subbotniks within the narrative of Russian Jewry, a move Simon Dubnow and the other editors of *Jewish Antiquities* welcomed.

Galicia

The examples of the Karaites, Central Asian and Mountain Jews, and Subbotniks demonstrate the inclusiveness of the Russian Jewish identity the JHES advanced. The editors of *Jewish Antiquities* also accommodated a countervailing narrative that was chiefly advanced by a group of professional historians based in Austrian Galicia and led by Balaban. This group articulated a vision of Ashkenazic identity that included Galicia—indeed, was centered on Galicia—but excluded non-Ashkenazic Jews such as the Karaites. Rather than looking east to Central Asia for inspiration, they looked west to German Jews. The orientalist impulse that interested the Jewish elites of St. Petersburg was largely absent in Austrian Galicia, where the local Jews sought nothing more than to be considered European. Balaban, for instance, published an article in *Jewish Antiquities* that argued that in the early period of the Polish-Lithuanian Commonwealth, Red Ruthenian (Galician) Karaites retained completely separate existences from rabbinical Jews. They even used Tatar as their spoken language until the seventeenth century.[54] Balaban's Galician colleague Ignacy Schipper shared this opinion, pointing out that many cities in the fifteenth century registered the Karaites as a separate community.[55] Balaban's vision of Polish Jewry was far more connected to the Ashkenazic Jews of Western Europe than to the Karaites and Mountain Jews of the imperial Russian vision. His analysis of the legal history of Jews in Poland argued that Polish Jewish culture was derived first and foremost from that of Germany Jewry.

Although most scholars affiliated with the JHES recognized the tremendous impact migrations from Western and Central Europe had had on Russian Jewish history, the historical narrative Dubnow and others promoted nevertheless began with the Khazars. Even those who questioned the Khazar theory of the ethnic origin of Russian Jewry and denied cultural, ethnic, or spiritual linkages between the two groups still sometimes regarded the Khazars as the progenitors of Russian Jewry, often for no other reason than that they were among the first Jews to occupy the territorial space of what would become the Russian Empire. But Balaban rejected all attempts to trace the origins of modern Russian Jewry to the Khazars and argued that the German migrations of the thirteenth century provided the origins of Polish Jewry. Although some early settlers came from Khazaria, Balaban continued, it was from the later settlements of German Jews that Polish Jewry derived its cultural, religious, and legal traditions. Balaban argued that this is most evident in the thirteenth century privilege granted by Boleslav of Kalisz (1264), which he showed was clearly based on the prototypes of earlier privileges granted to the Jews of Austria by Friedrich II in 1244, which in turn were based on earlier eleventh-century privileges.[56] Balaban had no tolerance for speculation about Oriental Jewish origins: the Jews of Poland, he insisted, were thoroughly European.

In contrast to Dubnow, Gessen, and other members of the JHES based in the imperial capital who made their reputations on grand narratives of Jewish history in Russia, Balaban emphasized local history. The communities he studied were smaller entities, provinces (Galicia), cities (Lemberg), towns (Żółkiew), and even a single street (Lemberg's Ulica Żydowska). His focus on local history implicitly challenged the grand imperial narratives of the JHES. Although no consensus on the nature of Russian Jewry emerged, *Jewish Antiquities* and the JHES became important forums for delimiting, articulating, and propagating Jewish public history in the Russian Empire.

Conclusion: This World and the Next

For the Jewish community of the Russian Empire, the Great War was a battle between this world and the next. Fighting on the side of *this* world were the innumerable relief organizations, international aid societies, hospitals, soup kitchens, theater societies, literary groups, artists, and ordinary people who worked to maintain what they could of a normal social and cultural life in what was evidently a flawed but (some would say) ultimately salvageable world.[1] Fighting for the next world was a diverse group that included socialist revolutionaries, religious extremists, and diplomatic visionaries, all of whom were convinced that they could harness the raw energy of war to create another and better utopian world in place of the one the ideologues and tanks were destroying. Nowhere was the triumph of the "next-worldniks" greater than in Soviet Russia, where the thirst to destroy was insatiable.

One of the most powerful accounts of that war and the destruction it wrought among the Jewish community of Eastern Europe was written by S. An-sky, whose *Khurbn Galitsye* (Destruction of Galicia) chronicled the Jewish community of Austrian Galicia during these turbulent times. An-sky not only documented the destruction but also helped bring aid to the affected populations and worked with the JHES to preserve the cultural legacy of the Jewish communities under threat. Like many other associations and societies of the era, the JHES responded to the chaos of total war by reinventing itself as a voluntary aid society and playing an important role in collecting and preserving Jewish artifacts.

In the fall of 1915, the JHES leadership voted to embark on a campaign to transfer articles of historic and ethnographic value from the war zone to synagogues and other social institutions far from the front, where they could be preserved in relative safety. The JHES authorized An-sky, who was in the Pale of Settlement at the time conducting his ethnographic expedition, to take charge of such activity.[2] In January 1916, the committee decided to place advertisements in all the major Russian Jewish journals urging those who lived in the war zone to send objects or writings of "national significance" to the JHES for preservation. The society sent funds to B. N. Rubenshteyn, a member of the society who was in the Pale, to collect such items. The society also asked the Petrograd synagogue for permission to store Torah scrolls retrieved from the war zone in its sanctuary and sought additional resources from the Jewish Committee for the Relief of War Victims.[3] Rubenshteyn spent the next two months trying to negotiate a way to bring the holy objects and archival material to the newly renamed capital, Petrograd, before concluding that it could not be done without investing at least 1,000 rubles and that taking the items directly to Petrograd would not be possible. He recommended first collecting the objects in an urban center within the Pale, such as Minsk or Vitebsk, and from there arranging for relocation to the capital.[4] By March 1916, Rubenshteyn was working on collecting materials from the Vitebsk region, while An-sky was broadening his efforts to save material from the Kiev region. The JHES followed Rubenshteyn's advice and allocated an additional thousand rubles toward the effort while simultaneously asking the Petrograd synagogue to match its donation with another thousand rubles.[5] A private philanthropist helped fund the frantic effort with a donation of 3,000 rubles, but additional funds were still needed from the Petrograd Jewish Assistance Committee.[6] Unfortunately, wartime tariffs prevented the evacuation of the Torah scrolls from proceeding as planned.[7] By August it had become clear that the evacuation work had failed: Rubenshteyn was instructed to switch his efforts from recovery to documenting lost treasures.[8] In December, hope was restored when the Academy of Sciences announced a plan to rescue items of historic importance from the war zones. The JHES sent a letter detailing the inventory it had composed and asked the academy to continue the work it had begun.[9] Late in the year, the society succeeded in opening a Jewish Ethnographic Museum in Petrograd that included materials rescued from the front. However, the society closed the museum the following summer as revolutionary unrest swept through the capital, and it did not reopen it until 1923. In 1929, the Soviet government closed the museum and dispersed its collection to various academies and museums.[10] Without the expertise and devotion of the JHES, though, the project was never fully realized.

It was not just the JHES that moved from creative activity into preservation mode. The Warsaw Hazomir Society, which in better days had hosted Warsaw's Jewish literati, was converted into a homeless shelter: "There were more than fifty thousand homeless in the city," wrote An-sky. "Most of them were provisionally housed in all types of Jewish institutions. Several hundred people, particularly women and children, were sheltered in the Jewish literary club Hazomir. . . . The large hall was packed from wall to wall with beds, benches, and crates on which children were sitting and lying, three or four to a bed."[11] Peretz, who was accustomed to regaling middle-class audiences with his magical realism in this hall, was instead running around trying to find beds for the newcomers. Throughout the region, public spaces once reserved for theater, circus, and musical performances became homeless shelters, refugee camps, and morgues.

The total destruction of the old world, though, brought with it hope for a newer, better world. Despite wartime censorship and a ban on the usage of Hebrew typeface, Jewish culture flourished. In the words of one observer, "The First World War broke the framework of shtetl life and shattered its very foundations. . . . [It] shattered traditional lifestyles, dreams, and illusions, and this prepared the groundwork for vital changes in the strivings and hopes of the youth."[12] Some regions were transformed by refugees, others by new overlords. Many towns that had been ruled by Russia found themselves under German occupation during the war and witnessed a new flowering of cultural activity. In Ivye, near Vilna, for instance, a drama circle formed during this period as well as a library and Jewish schools, all of which were encouraged by the local German commandant, who was interested in cultural activity and supported its development.[13] Similarly, in Horkhiv (Volhynia Province), new schools were established as well as a drama circle that presented plays by Jacob Gordin and others. Despite an inauspicious beginning—during its first production, a lamp that was hanging on the curtain fell, setting the town hall ablaze—the theater was not deterred and continued to perform throughout the war until it eventually succumbed to political infighting and split into two ensembles—a Yiddish troupe and a Zionist Hebrew troupe.

On a larger scale, several of the most successful Jewish theatrical experiments emerged during the war. The Yiddish-language Vilner Trupe, established in 1916, brought a level of professionalism and aesthetic heights unknown to previous troupes, while the Hebrew-language Habimah Theater, formed in 1918, attracted critical acclaim from around the world. Both achieved their greatest successes with adaptations of An-sky's play *Dybbuk: tsvishn tsvey veltn* (The Dybbuk: Between Two Worlds), a text (based in part on folklore An-sky collected during his ethnographic expeditions) about the conflicting rights of those living in *this* world with the spirits that inhabit the next. Ultimately, the rabbinical court that is convened to settle the dispute concludes that the rights of *this* world trump those of the next but that the obligations of the living to remember the dead must be enforced. It was a message that resonated in the aftermath of total war.

The public's fascination with migratory spirits was in part a reflection of real-life dislocation. Massive migration transformed the cultural and social life of the region. Half a million Jewish residents along Russia's western border were displaced, forced to move eastward away from enemy lines because the tsarist government regarded Jews as untrustworthy and as potential traitors. As this population fled, they carried the ideas and movements to which they had been exposed through their proximity to the other side of the border.[14] Even a large city like Kamenets-Podolsk was transformed when refugees from the neighboring town of Zhvanets flooded the city when the Jews were exiled from towns along the River Zbruch. Although Zhvanets was a much smaller town, its population was ardently Zionist and active in the Jewish self-defense movement, which had existed there since 1904–1905. In addition, a Poalei Tsion Zionist workers' movement had formed there in 1908. Refugees from Zhvanets played an important role in the Zionist movement in Kamenets-Podolsk as it matured during the war.[15]

The vast movement of peoples across borders and rivers intensified the process of cultural standardization taking place. The world shrank as refugees traversed cultural lines and language boundaries. In Luboml:

> At the beginning of the summer of 1916, groups of young men came to the shtetl from surrounding areas—Lutsk, Rovno, Rozhishch and elsewhere. They were of mobilization age and some were deserters from the Russian army. Fearing their own towns would be retaken by the Russians, they settled temporarily in our town. Most had had a high school education, and their influence on the youth of the shtetl soon became evident. We admired them and absorbed every word they uttered. Most spoke a perfect Russian, and some also knew German. . . . Binyomen Farshtey from Lutsk together with other young people formed a cultural group. Its members used to gather on Sabbath afternoons in the hall of the kitchen and sit for hours in rapt attention, listening to the readings of Graetz's *History of the Jews*, followed by fascinating discussion and explanations. I often snuck over with my friend Veyner to listen to these readings while standing under a window. The group became a nucleus for widespread cultural activities that lasted in the shtetl from 1918 to 1919, the year when Poland annexed our area.[16]

Youth who had fled their towns for larger cities during the war returned home having encountered new ideas in the urban centers and having become acquainted with broad political and cultural movements. Yaakov

Plot wrote of his return at the end of 1918 to Kamin-Kashirskii (Volhynia Province):

> Coming from Kiev, which was the capital of Ukraine, where all the central Zionist organizations could be found, where there was broad multi-branched Zionist activity in all fields, where I was also active and belonged to the "Young Zion" faction, I decided that also in Kamin a Zionist organization must be founded. I succeeded after much difficulty in arranging a meeting with my old friends as well as many other people. . . . I brought various Zionist brochures and weekly newspapers. . . . After a discussion everybody registered as members of the Zionist organization.[17]

Later the group held a larger meeting that established a cultural committee. The group organized regular readings and arranged with a newspaper dealer in Kovel to send them all the daily Zionist newspapers. Thus, through the Zionist organization, the Jewish youth of Kamin were able to establish regular contact with both Jews from smaller neighboring towns and with Jews from larger urban centers.

Kapresht in Bessarabia also benefited from refugees who fled west after the war. "With the end of the First World War and the annexation of Bessarabia, in the year 1918, to Romania, a renaissance of Jewish cultural life occurred in Bessarabia. Not a few refugees who arrived from Russia and settled there contributed. Among the refugees were poets and writers, teachers and public activists who found for themselves spacious meadows for cultural and public activity among the healthy Jewry there."[18] These refugees, most of whom were from Ukraine, played a dominant role in the founding of a Jewish theater in Kapresht as well as in the founding of a branch of the Zionist Hekhalutz (Pioneers) in the town in 1920, the first branch in Bessarabia.[19] According to a witness, during the chaos and horror of World War I, "the youth began to dream a new dream—the dream of making *aliyah* to the Land of Israel. . . . Hebrew conversation filled the streets."[20]

In Volhynia and other regions that were still under Russian rule, the February Revolution of 1917 was a major turning point. The lifting of all restrictions on Jews led to a brief flourishing of Jewish cultural activity, which was attested to in numerous memoirs. From Lutsk, one memoirist reported: "A radical change took place with the outbreak of the February Revolution in 1917. . . . A radical change also took place regarding the social and spiritual condition of the shtetl. Like mushrooms after a rain, various organizations, unions, and political parties were organized."[21] Another memoirist from the same city recalled: "In 1917, after the February Revolution, a ray of the light of freedom penetrated our dark Jewish life. We believed that a new epoch of true freedom for all people including Jews was coming."[22] Similar recollections are recorded from Ostrog:

> After the outbreak of the February Revolution in the year 1917, when Russia was freed from the repressive tsarist regime, Jewish social life in Ostrog was enlivened. The Zionist organization, which was semi-legal, began to lead broad and varied activities. In the shtetl at that time, there were demonstrations, manifestoes; people were full of hope for a better future. It was only natural then that the Bund activists also came to life.[23]

In Zvhil as well, Zionist and Bundist movements began after the February Revolution that "came with the first rays of spring. Everyone thought that freedom for the Russian people would come with spring. The activities of the political parties burst through like a mighty stream with the breach of a dam."[24]

By the time the fighting of World War I and the Civil War had begun to die down, the region had been largely cleared of "this-worldniks." Many had gone to the next world when they succumbed to typhus, flu, or hunger; others perished on the battlefield or were murdered in pogroms. A. Vayter's life in this world ended during the Vilna pogrom of April 1919, closing his story like the plot of one of the literary plays he had worked so hard to champion. Peretz died in Warsaw in 1915. An-sky recalled that he was "already a sick, tired, and broken man from all the troubles. The whole time he remained in the midst of the absolute hell that was the Jewish catastrophe."[25] Others, including many leaders of the generation that had inaugurated Jewish public culture, died in peace (of body, if not of soul): Sholem Aleichem in New York in 1916, Mendele in Odessa in 1917, and An-sky in Otwock in 1920. Dubnov survived until the next war; he was murdered in Riga by Latvian militiamen in 1941. An even greater number fled the territories of the former Russian Empire for the New World, carrying with them cultural memories that would significantly shape the development of American public and popular culture.[26]

In the lands of the former Russian Empire, new forms of Jewish culture developed in the interwar period. Jewish writers of poetry and prose found inspiration in the violence and tragedy of war: Isaac Babel (1894–1940) in Russian, Peretz Markish (1895–1952) in Yiddish, Antoni Slonimski (1895–

1976) in Polish, and Leonid Pervomaisky (1908–1973) in Ukrainian. The Yiddish and Hebrew poet Uri Zvi Greenberg (1896–1981), who migrated from Austrian Galicia to Palestine after fighting in the war, was fired by a militaristic poetic rage.[27] New literary and artistic groups emerged, only to be co-opted by the mass political movements that began to take over local public culture.[28] Throughout the newly independent states of Eastern Europe, Jewish voluntary associations, which were originally formed as independent and local public cultural projects, came under the authority of larger, often multinational organizations, such as Kultur-Lige (Culture League), which dominated Yiddish organizations, and Tarbut (Culture), which dominated Hebrew organizations.[29] When the Bolsheviks seized power in October 1917, the Soviet state and the Jewish sections of the Communist Party began eradicating independent political, social, and cultural organizations in Russia, eastern Ukraine, and Belarus.[30] By the end of the next world war, Jewish cultural associations throughout Eastern Europe had been eradicated, along with the people who had enjoyed them.

. . . And They Gathered

In the waning years of the Russian Empire, a group of predominantly liberal nationalists sought to construct and promote a Jewish public culture that accommodated the political climate in which they found themselves. They eschewed clandestine activity, instead believing that they could work for the advancement of Jewish interests openly, in public, and within the bounds of tsarist restrictions and legalities. They recognized the futility of revolutionary change and hoped instead to make possible gradual cultural and social improvements in the material and spiritual conditions of Russian Jewry through building institutions. Despite political differences, they believed that constructing culture was a public matter and that while it might be guided by intellectuals and elites, it was essential that the community as a whole participate.

Their efforts met some success. After the political turbulence and pogrom violence that accompanied the Revolution of 1905 died down, the Jewish community of the Russian Empire experienced almost a decade of relative calm—relative, that is, to what had come before and certainly to what would come after. The political struggles and infighting that had characterized the first two years of the Russian parliamentary experiment died down temporarily with the dissolution of the Second Duma in June 1907, when all the Jewish political parties were equalized in their exclusion from political life. It was during this period that liberals throughout the empire began to realize the potential offered by the March 1906 Temporary Regulations on Societies and Unions.

Invigorated by their newfound freedom, Jews of the Russian Empire embraced the cultural opportunities modernity afforded, and they were well-situated to do so. Concentrated in the western provinces of the Pale of Jewish Settlement and the Kingdom of Poland, much of the Jewish population lived in close proximity to the cultural renaissance of Central Europe. By the 1900s, the culture of fin-de-siècle Vienna had arrived in Austria's eastern provinces and was carried across the border by the many Jews who traversed it. Modern culture was first and foremost an urban culture. And in the Ukrainian, Belorussian, Lithuanian, and Polish lands of the Russian Empire, the urban centers were populated by Jews. In these urban centers, whether in major metropolitan areas or smaller market towns, a modern Jewish public culture that merged parochial Jewish concerns with broader European civilization came into being. Growing numbers of young Jews across the empire exchanged prayer halls and synagogue pulpits for public libraries and theatrical stages, while some, often their parents, resisted these changes with all their might. Still others, perhaps most, sought some balance between the two.

It became increasingly difficult for even the most traditional to remain completely aloof from the influences of modern culture. Local and national happenings, such as the visit of a Jewish poet to town, an amateur performance of a Yiddish play, the opening of a local library, or the death of a great Russian writer, infiltrated deep into the Jewish community. What differentiated these occurrences from other events, such as visits by itinerant preachers, *purimshpils,* groundbreaking ceremonies for prayer halls, and the deaths of rabbinic leaders, was their secular orientation and ecumenical meaning. For the most part, Jews of the region remained firmly grounded in a religious way of life, but many spent increasing amounts of time in secular pursuits. More and more Jews were willing to risk paradise in the next world for cultural fulfillment in this world.

The Torah portion Vayakhel (Hebrew for "and they gathered"), which recounts the construction of the Tabernacle, celebrates how "the whole community of Israelites," "men and women" participated in constructing this sacred object by gathering and providing "gold, silver, and copper; blue, purple, and crimson yarns, fine linen, and goats' hair; tanned ram skins, dolphin skins, and acacia wood; oil for lighting, spices for the anointing oil and for the aromatic incense; lapis lazuli and other stones for setting, for the ephod and the breastpiece" (Exodus 35:5–9). Each brought to the Tabernacle what they could: "The Israelites, all the men and women whose hearts moved them to bring anything for the work that the Lord, through Moses, had commanded to be done, brought it as a freewill offering to the lord" (Exodus 35:29). Rabbinical commentators have often pointed to the portion's title, Vayakhel, to underscore the project of fusing individual people into a community, a *kahal*. Few note that the task that unites the community is the construction of a public cultural object. The portion also provides a model for the role of elites in the project, which despite its communal aspects was distinctly guided by Moses and the master craftsman Bezalel, who the Lord "singled out by name" and was endowed "with a divine spirit of skill, ability, and knowledge in every kind of craft and has inspired him" (Exodus 35:30–31). In their enactment and articulation of a public culture encapsulated in voluntary associations, Jewish cultural activists and their audiences emulated one of the first communal projects of cultural construction in Jewish historical memory.

NOTES

Introduction

1. Ahad Ha'am, *Selected Essays of Ahad Ha'am*, trans., ed., and with an introduction by Leon Simon (Cleveland, Ohio: World Publishing Co., 1962), 259.

2. For theorizations of notions of public culture, see *Public Culture* 1, no. 1 (Fall 1988). The term "social imaginaries" comes from Charles Taylor, *Modern Social Imaginaries* (Durham, N.C.: Duke University Press, 2004).

3. For discussions of the classification of societies and organizations, see A. S. Tumanova, *Samoderzhavie i obshchestvennye organizatsii v Rossii, 1905–1917 gody* (Tambov: Tambovskii gosudarstvennyi universitet, 2002), 458–461; and T. A. Ivenina, *Kul'turno-prosvetitel'nyie organizatsii i uchrezhdeniia obshchestvennoi i chastnoi initsiativy v dorevoliutsionnoi rossii (1900–1916 gg.)* (Moscow: Frantera, 2003).

4. For critical approaches to Jewish memoir literature, see Michael Stanislawski, *Autobiographic Jews: Essays in Jewish Self-Fashioning* (Seattle: University of Washington Press, 2004); and Marcus Moseley, *Being for Myself Alone: Origins of Jewish Autobiography* (Stanford, Calif.: Stanford University Press, 2006).

5. For more on the history and uses of *yizker bikher*, see Jack Kugelmass and Jonathan Boyarin, eds. and translators, *From a Ruined Garden: The Memorial Books of Polish Jewry*, 2nd ed. (Bloomington: Indiana University Press, 1998); Rosemary Horowitz, *Literacy and Cultural Transmission in the Reading, Writing, and Rewriting of Jewish Memorial Books* (San Francisco, Calif.: Austin & Winfield, 1998); and Abraham Wein, "'Memorial Books' as a Source for Research into the History of Jewish Communities in Europe," *Yad Vashem on the European Jewish Catastrophe and Resistance* (Jerusalem: Yad Vashem, 1973), 9:255–272.

1. The Jews of This World

1. Dr. A. Mukdoyni, "Di lebens-kunst," *Der fraynd*, 13 June 1910.

2. Ibid.

3. Jeremiah 29: 5–9. Translation adapted from the New Revised Standard Version.

4. See, for instance, Judah ben Samuel, *Sefer hasidim* (Warsaw: Levin Epshtain, 1909), 42.

5. Translation from Solomon Ganzfried, *Code of Jewish Law (Kitzur Schulchan Aruch): A Compilation of Jewish Laws and Customs,* trans. Hyman E. Goldin (New York: Star Hebrew Book Company, 1927), 1;100.

6. Moses Hayyim Luzatto, *Mesilat yesharim* (Jerusalem and New York: Feldheim Publishers, 1974), 178–191.

7. Hanokh Henikh Teitelbaumm, *Mefaʿneach neʿelamim* (New York: A. M. Meisels, 2000), in Global Jewish Database, version 15, CD-ROM.

8. M. Z. Feierberg, *Kitve M. Z. Feierberg* (Tel Aviv: Keneset, 1951), 69.

9. A. Litvak, *Vos geven: etyudn un zikhroynes* (Vilna: B. Kletskin, 1925), 151.

10. Y. L. Peretz, "Di toyte shtodt," in *Ale verk fun Y. L. Peretz* (Vilna: B. Kletskin, 1925), 6:113.

11. Zalman Shneour, *Fertsik yor: lider un poemen, 1903–1944* (New York: Yidishn natsionalen arbeter-farband, 1945), 166.

12. Mikhail Artsybashev, *Sanin: A Novel,* trans. Michael R. Katz (Ithaca, N.Y.: Cornell University Press, 2001), 33–34.

13. Jürgen Habermas, *The Structural Transformation of the Public Sphere: An Inquiry into a Category of Bourgeois Society,* trans. Thomas Burger (Cambridge: MIT Press, 1989), 27.

14. Jürgen Habermas, Sara Lennox, and Frank Lennox, "The Public Sphere: An Encyclopedia Article (1964)," *New German Critique* no. 3 (Autumn 1974): 49.

15. For similar debates in China see Heath B. Chamberlain, "On the Search for Civil Society in China," *Modern China* 19, no. 2 (April 1993): 200.

16. Jacob Walkin, *The Rise of Democracy in Pre-Revolutionary Russia* (New York: Frederick A. Praeger, 1962); A. S. Tumanova, *Samoderzhavie i obshchestvennye organizatsii v Rossii, 1905–1917 gody* (Tambov: Tambovskii gosudarstvennyi universitet, 2002); Joseph Bradley, "Subjects into Citizens: Societies, Civil Society, and Autocracy in Tsarist Russia," *American Historical Review* 107, no. 4 (October 2002): 1094–1123; Laura Engelstein, "The Dream of Civil Society in Tsarist Russia: Law, State, and Religion," in *Civil Society before Democracy: Lessons from Nineteenth-Century Europe,* ed. Nancy Bermeo and Philip Nord (Lanham, Md.: Rowman & Littlefield, 2000), 23–41; Manfred Hagen. *Die Entfaltung Politischer Öffentlichkeit in russland, 1906–1914* (Wiesbaden: Franz Steiner Verlag, 1982).

17. See David Wartenweiler, *Civil Society and Academic Debate in Russia, 1905–1914* (Oxford: Clarendon Press, 1999); Edith W. Clowes, Samuel D. Kassow, and James L. West, *Between Tsar and People: Educated Society and the Quest for Public Identity in Late Imperial Russia* (Princeton, N.J.: Princeton University Press, 1991); Douglas Smith, *Working the Rough Stone: Freemasonry and Society in Eighteenth-Century Russia* (DeKalb: Northern Illinois University Press, 1999); Louise McReynolds, *The News under Russia's Old Regime: The Development of a Mass-Circulation Press* (Princeton, N.J.: Princeton University Press, 1991); Olga Crisp, *Civil Rights in Imperial Russia* (Oxford: Clarendon Press, 1989); Adele Lindenmeyr, *Poverty Is Not a Vice: Charity, Society, and the State in Imperial Russia* (Princeton, N.J.: Princeton University Press, 1996); Daniel R. Brower, *The Russian City: Between Tradition and Modernity, 1850–1900* (Berkeley: University of California Press, 1990); Murray Frame, *School for Citizens: Theatre and Civil Society in Imperial Russia* (New Haven, Conn.: Yale University Press, 2006); E. Anthony Swift, *Popular Theater and Society in Tsarist Russia* (Berkeley: University of California Press, 2002); Louise McReynolds, *Russia at Play: Leisure Activities at the End of the Tsarist Era* (Ithaca, N.Y.: Cornell University Press, 2003); and Richard Stites, *Serfdom, Society, and the Arts in Imperial Russia: The Pleasure and the Power* (New Haven, Conn.: Yale University Press, 2005).

18. Edward Shils, "The Virtue of Civil Society," *Government and Opposition* 26, no. 1 (January 1991): 16.

19. See Geoff Eley, "Nations, Publics and Political Culture," in *Habermas and the Public Sphere,* ed. Craig Calhoun (Cambridge: MIT Press, 1992), 289–339; Mary P. Ryan, "Gender and Public Access," in Calhoun, *Habermas and the Public Sphere,* 259–288; and Harold Mah, "Phantasies of the Public Sphere: Rethinking the Habermas of Historians," *Journal of Modern History* 72, no. 1 (March 2000): 153–182.

20. Isaac Levitats, *The Jewish Community in Russia, 1844–1917* (Jerusalem: Posner and Sons, 1981), 70. For other studies of Jewish institutional life in the Russian Empire, see Ilya Trotsky, "Jewish Institutions of Social Welfare, Education, and Mutual Assistance," in *Russian Jewry, 1860–1917,* ed. Jacob Frumkin, Gregor Aronson, and

Alexis Goldenweiser (South Brunswick, N.J.: Thomas Yoseloff, 1966), 416–433; John Klier, "Russkaia voina protiv Khevra Kaddisha," *Trudy po iudaike* 1 (1993): 109–115; Abraham Yaari, "*Ner Tamid* Societies in Poland and Lithuania," *Jewish Social Studies* 21, no. 1 (1959): 118–131; and François Guesnet, *Polnische Juden im 19. Jahrhundert. Lebensbedingungen, Rechtsnormen und Organisation im Wandel* (Cologne: Böhlau, 1998), especially 333–412.

21. For evidence of the continued existence of religiously based societies, see *fond* 821, *opis'* 8, *delo* 173 (delo o razreshenii evreiskii dukhovnym i blagotvoritel'nymi uchrezhdeniia, 1900–1910), Rossiskii gosudarstvennyi istoricheskii arkhiv.

22. Christoph Gassenschmidt, *Jewish Liberal Politics in Tsarist Russia, 1900–1914* (New York: New York University Press, 1995), 134. Gassenschmidt's primary focus remains the political sphere, and his ventures into nonpolitical associations are mostly limited to economic cooperatives, mutual aid societies, and educational institutions. Other specialized studies of individual communities have stressed the importance of communal organizations in the nineteenth and early twentieth centuries.

For Jewish voluntary associations in the Russian Empire, see M. Polishchuk, *Evrei Odessy i Novorosii. Sotsial'no-politicheskaia istoriia evreev Odessy i drugikh gorodov Novorossii, 1881–1904* (Jerusalem: Gesharim; Moscow: Mosty Kul'tury, 2002); Natan M. Meir, "Jews, Ukrainians, and Russians in Kiev: Intergroup Relations in Late Imperial Associational Life," *Slavic Review* 65, no. 3 (Fall 2006): 475–501; Heinz-Dietrich Löwe, "From Charity to Social Policy: The Emergence of Jewish 'Self-Help' Organizations in Imperial Russia, 1800–1914," *East European Jewish Affairs* 27, no. 2 (1997): 53–75; Steven Zipperstein, "The Politics of Relief: The Transformation of Russian Jewish Communal Life during the First World War," in *Studies in Contemporary Jewry,* vol. 4, *The Jews and the European Crisis, 1914–1921,* ed. Jonathan Frankel (New York: Oxford University Press, 1988), 22–40; and Scott Ury, "Red Banner, Blue Star: Radical Politics, Democratic Institutions and Collective Identity among Jews in Warsaw, 1904–1907" (Ph.D. diss., Hebrew University of Jerusalem, 2006). For other important studies of Jewish voluntary associations elsewhere in Europe, see Moshe Kligsberg, "Di yidishe yugnt-bavegung in Poyln tsvishn beyde velt-milkhomes (A sotsiologishe shtudie)," in *Studies on Polish Jewry, 1919–1939,* ed. Joshua Fishman (New York: YIVO Institute for Jewish Research, 1974), 137–228; Michael Brenner, *The Renaissance of Jewish Culture in Weimar Germany* (New Haven, Conn.: Yale University Press, 1996); and Derek Penslar, *Shylock's Children: Economics and Jewish Identity in Modern Europe* (Berkeley: University of California Press, 2001).

23. For two seminal works on the relationship between Jews and European modernity, see Yuri Slezkine, *The Jewish Century* (Princeton, N.J.: Princeton University Press, 2004); and Peter Gay, *Freud, Jews, and Other Germans: Masters and Victims in Modernist Culture* (New York: Oxford University Press, 1978). For works that discuss the role of Jews in modern movements in individual locales and contexts, see Carl E. Schorske, *Fin-de-Siècle Vienna: Politics and Culture* (New York: Knopf, 1979); Peter Jelavich, *Berlin Cabaret* (Cambridge, Mass.: Harvard University Press, 1993); Peter Jelavich, *Munich and Theatrical Modernism: Politics, Playwriting, and Performance, 1890–1914* (Cambridge, Mass.: Harvard University Press, 1985); Peter Paret, *The Berlin Secession: Modernism and Its Enemies in Imperial Germany* (Cambridge, Mass.: Belknap Press of Harvard University Press, 1980); John Lukacs, *Budapest 1900: A Historical Portrait of a City and Its Culture* (New York: Grove, 1990); Marline Otte, *Jewish Identities in German Popular Entertainment, 1890–1933* (Cambridge: Cambridge University Press, 2006); Steven Beller, *Vienna and the Jews, 1867–1938: A Cultural History* (Cambridge:

Cambridge University Press, 1989); and Mary Gluck, "The Budapest Flâneur: Urban Modernity, Popular Culture, and the 'Jewish Question' in Fin-de-Siècle Hungary," *Jewish Social Studies* 10, no. 3 (Spring/Summer 2004): 1–22.

24. For a problematization of normative models of cultural modernism as it relates to the emergence of a liberal bourgeoisie, see David Blackbourn and Geoff Eley, *The Peculiarities of German History: Bourgeois Society and Politics in Nineteenth-Century Germany* (New York: Oxford University Press, 1984). For a review of works on the German bourgeoisie, see Jonathan Sperber, "Bürger, Bürgertum, Bürgerlichkeit, Bürgerliche Gesellschaft: Studies of the German (Upper) Middle Class and Its Sociocultural World," *Journal of Modern History* 69, no. 2 (June 1997): 271–297. For the application of modernization models to Russian Jewry, see Eli Lederhendler, "Modernity without Emancipation or Assimilation?" in *Assimilation and Community: The Jews in Nineteenth-Century Europe,* ed. Jonathan Frankel and Steven Zipperstein (New York: Cambridge University Press, 1991), 324–343; and Eli Lederhendler, *The Road to Modern Jewish Politics: Political Tradition and Political Reconstruction in the Jewish Community of Tsarist Russia* (New York: Oxford University Press, 1989).

25. Shmuel Feiner notes that the early Haskalah of the eighteenth century was characterized by Jewish perceptions of their own intellectual inferiority. See his *The Jewish Enlightenment* (Philadelphia: University of Pennsylvania Press, 2004), especially 21–35.

26. A. Lehrerin, "Der tsuzamenfor fun di bildungs-tuer," *Der fraynd,* 4, 6, 7, and 8 January 1908; quote from 7 January.

27. For recent scholarship that has demonstrated how modern cultural associations affected the Russian provinces, see T. A. Andreeva, ed., *Sotsial'no-politicheskie instituty provintsial'noi Rossii (XVI-nachalo XX vv)* (Cheliabinsk: Cheliabinskii gosudarstvennyi universitet, 1993); and A. S. Tumanova, *Obshchestvennye organizatsii goroda Tambova na rubezhe XIX–XX vekov* (Tambov: Tambovskii gosudarstvennyi universitet, 1999).

28. Mark Zborowski and Elizabeth Herzog, *Life Is with People: The Culture of the Shtetl* (New York: Schocken Books, 1962). For studies of popular and literary portrayals of the shtetl, see Steven Zipperstein, *Imagining Russian Jewry: Memory, History, Identity* (Seattle: University of Washington Press, 1999); Ben Cion Pinchuk, "Jewish Discourse and the Shtetl," *Jewish History* 15, no. 2 (June 2001): 169–179; Barbara Kirshenblatt-Gimblett, "Imagining Europe: The Popular Arts of American Jewish Ethnography," in *Divergent Jewish Cultures: Israel and America,* ed. Deborah Dash Moore and Ilan Troen (New Haven, Conn.: Yale University Press, 2001), 166–191; and Dan Miron, *The Image of the Shtetl and Other Studies of Modern Jewish Literary Imagination* (Syracuse, N.Y.: Syracuse University Press, 2000). See also Antony Polonsky, ed., *Polin,* vol. 17, *The Shtetl: Myth and Reality* (Oxford: Littman Library of Jewish Civilization, 2004); Steven T. Katz, ed., *The Shtetl: New Evaluations* (New York: New York University Press, 2007); and Benjamin Harshav, *Language in Time of Revolution* (Berkeley: University of California Press, 1993).

29. Charles Taylor, "Nationalism and Modernity," in *The Morality of Nationalism,* ed. Robert McKim and Jeff Mc Mahan (New York: Oxford University Press, 1997), 46. See also Charles Taylor, *Multiculturalism: Examining the Politics of Recognition,* ed. Amy Gutman (Princeton, N.J.: Princeton University Press, 1994).

30. See Will Kymlicka, *Multicultural Citizenship: A Liberal Theory of Minority Rights* (Oxford: Clarendon Press, 1995).

31. S. Dubnov, "Pis'ma o starom i novom evreistve. Pis'mo sed'moe. Avtonomizm, kak osnova natsional'noi programmy," *Knizhki voskhoda* no. 12 (1901): 34.

32. For Buber's seminal article, see Martin Buber, "Jüdische Renaissance," *Ost und West* 1, no. 1 (January 1901): 7–10. For more on Ahad Ha'am, see Steven Zipperstein, *Elusive Prophet: Ahad Ha'am and the Origins of Zionism* (Berkeley: University of California Press, 1993). For Buber's secular ideologies, see Donald J. Moore, *Martin Buber: Prophet of Religious Secularism* (Philadelphia, Pa.: Jewish Publication Society of America, 1974). For a comparative analysis of Dubnow and Ahad Ha'am, see David H. Weinberg, *Between Tradition and Modernity: Haim Zhitlowski, Simon Dubnow, Ahad Ha-am, and the Shaping of Modern Jewish Identity* (New York: Holmes and Meier, 1996). For Dubnov's autobiography, see S. M. Dubnov, *Kniga zhizni: vospominaniia i razmyshleniia: materialy dlia istorii moego vremeni,* ed. Viktor Kel'ner (St. Petersburg: Peterburgskoe vostokovedenie, 1998). See also Sophia Dubnova-Erlikh, *Life and Work of S. M. Dubnov: Diaspora Nationalism and Jewish History,* ed. Jeffrey Shandler (Bloomington: Indiana University Press, 1991).

33. Gilya G. Schmidt, ed., *The First Buber: Youthful Zionist Writings of Martin Buber* (Syracuse, N.Y.: Syracuse University Press, 1999), 24. Originally published as "Gegenwarsarbeit," *Die Welt* 5, no. 6 (8 February 1901): 4–5.

34. S. Dubnov, "Pis'ma o starom i novom evreistve. Pis'mo IV. Etika natsionalizma i tsionizma," *Voskhod* no. 6 (1899): 61.

35. S. Dubnov, "Pis'ma o starom i novom evreistve. Pis'mo sed'moe. Avtonomizm, kak osnova natsional'noi programmy," *Knizhki voskhoda* no. 12 (1901): 40.

36. For analyses of the role of culture in national identity, see Prasenjit Duara, *Sovereignty and Authenticity: Manchukuo and the East Asian Modern* (Lanham, Md.: Rowman & Littlefield Publishers, 2004); Joseph Raz, *The Morality of Freedom* (Oxford: Clarendon Press, 1986); and Michael Walzer, "Multiculturalism and the Politics of Interest," in *Insider/Outsider: American Jews and Multiculturalism,* ed. David Biale, Michael Galchinsky, and Susannah Heschel (Berkeley: University of California Press, 1998).

37. Elias Tcherikover, *Istoriia obshchestva dlia rasprostraneniia prosveshcheniia mezhdu evreiami v Rossii (Kul'turno-obshchestvennyiia techeniia v russkom evreisve), 1863–1913* (St. Petersburg: I. Lur'e 1913); and Leon Rosenthal, *Toldot Hevrat marbe haskalah be-Yisrael be-erets Rusya mi-shenat hityasdutah 624 (1863) 'ad shenat 646 (1885)* (St. Petersburg: Bi-defus H. Ts. H. Pines, 1885–1890). For more on the OPE, see Brian Horowitz, "The Society for the Promotion of Enlightenment among the Jews of Russia and the Evolution of the St. Petersburg Russian-Jewish Intelligentsia, 1893–1905," in *Studies in Contemporary Jewry,* vol. 19, *Jews and the State: Dangerous Alliances and the Perils of Privilege,* ed. Ezra Mendelsohn, 195–213 (New York: Oxford University Press, 2004).

38. Tumanova, *Samoderzhavie i obshchestvennye organizatsii,* 83.

39. Ibid., 28–92; Walkin, *The Rise of Democracy in Pre-Revolutionary Russia,* 121–152.

40. For general works on the Revolution of 1905 that highlight the effects of the revolution on Jewish politics, see Abraham Ascher, *The Revolution of 1905,* vol. 1, *Russia in Disarray* (Stanford, Calif.: Stanford University Press, 1988); Abraham Ascher, *The Revolution of 1905,* vol. 2, *Authority Restored* (Stanford, Calif.: Stanford University Press, 1992); Robert Weinberg, *The Revolution of 1905 in Odessa: Blood on the Steps* (Bloomington: Indiana University Press, 1993); and Sidney Harcave, *First Blood: The Russian Revolution of 1905* (New York: Macmillan, 1964).

41. "Peterburg, dem 24-ten oktober," *Der fraynd,* 25 October 1905.

42. *Polnoe sobranie zakonov Rossiiskoi Imperii,* Series III (St. Petersburg: Gos. Tip., 1830–1913), 26:27479.

43. See Sidney Harcave, "The Jewish Question in the First Russian Duma," *Jewish Social Studies* 6 (1944): 155–176. For the first three dumas, see Vladimir Levin, "Russian

Jewry and the Duma Elections, 1906–1907," in *Jews and Slavs,* ed. Wolf Moskovich, Leonid Finberg, and Martin Feller (Jerusalem: Hebrew University of Jerusalem Center for Slavic Languages and Literatures / the Institute of Jewish Studies, 2000), 7:233–264.

44. For general works on Russian political party formation, see Terence Emmons, *The Formation of Political Parties and the First National Elections in Russia* (Cambridge, Mass.: Harvard University Press, 1983); Victoria E. Bonnell, *Roots of Rebellion: Workers' Politics and Organizations in St. Petersburg and Moscow, 1900–1914* (Berkeley: University of California Press, 1983); and Leopold Haimson, *The Politics of Rural Russia, 1905–1914* (Bloomington: Indiana University Press, 1979).

For Jewish politics in Russia, see Jonathan Frankel, *Prophecy and Politics: Socialism, Nationalism, and the Russian Jews, 1862–1917* (Cambridge: Cambridge University Press, 1981); Gassenschmidt, *Jewish Liberal Politics;* Gitelman, *The Emergence of Modern Jewish Politics;* Ezra Mendelsohn, *Class Struggle in the Pale* (New York: Cambridge University Press, 1981); Moshe Mishkinsky, *Reshit tenu'at ha-poalim ha Yehudit be-Rusyah* (Tel Aviv: Hakibutz Hamechad, 1981); Lederhendler, *The Road to Modern Jewish Politics;* and David Vital, *The Origins of Zionism* (Oxford: Clarendon Press, 1975).

45. Frankel, *Prophecy and Politics,* 139.

46. Gassenschmidt, *Jewish Liberal Politics,* 47, 45.

47. Ibid., 19.

48. Litvak, *Vos geven,* 268.

49. Gassenschmidt, *Jewish Liberal Politics,* 70.

50. Vladimir Medem, *Fun mayn lebn* (New York: Vladimir Medem Komite, 1923), 2:196. See also Sophia Dubnova-Erlikh, "In di yorn fun reaktsye," in *Di geshikhte fun bund,* ed. Jacob Sholem Hertz, Grigor Aronson, and Sophia Dubnova-Erlikh (New York: Unzer tsayt, 1960), 2:539–626.

51. Dubnova-Erlikh, "In di yorn," 539.

52. Ibid., 542. See also Litvak, *Vos geven,* 148–165.

53. The term is borrowed from Polish historiography, in which "organic work" is taken to mean concentrating on economic and social development instead of armed insurrection as a path to nationhood. For more on the topic, see Stanislaus A. Blejwas, "The Origins and Practice of Organic Work in Poland: 1795–1863," *Polish Review* 15, no. 4 (1970): 23–54.

54. Y. Uner, "Fun Lodzer leben," *Der fraynd,* 17 January 1911.

55. Dubnov, *Kniga zhizni,* 297.

56. Joshua D. Zimmerman, *Poles, Jews, and the Politics of Nationality* (Madison: University of Wisconsin Press, 2004): 227–254; Dubnova-Erlikh, "In di yorn"; David E. Fishman, "The Bund and Modern Yiddish Culture," in *The Emergence of Modern Jewish Politics: Bundism and Zionism in Eastern Europe,* ed. Zvi Gitelman (Pittsburgh, Pa.: University of Pittsburgh Press, 2003), 107–119.

57. Dubnova-Erlikh, "In di yorn," 551. For more on the conference, see Avrom Reyzen, *Epizodn fun mayn lebn: literarishe erinerungen* (Vilna: B. Kletskin, 1929), 3:327–339.

58. Dubnova-Erlikh, "In di yorn," 552.

59. For scholarship on the major literary figures of the period see Dan Miron, *A Traveler Disguised: The Rise of Modern Yiddish Fiction in the Nineteenth Century* (Syracuse, N.Y.: Syracuse University Press, 1996; reprint, New York: Schocken Books, 1973); Ken Frieden, ed., *Classic Yiddish Stories of S. Y. Abramovitsh, Sholem Aleichem, and I. L. Peretz* (Syracuse, N.Y.: Syracuse University Press, 2004); and Ruth R. Wisse, *I. L. Peretz and the Making of Modern Jewish Culture* (Seattle: University of Washington Press, 1991).

For cultural activity, see David E. Fishman, *The Rise of Modern Yiddish Culture* (Pittsburgh, Pa.: University of Pittsburgh Press, 2005). See also Kenneth Benjamin Moss, "'A Time for Tearing Down and a Time for Building Up': Recasting Jewish Culture in Eastern Europe, 1917–1921" (Ph.D. diss., Stanford University, 2003); Mikhail Krutikov, *Yiddish Fiction and the Crisis of Modernity, 1905–1914* (Stanford, Calif.: Stanford University Press, 2001); Gennady Estraikh, *In Harness: Yiddish Writers' Romance with Communism* (Syracuse, N.Y.: Syracuse University Press, 2005). For popular culture, see Michael C. Steinlauf and Antony Polonsky, eds., *Polin,* vol. 16, *Jewish Popular Culture and Its Afterlife* (Oxford: Littman Library of Jewish Civilization, 2003).

For folklore, see Itzik Nakhmen Gottesman, *Defining the Yiddish Nation: The Jewish Folklorists of Poland* (Detroit, Mich.: Wayne State University Press, 2003); Mark W. Kiel, "A Twice Lost Legacy: Ideology, Culture and Pursuit of Jewish Folklore in Russia until Stalinization (1930–1931)" (Ph.D. diss., Jewish Theological Seminary, 1991); and Adam Rubin, "From Torah to Tarbut: Hayim Nahman Bialik and the Nationalization of Judaism" (Ph.D. diss., University of California, Los Angeles, 2000). For academia, see Cecile Esther Kuznitz, "The Origins of Yiddish Scholarship and the YIVO Institute for Jewish Research" (Ph.D. diss., Stanford University, 2000); and David N. Myers, *Re-Inventing the Jewish Past: European Jewish Intellectuals and the Zionist Return to History* (New York: Oxford University Press, 1995). For art, see Michael Stanislawski, *Zionism and the Fin-de-Siècle: Cosmopolitanism and Nationalism from Nordau to Jabotinsky* (Berkeley: University of California Press, 2001), 98–115; Ezra Mendelsohn, *Painting a People: Maurycy Gottlieb and Jewish Art* (Hanover: Brandeis University Press, 2002); Emily D. Bilski, ed., *Berlin Metropolis: Jews and the New Culture, 1890–1918* (Berkeley: University of California Press, 1999); Susan Tumarkin Goodman, *Russian Jewish Artists in a Century of Change, 1890–1990* (Munich: Prestel, 1995); Ruth Apter-Gabriel, ed., *Tradition and Revolution: The Jewish Renaissance in Russian Avant-Garde Art, 1912–1928* (Jerusalem: The Israel Museum, 1987); Benjamin Harshav, *Marc Chagall and His Times: A Documentary Narrative* (Stanford, Calif.: Stanford University Press, 2004); Seth Wolitz, "A Jewish *Kulturkampf* in the Plastic Arts," in *The Emergence of Modern Jewish Politics: Bundism and Zionism in Eastern Europe,* ed. Zvi Gitelman (Pittsburgh, Pa.: University of Pittsburgh Press, 2003), 151–177; and Alina Orlov, "Natan Altman and the Problem of Jewish Art in the 1910s" (Ph.D. diss., University of Southern California, 2003). For the performing arts, see Jeffrey Veidlinger, *The Moscow State Yiddish Theater: Jewish Culture on the Soviet Stage* (Bloomington: Indiana University Press, 2000); Joel Berkowitz, ed., *Yiddish Theater: New Approaches* (Oxford: Littman Library of Jewish Civilization, 2003); Mordechai Altshuler, *Hate'atron hayehudi bevrit ha-mo'atsot* (Jerusalem: Hebrew University of Jerusalem Press, 1996); and Brigitte Dalinger, *"Verloschene Sterne": Geschichte des jüdischen Theaters in Wien* (Vienna: Picus Verlag, 1998).

60. S. An-sky, "Di Yudishe folks-shafung," in An-sky, *Gezamlte shriften* (Warsaw: An-sky, 1928), 15:27–95. For more on An-sky and his influence, see Gabriella Safran and Steven J. Zipperstein, eds., *The Worlds of S. An-sky: A Russian Jewish Intellectual at the Turn of the Century* (Stanford, Calif.: Stanford University Press, 2006).

2. Libraries

1. *"S'iz geven akorsht nit lang, mit a tsen yor tsurik. Hot a kleynshtetldike yugnt ba zikh a idishe bibliotek gegrindet. . . . Oysgeputst a sforim-almer un in untn fun kloyz, in talmud-toyre im bishtike avekgeshtelt. Derbay, vi der seyder iz, an efenung-yontev gemakht un yontevdike droshes gehaltn: Ot der sforim-almer . . . vet undzer nayer orn vern, fun oybn*

fun kloiz vet aher di shkhine arop, vayl do gefint zikh shoyn di naye idishe toyre."
Y. Dobrushin, *Gedankengang* (Kiev: Kultur-Lige, 1922), 31.

2. Richard D. Altick, *The English Common Reader: A Social History of the Mass Reading Public, 1800–1900* (Chicago: University of Chicago Press, 1957), 5.

3. Khayim Rabinovitsh, "Haskalah, bund, zelbshuts," in *Sefer Deretsin*, ed. Y. Raban (Tel Aviv: Irgun yotse'e Deretsin, 1971 or 1972), 81.

4. Dvoyre Kutnik, "Di ershte yidishe bibliotek," in *Yizkor kehilot Luninyets / Koz'anhorodok*, ed. Yosef Ze'evi (Tel Aviv: Irgun yots'e Luninyets ve-Koz'anhorodok, 1952), 147.

5. Falik Zolf, *Di letste fun a dor: heymishe geshtaltn* (Winnipeg: The Israelite Press, 1952), 195.

6. Quoted in Simhah Assaf, *Am ha-sefer veha-sefer* (Safed: ha-Muze'on le-'omanut ha-defus, 1964), 65.

7. Ibid., 66.

8. Gershon David Hundert, "The Library of the Study Hall in Volozhin, 1762: Some Notes on the Basis of a Newly Discovered Manuscript," *Jewish History* 14, no. 2 (June 2000): 225–244; and Hagit Cohen, *Ba-hanuto shel mokher ha-sefarim: hanuyot sefarim Yehudiyot be-Mizrah Eropah ba-mahatsit ha-sheniya shel ha-me'ah ha-tesha esreh* (Jerusalem: Hebrew University Magnes Press, 2006), 9–22.

9. Rabinovitsh, "Haskalah, bund, zelbshuts," 81.

10. Moshe Reuveni (Rostovski), "Ha-sifriyah," in *Sefer Mir*, ed. N. Blumental (Jerusalem: Entsiklopedyah shel galuyot, 1962), 227–232.

11. Avrom Reyzen, *Epizodn fun mayn lebn: literarishe erinerungen* (Vilna: B. Kletskin, 1929), 1:45.

12. S. An-sky, *Gezamelte shriften* (Vilna, Warsaw, and New York: An-sky, 1922), 10:5–6. Translation from S. An-sky, *The Dybbuk and Other Writings*, ed. David Roskies, trans. Golda Werman (New York: Schocken Books, 1992), 71–72.

13. Mikhal Rubenshteyn, "Ivenits un ire tsionistn," in *Sefer Ivenits, Kamin, veha-sevivah* (Tel Aviv: Defus Arazi, 1973), 79.

14. Avrom Kotik, *Dos lebn fun a idishn inteligent* (New York: H. Toybenshlag, 1925), 61–64.

15. S. M. Dubnov, *Kniga zhizni: vospominaniia i razmyshleniia: materialy dlia istorii moego vremeni*, ed. Viktor Kel'ner (St. Petersburg: Peterburgskoe vostokovedenie, 1998), 67.

16. Y. L. Peretz, "Mayn zikhroynes," in *Ale verk fun Y. L. Peretz* (Vilna: B. Kletskin, 1925), 12:126.

17. Ibid., 127.

18. M. Z. Feierberg, *Kitve M. Z. Feierberg* (Tel Aviv: Keneset, 1951), 86.

19. Avrom Kotik, "Dos bukh un der leyzer," *Der fraynd*, 8 July 1911.

20. "Luakh akhiasaf," supplement to *Akhiasaf* (1904–1905): 4–5. Population statistics for Bobruisk are based on the 1897 census. Tsentral'nyi statisticheskii komitet, *Pervaia vseobshchaia perepis' naseleniia Rossiiskoi Imperii 1897 g.* (St. Petersburg: Izd. Tsentral'nago statisticheskago komiteta Ministerstva vnutrennikh diel, 1899–1905).

21. Ts. Ts-n, "K kharakteristike chitatelia-evreia," *Voskhod* 26, no. 8 (1906): 42.

22. A. I[zrailitin], "Khronika russko-evreiskago bibliotechnago dela," *Voskhod* 25, no. 34 (25 August 1905): 23–24.

23. "Vopros ob uchrezh. otdela iudaika pri kharkovsk. biblioteka," *Voskhod* 23, no. 18 (1 May 1903). See also Kharkovets, "Kharkov," *Razsvet* 5, no. 45 (4 November 1911): 31–32.

24. A. Izrailitin, "Obshchedostupnyia biblioteki i zhargonnaia literature," *Voskhod* 25, no. 26 (29 June 1905): 29–33.

25. "Za nedeliu," *Voskhod* 24, no. 5 (5 February 1904): 15.

26. "Provints (fun undzere korespondenten)," *Der fraynd,* 14 January 1908.

27. On private libraries in Russia, see N. V. Zdobnov, *Istoriia russkoi bibliografii do nachala XX veka,* 2nd ed. (Moscow: Akademii nauk SSSR, 1951), 133–137.

28. Judah ben Samuel, *Sefer hasidim* (Warsaw: Levin Epshtain, 1909), 186.

29. Assaf, *Am ha-sefer,* 14–21.

30. Reuven Brainin, *Fun mayn lebns-bukh* (New York: YKUF, 1946), 246.

31. Osip Mandelstam, *The Noise of Time: Selected Prose,* trans. Clarence Brown (Evanston, Ill.: Northwestern University Press, 2002), 78–79.

32. Khaykl Lunski, "Di strashun bibliotek in Vilne," in *Vilne: a zamelbukh gevidmet der shtot Vilne,* ed. Yefim Yeshurin (New York: Vilner Brentsh 367 Arbeyter Ring, 1935), 273–287; and Aviva Astrinsky, Mordekhai Zalkin, and Yermiyahu Taub, eds., *Mattityahu Strashun 1817–1885: Scholar, Leader, and Book Collector* (New York: YIVO Institute for Jewish Research, 2001).

33. "Be-artsenu," *Hamelits,* 2 July 1903.

34. "Be-artsenu," *Hamelits,* 18 April 1902.

35. For more on Lunski, see N. Vaynig, "Khaykl Lunski," *Literarishe bleter* 10, no. 12 (1933): 188; and Hirsh Abramovitsh, "Der bibliotekor," *Literarishe bleter* 2, no. 58 (1925): 4.

36. Lunski, "Di strashun bibliotek in Vilne," 273.

37. Quoted in Astrinsky, Zalkin, and Taub, *Mattityahu Strashun,* 18.

38. Avrom Yitskhak Slutski, "Der kultureler matsev in undzer shtetl," in *Kehilat Lenin: sefer zikaron,* ed. Moshe Tamari (Tel Aviv: Vaad yotse'e Lenin, 1956 or 1957), 253.

39. A. I. Paperna, "Iz Nikolaevskoi epohki," in *Evrei v Rossii: XIX vek,* ed. Viktor Efimovich Kel'ner (Moscow: Novoe literaturnoe obozrenie, 2000), 44.

40. Yekhezkel Kotik, *Mayne zikhroynes* (Berlin: Klal, 1922), 1:312.

41. Kutnik, "Di ershte yidishe bibliotek," 147.

42. Zolf, *Di letste fun a dor,* 189.

43. Ibid., 189–190.

44. Ibid., 190–191.

45. Ibid., 192.

46. Alter Trus and Julius Cohen, *Braynsk sefer ha-zikaron: a bashraybung fun unzer heym* (New York: Braynsker relif komitet, 1948), 147–149.

47. Slutski, "Der kultureler matsev in undzer shtetl," 253.

48. Kotik, *Mayne zikhroynes,* 230–231.

49. Paperna, "Iz Nikolaevskoi epokhi," 142.

50. Kotik, *Mayne zikhroynes,* 231.

51. S. Y. Abramovitsh, "Dos kleyne mentshele," in *Ale verk fun Mendele Moykher Sforim* (New York: Hebrew Publishing Company, 1920), 3:5–6.

52. Nakhman Huberman, *Bershad: be-tsel 'ayarah* (Jerusalem: Hotsaat Entsiklopedyah shel galuyot, 1956), 102–103.

53. Slutski, "Der kultureler matsev in undzer shtetl," 253.

54. Avrom Yaron, "A lebn iz untergegangn," in *Seyfer Hosht: yizker-bukh,* ed. Reuven Fink (Tel Aviv: Irgun yotse'e Hosht, 1957), 149–150.

55. Ibid., 150. For more on workers' libraries and the development of clandestine libraries in the 1890s, see David Shavit, "The Emergence of Jewish Public Libraries in

Tsarist Russia," *Journal of Library History, Philosophy, and Comparative Librarianship* 20, no. 3 (Summer 1985): 239–252.

56. L. Berman, *In loyf fun yorn: zikhroynes fun a yidishn arbeter* (New York: Farlag Unzer Tsayt, 1945), 145–149.

57. A. Litvak, *Vos geven: etyudn un zikhroynes* (Vilna: B. Kletskin, 1925), 155.

58. Ibid., 153.

59. Ibid., 152.

60. Berman, *In loyf fun yorn*, 146–147.

61. Jack Kugelmass and Jonathan Boyarin, eds. and trans., *From a Ruined Garden: The Memorial Books of Polish Jewry*, 2nd ed. (Bloomington: Indiana University Press, 1998), 60–61.

62. Kotik, *Dos lebn fun a idishn intelligent*, 61–64.

63. Moyshe Shmuel Shklarski, "Kontrabandshtshik fun yidisn bukh," in *Lite*, ed. Mendl Sudarski, Urieh Katsenelbogen, and Y. Kisin (New York: Kultur-gezelshaft fun litvishe yidn, 1951), 1:1290.

64. "Be-artsenu," *Hamelits*, 19 November 1900.

65. "Be-artsenu," *Hamelits*, 21 March 1903.

66. Tsipporah Katsenelson-Nakhumov, "Yitskhak Katsenelsons geburt-shtetl," in *Korolits-Korelitsh: hayeha ve-hurbanah shel kehilah Yehudit=kiyum un hurbn fun a Yidisher kehile*, ed. Mikhael Valtser-Fas (Tel Aviv: Akhdut, 1973), 53.

67. For libraries in the United States and Great Britain, see Robert Snape, *Leisure and the Rise of the Public Library* (London: Library Association, 1995); and Alistair Black, *A New History of the English Public Library: Social and Intellectual Contexts, 1850–1914* (London: Leicester University Press, 1996).

68. For the legal status of Russian libraries, see E. Zviagintsev, *Pravovoe polozhenie narodnykh bibliotek za 50 let* (Moscow: Izdanie knizhnago sklada "dlia samoobrazovaniia biblioteki i shkoli," E. D. Trautskoi, 1916); A. N. Vaneev, *Razvitie bibliotekovedcheskoi mysli v Rossii v nachale XX veka: uchebnoe posobie* (St. Petersburg: Sankt-Peterbergskaia gos. Akademiia kul'tury, 1999), 32–39; and "Pravila o bezplatnykh narodnykh chital'niakh i o poriadke nadzora za nimi," *Russkaia shkola* no. 7 (1890): 3–6. For censorship in general, see "Tsenzura v Rossii vo vtoroi polovine XIX–nachale XX v: Zakony i praktika," in *Tsenzura v Rossii v kontse XIX-nachale XX veka: Sbornik vospominanii*, ed. M. A. Benina (St. Petersburg: Dmitri Bulanin, 2003), 8–42; Daniel Balmuth, *Censorship in Russia, 1865–1905* (Washington, D.C.: University Press of America, 1979); and Charles A. Rudd, *Fighting Words: Imperial Censorship and the Russian Press, 1804–1906* (Toronto: University of Toronto Press, 1982).

69. Many Russian terms were used for public libraries, all of which were used slightly differently by different organizations. In general, *publichnaia* and *obshchestvennaia biblioteka* were used synonymously to refer to libraries for general education. A *publichnaia biboteka* was usually funded by membership dues or borrowing fees and could be a commercial venture, whereas an *obshchestvennaia biblioteka* was generally funded by a charitable or voluntary association. A *narodnaia biblioteka* could be distinguished from a *publichnaia* and *obshchestvennaia biblioteka* in that it would be expected to serve primarily those with only primary education or the poor and would be more likely to be found in rural regions, serving peasant populations. Although it is usually assumed that a *narodnaia biblioteka* was free, there are indications that some charged fees. An *obshchedostupnaia biblioteka,* in contrast, was a public library that was either free or had nominal fees for the poor. For an attempt to unravel the terms, see Vaneev, *Razvitie bibliotekovedcheskoi mysli*, 21–31; E. I. Shamurin, *Slovar'*

knigovedcheskikh terminov dlia bibliotekarei, bibliografov, rabotnikov pechati i knizhnoi torgovli (Moscow: Izdatel'stvo Sovetskaia Rossiia, 1958); and L. B. Khavkina, *Slovari bibliotechno-bibliograficheskikh terminov* (Moscow: Izdatel'stvo vsesoiuznoi knizhnoi palaty, 1952).

70. M. Iu. Matveev, "Zemskie narodnye biblioteki v dorevoliutsionnoi Rossii: stanovlenie i razvitie," in *Istoriia bibliotek: issledovaniia, materially, dokumenty* (St. Petersburg: Izdatel'stvo Rossiiskoi natsional'noi biblioteki, 2000), 3:15; V. F. Abramov, "Zemskie biblioteki v Rossii," in *Istoriia bibliotek: issledovanisia, materially, dokumenty* (St. Petersburg: Izdatel'stvo Rossiiskoi natsional'noi biblioteki, 1999), 2:16–17.

71. See Alfred Erich Senn, *Nicholas Rubakin: A Life for Books* (Newtonville, Mass.: Oriental Research Partners, 1977).

72. Subsequent volumes of *Sredi knig* appeared in 1913 and 1915 (Moscow: Knigaizdatel'stvo nauka, 1911–1915). See also Nikolai Rubakin, *Etiudy o russkoi chitaiushchei publike: fakty, tsifry i nabliudeniia* (St. Petersburg: Sklad izd. knizhnykh magazinakh N. P. Karbasnikova, 1895).

73. Matveev, "Zemskie narodnye biblioteki," 17.

74. See Joel Perlman, "Russian-Jewish Literacy in 1897: A Reanalysis of Census Data," in *Proceedings of the Eleventh World Congress of Jewish Studies, Jerusalem, June 22–29, 1993*, vol. 2, part 3 (Jerusalem: World Union of Jewish Studies, 1994), 23–30.

75. For a recent article questioning the extent of the spread of Haskalah ideology, see Alyssa Pia Quint, "Yiddish Literature for the Masses"? A Reconsideration of Who Read What in Jewish Eastern Europe," *AJS Review* 29, no. 1 (2005): 61–89.

76. For a detailed analysis of this survey, see A. I. Izrailitin, "O merakh k razvitiiu obshchedostupnykh bibliotek sredi evreiskago naseleniia v Rossii," *Knizhki voskhoda* no. 2 (February 1905): 99–113; and A. I. Izralitin, "Russko-evreiskii obshchedostupnyia biblioteki," *Knizhki voskhoda* no. 5 (May 1905): 125–135. Izrailitin recognized that the OPE figures he used were incomplete, but he maintained that his conclusion that Jewish public libraries were woefully inadequate was still accurate. See also "Zasedanie bibliotechnago otdela shkol'no-uchebnoi kommissii Obshchestva prosveshcheniia," *Voskhod* 25, no. 3 (22 January 1905): 15–16.

77. I. Edel'man, "Evreiskiia biblioteki v Mogilevskoi i Vitebskoi gub v 1911," *VOPE*, no. 16 (November 1912): 37–55.

78. I. S., "Melitopol'," *Razsvet* 3, no. 35 (30 August 1909): 25.

79. "Bibliotechnaia khronika," *VOPE*, no. 5 (March 1911): 115.

80. See M. Polishchuk, *Evrei Odessy i Novorosii. Sotsial'no-politicheskaia istoriia evreev Odessy i drugikh gorodov Novorossii, 1881–1904* (Jerusalem: Gesharim; Moscow: Mosty Kul'tury, 2002), 169–181.

81. See Abramov, "Zemskie biblioteki."

82. See Mary Stuart, "'The Ennobling Illusion': The Public Library Movement in Late Imperial Russia," *The Slavonic and East European Review* 76, no. 3 (July 1998): 401–440. See also Harold M. Leich, "The Society for Librarianship and Russian Librarianship in the Early Twentieth Century," *Journal of Library History* 22 no. 1 (Winter 1987): 42–57.

83. Matveev, "Zemskie narodnye biblioteki," 19.

84. Abramov, "Zemskie biblioteki," 22–23.

85. In 1915, Kirzhnits was exiled to Siberia for his participation in the Bundist workers' movement. He returned after the October Revolution and joined the Communist Party. During the 1920s he published several books on the Jewish press and the Jewish workers' movement. He was arrested in the 1930s and died in prison, probably in 1938. A. Greenbaum, "Avraham Kirzhnits," in *Leksikon fun der nayer yiddisher literatur*, ed.

Shmuel Niger and Jacob Shatzky (New York: Alveltlekhn yidishn kultur-kongres, 1981), 8:200–201.

86. S. Kotsyna and A. Verblovskaia, "Obraztsy chtenii s podborom posobii," *Evreiskaia shkola* 2, no. 3 (March 1905): 71–80. In the Soviet period, Kotsyna continued her library and archival work and held leadership positions at the Jewish People's University and the Institute of Jewish History in Moscow.

87. Izrailitin, "O merakh k razvitiiu obshchedostupnykh bibliotek," 104.

88. See Kotsyna archive, *fond* 9535, *opis'* 1, *delo* 2, Gosudarstvennyi arkhiv rossiiskoi federatsii. Accessed at Central Archives for the History of the Jewish People.

89. Kotsyna archive, *fond* 9535, *opis'* 1, *delo* 6, Gosudarstvennyi arkhiv rossiiskoi federatsii. Accessed at Central Archives for the History of the Jewish People. The Moscow OPE subsidized twenty libraries in Mogilev Province. Six were established by public institutions and the rest by private individuals; *Otchet obshchestva dlia rasprostraneniia prosveshcheniia mezhdu evreiami v Rossii za 1910 god* (St. Petersburg: Obshchestvo dlia rasprostraneniia prosveshcheniia mezhdu evreiami v Rossii, 1911), 60–61. See also "Bibliotechnaia tetrad' S. R. Kotsynoi," Kotsyna archive, *fond* 9535 *opis'* 1, *delo* 2, *list* 23–28, Gosudarstvennyi arkhiv rossiiskoi federatsii.

90. "Zasedanie bibliotechnago," 16. The meeting took place on 4 January 1905. See Izrailitin, "O merakh k razvitiiu obshchedostupnykh bibliotek"; and Izrailitin, "Russko-evreiskii obshchedostupnyia biblioteki."

91. See, for instance, "Baron Gintsburgs bibliotek," *Der fraynd,* 18 January 1911.

92. N. Pereferkovich, "O bibliotekakh, knigakh, i eshche koi o chem," *Voskhod* 24, no. 2 (16 January 1904): 48.

93. *Otchet obshchestva dlia rasprostraneniia prosveshcheniia mezhdu evreiami v Rossii za 1910 god,* 21.

94. A. D. Kirzhnits, "Vserossiiskii s"ezd po bibliotechnomy delu," *VOPE,* no. 8 (October 1911): 47–60; I. L., "Bibliotechnyi s"ezd," parts 1 and 2, *Razsvet* 5, no. 24 (12 June 1911): 21 and no. 25 (19 June 1911): 35–36.

95. In 1912, S. L. Tsinberg compiled a catalogue of Hebrew books for adults, Kh. Kh. Fialkov compiled a catalog of Hebrew children's books, and D. Gokhberg compiled a catalog of Yiddish books for teachers . See "Iz deiatel'nosti Obshchestva prosveshcheniia," *VOPE,* no. 16 (October 1912): 104.

96. "Deiatel'nost' Bibliotechnoi Komissii pri Komitete OPE," *VOPE,* no. 11 (January 1912): 106–108.

97. "Deiastel'nost' OPE v 1911 g. (Izvlechenie iz pechataemago otcheta)," *VOPE,* no. 19 (January 1913): supplement 1–8.

98. The Moscow OPE gave 7,865 rubles in subsidies to fifty-five preexisting and new libraries and 9,217 rubles in subsidies to schools. See *Otchet Moskovskago otdela obshchestva dlia rasprostraneniia prosveshcheniia mezhdu evreiami v Rossii za 1912 god* (Moscow: Obshchestvo dlia rasprostraneniia prosveshcheniia mezhdu evreiami v Rossii, 1913).

99. "Soveshchanie po bibliotechnomu delu," *VOPE,* no. 17 (November 1912): 133–140; Nokhri, "Soveshchanie evr. bibliotechykh deiatelei," *Razsvet* 6, no. 45 (9 November 1912): 16–18.

100. "Iz deiatel'nosti Obshchestva Prosveshcheniia," *VOPE,* no. 18 (December 1912): 89.

101. Obshchestvo dlia rasprostraneniia prosveshcheniia mezhdu evreiami v Rossii, *Spravochnik po evreiskomu bibliotechnomu* (St. Petersburg: Tip. I. Fleitmana, 1914), 128–129.

102. A. D. Kirzhnits, "Itogi obsledovaniia evreiskikh bibliotek," *VOPE,* no. 19 (January 1913): 34–35.

103. See for instance, N. B., "K voprosu o bibliotekakh," *Voskhod* 25, no. 15 (April 14, 1905): 9–12 and Izrailitin's response, "Po povodu stat'i g. N. B-ka 'K voprosu bibliotekakh,'" *Voskhod* 25, no. 16 (April 23, 1905): 32.

104. "Biblioteka v m. Fastove, Kievskoi gub," *VOPE*, no. 7 (September 1911): 129–130.

105. A. D. Kirzhnits, "Bibliotechnoe delo u evreev i zadachi Obshchestva Prosvesheniia (Vnutrenniaia organizatsiia evreiskikh bibliotek)," *VOPE*, no. 13 (March 1912): 13.

106. Ibid., 27.

107. "Bibliotechnaia khronika," *VOPE*, no. 3 (January 1911): 113.

108. Kirzhnits, "Bibliotechnoe delo," 13.

109. Kirzhnits, "Itogi obsledovaniia evreiskikh bibliotek," 41.

110. Kirzhnits, "Bibliotechnoe delo," 12.

111. For a survey of librarians in Mogilev and Vitebsk, see I. Edel'man, "Evreiskiia biblioteki v Mogilevskoi i Vitebskoi gub v 1911," *VOPE*, no. 16 (November 1912).

112. Edel'man, "Evreiskiia biblioteki"; Kirzhnits, "Itogi obsledovaniia evreiskikh bibliotek," 40.

113. Jacob Plot, "Di arlozorov bibliotek," in *Sefer ha-zikaron li-kehilat Kamin-Koshirski veha-sevivah*, ed. Abraham Samuel Stein, Y. Krust, and A. M. Orz'itser (Tel Aviv: Irgun yot'se Kamin-Koshirski veha-sevivah be-Yisra'el, 1965), 487–490.

114. *Otchet obshchestva dlia rasprostraneniia prosveshcheniia mezhdu evreiami v Rossii za 1910 god*, 57–58.

115. "Bibliotechnaia khronika," *VOPE*, no. 14 (April 1912): 120–121; "Bibliotechnaia khronika," *VOPE*, no. 13 (March 1912): 128–129; Obshchestvo dlia rasprostraneniia mezhdu evreiami v Rossii, *Spravochnik po evreiskomu bibliotechnomu*, 133.

116. In Kharkov Province, for instance, the average Russian library had 160–190 members, about 100 less than the average Jewish library in Mogilev and Vitebsk. "Narodnyia biblioteki v Kharkovskoi gubernii," *Bibliotekar* 4, no. 2 (1913): 95–96.

117. *Pervaia vseobshchaia perepis,'* 3:131.

118. A. I., "Khronika russko-evreiskago bibliotechnago dela," *Voskhod* 25, no. 12 (24 March 1905): 25.

119. *Pervaia vseobshchaia perepis,'* 3:108.

120. Kirzhnits, "Bibliotechnoe delo." My figures are also derived from dozens of reports sent to the OPE by local libraries and published in the OPE newsletter.

121. Altick, *English Common Reader,* 236.

122. N. A. Rubakin, *Etiudy o russkoi chitaiushchei publike* (St. Petersburg: Popova, 1895), 83–86.

123. *Otchet obshchestva dlia rasprostraneniia prosveshcheniia mezhdu evreiami v Rossii za 1910 god*, 55–57.

124. Ibid., 57–58.

125. Obshchestvo dlia rasprostraneniia mezhdu evreiami v Rossii, *Spravochnik po evreiskomu bibliotechnomu*, 134–135. In Vilna, there were 1,436 readers in 1912 and 30,644 requests for books. In Voronezh there were 171 members and 3,668 requests.

126. Ibid., 135. There were 2,818 members and 52,647 book requests by the end of 1912.

127. "Narodnyia biblioteki v Kharkovskoi gubernii," *Bibliotekar* 4, no. 2 (1913): 96.

128. A. D. Kirzhnits, "Bibliotechnoe delo u evreev i zadachi Obshchestva Prosveshcheniia (Vnutrenniaia organizatsiia evreiskikh bibliotek)," *VOPE*, no. 13 (March 1912): 8.

129. Rubakin, *Etiudy o russkoi chitaiushchei publike,* 90–91.

130. Ts. Ts-n, "K kharakteristike chitatelia-evreia," *Evreiskaia shkola* 1, no. 8 (August 1904): 44.

131. See Edel'man, "Evreiskiia biblioteki," 43–44.

132. "Bibliotechnaia khronika," *VOPE*, no. 7 (September 1911): 122–123; "Bibliotechnaia khronika," *VOPE*, no. 6 (April 1911): 130.

133. Edel'man, "Evreiskiia biblioteki," 42.

134. "Provints," *Der fraynd*, 13 January 1908.

135. "Bibliotechnaia khronika," *VOPE*, no. 12 (February 1912): 126. In 1907, 27 percent of the members of the Kovno community library were women; "Provints," *Der fraynd*, 13 January 1908.

136. "Bibliotechnaia khronika," *VOPE*, no. 14 (April 1912): 121–122.

137. "Bibliotechnaia khronika," *VOPE*, no. 7 (September 1911): 122–123; "Bibliotechnaia khronika," *VOPE*, no. 6 (April 1911): 130; *Otchet obshchestva dlia rasprostraneniia prosveshcheniia mezhdu evreiami v Rossii za 1910 god*, 55–57.

138. D. Svailikh, "Bibliotechnoe delo v Shklove, Mogil. gub.," *VOPE*, no. 5 (March 1911): 128–129; Bibliotechnaia khronika," *VOPE*, no. 6 (April 1911): 129; "Biblioteka prikazchikov-evreev v Odesse (po otchetu za 1910 g)," *VOPE*, no. 7 (September 1911): 124–127.

139. Edel'man, "Evreiskiia biblioteki," 39.

140. Rubakin, *Etiudy o russkoi chitaiushchei publike*, 89.

141. Kharkovskaia gubernskaia zemskaia uprava, *Narodnyia biblioteki kharkovskoi gubernii za 1912 god* (Kharkov: S. P. Iakovlen, 1914), 47.

142. *Pervaia vseobshchaia perepis,'* 3:131.

143. *Pervaia vseobshchaia perepis,'* 41:115. There were 1,500 literate Jewish women and 2,200 literate Jewish men in Melitopol.

144. *Pervaia vseobshchaia perepis,'* 23:135.

145. See Nils H. Roemer, *Jewish Scholarship and Culture in Nineteenth-Century Germany: Between History and Faith* (Madison: University of Wisconsin Press, 2005), 139–141.

146. B. Zaks, "Neskol'ko dannykh po statistike russkago bibliotechnago dela," *Bibliotekar,'* no. 3 (1914): 305.

147. T. A. Ivenina, *Kul'turno-prosvetitel'nyie organizatsii i uchrezhdeniia obshchestvennoi i chastnoi initsiativy v dorevoliutsionnoi rossii (1900–1916 gg.)* (Moscow: Frantera, 2003), 126.

148. For more on modernization in New Russia, see M. Polishchuk, *Evrei Odessy i Novorosii. Sotsial'no-politicheskaia istoriia evreev Odessy i drugikh gorodov Novorossii, 1881–1904* (Jerusalem: Gesharim; Moscow: Mosty Kul'tury, 2002); and Steven J. Zipperstein, *Jews of Odessa: A Cultural History, 1794–1881* (Stanford, Calif.: Stanford University Press, 1985).

149. A. D. Kirzhinits, "Bibliotechnoe delo u evreev i zadachi Obshchestva Prosveshcheniia," *VOPE*, no. 11 (January 1912): 5.

150. P., "Glukhov," *Razsvet* 6, no. 46 (16 November 1912): 31.

151. Ts. Khius, "Provints (fun unzere korespondenten) Baku," *Der fraynd*, 18 September 1908.

152. For one such suggestion, see A. I[zrailitin], "Khronika russko-evreiskago bibliotechnago dela," *Voskhod* 25, no. 13 (31 March 1905): 24.

153. A. D. Kirzhnits, "Bibliotechnoe delo u evreev i zadachi Obshchestva Prosveshcheniia," *VOPE*, no. 11 (January 1912): 3–21.

154. "Tiraspol,' Khers. Gub. (Ot nashego korrespondenta)," *Razsvet* 2, no. 5 (2 February 1908): 26–27.

155. "Biblioteka v m. Fastove, Kievskoi gub," *VOPE*, no. 7 (September 1911): 129–130.

156. B. P-al, "Fastov," *Razsvet* 5, no. 48 (25 November 1911): 35. See also Z. Zlatkin, "Fastov," *Razsvet* 5, no. 12 (20 March 1911): 24–25.

157. Kirzhnits, "Itogi obsledovaniia evreiskikh bibliotek," 32–33.

158. Obshchestvo dlia rasprostraneniia mezhdu evreiami v Rossii, *Spravochnik po evreiskomu bibliotechnomu*, 136.

159. "Kul'turnaia zhizn,'" *Razsvet* 7, no. 22 (31 May 1913): 24.

160. Obshchestvo dlia rasprostraneniia mezhdu evreiami v Rossii, *Spravochnik po evreiskomu bibliotechnomu*, 134.

161. Kirzhnits, "Itogi obsledovaniia evreiskikh bibliotek," 33.

162. I[zrailitin], "Kronika russko-evreiskago bibliotechnago dela," 23–24.

163. "Bibliotechnaia khronika," *VOPE*, no. 4 (February 1911): 100. For more on the Orgeev Public Library, see "Iz otcheta Orgeevskoi obshchestvennoi biblioteki-chital'ni za 1904 g," *Evreiskaia shkola* 2, no. 5 (May 1905): 53–54.

64. See T. Rotenberg, "K bibliotechnomu delu," *Evreiskaia shkola* 2, nos. 8–9 (August–September 1905): 76–77.

165. "Bibliotechnaia khronika," *VOPE*, no. 5 (March 1911): 115. Population statistics from Evreiskoe statisticheskoe obshchestvo, *Evreiskoe naselenie Rossii po dannym perepisi 1897 g i po noveishim istochnikam* (Petrograd: Kadima, 1917), 29.

166. Kirzhnits, "Bibliotechnoe delo u evreev i zadachi Obshchestva Prosveshcheniia," 11. The Voznesenskii situation was reported in "Bibliotechnaia khronika," *VOPE*, no. 6 (April 1911): 131. Population statistics for 1910 on Voznesenskii come from *Evreiskoe naselenie*, 69.

167. "Kishinev," *Razsvet* 3, no. 48 (29 November 1909): 27.

168. Ibid.; "Bibliotechnaia khronika," *VOPE*, no. 3 (January 1911): 114.

169. Kharkovets, "Kharkov," *Razsvet* 5, no. 45 (4 November 1911): 31–32.

170. "Bibliotechnaia khronika," *VOPE*, no. 4 (February 1911): 100.

171. Obshchestvo dlia rasprostraneniia mezhdu evreiami v Rossii, *Spravochnik po evreiskomu bibliotechnomu*, 68.

172. Kirzhnits, "Bibliotechnoe delo u evreev i zadachi Obshchestva Prosveshcheniia," 20.

173. See James Howard Wellard, *The Public Library Comes of Age* (London: Increased Book Service through Library Publicity in Community Studies, 1940), 1–16; Joseph L. Wheeler, *The Library and the Community* (Chicago: American Library Association, 1924); and Ronald C. Benge, *Libraries and Cultural Change* (London: Bingley, 1970).

174. N. Kroshinksy, "Inter der rusish-tsarisher hershaft," in *Baranovits: sefer zikaron*, ed. Avraham Shemuel Shtain (Tel Aviv: Irgun yotse'e baranovits be-yisrael, 1953), 72.

175. Plot, "Di arlozorov bibliotek," 487–490.

176. Dovid Zabludovsky, "Teater, kultur un farveylung in zabludovke," in *Zabludove yizker-bukh: di geshikhte fun der Yidisher kehile Zabludove fun ir breyshes biz ir fartilikung durkh di Natsishe rotshim*, ed. Shmuel Tsesler, Yosef Reznik, and Yitshak Tsesler (Buenos-Aires: Yizker-bukh komitet, 1961), 274.

177. Zolf, *Di letste fun a dor*, 192–193.

178. Quoted in Hundert, "The Library of the Study Hall in Volozhin," 229.

179. Paperna, *Iz Nikolaevskoi epokhi*, 36.

180. Peretz, "Mayn zikhroynes," 129.

181. Quoted in Jonathan Rose, *The Intellectual Life of the British Working Classes* (New Haven, Conn.: Yale University Press, 2001), 84.

182. L. N. Kogan, "Neskol'ko slov o evreiskikh bibliotekakh-chital'niakh," *Razsvet* 2, no. 8 (1 March 1908): 10–13.

183. Wheeler, *The Library and the Community.*

184. Ellen Kellman, "Dos yidishe bukh alarmirit! Towards the History of Yiddish Reading in Inter-War Poland," in *Polin,* vol. 16, *Jewish Popular Culture and Its Afterlife,* ed. Michael C. Steinlauf and Antony Polonsky (Oxford: Littman Library of Jewish Civilization, 2003), 213–242.

3. Reading

1. Richard D. Altick, *The English Common Reader: A Social History of the Mass Reading Public, 1800–1900* (Chicago: University of Chicago Press, 1957).

2. Guglielmo Cavallo and Roger Chartier, eds., *A History of Reading in the West,* trans. Lydia G. Cochrane (Amherst: University of Massachusetts Press, 1999), 2. For influential scholarship on the history of reading, see Robert Darnton, who first broached the topic in the series of essays that became *The Literary Underground of the Old Regime* (Cambridge, Mass.: Harvard University Press, 1982). For works on the history of reading in Russia, see Jeffrey Brooks, *When Russia Learned to Read: Literacy and Popular Literature, 1861–1917* (Princeton, N.J.: Princeton University Press, 1985); and Ben Eklof, *Russian Peasant Schools: Officialdom, Village Culture, and Popular Pedagogy, 1861–1914* (Berkeley: University of California Press, 1986). On the influence of the press in Russia, see Louise McReynolds, *The News under Russia's Old Regime* (Princeton, NJ: Princeton University Press, 1991).

3. Yuri Slezkine, *The Jewish Century* (Princeton, N.J.: Princeton University Press, 2004), 129–130.

4. Sh. Niger, *Geklibene shriftn,* vol. 1, *Lezer, dikhter, kritiker* (New York: Idisher Kultur Farlag, 1928), 1:16–17.

5. Daniel Boyarin, "Placing Reading: Ancient Israel and Medieval Europe," in *The Ethnography of Reading,* ed. Jonathan Boyarin (Berkeley: University of California Press, 1993), 13.

6. Ibid.15.

7. Solomon Ganzfried, *Code of Jewish Law (Kitzur Shulchan Aruch). A Compilation of Jewish Laws and Customs,* trans. Hymon E. Goldin (New York: Star Hebrew Book Company, 1927), 1:88–89.

8. Robert Bonfil, "Reading in the Jewish Communities of Western Europe in the Middle Ages," in *A History of Reading In the West,* ed. Guglielmo Cavallo and Roger Chartier, trans. Lydia G. Cochrane (Amherst: University of Massachusetts Press, 1999), 176.

9. Ganzfried, *Code of Jewish Law,* 1:88–89. See also Judah ben Samuel, *Sefer hasidim* (Warsaw: Levin Epshtain, 1909), 190.

10. For more on rabbinical rulings regarding the care of books, see Simhah Assaf, *Am ha-sefer veha-sefer* (Safed: ha-Muze'on le-'omanut ha-defus, 1964), 10–14.

11. Judah ben Samuel, *Sefer hasidim* (Warsaw: Levin Epshtain, 1909), 189–190.

12. A. I. Paperna, *Iz Nikolaevskoi epokhi,* in *Evrei v Rossii: XIX vek,* ed. V. Kel'ner (Moscow: Novoe literaturnoe obozrenie, 2000), 44.

13. Bonfil, "Reading in the Jewish Communities of Western Europe in the Middle Ages," 149–178. See also Assaf, *Am ha-sefer,* 14–21.

14. Paperna, *Iz Nikolaevskoi epokhi*, 134.

15. Khayim Rabinovitsh, "Haskalah, bund, zelbshuts," in *Sefer Deretsin,* ed. Y. Raban (Tel Aviv: Irgun yotse'e Deretsin, 1971): 81.

16. Reuven Brainin, *Fun mayn lebens-bukh* (New York: YKUF, 1946), 98.

17. S. An-sky, *The Dybbuk and Other Writings,* ed. David Roskies, trans. Golda Werman (New York: Schocken Books, 1992), 73.

18. Arnold Zweig, *The Face of East European Jewry,* ed., trans., and with an introduction by Noah Isenberg (Berkeley: University of California Press, 2004), 37–39.

19. Brainin, *Fun mayn lebens-bukh,* 82.

20. Leon Bernstein, *Ershte shprotsungen: zikhroynes* (Buenos Aires: Gezelshaft far yidish-veltlekhe shuln in Argentine, 1956), 133.

21. Ibid., 133.

22. S. An-sky, *The Dybbuk and Other Writings,* 73.

23. Zweig, *The Face of East European Jewry,* 36–37.

24. For a different interpretation of *maskilic* reading habits, see Iris Parush, *Reading Jewish Women: Marginality and Modernization in Nineteenth-Century Eastern European Jewish Society* (Waltham, Mass.: Brandeis University Press, 2004).

25. Brainin, *Fun mayn lebens-bukh,* 97.

26. Ibid., 90.

27. Moyshe Shmuel Shklarski, "Kontrabandshtshik fun yidisn bukh," in *Lite,* ed. Mendl Sudarski, Urieh Katsenelbogen, and Y. Kisin (New York: Kultur-gezelshaft fun litvishe yidn, 1951), 1:1289.

28. Avrom Kotik, *Dos lebn fun a idishn inteligent* (New York: H. Toybenshlag, 1925), 116.

29. Vladimir Medem, *Fun mayn lebn* (New York: Vladimir Medem Komite, 1923), 1:107.

30. Ibid., 109.

31. Falik Zolf, *Di letste fun a dor: heymishe geshtaltn* (Winnipeg: The Israelite Press, 1952), 189–190.

32. Ibid., 192.

33. Berakhot 4b.

34. Zolf, *Di letste fun a dor,* 8.

35. "Mendil Braynes," in *Ale verk fun Y. L. Peretz* (Vilna: B. Kletskin, 1925), 4:15.

36. *Moreh Nevuhim* (The Guide to the Perplexed), by Moses Maimonides, is a twelfth-century philosophical explication of scripture intended to ease the doubts of scholars who were perplexed by apparent inconsistencies. *Kuzari,* by Judah Halevi, is a twelfth-century apologetic defense of Judaism placed in the framework of the conversion of the king of the Khazars. *Ikkarim* (Principles), by Joseph Albo, is a fifteenth-century theological sermon that outlined fundamental principles of Jewish faith. *Hovot ha-levavot* (Duties of the Heart), by Bahya ibn Pakuda, is a twelfth-century homiletic work outlining the obligations incumbent upon a Jew. *Mesilat yesharim* (The Path of the Upright), by Moses Hayyim Luzzatto, is an eighteenth-century homiletic work about how to overcome obstacles to morality. The work became particularly popular among Eastern European Jews and was generally regarded as second only to ibn Pakuda's *Duties of the Heart* in the canon of homiletic literature. *Seder ha-dorot* (The Order of Generations), by Jehiel ben Solomon Heilpern (1660–1746), was a popular chronology and biography of major rabbinical figures in history. *The Book of Jossipon* is a Hebrew historical narrative of the Second Temple Period written anonymously in the tenth century. *Shalshelet ha-kabbalah* (The Chain of Tradition), by Gedaliah ben Yosef ibn Yahya (1515–1587), was a popular Hebrew history of the Jewish people from the Bible to the Renaissance.

37. Paperna, *Iz Nikolaevskoi epokhi,* 43.

38. Bernstein, *Ershte shprotsungen,* 129–130.

39. Kotik, *Dos lebn fun a idishn inteligent,* 132.

40. Michel de Certeau, "Reading as Poaching," in de Certeau, *The Practice of Everyday Life,* trans. Steven F. Rendall (Berkeley: University of California Press, 1984), 165–176.

41. For more on the polylingualism of Eastern European Jewish society, see Dovid Katz, *Words on Fire* (New York: Basic Books, 2004); and Benjamin Harshav, *The Meaning of Yiddish* (Stanford, Calif.: Stanford University Press, 1990).

42. See, for instance, Tcherikover, *Istoriia obshchestva dlia rasprostraneniia prosveshcheniia mezhdu evreiami v Rossii,* especially 65–77 and 110–126.

43. Abraham Cahan, *The Education of Abraham Cahan,* trans. Leon Stein, Abraham P. Conan, and Lynn Davidson (Philadelphia: Jewish Publication Society of America, 1969), 79.

44. Kotik, *Dos lebn fun a idishn inteligent,* 116.

45. Brainin, *Fun mayn lebens-bukh,* 95.

46. For usage of *vechernik,* see Bernstein, *Ershte shprotsungen,* 130. For a description of circle terminology, see A. Litvak, *Vos geven: etyudn un zikhroynes* (Vilna: B. Kletskin, 1925), 155.

47. Yehuda Slutsky, *Ha-'Itonut ha-yehudit-rusit ba-meʿah ha-'esrim, 1900–1918* (Tel Aviv: ha-Agudah le-Heker Toldot ha-Yehudim, ha-Makhon le-Heker ha-Tefutsot, 1978).

48. For more information about this expedition, see chapter 8.

49. S. A. An-sky, *Dos yudishe etnografishe program* (Petrograd: Yosef Lur'e, 1914), 113.

50. Ibid., 95.

51. Sholem Aleichem, *Fun'm yarid,* in *Ale verk fun Sholem Aleykhem* (New York: Sholem Aleykhem folks-fond oysgabe, 1923, 1942), 27:66.

52. Sonia Ayerof, "Ivie in di yorn 1904–1907," in *Sefer zikaron li-kehilat Ivyeh,* ed. Moshe Kahanovich (Tel Aviv: Irgune yots'e Ivyeh be-Yiśra'el uva-Amerikah, 1968).

53. Y. L. Peretz, "Di fershtoysene," in *Ale verk fun Y. L. Peretz* (Vilna: B. Kletskin, 1925), 2:186.

54. Sholem Aleichem, "Khave," in *Ale verk fun Sholem Aleykhem,* 5:124.

55. Sholem Aleichem, "Keyver oves," in *Ale verk fun Sholem Aleykhem,* 5:91–101.

56. For Jewish women's reading in nineteenth-century Eastern Europe, see Parush, *Reading Jewish Women;* David Roskies, "Yiddish Popular Literature and the Female Reader," *Journal of Popular Culture* 10, no. 4 (1976–1977): 852–858; Shaul Stampfer, "Gender Differentiation and Education of the Jewish Woman in Nineteenth-Century Eastern Europe," in *Polin,* vol. 7, *Jewish Life in Nazi-Occupied Warsaw,* ed. Antony Polonsky (Oxford: Littman Library of Jewish Civilization, 1992): 63–85; and Sh. Niger, ed., *Der Pinkes* (Vilna: B. Kletskin, 1913), 85–138. For a criticism of Parush's argument that women had greater access to Russian literature than men, see Shaul Stampfer's review of her book in *Jews in Russia and Eastern Europe* 52, no. 1 (Summer 2004): 244–248. See also Tova Cohen, "'Information about Women Is Necessarily Information about Men: On Iris Parush's 'Reading Women,'" *Journal of Israeli History* 21, nos. 1–2 (2002): 169–191.

57. See, for instance, Edel'man, "Evreiskiia biblioteki."

58. Moyshe Shmuel Shklarski, "Kontrabandshtshik fun yidns bukh," in *Lite,* ed. Mendl Sudarski, Urieh Katsenelbogen, and Y. Kisin (New York: Kultur-gezelshaft fun litvishe yidn, 1951), 1:1289.

59. See Sarah Abrevaya Stein, *Making Jews Modern: The Yiddish and Ladino Press in the Russian and Ottoman Empires* (Bloomington: Indiana University Press, 2004).

60. Dvoyre Kutnik, "Di ershte yidishe bibliotek," in *Yizkor kehilot Luninyets /
Koz'anhorodok*, ed. Yosef Ze'evi (Tel Aviv: Irgun yots'e Luninyets ve-Koz'anhorodok,
1952), 146–147.

61. Perets Hirschbein, *In gang fun lebn* (New York: Central Yiddish Culture
Organization, 1948), 1:95–96.

62. For Yiddish publishing in Warsaw, see Avrom Reyzen, *Epizodn fun mayn lebn:
literarishe erinerungen* (Vilna: B. Kletskin, 1929), 2:5–10.

63. Ibid., 112.

64. D. A. El'iashevich, *Pravitel'stvennaia politika i evreiskaia pechat' v Rossii, 1797–
1917* (St. Petersburg: Mosty Kul'tury; and Jerusalem: Gesharim, 1999), 453–454. For more
on the Yiddish press in Russia, see Stein, *Making Jews Modern*, especially 23–54; and
Slutsky, *Ha-'Itonut ha-yehudit-rusit*.

65. Stein, *Making Jews Modern*, 48. See also Moshe Grossman and Chaim Finkelstein,
"Haynt," in *Fun noentn over: monografyes un memuarn* (New York: Tsiko, 1956): 2:31.

66. "Kul'turno-prosvetitel'naia khronika," *VOPE*, no. 6 (April 1911): 133. In 1910, a
total of 6,737 books were published in Russia in forty-three non-Russian languages.

67. See Kotsyna archive, *fond* 9535, *opis'* 1, *delo* 2, Gosudarstvennyi arkhiv rossiiskoi
federatsii.

68. A Yudisher arbeyter, "Efentlikhe biblioteken," *Der fraynd*, 3 January 1910.

69. "Provints," *Der fraynd*, 9 March 1908.

70. A. D. Kirzhnits, "Bibliotechnoe delo u evreev i zadachi Obshchestva
Prosvesheniia (Vnutrenniaia organizatsiia evreiskikh bibliotek)," *VOPE*, no. 13 (March
1912): 5.

71. "Biblioteka prikazchikov-evreev v Odesse (po otchetu za 1910 g)," *VOPE*, no. 7
(September 1911): 124–127.

72. A. D. Kirzhnits, "K kharakteristike," *VOPE*, no. 2 (December 1910): 52–53.

73. "Bibliotechnaia khronika," *VOPE*, no. 16 (October 1912): 114–115.

74. Edel'man, "Evreiskiia biblioteki," 47–51.

75. Ts. Ts-n, "K kharakteristike chitatelia-evreia," *Voshkod* 26, no. 8 (1906): 41–48.

76. Tsentral'nyi statisticheskii komitet, *Pervaia vseobshchaia perepis' naseleniia
Rossiiskoi Imperii 1897 g.* (St. Petersburg: Izd. Tsentral'nago statisticheskago komiteta
Ministerstva vnutrennikh diel, 1899–1905), 17:127. "Bibliotechnaia khronika," *VOPE*,
no. 12 (February 1912): 127. See also S. T., "Kovno," *Razsvet* 3, no. 31 (2 August 1909):
19–20.

77. "Bibliotechnaia khronika," *VOPE*, no. 11 (January 1912): 118.

78. "Kul'turno-prosvetitel'naia khronika," *VOPE*, no. 13 (March 1912): 131;
"Bibliotechnaia khronika," *VOPE*, no. 4 (February 1911): 100–101.

79. "Bibliotechnaia khronika," *VOPE*, no. 14 (April 1912): 120.

80. *Otchet obshchestva dlia rasprostraneniia prosveshcheniia mezhdu evreiami v Rossii
za 1910 god* (St. Petersburg: Obshchestvo dlia rasprostraneniia prosveshcheniia mezhdu
evreiami v Rossii, 1911), 58.

81. L. Dynin, "Kiev," *Razsvet* 3, no. 40 (4 October 1909): 20–21.

82. Z. Zlatkin, "Fastov," *Razsvet* 5, no. 12 (20 March 1911): 24–25.

83. Tsentral'nyi statisticheskii komitet, *Pervaia vseobshchaia perepis' naseleniia
Rossiiskoi Imperii 1897 g.* (St. Petersburg: Izd. Tsentral'nago statisticheskago komiteta
Ministerstva vnutrennikh diel, 1899–1905), 41:113, 161.

84. "Bibliotechnaia khronika," *VOPE*, no. 7 (September 1911): 122–123;
"Bibliotechnaia khronika," *VOPE*, no. 6 (April 1911): 130.

85. "Bibliotechnaia khronika," *VOPE*, no. 14 (April 1912): 121–122.

86. For Jewish acculturation in New Russia, see M. Polishchuk, *Evrei Odessy i Novorosii. Sotsial'no-politicheskaia istoriia evreev Odessy i drugikh gorodov Novorossii, 1881–1904* (Jerusalem: Gesharim; Moscow: Mosty Kul'tury, 2002).

87. Tsentral'nyi statisticheskii komitet, *Pervaia vseobshchaia perepis','* 22:95; "Bibliotechnaia khronika," *VOPE*, no. 4 (February 1911): 101. In 1911, less than 60 percent of the holdings of the Jewish library in Bobruisk were in Russian, most likely because of significant gains in Jewish-language books between 1909 and 1911. A preference for Russian over Hebrew can be observed in Brest-Litovsk, where between May 1907 and December 1907, the 779 Hebrew books in the collection circulated 2,082 times, whereas the 587 Russian books circulated 3,093 times. See "Provints (fun undzere dorespondenten)," *Der fraynd,* 14 January 1908.

88. Tsentral'nyi statisticheskii komitet, *Pervaia vseobshchaia perepis','* 22:131.

89. Kirzhnits, "K kharakterstike," 53.

90. Ts. Ts-n, "K kharakteristike," 41–48. See also "Zhargonnia literatura i eia chitateli," *Voskhod* 23, no. 4 (23 January 1903): 21.

91. Hebrew books were also circulated in greater proportion to their holdings, although it is impossible to determine exactly how much greater, as the statistics on holdings group Hebrew-language books together with German-language books. "Bibliotechnaia khronika," *VOPE*, no. 13 (March 1912): 128–129.

92. "Bibliotechnaia khronika," *VOPE*, no. 13 (March 1912): 129–130.

93. "Bibliotechnaia khronika," *VOPE*, no. 3 (January 1911): 112–113.

94. A. Izrailitin, "Obshchedostupnyia biblioteki i zhargonnaia literatura," *Voskhod* 25, no. 26 (29 June 1905): 29–33.

95. Kirzhnits, "Bibliotechnoe delo u evreev i zadachi Obshchestva Prosvesheniia (Vnutrenniaia organizatsiia evreiskikh bibliotek)," 6.

96. Izrailitin, "Obshchedostupnyia biblioteki."

97. Tsipporah Katsenelson-Nakhumov, "Yitskhak Katsenelsons geburt-shtetl," in *Korolits-Korelitsh: hayeha ve-hurbanah shel kehilah Yehudit=kiyum un hurbn fun a Yidisher kehile,* ed. Mikhael Valtser-Fas (Tel Aviv: Akhdut, 1973), 53.

98. Amos Oz, *A Tale of Love and Darkness,* trans. Nicholas de Lange (Orlando: Harcourt, 2004), 38.

99. "Bibliotechnaia khronika," *VOPE,* no. 13 (March 1912): 129–130; "Biblioteka prikazchikov-evreev v Odesse (po otchetu za 1910 g)," *VOPE,* no. 7 (September 1911): 126; *Otchet obshchestva dlia rasprostraneniia prosveshcheniia mezhdu evreiami v Rossii za 1910 god,* 57–58; "Bibliotechnaia khronika," *VOPE,* no. 6 (April 1911): 130; "Bibliotechnaia khronika," *VOPE,* no. 7 (September 1911): 122–123.

100. Mary Stuart, "'The Ennobling Illusion': The Public Library Movement in Late Imperial Russia," *The Slavonic and East European Review* 76, no. 3 (July 1998): 413; "Narodnyiia biblioteki v Kharkovskoi gubernii," *Bibliotekar* 4, no. 2 (1913): 95; A. Peshekhonova, "Iz zhizni odnoi bezplatnoi biblioteki," *Bibliotekar* 4, no. 3 (1913): 176.

101. Nikolai Rubakin, "Knizhnyi priliv i knizhnyi otliv," *Sovremennyi mir,* no. 12 (1909): 8.

102. Nikolai Rubakin, *Etiudy o russkoi chitaiushchei publike: fakty, tsifry i nabliudeniia* (St. Petersburg: Sklad izd. v knizhnykh magazinakh N. P. Karbasnikova, 1895), 123.

103. D. Svailikh, "Bibliotechnoe delo v Shklove, Mogil. gub.," *VOPE*, no. 5 (March 1911): 128–129; "Biblioteka prikazchikov-evreev v Odesse (po otchetu za 1910 g)," *VOPE*, no. 7 (September 1911): 127; "Bibliotechnaia khronika," *VOPE*, no. 14 (April 1912): 120–121; A. Kirzhnits, "K kharakteristike sovremennago chitatelia-evreia," *VOPE*, no. 1 (November 1910): 41.

104. For an analysis of the impact of Verbitskaia on the Russian provinces, see "Chto chitaet provintsiia. Provintsial'noe obozrenie," *Vestnik evropy,* no. 6 (1911): 369–375.

105. For more on these novels, see the introductions to Anastasiia Verbitskaia, *Keys to Happiness: A Novel,* trans. and ed. Beth Holmgren and Helene Goscilo (Bloomington: Indiana University Press, 1999); and Mikhail Artsybashev *Sanin: A Novel,* trans. Michael R. Katz, introduction by Otto Boele, afterword by Nicholas Luker (Ithaca, N.Y.: Cornell University Press, 2001). See also Louise McReynolds, "Reading the Russian Romance: What Did the Keys to Happiness Unlock?" *Journal of Popular Culture* 31, no. 4 (Spring 1998): 95–108; N. M. Zorkaia, *Na rubezhe stoletii: U istokov massovogo iskusstva v Rossii, 1900–1910 godov* (Moscow: Nauka, 1976); A. N. Ostrogorskii, "Pedagogicheskie ekskursii v oblast' literatury ('Sanin' Artsybasheva: K voprosu o besedakh po polovomu voprosu)," *Russkaia shkola,* no. 3, (1908): 1–22.

106. Sh. Menakhem, "Di tsionistishe bavegung in Slutsk," in *Pinkas Slutsk u-venoteha,* ed. Shimshon Nakhmani (New York: Hotsa'at Va'ad ha-sefer, 1962), 299–300.

107. A. Almi, *Momentn fun a lebn: zikhroynes, bilder un epizodn* (Buenos Aires: Tsentral-farband fun Poylishe Yidn in Argentine, 1948), 169–170.

108. For more on the associations between Jews, prostitution, and pornography in Russia during this period, see Laura Engelstein, *The Keys to Happiness: Sex and the Search for Modernity in Fin-de-Siècle Russia* (Ithaca, N.Y.: Cornell University Press, 1992), 299–333.

109. Obshchestvo dlia rasprostraneniia mezhdu evreiami v Rossii, *Spravochnik po evreiskomu bibliotechnomu,* 69.

110. Ts. Ts-n, "K kharakteristike," 46.

111. Quoted in "Bibliotechnaia khronika," *VOPE,* no. 12 (February 1912): 125.

112. A. I[zrailitin], "Khronika russko-evreiskago bibliotechnago dela," *Voskhod* 25, no. 37 (16 September 1905): 28. See also A. Izr[ailitin], "Khronika russko-evreiskago bibliotechnago dela," *Voskhod* 25, no. 39 (29 September 1905): 36–38.

113. S. An-sky, *Narod i kniga: opyt kharakteristiki narodnago chitatelia* (Moscow: L. A. Stoliar, 1914).

114. M. B., "Baranovichi," *Razsvet* 5, no. 5 (30 January 1911): 34. The writer neglected to mention that *Znanie* also published Asch extensively.

115. There have been several studies of Tolstoy's attitudes toward Jews but very few studies on Jewish attitudes toward Tolstoy. For the former, see Harold K. Schefski, "Tolstoi and the Jews," *Russian Review* 41, no. 1 (January 1982): 1–10; L. B., "Tolstoy vegen yuden," *Der fraynd,* 27 and 28 April and 2 May 1910; and A. Tenerama, *L. N. Tolstoy vegen iden* (New York: Di internatsionale bibliotek, 1911). For an example of the latter, see Aaron Riklis, *Liev Tolstoy (zayn leben un zayne verk)* (Warsaw: velt-bibliotek, 1910).

116. Nun, "Vokhendige shmuesen," *Der fraynd,* 5 November 1910.

117. Ts. Ts-n, "K kharakteristike," 41.

118. For some examples see *Knizhnaia letopis'* 3, no. 25 (27 June 1909): 26.

119. *Knizhnaia letopis'* 8, no. 20 (25 May 1913): 30.

120. For more on the genre of the feuilleton, see Katia Dianina, "The Feuilleton: An Everyday Guide to Public Culture in the Age of the Great Reforms," *Slavic and East European Journal* 47, no. 2 (2003): 187–210; and McReynolds, *The News under Russia's Old Regime,* 66–72.

121. See, for instance, *Knizhnaia letopis'* 4, no. 12 (27 March 1910): 21.

122. I. L. Peretz, *Razskazy i skazki,* trans. S. G. Frug (St. Petersburg: Pechatnyi trud, 1909). *Razskazy i skazki* had a press run of 2,000; see *Knizhnaia letopis'* 3, no. 28 (18

July 1909): 18. The third volume of Sholem Asch, *Razskazy i p'esi*, trans. S. G. Frug (St. Petersburg: Znanie, 1909) had a press run of 5,300; see *Knizhnaia letopis'* 3 no. 18 (2 May 1909): 2. By contrast, the third volume of his *Ertsehlungen* had a print run of only 1,000; see *Knizhnaia letopis'* 3 no. 22 (30 May 1909): 17.

123. Mordecai Ze'ev Fayerberg, *Vuhin? ertsehlung*, trans. Leon [Avrom Leyb Yakubovitch] (Warsaw: Velt bibliotek, 1909).

124. Heinrich Heine, *Heynrikh Heynes verk mit zayn biografye*, trans. Leon [Avrom Leyb Yakubovitch], 2 vols. (Warsaw: Velt bibliotek, 1909). See also Heinrich Heine, *Di hartsrayze*, trans. Zalmen Reyzen (Warsaw: Velt bibliotek, 1911).

125. *Knizhnaia letopis'* 3, no. 45 (21 November 1909): 19.

126. Arthur Schnitzler, *Gezamelte shriften*, trans. B. K., ed. H. D. Nomberg, 3 vols. (Warsaw: Velt bibliotek, 1909); *Knizhnaia letopis'* 4, no. 4 (30 January 1910): 28.

127. Most of these translations were done by Avrom Leyb Yakubovitch under the pseudonym "Leon." He translated *Whither?*, the collected works of Heine, Rudyard Kipling's *The Jungle Book*, Guy de Maupassant's *Yvette*, and Knut Hamsun's *The Editor*. He also translated Arthur Conan Doyle, Charles Dickens, and Jack London.

128. His *Between Heaven and Earth* was published in two volumes, each with a print run of 3,000. For publication figures, see *Knizhnaia letopis'* 3 no. 45 (21 November 1909): 19. For other Anokhi works published by Velt bibliotek, see Zalman Yitzkhok Anokhi, *Tsvishen himel un erd* (Warsaw: Velt bibliotek, 1908); Anokhi, *Reb Elhonon, un andere ertsehlungen* (Warsaw: Velt bibliotek, 1910); Anokhi, *Z. Y. Anokhis shriften*, 2 vols. (Warsaw: Velt bibliotek, 1909); and Anokhi, *Reb Abe* (Warsaw: Velt bibliotek, 1910 or 1911).

129. Max Nordau, *Oysgevehlte shriften*, trans. B. K-Y (Warsaw: Velt bibliotek, 1909), 5–6.

130. See Hamutal Bar Yosef, "The Heine Cult in Hebrew Literature of the 1890s and Its Russian Context," in *The Jewish Reception of Heinrich Heine*, ed. Mark H. Gelber (Tübingen: Max Niemeyer Verlag, 1992), 127–138; and Sol Liptzin, "Heine and the Yiddish Poets," in ibid., 67–76.

131. *Tevye in Erets Yisroel* began serialization on 14 February 1909; "Di revolutsie in kleynem beys-midrash," *Der fraynd*, 23 March 1909.

132. *Ivanhoe* ran in *Der fraynd* from 28 May 1910 to 13 September 1910. Serialization of Dickens's *Barnaby Rudge* in *Der fraynd* began on 10 September 1910. For more on Yiddish translations of Dickens and his influence on Yiddish writers, see Leonard Prager, "Charles Dickens in Yiddish (A Survey)," *Jewish Language Review* 4 (1984): 158–178. For *The Man Who Laughs*, see "Dos mentsh vos lakht," *Der fraynd*, 17 June–29 December 1911.

Lamed Shapiro's translation of *Les Miserables* was later published independently with Shimin's press in 1911, *Ivanhoe* with Bikher far ale in 1912, and *Barnaby Rudge* with Kletskin in 1924. In 1912, Lamed Shapiro published his translation of Rudyard Kipling's *Jungle Book*.

133. Edel'man, "Evreiskiia biblioteki," 50.

134. Osip Mandelstam, *The Noise of Time: Selected Prose*, trans. Clarence Brown (Evanston, Ill.: Northwestern University Press, 2002), 70.

135. Reyzen, *Epizodn fun mayn lebn*, 2:7.

136. N. A. Rubakin, *Vi leben di khayes? Bilder fun zeyer leben* (Warsaw: Progres, 1902); *Di vunderlikhe erfindungen* (Warsaw: Progres, 1904); and *Der zayde tsayt oder di entviklung fun der velt, der erd un alts vos es lebt oyf ihr* (Warsaw: Bildung, 1901).

137. N. A. Rubakin, *Al-miftan yeme ha-benayim: sipur yesodato be-divre ha-yamim* (Vilna: Sh. P. Garber, 1893).

138. For more on natural science writing in Russia, see Brooks, *When Russia Learned to Read,* 295–352.

139. *Di greste krimenal protsesen* (Warsaw: Idishes tagenblat, 1909); publication data from *Knizhnaia letopis'* 3, no. 9 (28 February 1909): 20. *Di parizer komuna* (Warsaw: Idishes tagenblat, 1908); publication data from *Knizhnaia letopis'* 2, no. 39 (4 October 1908): 19.

140. *A rayze iber eyrope* (Warsaw: Idishes tagenblat, 1908); *Di khinizer* (Warsaw: Idishes tagenblat, 1908); *Epan* (Warsaw: Idishes tagenblat, 1908). Publication data from *Knizhnaia letopis'* 2, no. 39 (4 October 1908): 18–21.

141. See, for instance, *Napoleons anekdoten un maselekh* (Warsaw: Kultur, 1912); and *Napoleon un froyen* (Warsaw: Kultur, 1912).

142. *Idishe pogrom-protsessen,* 3 vols. (Warsaw: Idishes tagenblat, 1908–1909); *Di shreklekhste momenten in der idisher istoriye,* 3 vols. (Warsaw: Idishes tagenblat 1908); *Di geshikhte fun iden poyln;* and *Di falshe meshikhim bay idn* (Warsaw: Idishes tagenblat, 1908). Publication data from *Knizhnaia letopis'* 3, no. 3 (17 January 1909): 23; *Knizhnaia letopis'* 3, no. 4 (24 January 1909): 22; *Knizhnaia letopis'* 2, no. 35 (6 September 1908): 20; *Knizhnaia letopis'* 2, no. 42 (25 October 1908): 13; and *Knizhnaia letopis'* 2, no. 39 (October 4 1908): 19.

143. *Di idn in khino* (Warsaw : Idishes tagenblat, 1908). Publication data from *Knizhnaia letopis'* 3, no. 4 (24 January 1909): 21.

144. A. D. Kirzhnits, "K kharakteristike," *VOPE,* no. 2 (December 1910): 44. Publication data from *Knizhnaia letopis'* 3, no. 21 (23 May 1909): 4.

145. S. M. Dubnov, *Uchebnik evreiskoi istorii dlia shkoly i samoobraovzniia* (St. Petersburg, 1909); Dubnov, *Kniga zhizni,* 585. Publication data from *Knizhnaia letopis'* 3, no. 29 (25 July 1909): 8.

146. Publication data from *Knizhnaia letopis'* 2, no. 35 (6 September 1908): 19; *Knizhnaia letopis'* 2, no. 45 (15 November 1908): 1; *Knizhnaia letopis'* 3, no. 8 (21 February 1909): 22.

147. L-N., *Der veg tsum glik* (Warsaw: Idishes tagenblat, 1908). Publication data from *Knizhnaia letopis'* 2, no. 49 (13 December 1908): 34.

148. Kirzhnits, "K kharateristike sovremennago," 40; and "Biblioteka prikazchikov-evreev v Odesse (po otchetu za 1910 g)," *VOPE,* no. 7 (September 1911): 126.

149. Kirzhnits, "K kharateristike sovremennago," 40; "Biblioteka prikazchikov-evreev v Odesse (po otchetu za 1910 g)," *VOPE,* no. 7 (September 1911): 126; and Edel'man, "Evreiskiia biblioteki," 47–51.

150. Beth Holmgren and Helen Goscilo note that *Sex and Character* had a total print run of 35,000, the same as each volume of *Keys to Happiness.* For the influence of Weininger on Verbitskaia, see Verbitskaia, *Keys to Happiness,* xix.

151. For the role of sexuality in modernist and Jewish philosophies, see George L. Mosse, "Nationalism and Respectability: Normal and Abnormal Sexuality in the Nineteenth Century," *Journal of Contemporary History* 17, no. 2 (April 1982): 221–246.

152. Edel'man, "Evreiskiia biblioteki," 46–47. Interest in Mark Twain was also evident in articles that appeared in the Yiddish-language press, such as "Mark Tven vegen yuden," *Der fraynd,* 6 May 1910.

153. Peshekonova, "Iz zhizni odnoi bezplatnoi biblioteki," 175. These debates echoed the debate over "the fiction question" that had taken place among English public librarians a generation earlier. See Altick, *The English Common Reader,* 231–236.

154. Sh. Biber, "Vegen a teater far kinder," *Der fraynd,* 26 April 1910.

155. "Di yerlikhe ferzamlung fun der literarisher gezelshaft," *Der fraynd,* 26 January 1911.

156. "Kul'turno-prosvetitel'naia khronika," *VOPE,* no. 12 (February 1912): 127–128; "Varia," *Razsvet* 5, no. 19 (9 May 1911): 23; M. Zalmenson, "Bibliotechnoe soveshchanie," *Razsvet* 7, no. 47 (22 November 1913): 19–20. For more on Yiddish children's literature, see Chone Shmeruk, "Yiddish Adaptations of Children's Stories from World Literature," in *Studies in Contemporary Jewry,* vol. 6, *Arts and Its Uses: The Visual Image and Modern Jewish Society,* ed. Ezra Mendelsohn, 186–200 (New York and Oxford, 1990); and Chone Shmeruk, "Sholem Aleichem un di onheybn fun der yidisher literatur far kinder," *Di goldene keyt* 112 (1984): 39–53. He notes that even when stories by the Brothers Grimm and Hans Christian Andersen were translated into Yiddish after World War I, they came through the intermediary languages of Polish and Russian.

157. For Russia, see McReynolds, *The News under Russia's Old Regime;* and Brooks, *When Russia Learned to Read.* For the impact of the press on the Jewish community of Russia, see, among others, Yehuda Slutsky, *Ha-itonut ha-yehudit-rusit ba-me'ah ha-tesha'-'esreh* (Jerusalem: Mosad Byalik, 1970); Jacob Shatsky, *Zamlbukh lekoved dem tsvey hundert un fuftikstn yovl fun der yiddisher prese* (New York: YIVO, 1937); and Sarah Stein, *Making Jews Modern.*

158. See Brooks, *When Russia Learned to Read,* 111–117.

159. On *Di literarishe monatsshriften,* see Kenneth Moss, "Jewish Culture between Renaissance and Decadence: *Di Literarishe Monatsshriften* and Its Critical Reception," *Jewish Social Studies* 8, no. 1 (Fall 2001): 153–198.

4. Literary Societies

1. Quoted in Isaiah Berlin, *Vico and Herder: Two Studies in the History of Ideas* (London: The Hogarth Press, 1976), 165.

2. Natan M. Meir, "Jews, Ukrainians, and Russians in Kiev: Intergroup Relations in Late Imperial Associational Life," *Slavic Review* 65, no. 3 (Fall 2006): 484–485.

3. Vladimir Levin, "Russian Jewry and the Duma Elections, 1906–1907," in *Jews and Slavs,* ed. Wolf Moskovich, Leonid Finberg, and Martin Feller (Jerusalem: Hebrew University of Jerusalem Center for Slavic Languages and Literatures and the Institute of Jewish Studies, 2000), 238.

4. See Aleksandr Lokshin, "Fantasmagoriia ili gesheft? Sionistskoe dvizhenie glazami tsarskoi administratsii," *Rodina,* nos. 4–5 (2002): 95–101.

5. Y. A. Bar-Levi (Vaysman), "Kaminits-Podolsk," in *Kaminits-Podolsk ve-sevivatah,* ed. Avraham Rosen, H. Sarig, and Y. Bernshtain (Tel Aviv: Irgun yots'e Kaminits-Podolsk u-sevivatah be-Yisra'el, 1965), 19–46.

6. Mikhal Rubenshteyn, "Ivenits un ire tsionistn," in *Sefer Ivenits, Kamin, veha-sevivah* (Tel Aviv: Defus Arazi, 1973), 80.

7. B. V., "Horodnitsah," in *Zvhil (Novogrodvolinsk),* ed. Azri'el Uri and Moredkhai Boneh (Tel Aviv: ha-Igud ha-artsi shel yots'e Zvhil veha-sevivah, 1962), Part 1, 258–260.

8. *Fond 2, opis' 7, delo* 55, Derzhavnyi arkhiv Odeskoi oblasti. Accessed at Central Archives for the History of the Jewish People, RU 389.

9. "Obshchestvennaia zhizn,'" *Razsvet* 1, no. 19 (19 May 1907).

10. "Ustav obshchestva liubitelei evreiskago iazyka 'Agudas khovevei sfas eiver,'" *fond 2, opis' 7, delo* 265, Derzhavnyi arkhiv Odeskoi oblasti. Accessed at Central Archives for the History of the Jewish People, RU395, 11.

11. *Fond 2, opis' 7, delo* 265, Derzhavnyi arkhiv Odeskoi oblasti. Accessed at Central Archives for the History of the Jewish People, RU395, 3.

12. Iwri, "Pervoe obshchee sobranie obshchestva 'Khoveve sfat ever' v S. Peterburge," *Razsvet* 2, no. 2 (12 January 1908): 17–18.

13. "Obshchee sobranie 'Khoveve-sfat ever' v S. Peterburge," *Razsvet* 5, no. 20 (15 May 1911): 30.

14. "Varia," *Razsvet* 1, no. 47 (1 December 1907): 21.

15. "Kul'turno-prosvetitel'naia khronika," *VOPE*, no. 19 (January 1913): 113.

16. Yosef Katz and Yehudah Vaynshtayn, "Agudat ha-Tsionim be-Zgierz," in *Sefer Zgyerz: mazkeret netsakh li-kehilah Yehudit be-Polin,* ed. David Sztokfisz (Tel Aviv: Irgun yots'e Zgyerz be-Yisra'el, 1975), 295–297.

17. Iu. S., "Sobranie O-va 'Khoveve-sfat-ever' v S.-Peterburge," *Razsvet* 5, no. 48 (25 November 1911): 32.

18. "M. L-l, Belostok," *Razsvet* 3, no. 32 (9 August 1909): 19.

19. Aryeh Avatikhi, "Agudat Khovevei Sefat Ever," in *Rovneh: Sefer Zikaron,* ed. Aryeh Avatikhi (Tel Aviv: Irgun yots'e Rovneh be-Yisra'el, 1956), 192.

20. I. O-nskii, "Kovno," *Razsvet* 5, no. 52 (23 December 1911): 33.

21. "V obshchestvakh," *Razsvet* 5, no. 4 (23 January 1911).

22. "Varia," *Razsvet* 2, no. 46 (30 November 1908).

23. A. Tarnopol'skii, "Elizavetgrad (ot nashego korrespondenta)," *Razsvet* no. 41 (9 October 1911): 31.

24. "Provints (me shraybt undz) fun Soroki," *Der fraynd,* 10 August 1908.

25. Pinhas Tsitron, *Sefer Kelts* (Tel Aviv: Irgun ole Kelts be-Yisra'el, 1957), 63.

26. "Ot komiteta Obshchestva Prosveshcheniia," *VOPE*, no. 14 (April 1912): 128.

27. Yisroel Gindel, "Ideishe shtremungen bay der liutsker yugnt," in *Sefer Lutsk* (Tel Aviv: Irgun yots'e Lutsk be-Yisra'el, 1961), 171–177.

28. "Ot kul'turnoi organizatsiia," *Razsvet* no. 26, no. 5 (27 June 1911): 26–27.

29. "Tsu der yudisher konferents," *Der fraynd,* 17 August 1908.

30. Published in "Di yudishe literarishe gezelshaft," *Der fraynd,* 26 June 1908.

31. S. M. Dubnov, *Kniga zhizni: vospominaniia i razmyshleniia: materialy dlia istorii moego vremeni,* ed. Viktor Kel'ner (St. Petersburg: Peterburgskoe vostokovedenie, 1998), 296–297.

32. A. I., "Evreiskoe literaturnoe Obshchestvo," *Razsvet* 5, no. 28 (10 July 1911).

33. "Kul'turno-prosvetitel'naia khronika," *VOPE*, no. 2 (December 1910): 113.

34. Dovid Roykhl, "Vi m'hot amol farshpreyt yidishe literature," in *Pinkas Kremnits: sefer zikaron,* ed. Abraham Samuel Stein (Tel Aviv: Hotsa'at irgun 'ole Kremnits be-Yisra'el, 1954), 377.

35. "Kul'turno-prosvetitel'naia khronika," *VOPE*, no. 5 (March 1911): 118–121; "Kul'turno-prosvetitel'naia khronika," *VOPE*, no. 4 (February 1911): 105; "Kul'turno-prosvetitel'naia khronika," *VOPE*, no. 2 (December 1910): 113; Bibliotechnaia khronika," *VOPE*, no. 3 (January 1911): 115.

36. "Lira un di yidishe literarishe gezelshaft," in *Tshenstokhover yidn,* ed. Raphael Mahler (New York: OFG, 1947), 81.

37. M. B., "Baranovichi (ot nashego korrespondenta)," *Razsvet* 5, no. 5 (30 January 1911).

38. M. Leivi, "Pinsk," *Razsvet* 5, no. 51 (16 December 1911): 30.

39. "Kul'turno-prosvetitel'naia khronika," *VOPE*, no. 1 (November 1910): 110; "Kul'turno-prosvetitel'naia khronika," *VOPE*, no. 2 (December 1910): 113.

40. "Kul'turno-prosvetitel'naia khronika," *VOPE*, no. 4 (February 1911): 104–105.

41. *Fond* 2, *opis'* 7, *delo* 351, Derzhavnyi arkhiv Odeskoi oblasti, accessed at Central Archives for the History of the Jewish People, RU 346.

42. Sophia Dubnova-Erlikh, "In di yorn fun reaktsye," in *Di geshikhte fun bund,* ed. Jacob Sholem Hertz, Grigor Aronson, and Sophia Dubnova-Erlikh (New York: Unzer tsayt, 1960), 556.

43. "Varia," *Razsvet* 2, no. 48 (14 December 1908): 41.

44. Kh., "Iur'ev (ot nashego korrespondenta)," *Razsvet* 4, no. 51 (16 December 1911): 30.

45. M. Reveun, "A kultur pruv," in *Sefer Byalah-Podlaskah,* ed. M. Feigenbaum (Tel Aviv: Kupat gemilut hesed a. sh. kehilat Byalah-Podlaskah, 1961), 234–235.

46. Kalif, "Fun der yudisher gas," *Der fraynd,* 20 January 1911.

47. "Sobranie 'Evr. Literaturnago obshchestva,'" *Razsvet* 2, no. 40 (19 October 1908): 22.

48. "Sobranie 'Evreiskago literaturnago o-va' v Peterburge," *Razsvet* 2, no. 42 (2 November 1908): 22–24.

49. K., "Sobranie 'Evreiskago literaturnago O-va' v Peterburge," *Razsvet* 2, no. 44 (16 November 1908): 19–20.

50. For more on language debates within the society. see "In der yudisher literarisher gezelshaft," *Der fraynd,* 3 February 1910; and "A brief in redaktsie," *Der fraynd,* 15 February 1910.

51. "Varia," *Razsvet* 2, no. 41 (26 October 1908): 27–28.

52. Ia. K., "Sobranie Evr. Lit. Obshchestva v S-Peterburge," *Razsvet* 3, no. 43 (25 October 1909).

53. "Obshchinnaia zhizn,'" *Razsvet* 3, no. 43 (25 October 1909): 25.

54. M. Vinokur, "Berdichev," *Razsvet* 5, no. 6 (6 February 1911): 30–31.

55. "Lira un di yidishe literarishe gezelshaft," 80.

56. "Undzer kultur arbayt," *Der fraynd,* 29 January 1910.

57. N. Kroshinksy, "Inter der rusish-tsarisher hershaft," in *Baranovits: sefer zikaron,* ed. Avraham Shemuel Shtain (Tel Aviv: Irgun yotse'e baranovits be-yisrael, 1953), 71.

58. Dovid Roykhl, "Vi m'hot amol farshpreyt yidishe literature," in *Pinkas Kremnits: sefer zikaron,* ed. Abraham Samuel Stein (Tel Aviv: Hotsa'at irgun 'ole Kremnits be-Yisra'el, 1954), 377.

59. "Kul'turno-prosvetitel'naia khronika," *VOPE,* no. 4 (February 1910): 102–103.

60. *Fond* 2, *opis'* 7, *delo* 243, Derzhavnyi arkhiv Odeskoi oblasti. Accessed at Central Archives for the History of the Jewish People, RU394, 3.

61. *Fond* 2, *opis'* 7, *delo* 243, Derzhavnyi arkhiv Odeskoi oblasti. Accessed at Central Archives for the History of the Jewish People, RU394, 16–19. Excerpts of these documents were published in L. G. Belousova and T. E. Volkova, eds., *Evrei odessy i iuga ukrainy: istoriia v dokumentakh* (Odessa: Studiia Negotsiant, 2002), 1:100–103.

62. A. Sh., "Provints: fun unzere korespondenten, odes, a lektsie vegen dem poet Kh. N. Bialik," *Der fraynd,* 28 April 1908.

63. "Obshchinnaia zhizn,'" *Razsvet* 2, no. 16 (26 April 1908): 33.

64. Ben Ioir, "Bobruisk; ot nashego korrespondenta)," *Razsvet* 2, no. 36 (15 September 1908).

65. "Bibliotechnaia khronika," *VOPE,* no. 3 (January 1911): 116.

66. For the closure of the society, see "Zakrytie evr. Liter. O-va," *Razsvet* 5, no. 28 (10 July 1911): 21–22; A. I., "Evreiskoe Literaturnoe Obshchestvo," *Razsvet* 5, no. 28 (10 July 1911): 3–5; "Di kritishe lage fun der literarisher gezelshaft," *Der fraynd,* 3 July 1911;

Ben-Khayim, "Tsu der lage fun der yudisher literarisher gezelshaft," *Der fraynd,* 3 July 1911; "Tsum fermakhen di yudishe literarishe gezelshaft," *Der fraynd,* 6 July 1911.

67. Quoted in T. A. Ivenina, *Kul'turno-prosvetitel'nyie organizatsii i uchrezhdeniia obshchestvennoi i chastnoi initsiativy v dorevoliutsionnoi rossii (1900–1916 gg.)* (Moscow: Frantera, 2003), 36.

68. See "Obshchestvennaia zhizn,'" *Razsvet* 6, no. 14 (6 April 1912): 35.

69. For the controversies within the society, see Iu. S., "Obshchee sobranie 'Nauchno-literaturnago obshchestva' v S.-Peterburge," *Razsvet* 6 no. 6 (10 February 1912): 25; and Iu. S., "Obshchee sobranie 'Nauchno-literaturnago obshchestva' v S.-Peterburge," *Razsvet* 6, no. 3 (20 January 1912): 35–36.

70. I. L., "B Evr. Literaturno-nauchnom obshchestve," *Razsvet* 7, nos. 14–15 (5 April 1913): 40.

71. *Fond 2, opis' 7, delo* 506, Derzhavnyi arkhiv Odeskoi oblasti. Accessed at Central Archives for the History of the Jewish People, RU 404, 12.

72. Ibid., 18.

73. Ibid., 21–30.

74. "Lira un di yidishe literarishe gezelshaft," 82.

75. "Kul'turno-prosvetitel'naia khronika," *VOPE,* no. 12 (February 1912): 128.

76. "Kul'turno-prosvetitel'naia khronika," *VOPE,* no. 13 (March 1912): 131.

77. "Kul'turno-prosvetitel'naia khronika," *VOPE,* no. 18 (December 1912): 102.

78. "Kul'turno-prosvetitel'naia khronika," *VOPE,* no. 22 (April 1913): 130.

79. *Fond 2, opis' 7, delo* 265, Derzhavnyi arkhiv Odeskoi oblasti. Accessed at Central Archives for the History of the Jewish People, RU 395, 18–20.

80. *Fond 2, opis' 7, delo* 265, Derzhavnyi arkhiv Odeskoi oblasti. Accessed at Central Archives for the History of the Jewish People, RU 395 21–33. Excerpts of these documents were published in Belousova and Volkova, *Evrei odessy,* 98–100.

81. David Vital, *Zionism: The Crucial Phase* (Oxford: Clarendon Press, 1987), 53.

82. Pierre Bourdieu, "Intellectual Field and Creative Projects," *Social Science Information Bulletin* 8, no. 2 (April 1969): 90. See also Fritz Ringer, "The Intellectual Field, Intellectual History and the Sociology of Knowledge," *Theory and Society* 19, no. 3 (June 1990): 269–294.

5. Cultural Performance

1. Milton Singer, *When a Great Tradition Modernizes: An Anthropological Approach to Indian Civilization* (New York: Praeger, 1972), 71.

2. Ibid.

3. Richard Bauman, ed., *Folklore, Cultural Performances, and Popular Entertainments: A Communications-Centered Handbook* (New York: Oxford University Press, 1992), 41. See also Victor Turner, *The Anthropology of Performance* (New York: PAJ Publications, 1986).

4. "Di yudishe literarishe gezelshaft," *Der fraynd,* 26 June 1908.

5. See Ben Ioir, "Bobruisk (ot nashego korrespondenta)," *Razsvet* 2, no. 36 (15 September 1908): 17.

6. Avrom Reyzen, "Der alter moged," in Reyzen, *Ale verk: in 12 bender* (New York: Idish, 1917), 3:164–174.

7. For more on the tradition of preaching, see Joseph Heinemann and Louis Jacobs, "Preaching," in *Encyclopedia Judaica,* 2nd ed., ed. Michael Berenbaum and Fred Skolnik,

(Detroit: Macmillan Reference, 2007), 467–475; Marc Saperstein, *Jewish Preaching, 1200–1800: An Anthology* (New Haven, Conn.: Yale University Press, 1989); Marc Saperstein, *"Your Voice Like a Ram's Horn": Themes and Texts in Traditional Jewish Preaching* (Cincinnati, Ohio: Hebrew Union College Press, 1996); David B. Ruderman, ed., *Preachers of the Italian Ghetto* (Berkeley: University of California Press, 1992); Alexander Altmann, "The New Style of Preaching in Nineteenth-Century German Jewry," in *Studies in Nineteenth-Century Jewish Intellectual History,* ed. Alexander Altmann (Cambridge, Mass.: Harvard University Press, 1964), 65–116; Shimon Zeev Gries, "Preachers and Preaching," in *The YIVO Encyclopedia of Jews in Eastern Europe,* ed. Gershon David Hundert (New Haven, Conn.: Yale University Press, 2008), 1450–1453.

8. Barbara Kirshenblatt-Gimblett, "The Concept and Varieties of Narrative Performance in East European Jewish Culture," in *Explorations in the Ethnography of Speaking,* ed. Richard Bauman and Joel Sherzer (Cambridge: Cambridge University Press, 1974), 297.

9. Zalman Shazar, "Ha-magid mi-Minsk," in *Minsk, 'ir ve-em, korot, ma'asim, ishim, havai,* ed. David Kohen and Shelomoh Even-Shoshan (Tel Aviv: Irgun tose Minsk u-benoteha be-Yisrael, 1975–1985), 501.

10. Pinhas Tsitron, *Sefer Kelts* (Tel Aviv: Irgun ole Kelts be-Yisra'el, 1957), 58–59.

11. Sholem Aleichem, "Mayn bekantshaft mit Kh. N. Bialik," in *Ale verk fun Sholem Aleykhem* (New York: Sholem Aleykhem folks-fond oysgabe, 1923), 15:101–102.

12. A. Mukdoyni, *Yitshak Leybush Perets un dos Yidishe teater* (New York: Yidisher kultur farband, 1949), 157.

13. "Lira un di yidishe literarishe gezelshaft," in *Tshenstokhover yidn,* ed. Raphael Mahler (New York: OFG, 1947), 83.

14. "Kul'turno-prosvetitel'naia khronika," *VOPE,* no. 12 (February 1912): 128–129.

15. Avrom Reyzen, *Epizodn fun mayn lebn: literarishe erinerungen* (Vilna: B. Kletskin, 1929), 3:199.

16. Perets Hirschbein, *In gang fun lebn* (New York: Central Yiddish Culture Organization, 1948), 1:108.

17. Mukdoyni, *Yitshak Leybush Perets,* 139.

18. Swoj, "Literaturnaia poezdka Mendele Moikher-Sforim," *Razsvet* 3, no. 28 (20 September 1909): 16.

19. Sholem Aleichem to Ernestina Rabinovitsh, 22 April 1905, in *Dos Sholem-Aleykhem bukh,* ed. Y. D. Berkowitz (New York: Sholem Aleykhem bukh komitet, 1926), 63.

20. "Lira un di yidishe literarishe gezelshaft," 85.

21. Sh. Rozenfeld, "Kh. N. Bialik in Peterburg," *Der fraynd,* 6 March 1908.

22. M. Sen-ski, "Provints (fun unzer korespondent): Vilno, a tsionistisher ovend," *Der fraynd,* 10 March 1908.

23. A. Sh., "Provints fun unzere korespondenten) Odes, a lektsie vegen dem poet Kh. N. Bialik," *Der fraynd,* 28 April 1908.

24. Hirschbein, *In gang fun lebn,* 1:257–264.

25. Quoted in Y. L. Peretz, "Briv un redes," in *Ale verk fun Y. L. Peretz* (Vilna: B. Kletskin, 1929), 19:243.

26. These were Y. L. Peretz, *Dray ertsehlungen* (Warsaw: Progres, 1908); and Peretz, *In yener tsayt* (Warsaw: Familien bibliotek, 1909).

27. T. A. Ivenina, *Kul'turno-prosvetitel'nyie organizatsii i uchrezhdeniia obshchestvennoi i chastnoi initsiativy v dorevoliutsionnoi rossii (1900–1916 gg.)* (Moscow: Frantera, 2003), 100.

28. Mary Kupiec Cayton, "The Making of an American Prophet: Emerson, His

Audiences, and the Rise of the Culture Industry in Nineteenth-Century America," *American Historical Review* 92, no. 3 (June 1987): 598.

29. Reyzen, *Epizodn fun mayn lebn*, 3:200–203.

30. Quoted in Peretz, "Briv un redes," 243.

31. Ibid., 19:247.

32. Sh. Rozenfeld, "Kh. N. Bialik in Peterburg," *Der fraynd*, 6 March 1908.

33. "Provints. Minsk. Ruka oyf yudish," *Der fraynd*, 7 July 1908.

34. Alter Epshteyn, "Ponevezsh in yor 1906," in *Lite*, ed. Mendl Sudarski, Urieh Katsenelbogen, and Y. Kisin (New York: Kultur-gezelshaft fun litvishe yidn, 1951), 1:1414.

35. Richard Bauman, *Verbal Art as Performance* (Rowley, Mass: Newbury House, 1978), 11.

36. All these events are described in "Kul'turno-prosvetitel'naia khronika," *VOPE*, no. 5 (March 1911): 118–121.

37. "Kul'turno-prosvetitel'naia khronika," *VOPE*, no. 12 (February 1912): 127–128.

38. "Kul'turno-prosvetitel'naia khronika," *VOPE*, no. 11 (January 1912): 119; "Kul'turno-prosvetitel'naia khronika," *VOPE*, no. 17 (November 1912): 150; "Kul'turno-prosvetitel'naia khronika," *VOPE*, no. 18 (December 1912): 102–103.

39. "Vitebskoe evreiskoe lit-muz obshchestvo," *fond* 9532, *opis'* 1, *delo* 52, *list* 10–21, Gosudarstvennyi arkhiv rossiiskoi federatsii.

40. According to Nakhman Mayzel, Peretz began the custom of *kestl ovntn* in 1914 at the Hazomir Society. See Peretz, "Briv un redes," 272.

41. Donald M. Scott, "The Popular Lecture and the Creation of a Public in Mid-Nineteenth-Century America," *Journal of American History* 66, no. 4 (March 1980): 801.

42. "Lodz (fun unzer korespondent)," *Der fraynd*, 12 January 1910.

43. M. Reveun, "A kultur pruv," in *Sefer Byalah-Podlaskah*, ed. F. Feigenbaum (Tel Aviv: Kupat gemilut hesed a. sh. kehilat Byalah-Podlaskah, 1961), 234–235.

44. "Varia," *Razsvet* 5, no. 11 (13 March 1911): 38.

45. "Kul'turno-prosvetitel'naia khronika," *VOPE*, no. 5 (May 1911): 118.

46. "Kul'turno-prosvetitel'naia khronika," *VOPE*, no. 2 (December 1910): 113.

47. "Kul'turno-prosvetitel'naia khronika," *VOPE*, no. 5 (May 1911): 118.

48. Singer, *When a Great Tradition Modernizes*, 75.

49. Scott, "The Popular Lecture," 808.

50. Walter J. Ong, *Rhetoric, Romance, and Technology: Studies in the Interaction of Expression and Culture* (Ithaca, N.Y.: Cornell University Press, 1971), 285; Daniel Boyarin, "Placing Reading: Ancient Israel and Medieval Europe," in *The Ethnography of Reading*, ed. Jonathan Boyarin (Berkeley: University of California Press, 1993), 10–37; Michael Wex and Barbara Kirshenblatt-Gimblett, "Talk," in *The YIVO Encyclopedia of Jews in Eastern Europe*, ed. Gershon David Hundert (New Haven, Conn.: Yale University Press, 2008), 1828–1832.

51. Martin S. Jaffee, *Torah in the Mouth: Writing and Oral Tradition in Palestinian Judaism 200 BCE–400 CE* (New York: Oxford University Press, 2001).

52. Ong, *Rhetoric, Romance, and Technology*, 284; Walter J. Ong, *Orality and Literacy: The Technologizing of the Word* (London and New York: Methuen, 1982), 69.

53. Ong, *Rhetoric, Romance, and Technology*, 74.

54. Ibid.

55. For a characterization of the dominant theories of the distinction between oral and written communication, see Ruth Finnegan, *Literacy and Orality: Studies in the Technology of Communication* (Oxford: Basil Blackwell, 1988), 18.

56. Ong, *Orality and Literacy*, 42.

6. Theater

1. Murray Frame, *School for Citizens: Theatre and Civil Society in Imperial Russia* (New Haven, Conn.: Yale University Press, 2006), 1.

2. Arnold Zweig, *The Face of East European Jewry,* ed., trans., and with an introduction by Noah Isenberg (Berkeley: University of California Press, 2004), 124.

3. Ibid., 123.

4. Victor Turner, *The Anthropology of Performance* (New York: PAJ Publications, 1986), 31–32.

5. See M. Beregovskii, *Purimshpil. Evreiskie narodnye muzykal'no-teatral'nye predstavleniia* (Kiev: Dukh i litera, 2001); and Ahuva Belkin, *Ha-Purim shpil: 'iyunim ba-te'a·tron ha-Yehudi ha-'amami* (Tel Aviv: Mossad Bialik, 2002). See also Mikhl Weichert's memoirs of theater in 1900s Galicia: *Zikhroynes,* vol. 1 (Tel Aviv: Menora, 1960).

6. For more on the development of Jewish theater in Galicia and Bukovina, see Doris A. Karner, *Lachen unter Tränen: Jüdisches Theater in Ostgalizien und der Bukowina* (Vienna: Steinbauer, 2005).

7. Nakhman Mayzel, *Avrom Goldfadn: der foter fun yidishn teater* (Warsaw: Groshn bibliotek, 1935), 9.

8. Ibid., 25.

9. Richard Stites, *Serfdom, Society, and the Arts in Imperial Russia: The Pleasure and the Power* (New Haven, Conn.: Yale University Press, 2005), 44. For more on popular theater in Russia, see Frame, *School for Citizens;* E. Anthony Swift, *Popular Theater and Society in Tsarist Russia* (Berkeley: University of California Press, 2002); and Gary Thurston, *The Popular Theatre Movement in Russia, 1862–1919* (Evanston, Ill.: Northwestern University Press, 1998).

10. Stites, *Serfdom, Society, and the Arts,* 273.

11. For regulations for theater companies, see Swift, *Popular Theater and Society,* 88–130; Charles A. Rudd, *Fighting Words: Imperial Censorship and the Russian Press, 1804–1906* (Toronto: University of Toronto Press, 1982), 251; Louise McReynolds, *Russia at Play: Leisure Activities at the End of the Tsarist Era* (Ithaca, N.Y.: Cornell University Press, 2003), 19; D. A. El'iashevich, *Pravitel'stvennaia politika i evreiskaia pechat' v Rossii, 1797–1917* (St. Petersburg: Mosty Kul'tury; and Jerusalem: Gesharim, 1999), 473–480.

12. These phrases recur in different forms throughout the *Lexicon of Yiddish Theater.* The quoted phrases in this case come from the biography of Yakov Spivakovski (in Zalmen Zylbercweig, ed., *Leksikon fun yidishn teater* [Warsaw: Elisheva, 1934], 2:1528).

13. Mendl Elkin, "Fun mayn lebn," in *Bobroisk: sefer zikaron li-kehilat Bobroisk u-venoteha,* ed. Yehuda Slutsky (Tel Aviv: Yots'e Bobroisk bi-Medinat Yisra'el uva-Artsot-ha-Berit, 1967), 542. See also Mikhl Weichert's memories of German, Polish, and Ukrainian theatrical performances in Galicia: *Zikhroynes,* 1:127–133. "A large part of the tickets were bought up by Jews," he noted (128).

14. L. Berman, *In loyf fun yorn: zikhroynes fun a yidishn arbeter* (New York: Farlag Unzer Tsayt, 1945), 157.

15. Ibid., 158.

16. Vladimir Medem, *Fun mayn lebn* (New York: Vladimir Medem Komite, 1923), 1:127–128.

17. Quoted in Joel Berkowitz and Jeremy Dauber, "Introduction," in *Landmark Yiddish Plays: A Critical Anthology,* ed. Joel Berkowitz and Jeremy Dauber (Albany: State University of New York, 2006), 55.

18. See the account of the performance of *Jews* in the city of Dvinsk in "Men shraybt undz," *Der fraynd*, 6 June 1908.

19. "Gordin's 'Got, mentsh, un tayvl," *Der fraynd*, 28 January 1910.

20. Avrom Reyzen, "Di repetitsie: komedie in tsvey akten," in *Yohr-bukh "Progres": A zshurnal fir literature, vissenshaft un kritik*, ed. Avrom Reyzen (Warsaw: Progres, 1904), 1:41–55.

21. Berman, *In loyf fun yorn*, 156.

22. Mikhl Weichert, *Trupe Tanentsap: a Goldfadn-shpil in a Galitsish shtetl* (Tel Aviv: Menorah, 1966).

23. A. Borukhov, "Teatr i zhizn," *Razsvet* 2, no. 3 (18 January 1908): 12–13.

24. Medem, *Fun mayn leben*, 2:110.

25. For the debate on whether Yiddish theater was founded in Warsaw or Iasi, see L. Dushman, "Iz dos yidishe teater gegrindet in Varshe?" *Literarishe bleter* 13 (30 March 1928): 269.

26. These documents were published in Y. Riminik, "Redifes afn idishn teatr in rusland in di 80-er un 90-er yorn," in *Teater Bukh: zamlung tsum fuftsikyorikn yubiley funm Idishn teatr (1876–1927)* (Kiev: Kultur-Lige, 1927), 74–76. Riminik provides other examples of Sabbath performances being forbidden throughout New Russia.

27. For more on the ban on Yiddish-language theater productions, see John Klier, "'Exit, Pursued by a Bear': The Ban on Yiddish Theatre in Imperial Russia," in *Yiddish Theater: New Approaches*, ed. Joel Berkowitz (Oxford: Littman Library of Jewish Civilization, 2003), 159–174; El'iashevich, *Pravitel'stvennaia politika*, 473–480; and Riminik, "Redifes afn idishn teatr," 73–94.

28. A. Mukdoyni, *Teater* (New York: A. Mukdoyni yubili-komitet, 1927), 108.

29. "Be-artsenu," *Hamelits*, 16 January 1903, 3.

30. For more on early Yiddish theater in the Russian Empire, see Evgenii Binevich, "Gastroliori v Peterburge," Jewish Heritage Society preprints and reprints no. 9, available at www.jewish-heritage.org/prep9.htm; and Evgenii Binevich, "Vozrozhdenie: Evreiskii teatr v Rossii, 1896–1904," Jewish Heritage Society preprints and reprints no. 44, available at www.jewish-heritage.org/prep44.htm; and Y. Liubomirski, "Der idisher teatr in tsarishn rusland," in *Teater-bukh: zamlung tsum fuftsikyorikn yubiley funm Idishn teatr (1876–1927)* (Kiev: Kultur-Lige, 1927), 95–112.

31. Itzik Manger, "Araynfir-vort," in *Yidisher teater in Eyrope tsvishn beyde velt-milkhomest*, ed. Itzik Manger, Jonas Turkow, Moses Perenson (New York: Alveltlekhn yidishn kultur-kongres, 1968), 1:14–15.

32. See El'iashevich, *Pravitel'stvennaia politika*, 367.

33. "Provints (fun unzer korespondent)," *Der fraynd*, 19 February 1908.

34. "Varia," *Razsvet* 1, no. 30 (4 August 1907): 28.

35. "Unzer kultur-arbayt," *Der fraynd*, 29 January 1910.

36. "Obshchinnaia zhizn,'" *Razsvet* 2, no. 34 (31 August 1908): 28.

37. Isaac Turkow-Grudberg, *Di Mame Ester Rokhl* (Warsaw: Yidish bukh, 1953), 111–112.

38. "In yudishen teater," *Der fraynd*, 17 April 1908.

39. Y. Y. Roytberg, "Dos yudishe teater in Kiev," *Der fraynd*, 24 August 1908.

40. "In yudishen tekhum," *Der fraynd*, 15 December 1908.

41. "Varia," *Razsvet* 1, no. 14 (13 April 1907): 29.

42. Bernard Gorin, *Di geshikhte fun idishen teater* (New York: Idisher farlag far literatur un visenshaft, 1923), 2:193.

43. Perets Hirschbein, *In gang fun lebn* (New York: Central Yiddish Culture Organization, 1948), 313–314.

44. Z., "Undzer inteligents—un 'yulikel mit zelikel' (a brief in redaktsie)," *Der fraynd*, 20 January 1908.

45. "Dos yudishe teater un di diplomirte inteligents (a brief in redaktsie)," *Der fraynd*, 1 February 1908.

46. A. Revel'skii, "Evreiskii teatr v Odesse," *Razsvet* 5, no. 42 (14 October 1911): 10–11.

47. Kh. Sh., "Kishinev," *Razsvet* 5, no. 6 (6 February 1911): 31.

48. Y. Sannin, "Dos yudishe teater in Peterburg," *Der fraynd*, 11 March 1909.

49. "A groyse ferzamlung vegen yudishen teater," *Der fraynd*, 10 January 1910.

50. A. Yarkhi, "Etlikhe verter vegen yudishen teater," *Der fraynd*, 8 January 1908; see also A. Yarkhi, "Etlikhe verter fun yudishen teater," *Der fraynd*, 10 January 1908.

51. Sholem Asch, "Vegen a iudishen teater," *Der fraynd*, 24 March 1908.

52. Avrom Yitskhok Kaminski, "Vegen yudishen teater," *Der fraynd*, 8 April 1908.

53. "A groyse ferzamlung vegen yudishen teater," *Der fraynd*, 10 January 1910.

54. Avrom Reyzen, *Epizodn fun mayn lebn: literarishe erinerungen* (Vilna: B. Kletskin, 1929), 3:117.

55. "Sem Adler," in *Leksikon fun yidishn teater*, ed. Zalmen Zylbercweig (New York: Elisheva, 1931), 1:30–32.

56. Hirschbein, *In gang fun lebn*, 116–117.

57. Ibid., 269.

58. A. Mukdoyni, *Yitshak Leybush Perets un dos Yidishe teater* (New York: Yidisher kultur farband, 1949), 168–169.

59. "In yudishen teater," *Der fraynd*, 17 and 18 April 1908.

60. Liubomirski, "Der idisher teatr," 103. Among the most commonly performed literary plays, Liubomirski lists Asch: *Got fun nekome* (God of Vengeance), *Der zindiker* (The Sinner), *Mit'n shtrom* (With the Stream), *Amnon un Tamar* (Amnon and Tamar), and *Yikhes* (Pedigree); Sholem Aleichem: *Tsezeyt un tseshpreyt* (Scattered and Dispersed), *Doktor* (A Doctor), *Mazl-tov* (Congratulations!), *Get* (The Divorce Paper), *Mentshn* (People), and *An eytse* (Advice); Pinski: *Yankl the Smith, Family Zvi,* and *Mother;* Hirshbein: *Di puste kretchme* (The Idle Inn), *Oyf yener zayt takh* (On the Other Side of the River), *A farvorfn vinkl* (A Secluded Corner), and *Tkies kef* (The Handshake); Peretz: *Shvester* (Sister), *S'brent* (It Burns), and *Di goldene keyt* (The Golden Chain); Mark Arnstein: *Dos eybike lid* (The Eternal Song) and *Der vilner balebesl* (The Little Vilna Householder); and S. Nomberg: *Mishpokhe* (Family).

61. Nina Warnke, "Going East: The Impact of American Yiddish Plays and Players on the Yiddish Stage in Czarist Russia, 1890–1914," *American Jewish History* 92, no. 1 (March 2004): 16–17.

62. Reyzen, *Epizodn fun mayn lebn*, 3:132.

63. G. B., "Sobranie 'Evr. Literaturnogo obshchestva' v S-Peterburge," *Razsvet* 3, no. 40 (4 October 1909): 19–20.

64. Ibid.

65. Ibid.

66. "Oykh vegen teater," *Der fraynd*, 29 January 1910.

67. Mukdoyni, *Yitshak Leybush Perets*, 147.

68. Ibid., 155–156.

69. "A groyse ferzamlung vegen yudishen teater," *Der fraynd*, 10 January 1910.

70. F. Novik, "Brief in redaktsie," *Der fraynd*, 12 January 1911.

71. Dr. A. Mukdoyni, "Fun teater," *Der fraynd*, 15 January 1910.

72. Dr. A. Mukdoyni, "Yudishen teater," *Der fraynd*, 22 January 1910.

73. Quoted in Binevich, "Gastroliery v Peterburge."

74. A. Revel'skii, "Evreiskii teatr v Odesse," *Razsvet* 5, no. 42 (14 October 1911): 10–11.

75. "Bibliotechnaia khronika," *VOPE*, no. 3 (January 1911): 117; "A yudishe teater gezelshaft," *Der fraynd*, 11 January 1911.

76. "Kul'turno-prosvetitel'naia khronika," *VOPE*, no. 4 (February 1911): 105–106. For a report on Vayter's visit, see "Kievskiia pis'ma. O kreditnykh uchrezhdeniiakh—ob evreiskom teatre (Ot nashego korrespondenta)," *Razsvet* 5, no. 11 (13 March 1911): 29–30.

77. "Kul'turno-prosvetitel'naia khronika," *VOPE*, no. 5 (March 1911): 121.

78. Mukdoyni, *Yitshak Leybush Perets*, 207.

79. "Iz zhizni provintsii. Minsk (ot nashego korrespondenta)," *Razsvet* 3, nos. 36–37 (13 September 1909): 26.

80. "Minsk (fun unzer korespondent)," *Der fraynd*, 12 February 1910.

81. Zweig, *The Face of East European Jewry*, 123.

7. Musical and Dramatic Societies

1. M. Olgin, *Mayn shtedtel in Ukraine* (New York: M. Gurevitsh'es farlag, 1921), 21–22.

2. Quoted in Yehuda Slutsky, "Bobroisk (Monografie)," in *Bobroisk: sefer zikaron li-kehilat Bobroisk u-venoteha*, ed. Yehuda Slutsky (Tel Aviv: Yots'e Bobroisk bi-Medinat Yisra'el uva-Artsot-ha-Berit, 1967), 153.

3. "Provints," *Der fraynd*, 31 January 1908.

4. Sholem Aleichem, *Fun'm yarid*, in *Ale verk fun Sholem Aleykhem* (New York: Sholem Aleykhem folks-fond oysgabe, 1923, 1942), 27:67.

5. "In yudishen tehkum," *Der fraynd*, 28 December 1908.

6. Evgenii Binevich, "Vozrozhdenie: Evreiskii teatr v Rossii, 1896–1904," Jewish Heritage Society preprints and reprints no. 44, available at www.jewish-heritage.org/prep44.htm.

7. Eyzik Hurvits, "Der 'breshis' fun yidish teater in Dubosar," in *Dubosari: sefer zikaron*, ed. Yosef Rubin (Tel-Aviv: Irgun yots'e Dubosari ba-Amerikah, Argentinah ve-Yisra'el, 1965), 221.

8. Ibid., 224.

9. Nina Warnke, "Going East: The Impact of American Yiddish Plays and Players on the Yiddish Stage in Czarist Russia, 1890–1914," *American Jewish History* 92, no. 1 (March 2004): 1–29.

10. "Yitshok Katsenelson," in *Leksikon fun Yidishn teater*, ed. Zalmen Zylbercweig (Mexico City: Elisheva, 1967), 5:4690–4691.

11. "Lira un di yidishe literarishe gezelshaft," in *Tshenstokhover yidn*, ed. Raphael Mahler (New York: OFG, 1947), 81.

12. Dr. Nekhemieh Kroshinsky, "Prokim tsu der geshikhte fun Baranovitsh," in *Baranovitsh: sefer zikaron* (Tel Aviv: Irgun yots'e Baranovitsh in yisroel, 1953), 70–71.

13. Dovid Zabludovsky, "Teater, kultur un farveylung in zabludovke," in *Zabludove yizker-bukh: di geshikhte fun der Yidisher kehile Zabludove fun ir breyshes biz ir fartilikung durkh di Natsishe rotshim*, ed. Shmuel Tsesler, Yosef Reznik, and Yitshak Tsesler (Buenos-Aires: Yizker-bukh komitet, 1961), 274.

14. "Kul'turno-prosvetitel'naia khronika," *VOPE*, no. 6 (April 1911): 133.

15. "Ustav Mitavskogo evreiskago muz-lit obshchestvo Hazamir," *fond* 9532, *opis'* 1, *delo* 53, Gosudarstvennyi arkhiv rossiiskoi federatsii. See also "Kul'turno-prosvetitel'naia khronika," *VOPE*, no. 14 (April 1912): 122.

16. Yaacov Abramowich, "Basheftikung fun di Korelitsher yidn," in *Korolits-Korelitsh: hayeha ve-hurbanah shel kehilah Yehudit=kiyum un hurbn fun a Yidisher kehile*, ed. Mikhael Valtser-Fas (Tel Aviv: Akhdut, 1973), 155.

17. "Provints (fun unzere korespondenten)," *Der fraynd*, 30 January 1908.

18. Khanan Boledo, "Mosadot khanukh ve-tarbut be-lubats," in *Lubats u-delatits*, ed. K. Hilel (Haifa: Irgun yots'e lubtse ve-delatits), 175; "Provints," *Der fraynd*, 3 March 1908; "Provints (me shraybt undz) fun Ungeni," *Der fraynd*, 13 August 1908.

19. Alter Zimmerman, "Shartutim," in *Megilat Kurenits: ayarah be-hayeha uve-motah*, ed. Aharon Meirovits (Tel Aviv: Irgun yots'e Kurenits be-Yisrael, 1956), 76.

20. Zahava Rabinovich-Engel, "Ha-teatron be navahrdok," in *Pinkas Navaredok*, ed. E. Yerushalmi (Tel Aviv: Relif Komitet a. sh. Aleksander Harkavi be-Artsot ha-Berit, 1963), 118.

21. Meir Edlboym, *Di yidn-shtot Meziritsh* (Buenos Aries: Mezritsher landslayt fareyn in Argentine, 1957), 264.

22. Gedalihu Braverman, "Dramatishe krayzn," in *Sefer Byalah-Podlaskah*, ed. M. Feigenbaum (Tel Aviv: Kupat gemilut hesed a. sh. kehilat Byalah-Podlaskah, 1961), 243.

23. Al. Samoilov, "Nikolaev. (Ot nashego korrespond)," *Razsvet* 5, no. 11 (13 March 1911): 31.

24. Alter Trus and Julius Cohen, *Braynsk sefer ha-zikaron: a bashraybung fun unzer heym* (New York: Braynsker relif komitet, 1948), 150.

25. Pinhas Tsitron, *Sefer Kelts* (Tel Aviv: Irgun ole Kelts be-Yisra'el, 1957), 67.

26. "Provints (fun unzer korespondent)," *Der fraynd*, 18 March 1908.

27. Shlomoh Rubin, "Yidish teater," in *Yizker-bukh fun Rakishok un umgegnt*, ed. Meilech Bakalczuk-Felin (Johannesburg: Rakishker landsmanshaft in Yohanesburg, 1952), 262.

28. Avi-Rut, "Khugim dramatiim," in *Yizkor kehilot Luninyets / Koz'anhorodok*, ed. Yosef Ze'evi (Tel Aviv: Irgun yots'e Luninyets ve-Koz'anhorodok, 1952), 52–53; Rubin, "Yidish teater," 261.

29. Mordechai Zaytshik, "Dos kulturere lebn," in *Kehilat Lenin: sefer zikaron*, ed. Moshe Tamari (Tel Aviv: Vaad yotse'e Lenin, 1956 or 1957), 257.

30. Eliyahu Dubkin, "Beit Tsioni," in *Bobroisk: sefer zikaron li-kehilat Bobroisk u-venoteha*, ed. Yehuda Slutsky (Tel Aviv: Yots'e Bobroisk bi-Medinat Yisra'el uva-Artsot-ha-Berit, 1967), 417–418.

31. N. Kroshinsky, "Onhoyb fun yidishn teater in Baranovitsh," in *Baranovitsh: sefer zikaron* (Tel Aviv: Irgun yots'e Baranovitsh in yisroel, 1953), 69–70.

32. Itshe Akhtman, "Yidish Teater," in *Yizker-bukh Khelm*, ed. Meilech Bakalczuk-Felin (Johannesburg: Khelmer landsmanshaft, 1954), 229.

33. Avrom-Yitzkhok Slutski, "Der kulturerer matsev in undzer shtetl," in *Kehilat Lenin: sefer zikaron*, ed. Moshe Tamari (Tel Aviv: Vaad yotse'e Lenin, 1956 or 1957), 253–255.

34. Aaron Shuster, *Lipkan fun amol* (Montreal: A. Shuster, 1957), 65.

35. Yisroel Garmi, "World War I and Its Aftermath," in *Luboml: The Memorial Book of a Vanished Shtetl*, ed. Berl Kagan (Hoboken, N.J.: Ktav, 1977), 81–82.

36. Ibid., 81.

37. Jacob Gordin, *Yakov Gordin's dramen* (New York: Soyrkel fun Yakov Gordin's Fraynt, 1911), 1:37.

38. Perets Hirschbein, *Barg arop*, in Hirschbein, *Gezamelte shriften* (New York: Literarish-dramatishe fereynen in Amerike, 1916), 5:5–88.

39. Sholem Ash, *Mit'n shtrom* (Warsaw: Lidski, 1909), 16–17.

40. The play was first published in 1904 in Hebrew in *Hashiloah* under the Hebrew title *Yatseh ve hazar* and in Yiddish in *Yidishe bibliotek* under the Yiddish title *Tsurikgekumen*. The play was published in a new edition under the title *Mitn Shtrom* in 1909 by the Warsaw-based Progress Publishers.

41. Sholem Aleichem, "Tsezeyt un tseshpreyt," in *Ale verk fun Sholem Aleykhem*, 4:57. My translations are based on an unpublished translation of this play by Jeremy Dauber.

42. Ibid., 91.

43. Ibid., 34.

44. Ibid., 93.

45. Ibid., 93.

46. A. Mukdoyni, "Der repertuar fun'm yudishen teater in rusland far dem yohr tre"b," in *Der Pinkes*, ed. Sh. Niger (Vilna: B. Kletskin, 1913), 265–271.

47. Pinhas Tsitron, *Sefer Kelts* (Tel Aviv: Irgun ole Kelts be-Yisra'el, 1957), 67.

48. Ze'ev Yunis, "Di alte heym," in *Pinkes Mlave*, ed. Ya'akov Shatzky (New York: Velt-farband Mlaver yidn, 1950), 105.

49. Advertisement: "Originele yudishe muzik," *Der fraynd*, 7 January 1908.

50. "Proket ustava evreiskago myzykal'nogo obshchestva," *fond* 1747 *opis'* 1, *delo* 1, Tsentral'nyi gosudarstvennyi istoricheskii arkhiv Sankt Peterburga. For more on the Jewish Folk Music Society, see G. B. Kopytova, *Obshchestvo evreiskoi nadornoi muzyki v peterburge-petrograde* (St. Petersburg: EZRO, 1997); and James Benjamin Loeffler, "'The Most Musical Nation': Jews, Culture and Nationalism in the Late Russian Empire" (Ph.D. diss., Columbia University, 2006).

51. For the programs of performances, see *fond* 1747, *opis'* 1, *delo* 2 (protokoly), Tsentral'nyi gosudarstvennyi istoricheskii arkhiv Sankt Peterburga.

52. *Fond* 1747, *opis'* 1, *delo* 17 (perepiski), Tsentral'nyi gosudarstvennyi istoricheskii arkhiv Sankt Peterburga.

53. For branches, see *fond* 1747, *opis'* 1, *delos* 6, 7, 11, 12, 13, 14, and 15 (otdelenikh obshchestva), Tsentral'nyi gosudarstvennyi istoricheskii arkhiv Sankt Peterburga.

54. Loeffler, "'The Most Musical Nation'"; and Lynn Mary Sargeant, "Middle Class Culture: Music and Identity in Late Imperial Russia" (Ph.D. diss., Indiana University, 2001).

55. "Der aktyor Matisyahu (Matus) Kovalsky," in *Lubats u-delatits*, ed. K. Hilel (Haifa: Irgun yots'e lubtse ve-delatits, 1971), 214–215.

56. Leyb Kadison, "Kovner dramatish-muzikalishe gezelshaft un di 'Vilner Trupe,'" in *Lite*, ed. Mendl Sudarski, Urieh Katsenelbogen, and Y. Kisin (New York: Kultur-gezelshaft fun litvishe yidn, 1951), 535–540.

57. Nehamiah Vornik, "Zikhronot," in *Sefer Kobrin: megilat hayim ve-hurban*, ed. Betsalel Shvarts (Tel Aviv: Hadash, 1951), 61–62.

58. Mordechai Meyerovits, "Zikhroynes fun der alter heym," in *Korolits-Korelitsh: hayeha ve-hurbanah shel kehilah Yehudit=kiyum un hurbn fun a Yidisher kehile*, ed. Mikhael Valtser-Fas (Tel Aviv: Akhdut, 1973),119; and Yakov Abramowits, "Basheftikung fun di Korelitsher yidn," in ibid., 149–158.

59. Meir Edlboym, *Di yidn-shtot Meziritsh* (Buenos Aries: Mezritsher landslayt fareyn in Argentine, 1957), 265.

60. Vornik, "Zikhronot," 65.

61. Raye Shneur, "Teatron ve-tizmoret," in *Korolits-Korelitsh: hayeha ve-hurbanah shel kehilah Yehudit=kiyum un hurbn fun a Yidisher kehile,* ed. Mikhael Valtser-Fas (Tel Aviv: Akhdut, 1973), 174.

62. Binyomin Yoali (Yevelevski), "Zikhroynes fun der alter heym," in *Sefer Nisviz,'* ed. David Sztokfisz (Israel: Irgun yots'e Nisviz' be-Yisra'el uva-tefutsot, 1976), 343; Moyshe Vlotshinskii, "Funem Niesvizsher yidishn shteyger," in ibid., 340–342.

63. Aaron Shuster, *Lipkan fun amol* (Montreal: A. Shuster, 1957), 90–91.

64. Naftoli Gross, "Yosl Klezmer ratevet di shtot fun a sreyfe," in *Pinkes-Kolomey: geshikhte, zikhroynes, geshtaltn, hurbn,* ed. Shlomo Bickel (New York: Rausen Bros., 1957), 251–252. The story is set in Kolomeia in Galicia, on the other side of the Russian border.

65. T-Sh, "M. Dunaevtsy," *Razsvet* 5, no. 52 (23 December 1911): 32–33.

66. Kroshinsky, "Prokim tsu der geshikhte," 71.

67. Shlomoh Rubin, "Yidish teater," in *Yizker-bukh fun Rakishok un umgegnt,* ed. Meilech Bakalczuk-Felin (Johannesburg: Rakishker landsmanshaft in Yohanesburg, 1952), 261.

68. Bar-gash, "Provints: Byalistok. Sholem-Aleichem's forlezungen," *Der fraynd,* 13 June 1908.

69. "Varia," *Razsvet* 2, no. 48 (14 December 1908): 41.

70. "Kul'turno-prosvetitel'naia khronika," *VOPE,* no. 2 (December 1910): 115.

71. "Varia," *Razsvet* 3, no. 49 (6 December 1909): 39.

72. Banner advertisement on front page of *Der fraynd,* 31 January 1910.

73. Reyzen, *Epizodn fun mayn lebn,* 2:17–22.

74. For a description of one such event in Galicia, see Mikhl Weichert, *Zikhroynes,* 1:136–137.

75. *Der fraynd,* 29 February 1908, front page.

76. M. Sen-ski, "Provints (fun unzer korespondent): Vilno, a tsionistisher ovend," *Der fraynd,* 10 March 1908.

77. Jacob Levin, "Kobrin beshnot 1909–1913," in *Sefer Kobrin: megilat hayim ve-hurban,* ed. Betsalel Shvarts (Tel Aviv: Hadash, 1951), 88–89.

78. For more on the repertoire of Hebrew-language theater in the late nineteenth century, see Shmuel Avisar, *Ha-mahazeh veha-teatron ha-Ivri veha-Yidi* (Jerusalem: Re'uven Mas, 1996).

79. Aher, "Gomel," *Razsvet* 6, no. 28 (13 July 1912): 29.

80. Ibid.

81. "Novosti literatury i teatra," *Razsvet* 6, no. 8 (24 February 1912): 24.

82. Mikhl Weichert, *Teater un drame* (Warsaw: Yiddish, 1922), 10.

83. Ibid., 15. Peretz Hirschbein also theorized about many of these themes in his memoirs. See Hirschbein, *In gang fun lebn,* especially 324–326.

8. The Jewish Historical and Ethnographic Society

1. The most influential book on Jewish history and Jewish memory is probably Yosef Hayim Yerushalmi, *Zakhor: Jewish History and Jewish Memory* (Seattle: University of Washington Press, 1982). For different approaches to this subject, see Amos Funkenstein, *Perceptions of Jewish History* (Berkeley: University of California Press, 1993); David G. Roskies, *The Jewish Search for a Usable Past* (Bloomington: Indiana University Press, 1999); Michael Meyer, *Judaism within Modernity: Essays on Jewish History and Religion* (Detroit, Mich.: Wayne State University Press, 2001); Michael Meyer, "The Emergence of Jewish Historiography: Motives and Motifs," *History and Theory* 27, no. 4 (1988): 160–175; Michael Brenner, *Propheten des Vergangenen: Jüdische*

Geschichtsschreibung im 19. und 20. Jahrhundert (Munich: C. H. Beck, 2006); and Nils Roemer, *Jewish Scholarship and Culture in Nineteenth-Century Germany: Between History and Faith* (Madison: University of Wisconsin Press, 2005).

2. Ismar Schorsch, *From Text to Context: The Turn to History in Modern Judaism* (Hanover, N.H.: Brandeis University Press, 1994), 1.

3. For more on the Jewish community of St. Petersburg, see Benjamin Nathans, *Beyond the Pale: The Jewish Encounter with Late Imperial Russia* (Berkeley: University of California Press, 2002); and Mikhail Beizer, *The Jews of St. Petersburg: Excursions through a Noble Past* (Philadelphia, Pa.: The Jewish Publication Society, 1989).

4. For more on the education movement, see David Wartenweiler, *Civil Society and Academic Debate in Russia, 1905–1914* (Oxford: Clarendon Press, 1999), 165–215; and T. A. Ivenina, *Kul'turno-prosvetitel'nyie organizatsii i uchrezhdeniia obshchestvennoi i chastnoi initsiativy v dorevoliutsionnoi rossii (1900–1916 gg.)* (Moscow: Frantera, 2003).

5. See Schorsch, *From Text to Context*, 51–70.

6. David L. Preston, "The German Jews in Secular Education, University Teaching, and Science: A Preliminary Inquiry," *Jewish Social Studies* 38, no. 2 (1976): 99–116.

7. For studies of these historical societies, see Robert Liberles, "Postemancipation Historiography and the Jewish Historical Societies of America and England," in *Studies in Contemporary Jewry,* vol. 10, *Reshaping the Past: Jewish History and the Historians,* ed. Jonathan Frankel, 45–65 (New York: Oxford University Press, 1994); David Myers, *Re-Inventing the Jewish Past: European Jewish Intellectuals and the Zionist Return to History* (New York: Oxford University Press, 1995); Cecile Esther Kuznitz, "The Origins of Yiddish Scholarship and the YIVO Institute for Jewish Research" (Ph.D. diss., Stanford University, 2000); Roemer, *Jewish Scholarship and Culture;* and David N. Myers and David B. Ruderman, eds., *The Jewish Past Revisited: Reflections on Modern Jewish Historians* (New Haven, Conn.: Yale University Press, 1998). The Jewish Historical and Ethnographic Society is largely unstudied in contemporary literature. Even its leader, Simon Dubnow, still awaits an academic biography or critical monograph. His daughter Sophia Dubnova-Erlikh's biography, *Life and Work of S. M. Dubnov: Diaspora Nationalism and Jewish History,* ed. Jeffrey Shandler (Bloomington: Indiana University Press, 1991), is useful but nonacademic. Robert Seltzer's "Simon Dubnov: A Critical Biography of His Early Years" (Ph.D. diss., Columbia University, 1970) deals only with Dubnow's early years and is largely based on Dubnow's own autobiography. Several festschrifts on Dubnow have been published, including Aaron Steinberg, ed., *Simon Dubnov: The Man and His Work* (Paris: Section Française du Congré Juif Mondial, 1963); Shimon Ravidowicz, ed., *Sefer Shimon Dubnov* (London, Jerusalem, and Waltham, Mass.: Hotsa'at Erret, 1954); and Kristi Groberg and Avraham Greenbaum, eds., *A Missionary for History: Essays in Honor of Simon Dubnov* (Minneapolis: University of Minnesota,1998). The best analysis of Dubnow's philosophical thought is probably still Koppel Pinson's introduction to Simeon Dubnov, *Nationalism and History* (Philadelphia: Jewish Publication Society of America, 1958).

8. For *maskilic* history, see Shmuel Feiner, *Haskalah and History: The Emergence of a Modern Jewish Historical Consciousness,* trans. Chaya Naor and Sondra Silberston (Oxford and Portland, Ore.: The Littman Library of Jewish Civilization, 2002).

9. F. I. Leontovich, "Istoricheskoe obzor postanovlenii o evreiakh v Rossii," *Sion* 2, no. 19 (10 November 1861) through 2, no. 27 (5 January 1862) and 2, no. 41 (13 April 1862) through 2, no. 43 (27 April 1862).

10. Some of these documents were published in 1879 and 1880 in *Evreiskaia biblioteka,* and 662 documents were later published in a compilation; see S. A. Bershadskii, *Russko-evreiskii arkhiv: deokumenty i materialy dlia istorii evreev v Rossii* (St.

Petersburg: Obshchestva rasporstran. prosveshch. mezhdy evreiami v Rossii, 1882). Two more volumes were published later, and a fourth was planned but never completed.

11. For Orshanskii's writings on law, see "Russkoe zakonodatel'stvo o evreiakh," *Evreiskaia biblioteka* 3 (1873); and *Russkoe zakonodatel'stvo o evreiakh. Ocherki i issledovaniia* (St. Petersburg: A. E. Landau, 1877). See also I. G. Orshanskii, *Evrei v Rossii. Ocherki ekonomicheskago i obshchestvennago byta russkikh evreev* (St. Petersburg: O. I. bakst, 1877). For more on Orshanskii, see "Il'ia Grigo'evich Orshanskii," *Evreiskaia biblioteka* 6 (1878): 3–17; "I. G. Orshanskii (1846–1875): ego zhizn' i literaturnaia deiatel'nosti," in *Galleria evreiskikh deiatelei. Literaturno-biograficheskii ocherki*, ed. Iu. I. Gessen (St. Petersburg: A. E. Landau, 1898), 75–86; M. G. Morgulis, "I. Orshanskii i ego issledovaniia po russkomu pravu," *Vestnik prava* 10 (1900); M. G. Morgulis, *Il'ia Grigo'evich Orshanskii i ego literaturnaia deiatel'nost* (St. Petersburg: A. E. Landau, 1901); and Dr. P. Iampol'skii, "Vospominaniii ob I. G. Orshanskom," *Evreiskaia starina* 4 (1911): 55–70.

12. I. G. Orshanksii, "Prostonarodnyia pesni russkikh evreev," in Orshanskii, *Evrei v Rossii*.

13. For more on Orshanskii and the relationship between lawyers and Jewish history in Russia, see Benjamin Nathans, "On Russian-Jewish Historiography," in *Historiography of Imperial Russia: The Profession and Writing of History in a Multinational State*, ed. Thomas Sanders (Armonk, N.Y.: M. E. Sharpe, 1999), 397–432; and Nathans, *Beyond the Pale*, 315–325.

14. Genrikh Sliozberg, *Dela minuvshikh dnei: zapiski russkago evreia* (Paris: Pascal, 1933–1934), 2:224.

15. I. Berlin, "Avraam Iakovlevich Garkavi. K piatidesiatiletnemy iubileiu ego nauchno-literaturnoi deiatel'nosti," *Evreiskaia starina* 3 (1910): 593. The society's grants helped fund the publication of Bershadskii's *Russki-evreiskii arkhiv: dokumenty i materialy dlia istorii evreev v Rossii* (St. Petersburg: Obshchestva rasprostran. prosveshch. mezhdu evreiami v Rossii, 1882).

16. S. M. Dubnov, "Ob izuchenii istorii russkikh evreev i ob uchrezhdenii russko-evereiskago istoricheskago obshchestva," *Voskhod* 4, no. 9 (April–September 1891): 1–91.

17. Ibid., 1. Italics in original.

18. Shimon Dubnov, "Nahpesah ve-nahkorah," *Pardes* 1 (1892): 221–242.

19. S. M. Dubnov, *Kniga zhizni: vospominaniia i razmyshleniia: materialy dlia istorii moego vremeni*, ed. Viktor Kel'ner (St. Petersburg: Peterburgskoe vostokovedenie, 1998), 160.

20. See Paul Eric Soifer, "The Bespectacled Cossack: S. A. Bershadskii (1850–1896) and the Development of Russo-Jewish Historiography" (Ph.D. diss., Pennsylvania State University, 1975), 14–15; and M. Polishchuk, *Evrei Odessy i Novorosii. Sotsial'no-politicheskaia istoriia evreev Odessy i drugikh gorodov Novorossii, 1881–1904* (Jerusalem: Gesharim; Moscow: Mosty Kul'tury, 2002), 239–243. For more on the OPE, see I. M. Cherikover, *Istorii obshchestva dlia rasprostraneniia prosveshcheniia mezhdu evreiami v Rossii (Kul'turno-obshchestvennyiia techeniia v russkom evreistve), 1863–1913* (St. Petersburg: I. Fleitman / I Lur'e, 1913).

21. O. O. Gruzenberg, *Yesterday: Memoirs of a Russian-Jewish Lawyer*, trans. Don C. Rawson and Tatiana Tipton (Berkeley: University of California Press, 1981), 41–43.

22. M. Vinaver, *Nedavnee (Vospominaniia i kharakteristiki)* (Paris, Imp. d'Art Voltaire, 1926), 115.

23. Sh. Ginzburg, *Amolike Peterburg* (New York: Tsiko Bikher-Farlag, 1944), 110.

24. Ibid., 108.

25. Ibid., 105.

26. G. B. Sliozberg, "Dela minuvshikh dnei," in *Evrei v Rossii: XIX vek*, ed. Victor Efimovich Kel'ner (Moscow: Novoe literaturnoe obozrenie, 2000), 414.

27. Vinaver, *Nedavnee*, 114.

28. Ibid.

29. Ibid., 100–102.

30. M. Kulischer, *Das Leben Jesu: eine Sage von dem Schicksale und Erlebnissen der Bodenfrucht, insbesondere der sogenannten palästinensischen Erstlingsgarbe, die am Passahfeste im Tempel* (Leipzig: Otto Wigand, 1876).

31. Vinaver, *Nedavnee*, 260.

32. Sliozberg, *Dela minuvshikh dnei*, 3:114.

33. M. I. Kulisher, *Razvod i polozhenie zhenshchiny* (St. Petersburg: B. M. Vol'f, 1896).

34. Vinaver, *Nedavnee*, 258.

35. Biographical information on Kulisher was drawn from Sliozberg, *Dela minuvshikh dnei*, 112–118; and Vinaver, *Nedavnee*, 256–263.

36. Dubnov, *Kniga zhizni*, 163.

37. Sliozberg, *Dela minuvshikh dnei*, 3:111.

38. Ibid., 112.

39. *Regesty i nadpisi: svod materialov dlia istorii evreev v Rossii (80 g–1800 g)* (St. Petersburg: Obshchestvo dlia rasprostraneniia prosveshcheniia mezhdu evreiami v Rossii, 1899).

40. The 568-page work was initially serialized as a supplement to *Voskhod* throughout 1892 as "Sistematicheskii ukazatel' literatury o evreiakh na russkom iazyke so vremeni vvdeniia grazhdanskago shrifta (1708 g) po dekabr' 1889 g."

41. Sliozberg, *Dela minuvshikh dnei*, 3:121–124.

42. A. I., "Zasedanie istoriko-etnograficheskoi kommissii pri 'Obshchestve rasprostraneniia prsveshcheniia mezhdu evreiami,'" *Voskhod* 25, no. 12 (24 March 1905): 43–45.

43. "Zasedanie istoriko-etnograficheskoi kommissii," *Voskhod* 23, no. 15 (1903).

44. "Zhargonnaia literature i eia chitateli," *Voskhod* 23, no. 4 (23 January 1903): 19–21.

45. *Fond* 2129, *opis'* 1, *delo* 1, Tsentral'nyi gosudarstvennyi istoricheskii arkhiv Sankt Peterburga.

46. "Ustav evreiskago Istoriko-etnograficheskago obshchestva," *fond* 2129, *opis'* 1, *delo* 1, Tsentral'nyi gosudarstvennyi istoricheskii arkhiv Sankt Peterburga. The language of the charter can be compared to that in Dubnov, "Ob izuchenii istorii," 78–82.

47. *Fond* 2129, *opis'* 1, *delo* 54, *list* 1–2, Tsentral'nyi gosudarstvennyi istoricheskii arkhiv Sankt Peterburga. See also "Uchreditel'noe sobranie i publichnyia zasedaniia Evreiskago Istoriko-Etnograficheskago Obshchestva," *Evreiskaia starina* 1 (1909): 154–158.

48. "Uchreditel'noe sobranie i publichnyia zasedaniia Evreiskago Istoriko-Etnograficheskago Obshchestva," 154.

49. Ibid., 157.

50. S. M. Dubnov, "Chto takoe evreiskaia istoriia? Opyt filosofskoi kharakteristiki," *Voskhod* 13, nos. 10–11 (1893): 122.

51. Dubnov, *Kniga zhizni*, 153–154.

52. M. Vinaver, "Kak my zanimalis istoriei," *Evreiskaia starina* 1 (1909): 49.

53. Ibid., 52.

54. Dubnov, *Kniga zhizni*, 299. For more on the relationship between *Perezhitoe* and *Evreiskaia starina*, see Dubnov's review of the first issue of *Perezhitoe*, published in *Evreiskaia starina* 1 (1909): 288–302.

55. "Ot redaktsii," *Evreiskaia starina* 1 (1909) v. See also *fond* 2129, *opis'* 1, *delo* 54, *list* 4–7, Tsentral'nyi gosudarstvennyi istoricheskii arkhiv Sankt Peterburga.

56. "Ot redaktsii," *Evreiskaia starina* 1 (1909), vi.

57. *Fond* 2129, *opis'* 1, *delo* 54, *list* 14, Tsentral'nyi gosudarstvennyi istoricheskii arkhiv Sankt Peterburga.

58. M. A. Soloveichik, M. I. Kulisher, and L. A. Sev, eds., *Ocherki po evreiskoi istorii i kul'ture: istoricheskaia khrestomatiia* (St. Petersburg: Evreiskago istoriko-etnograficheskago obshchestvo, 1912). The book was reviewed in "Kritika i bibliografia," *Evreiskaia starina* 5 (1912): 95–96. The second volume was never published. Dubnov's *Textbook of Jewish History for Schools and Self-Education* was, in many ways, a similar effort. See S. M. Dubnov, *Uchebnik evreiskoi istorii dlia shkoly i samoobrazovaniia,* 3 vols. (Odessa, 1900–1907).

59. "Kul'turno-prosvetitel'naia khronika," *VOPE*, no. 11 (January 1912): 119.

60. For reports of large numbers of remainders of the first volume, see *fond* 2129, *opis'* 1, *delo* 60, *list* 17, Tsentral'nyi gosudarstvennyi istoricheskii arkhiv Sankt Peterburga.

61. "Izveshcheniia o premiiakh za nauchnye i uchebnye trudy," *Evreiskaia starina* 5, no. 1 (1912): 110.

62. "Ot komiteta," *Evreiskaia starina* 3, no. 43 (1910): 461–462. Emphasis in original.

63. Ibid.; emphasis in original.

64. See Dubnov, "Ob izuchenii," 46–76.

65. For hostility to the Gesamtarchiv, see Roemer, *Jewish Scholarship and Culture,* 119–120.

66. *Fond* 2129, *opis'* 1, *delo* 54, *list* 99, Tsentral'nyi gosudarstvennyi istoricheskii arkhiv Sankt Peterburga.

67. Ibid., 99–100.

68. *Otchet evreiskago istoriko-etnograficheskago obshchestvo za 1910 god* (St. Petersburg: I. Fleitman, 1911); *Otchet evreiskago istoriko-etnograficheskago obshchestvo za 1914 god* (St. Petersburg: I. Fleitman, 1915).

69. *Otchet evreiskago istoriko-etnograficheskago obshchestvo za 1912 god* (St. Petersburg: I. Fleitman, 1913), 3.

70. In 1912, the JHES gave a 100-ruble subsidy to the Riga department of the JHES to pay for the publication of documents relating to the Jews of Riga and Courland, which were being edited by I. Joffe. See "Otchet evreiskago istoriko-etnograficheskago obshchestvo za 1912 god."

71. *Fond* 2129, *opis'* 1, *delo* 54, *list* 12–13, Tsentral'nyi gosudarstvennyi istoricheskii arkhiv Sankt Peterburga.

72. S. D., "Pinkos 'velikogo grada' Dubno," *Evreiskaia starina* 4 (1911): 435. The publication was Hayyim Ze'eb Margalioth, *Dubna rabati toldot ha-'ir dubna ve ha-at'akot mi-pinkas ha-kahal shelah mi-shenat 475 ve-hal'ah . . .* (Warsaw: Bi-defus ha-Tsefirah, 1910).

73. "Soobshcheniia korrespondentov *Evreiskoi Stariny,*" *Evreiskaia starina* 2 (1909): 126–127.

74. "Prikliucheniia evreia vo vremia pol'skago vozstaniia," *Evreiskaia starina* 3 (1910): 390.

75. P. Sonin, "Vospominaniia o iuzhnorusskikh pogromakh 1881 goda," *Evreiskaia starina* 2 (1909): 207–218.

76. David Kogan, "Pervyia desiatiletiia evreiskoi obshchiny v Odesse i pogrom 1821 goda (po istochnikam i semeinym predaniiam)," *Evreiskaia starina* 4 (1911): 260–267.

77. D. Z., "Lipman Zel'tser. (Iz semeinykh vospominanii)," *Evreiskaia starina* 4 (1911): 293–298.

78. *Fond* 2129, *opis'* 1, *delo* 54, *list* 61, Tsentral'nyi gosudarstvennyi istoricheskii arkhiv Sankt Peterburga.

79. *Fond* 2129, *opis'* 1, *delo* 54, *list* 7, Tsentral'nyi gosudarstvennyi istoricheskii arkhiv Sankt Peterburga, 80.

80. S. Beilin, "Iz razskazov o kantonistakh," *Evreiskaia starina* 2 (1909): 115.

81. G. Barats, "Dva dokumenta 1828 goda," *Evreiskaia starina* 4 (1911): 95.

82. M. Merimzon, "Razskaz starago soldata," *Evreiskaia starina* 5 (1912): 290–301, 406–422; "Razskaz starago soldata," *Evreiskaia starina* 6 (1913): 86–95, 221–232. The memoirs were later published as Meir Merimson, *Zikhroynes fun a Nikolayever soldat* (Vilna: B. Kletskin, 1921).

83. I. Itskovich, "Vospominaniia arkhangel'skago kantonista," *Evreiskaia starina* 5 (1912): 54. For another article on cantonists, see Kh. Korobkin, "Evreiskaia rekrutchina v tsarstvovanie Nikolai I," *Evreiskaia starina* 6 (1913): 70–85, 233–244.

84. "Zametki i soobshcheniia," *Evreiskaia starina* 5 (1912): 85.

85. Ibid., 85–90.

86. I. Galant, "Offitsial'naia perepiska o prekrashchenii kolonizatsii evreev v Novorossiiskom krae (1862)," *Evreiskaia starina* 5 (1912): 330–334; "Goneniia na evreiskuiu odezhdu (1871)," *Evreiskaia starina* 5 (1912): 334–338.

87. Lev Shternberg, "Probelmy evreiskoi etnografii," *Evreiskaia starina* 12 (1928): 12–13.

88. Dubnov, *Kniga Zhizni*, 73.

89. See Christoph Daxelmüller, "Max Grunwald and the Origins and Conditions of Jewish Folklore at Hamburg," in *Proceedings of the Ninth Congress of Jewish Studies, Jerusalem, August 4–12, 1985: Division D, Volume 2, Art, Folklore, Theater, Music* (Jerusalem: World Union of Jewish Studies, 1986), 2:73–80; Adam Rubin, "Hebrew Folklore and the Problem of Exile," *Modern Judaism* 25, no. 1 (2005): 62–83.

90. See Itzik Nakhmen Gottesman, *Defining the Yiddish Nation: The Jewish Folklorists of Poland* (Detroit, Mich.: Wayne State University Press, 2003). Gottesman points out that the Polish folklore collectors, such as Menakhem Kipnis and Shmuel Lehman, often obtained material from family, friends within the intelligentsia, and their own memories. Much of the folklore collection in Poland was characterized by a tension between differing conceptions of the nature of the folk within the Eastern European Jewish tradition.

91. S. Beilin, "Iz razskazov o kantonistakh," *Evreiskaia starina* 2 (1909): 115–116.

92. S. Beilin, "Anekdoty o evreiskom bezpravii," *Evreiskaia starina* 2 (1909): 269.

93. Ibid., 278.

94. Ibid., 281.

95. Dubnov, *Kniga zhizni*, 306.

96. "Soobshchenie," *Evreiskaia starina* 8 (1915): 239–240. For more on An-sky, see Gabriella Safran and Steven J. Zipperstein, eds., *The Worlds of S. An-sky: A Russian Jewish Intellectual at the Turn of the Century* (Stanford, Calif.: Stanford University Press, 2006). For more on An-sky's ethnographic work, see Eleanor Moltek, ed., *S. Ansky (Shloyme-Zanvl Rappoport), 1863–1920: His Life and Work, Catalog of an Exhibition* (New York: YIVO, 1980); and Benjamin Lukin, "Ot narodnichestva k narodu (S. A. An-sky—etnograf vostochno-evropeiskogo evreistva)," in *Evrei v Rossii: Istoriia i kul'tura,* ed. D. A. El'iashevich (St. Petersburg: Peterburgskii evreiskii universitet, 1995). For documents on the expedition, see Irina Sergeeva, ed., "Khozhdenie v evreiskii narod:

etnograficheskie ekspeditsii Semena An-skogo v dokumentakh," *Ab Imperio, no.* 4 (2003): 395–428; and "Perepiska barona Gintsburga i S. An-skogo po povodu etnograficheskikh ekspeditsii v cherte evreiskoi osedlosti," *Ab Imperio, no.* 4 (2003): 429–473.

97. S. An-sky, "O evreiskoi narodnoi pesne," *Evreiskaia starina* 2 (1909): 56.

98. S. An-sky, "Novyi sbornik narodnykh pesen," *Evreiskaia starina* 4 (1911): 591–594.

99. For more on this debate, see Gottesman, *Defining the Yiddish Nation.*

100. S. An-sky, "Narodnyia detskiia pesni," *Evreiskaia starina* 3 (1910): 391.

101. Ibid., 393.

102. S. A. An-sky, *Dos yudishe etnografishe program* (Petrograd: Yosef Lur'e, 1914), 9.

103. Ibid., 13–15.

104. H. Gilernt, "Di anski-ekspeditsie in Kremenits," in *Pinkas Kremnits: sefer zikaron,* ed. Abraham Samuel Stein (Tel Aviv: Hotsa'at irgun 'ole Kremnits be-Yisra'el, 1954), 370.

9. Public History

1. For more on early Russian Jewish historiography, see Paul Eric Soifer, "The Bespectacled Cossack: S. A. Bershadskii (1850–1896) and the Development of Russo-Jewish Historiography" (Ph.D. diss., Pennsylvania State University, 1975); and Benjamin Nathans, "On Russian-Jewish Historiography," in *Historiography of Imperial Russia: The Profession and Writing of History in a Multinational State,* ed. Thomas Saunders (New York: M. E. Sharpe, 1999), 397–432. See also Joel Raba, *Between Remembrance and Denial: The Fate of the Jews in the Wars of the Polish Commonwealth during the Mid-Seventeenth Century as Shown in Contemporary Writings and Historical Research* (Boulder, Colo.: East European Monographs, 1995).

2. A. Ia. Harkavy, *Ob iazyke evreev zhivshikh v drevnee vremia na Rusi i o slavianskikh slovakh vstrechaemykh y evreiskikh pisatelei* (St. Petersburg: Imp. akademii nauk, 1865); Harkavy, "Rus i russkoe v sredne-vekovoi evreiskoi literature," *Voskhod* 1, no. 1 (1881): 62–84 and 2, no. 1 (1882): 239–225; and S. A. Bershadskii, *Litovskie evrei* (St. Petersburg: M. M. Stas'iulevicha, 1883), 395.

3. S. Dubnov, "Razgovornyi iazyk i narodnaia literatura pol'sko-litovskikh evreev v XVI i pervoi polovine XVII veka," *Evreiskaia starina* 1 (1909): 7–40. Notably, in one of the last articles Dubnow wrote, he argued that linguistic assimilation was not necessarily a sign of national assimilation because many of the greatest Jewish creative works had been written in non-Jewish languages. See S. Dubnov, "Russko-evreiskaia intelligentsia v istoricheskom aspekte," *Evreiskii mir ezhegodnik na 1939 god* (Paris: Ob'edinenie russko-evreiskoi intelligentsii, 1939): 11–16.

4. D. Maggid, "Inoiazychnye zagovory u russkikh evreev," *Evreiskaia starina* 3 (1910): 591.

5. Mikhail Kulisher, "Pol'sha s evreiam u rus' bez evreev," *Evreiskaia starina* 3 (1910): 214–234.

6. See Samuel Weissenberg, "Südrussische Amulette," *Verhandlungen der Berliner Gesellschaft für Anthropologie, Ethnologie und Urgeschichte* 29 (1897): 367–369; and John Efron, *Defending the Jewish Race* (New Haven, Conn.: Yale University Press, 1994), 109.

7. Quoted in Shmuel Feiner, *Haskalah and History: The Emergence of a Modern Jewish Historical Consciousness,* trans. Chaya Naor and Sondra Silberston (Oxford and Portland, Ore.: The Littman Library of Jewish Civilization, 2002), 193. For more on *maskilic* attitudes toward Jewish dress, see I. Klausner, "Ha-gezerah al tilboshot ha-yehudim," *Gal-Ed: On the History of the Jews of Poland* 6 (1982): 11–26.

8. "Goneniia na evreiskuiu odezhdu (1871)," *Evreiskaia starina* 5 (1912): 335. See also "Domashnii reglament v belorussii (1845)," *Evreiskaia starina* 3 (1910): 110–117.

9. *Otchet evreiskago istoriko-etnograficheskago obshchestva za 1915 god* (St. Petersburg: I. Fleitman, 1916). The minute books were eventually released as an independent volume as Simon Dubnov, ed., *Pinkas ha-medinah o Pinkas Va'ad hakehilot ha-rashiyot bi-medinat Lita* (Berlin: 'Ayanot, 1925).

10. See, for instance, Perets ben Barukh Asher Perles, *Geschichte der Juden in Posen* (Breslau: Verlag der Schletterschen Buchhandlung, 1865). For a list of other examples see S. D., "Akty evreiskago koronnago seima, ili 'Vaada chetyrekh oblastei,'" *Evreiskaia starina* 5 (1912): 70.

11. See S. D., "Akty evreiskago koronnago seima, ili 'Vaada chetyrekh oblastei,'" *Evreiskaia starina* 5 (1912): 70–84, 178–186, 453–459.

12. See his first letter, originally published as S. Dubnov, "Pis'ma o starom i novom evreistve," *Voskhod* 16, no. 11 (November 1897): 3–21.

13. S. Dubnov, "Pis'ma o starom i novom evreistve. Pis'mo sed'moe. Avtonomizm, kak osnova national'noi programmy," *Voskhod* 20, no. 12 (December 1901): 4–5.

14. David N. Myers, *Re-Inventing the Jewish Past: European Jewish Intellectuals and the Zionist Return to History* (New York: Oxford University Press, 1995), 114–115.

15. Feiner, *Haskalah and History*.

16. "Materyały do historyi Berka Ioselewicza," *Jedność*, no. 19 (1909). Numerous pamphlets, brochures, and articles were written about Joselewicz in the late nineteenth century, but the first scholarly monograph did not appear until 1909; see Ernest Luninski, *Berek Joselevicz i jego sy: zarys historyczny* (Warsaw: Nakl. Tow. Akc. S. Orgelbranda Synów, 1909).

17. David Kandel, "Berek Ioselewicz. Przemówiénie wygloszone w Kole historycznem na Universitecie Lembergskim, dnia 5 maja 1909," *Przegląd historyczny* 9, no. 3 (1909): 290–298. For the review, see Majer Balaban, "Obzor literatury po istorii evreev v Pol'she (1907–1908)," *Evreiskaia starina* 3 (1910): 312–314.

18. The paper was published as S. Mstislavskaia, "Berek Ioselevich i evo syn,'" *Evreiskaia starina* 2 (1909): 128–148. The talk was delivered by Dubnova on 18 October 1909. The quote is from page 128.

19. S. Dubnov, "Evreiskaia pol'sha v epokhu poslednykh razdelov," *Evreiskaia starina* 4 (1911): 455. The segments of the article dealing with Joselewicz are on pages 452–457.

20. "Uchastie vilenskikh evreev v traure po smerti Kostiushko," *Evreiskaia starina* 1 (1909), 114–116.

21. M. Balaban, "Galitsiiskie evrei vo vremia revoliutsii 1848 goda," *Evreiskaia starina* 5 (1912): 435.

22. S. Dubnov, "Protsessy gumanizatsii i nationalizatsii v noveishei istorii evreev," *Evreiskii mir*, no. 1 (January 1909): 42.

23. M. Balaban, "Galitsiiskie evrei vo vremia revoliutsii 1848 goda," *Evreiskaia starina* 5 (1912): 424.

24. The story of Kohn has recently been retold by Michael Stanislawski in *A Murder in Lemberg: Politics, Religion, and Violence in Modern Jewish History* (Princeton, N.J.: Princeton University Press, 2007).

25. M. Balaban, "Galitsiiskie evrei vo vremia revoliutsii 1848 goda," *Evreiskaia starina* 5 (1912): 439.

26. Ibid., 438.

27. S. Dubnov, "Protsessy gumanizatsii i nationalizatsii v noveishei istorii evreev": 29–30.

28. Ibid., 31.

29. Ibid., 32.

30. Ibid., 35.

31. Ibid., 29–49.

32. "Ustav evreiskago Istoriko-etnograficheskago obshchestva," *fond* 2129, *opis'* 1, *delo* 1, Tsentral'nyi gosudarstvennyi istoricheskii arkhiv Sankt Peterburga.

33. *Transactions: The Jewish Historical Society of London, Sessions 1902–1905* (Edinburgh and London: Ballantyne, Hanson, and Co., 1908), 317.

34. "Ot redaktsiia," *Evreiskaia starina* 1 (1909): iv.

35. For more on the cultural identity of Ostjuden, see Nathan Birnbaum, *Was sind Ostjuden? Zur ersten Information* (Vienna: R. Löwit, 1916).

36. For more on the Karaites, see Raphael Mahler, *Karaimer: a Yidishe geule-bavegung in Mitlalter* (New York: E. Shulman, 1947).

37. For Firkovich's findings, see A. Firkovich, *Sefer Avnei Zikaron: ha-measef reshimot ha-masevot 'al qivrey beney Yisrael be-hasi ha-iqirim* (Vilna: Sh. Y. Fin ve R. A. S. Rosenqrans, 1872).

38. Abraham Harkavy, *Altjüdische Denkmäler aus dem Krim mitgetheilt von Abraham Firkowitsch (1839–1872)* (St. Petersburg: Impr. De l'Acad, 1876). For more on the debate between Firkovich and Harkavy, see I. Berlin, "Avraam Iakovlevich Garkavi. K piatidesiatiletnemy iubileiu ego nauchno-literaturnoi deiatel'nosti," *Evreiskaia starina* 3 (1910): 592–598.

39. Iulii Gessen, "Bor'ba Karaimov g. Trok s Evreiami," *Evreiskaia starina* 3 (1910): 569–579.

40. For ethnography in Russia, see Yuri Slezkine, *Arctic Mirrors: Russia and the Small Peoples of the North* (Ithaca, N.Y.: Cornell University Press, 1994); Robert Geraci, *Window on the East: National and Imperial Identities in Late Tsarist Russia* (Ithaca, N.Y.: Cornell University Press, 2001); and Nathaniel Knight "Constructing the Science of Nationality: Ethnography in Mid-Nineteenth Century Russia" (Ph.D. diss., Columbia University, 1995).

41. L. Zaydel, "Evrei na ural," *Evreiskaia starina* 3 (1910): 422–426.

42. I. Markon, "David Lekhno," *Evreiskaia starina* 3 (1910): 599–602.

43. For more on Weissenberg, see John M. Efron, *Defenders of the Race: Jewish Doctors and Race Science in Fin-de-Siècle Europe* (New Haven, Conn.: Yale University Press, 1994), 91–122.

44. S. Vaisenberg, "Evrei v Turkestane," *Evreiskaia starina* 5 (1912): 390.

45. S. Vaisenberg, "Istoricheskiia gnezda Kavkaza i Kryma," *Evreiskaia starina* 6 (1913): 60.

46. Ibid., 69. See also S. Vaisenberg, "Familii karaimov i krymchakov," *Evreiskaia starina* 6 (1913): 384–399.

47. S. Vaisenberg, "Istoricheskiia gnezda Kavkaza i Kryma," *Evreiskaia starina* 6 (1913): 52.

48. M. Kozmin, "Proshloe i nastoiashchee sibirskikh sektantov-subbotnikov," *Evreiskaia starina* 6 (1913): 3. See also Kozmin, "Iz byta Subbotnikov," *Evreiskaia starina* 7 (1914): 443–458; and I. Neiman, "O Subbotnikakh na Amure," *Evreiskaia starina* 8 (1915): 183–185.

49. Kozmin, "Proshloe i nastoiashchee," 3.

50. Ibid., 6.

51. Ibid.

52. Ibid., 19–20.

53. Ibid., 180.

54. M. Balaban, "Iz istorii karaimov v Galitsii," *Evreiskaia starina* 4 (1911): 117–124.

55. I. Shipper, "Ranniia etadii evreiskoi kolonizatsii v Pol'she," *Evreiskaia starina* 4 (1911): 356–357.

56. M. Balaban, "Pravovoi stroi Evreev v Pol'she," *Evreiskaia starina* 3 (1910): 39–60, 161–191, 324–345; M. Balaban, "Pravovoi stroi Evreev v Pol'she," *Evreiskaia starina* 4 (1911): 40–54.

Conclusion

1. See Steven Zipperstein, "The Politics of Relief: The Transformation of Russian Jewish Communal Life during the First World War," in *Studies in Contemporary Jewry*, vol. 4, *The Jews and the European Crisis, 1914–1921*, ed. Jonathan Frankel, 22–40 (New York: Oxford University Press, 1988); and Oleg Budnitskii, ed., *Mirovoi krizis 1914–1920 godov i sud'ba vostochnoevropeiskogo evreistva* (Moscow: ROSSPEN, 2005). For the cultural impact of the Great War, see Aviel Roshwald and Richard Stites, eds., *European Culture in the Great War: The Arts, Entertainment, and Propaganda, 1914–1918* (Cambridge: Cambridge University Press, 1999); and Modris Eksteins, *Rites of Spring: The Great War and the Birth of the Modern Age* (New York: Houghton Mifflin, 1989).

2. *Fond* 2129, *opis'* 1, *delo* 60, *list* 38, Tsentral'nyi gosudarstvennyi istoricheskii arkhiv Sankt Peterburga.

3. *Fond* 2129, *opis'* 1, *delo* 77, *list* 1, Tsentral'nyi gosudarstvennyi istoricheskii arkhiv Sankt Peterburga.

4. *Fond* 2129, *opis'* 1, *delo* 60, *list* 7, Tsentral'nyi gosudarstvennyi istoricheskii arkhiv Sankt Peterburga.

5. Ibid., *list* 9.

6. Ibid., *list* 10–11.

7. Ibid., *list* 3.

8. Ibid., *list* 13.

9. Ibid., *list* 17.

10. For the fate of the Jewish Ethnographic Museum, see Igor Krupnik, "Jewish Holdings of the Leningrad Ethnographic Museum," in *Tracing An-Sky: Jewish Collections from the State Ethnographic Museum in St. Petersburg*, ed. Mariëlla Beukers and Renée Waale (Zwolle: Waanders Uitgevers, 1992), 16–12.

11. S. An-sky, *Khurbn Galitsye*, in An-sky, *Gezamelte shriften* (Vilna, Warsaw, and New York: An-sky, 1922), 4:21–22.

12. Yisroel Garmi, "World War I and Its Aftermath," in *Luboml: The Memorial Book of a Vanished Shtetl*, ed. Berl Kagan (Hoboken, N.J.: Ktav, 1997), 73.

13. "Teater in Ivie," in *Sefer zikaron li-kehilat Ivyeh*, ed. Moshe Kahanovich (Tel Aviv: Irgune yots'e Ivyeh be-Yiśra'el uva-Amerikah, 1968), 388–390.

14. For more on World War I in Russia, especially the movement of peoples, see Eric Lohr, *Nationalizing the Russian Empire: The Campaign against Enemy Aliens during World War I* (Cambridge, Mass.: Harvard University Press, 2003); and Peter Gatrell, *A Whole Empire Walking: Refugees in Russia during World War I* (Bloomington: Indiana University Press, 2005).

15. Y. A. Bar-Levi (Vaysman), "Kaminits-Podolsk," in *Kaminits-Podolsk ve-sevivah*, ed. Avraham Rosen, H. Sarig, and Y. Bernshtain (Tel Aviv: Irgun yots'e Kaminits-podolsk u sevivatah be-Yisra'el, 1965), 19–46. See also A. Stit, "Ha-haganah be-Zhbanits," in ibid., 161–169.

16. Garmi, "World War I and Its Aftermath," 77–79.

17. Yakov Plot, "Der onhoyb fun der tsionistisher bavegung in Kamin-Kashirski," in *Sefer ha-zikaron li-kehilat Kamin-Koshirski veha-sevivah*, ed. Abraham Samuel Stein,

Y. Krust, and A. M. Orz'itser (Tel Aviv: Irgun yot'se Kamin-Koshirski veha-sevivah be-Yisra'el, 1965), 426.

18. Barukh Yanovits, "Hayei tarbut," in *Kapresht 'ayaratenu,* ed. Barukh Yanovits (Haifa: Irgun yots'e Kapresht be-Yisra'el, 1980), 86.

19. Dov Tabachnik, "He-halutz be-Kapresht," in *Kapresht 'ayaratenu,* ed. Barukh Yanovits (Haifa: Irgun yots'e Kapresht be-Yisra'el, 1980), 114–115.

20. Hayim Dan, "Mekorot ha-yanikah shelanu," in *Sefer Horokhov,* ed. Hayim Dan (Tel Aviv: Irgun yots'e Horokhov be-Yisra'el, 1966), 82.

21. Pinkhas Tshetshotka, "Tsvishn 1915 un 1918," in *Sefer Lutsk* (Tel Aviv: Irgun yots'e Lutsk be-Yisra'el, 1961), 117.

22. Avraham Vaksman, "Tsionistn un tsionizm in Liutsk," in *Sefer Lutsk* (Tel Aviv: Irgun yots'e Lutsk be-Yisra'el, 1961), 133.

23. Freyda (Gorin) Kolpanitski, "Di linke arbeter-bavegung in Ostrah," in *Sefer Ostra'ah (Vohlin): matsever zikaron li-kehilah kedoshah,* ed. Yitzhak Alperowitz and Chaim Finkel (Tel Aviv: Irgun yot'se Ostra'ah be-Yisra'el: 1987), 89.

24. Yonatan Shlain, "R. Ayzik Arbtman—peiloto ha-tsionit ve-eskiv," in *Zvhil (Novogrodvolinsk),* ed. Azri'el Uri and Moredkhai Boneh (Tel Aviv: ha-Igud ha-artsi shel yots'e Zvhil veha-sevivah, 1962), Part 1, 197.

25. An-sky, *Khurbn Galitsye,* 4:21–22.

26. For the influence of Jewish immigrants in American culture, see Irving Howe, *World of Our Fathers: The Immigrant Jews of New York, 1881 to the Present* (London: Routledge and Keegan Paul, 1976); Steven Cassedy, *To the Other Shore: The Russian Jewish Intellectuals Who Came to America* (Princeton, N.J.: Princeton University Press, 1997); Neal Gabler, *An Empire of Their Own: How the Jews Invented Hollywood* (New York: Anchor Doubleday, 1989); Michael Rogin, *Blackface, White Noise: Jewish Immigrants in the Hollywood Melting Pot* (Berkeley: University of California Press, 1996); and Andrea Most, *Making Americans: Jews and the Broadway Musical* (Cambridge, Mass: Harvard University Press, 2004).

27. For Jewish literary responses to the war, see David Roskies, *Against the Apocalypse: Responses to Catastrophe in Modern Jewish Culture* (Syracuse, N.Y.: Syracuse University Press, 1984).

28. See Aviel Roshwald, "Jewish Cultural Identity in Eastern and Central Europe during the Great War," in Stites and Roshwald, *European Culture in the Great War,* 89–126; and Ruth Apter-Gabriel, ed., *Tradition and Revolution: The Jewish Renaissance in Russian Avant-Garde Art, 1912–1928* (Jerusalem: The Israel Museum, 1987).

29. For English works on Yiddish in interwar Poland, see David E. Fishman, *The Rise of Modern Yiddish Culture* (Pittsburgh, Pa.: University of Pittsburgh Press, 2005), 85–153; Ezra Mendelsohn, *The Jews of East Central Europe between the Two World Wars* (Bloomington: Indiana University Press, 1985), 11–84; Yisrael Gutman, Ezra Mendelsohn, Jehuda Reinharz, and Chone Shmeruk, *The Jews of Poland between Two World Wars* (Hanover, N.H.: University Press of New England, 1989); and Michael C. Stenlauf and Antony Polonsky, eds., *Polin,* vol. 16, *Jewish Popular Culture and Its Afterlife* (Oxford: Littman Library of Jewish Civilization, 2003). For the Zionist movement, see Ezra Mendelsohn, *Zionism in Poland: The Formative Years* (New Haven, Conn.: Yale University Press, 1982).

30. For recent scholarship on the fate of Jews during the revolutionary period, see Oleg V. Budnitskii, *Rossiiskie evrei mezhdu krasnymi i belymi: 1917–1920* (Moscow: ROSSPEN, 2005).

BIBLIOGRAPHY

Archival Collections

Derzhavnyi arkhiv Odeskoi oblasti (State Archive of the Odessa Region), accessed at Central Archives for the History of the Jewish People, Jerusalem

Fond 2 Upravlenie odesskago gradonachal'nika

Gosudarstvennyi arkhiv rossiiskoi federatsii (State Archive of the Russian Federation), accessed at Central Archives for the History of the Jewish People, Jerusalem

Fond 9532 Motylev, Lazar Evnovich

Fond 9535 Kotsyna, Sofia Rafailovna

Rossiskii gosudarstvennyi istoricheskii arkhiv (Russian State Historical Archive), St. Petersburg, Russia

Fond 821 Departament dukhovnykh del inostrannykh ispovedanii

Tsentral'nyi gosudarstvennyi istoricheskii arkhiv Sankt Peterburga (Central State Historical Archive of St. Petersburg), St. Petersburg, Russia

Fond 1747 Obshchestvo evreiskoi narodnoi muzyki

Fond 2129 Evreiskoe istoriko-etnograficheskoe obshchestvo

Fond 1720 Obshchestvo rasprostraneniia pravil'nikh svedenii o evreiakh i evreistve

Journals and Newspapers

Ahiasaf

Bibliotekar

Den'

Der fraynd

Evreiskaia biblioteka

Evreiskii mir

Evreiskaia shkola

Evreiskaia starina

Hamelits

Knizhnaia letopis'

Knizhki voskhoda

Literarishe bleter

Perezhitoe

Przegląd historyczny

Razsvet

Russkaia shkola

Sion

Sovremennyi mir

Vestnik evropy

Vestnik prava

VOPE (Vestnik obshchestva rasprostraneniia prosveshcheniia mezhdu evreiami v Rossii)

Voskhod

Other Primary Source Material

Abramovitsh, S. Y. *Ale verk fun Mendele Moykher Sforim.* 10 vols. New York: Hebrew Publishing Company, 1920.

————. *Dray ertsehlungen.* Warsaw: Progres, 1908.

————. *In yener tsayt.* Warsaw: Familien bibliotek, 1909.

Almi, A. *Momentn fun a lebn: zikhroynes, bilder un epizodn.* Buenos Aires: Tsentralfarband fun Poylishe Yidn in Argentine, 1948.

Alperowitz, Yitzhak, and Chaim Finkel, eds. *Sefer Ostra'ahh (Vohlin): matsever zikaron li-kehilah kedoshah.* Tel Aviv: Irgun yot'se Ostra'ah be-Yisra'el: 1987.

Anokhi, Z. Y. *Anokhis shriften.* 2 vols. Warsaw: Velt bibliotek, 1909.

————. *Reb Abe.* Warsaw: Velt bibliotek, 1910 or 1911.

————. *Reb Elhonon, un andere ertsehlungen.* Warsaw: Velt bibliotek, 1910.

————. *Tsvishen himel un erd.* Warsaw: Velt bibliotek, 1908.

An-sky, S. *The Dybbuk and Other Writings.* Ed. David Roskies, trans. Golda Werman. New York: Schocken Books, 1992.

————.*Gezamelte shriften.* 15 vols. Vilna-Warsaw-New York: An-sky, 1922–1928.

————. *Narod i kniga: opyt kharakteristiki narodnago chitatelia.* Moscow: L. A. Stoliar, 1914.

————, ed., *Dos yudishe etnografishe program.* Petrograd: Yosef Luria, 1914.

Artsybashev, Mikhail. *Sanin: A Novel.* Trans. Michael R. Katz, introduction by Otto Boele, afterward by Nicholas Luker. Ithaca, N.Y.: Cornell University Press, 2001.

Asch, Sholem. *Gezamelte shriften.* 12 vols. New York: Sholem Ash Komite, 1923–1938.

————. *Mit'n shtrom.* Warsaw: Lidski, 1909.

————. *Razskazy i p'esi.* Trans. S. G. Frug. St. Petersburg: Znanie, 1909.

Avatikhi, Aryeh, ed. *Rovneh: Sefer Zikaron.* Tel Aviv: Irgun yots'e Rovneh be-Yisra'el, 1956.

Bakalczuk-Felin, Meilech, ed. *Yizker-bukh fun Rakishok un umgegnt.* Johannesburg: Rakishker landsmanshaft in Yohanesburg, 1952.

————. *Yizker-bukh Khelm.* Johannesburg: Khelmer landsmanshaft, 1954.

Baranovitsh: sefer zikaron. Tel Aviv: Irgun yots'e Baranovitsh in yisroel, 1953.

Belousova, L. G., and T. E. Volkova, eds. *Evrei odessy i iuga ukrainy: istoriia v dokumentakh.* 2 vols. Odessa: Studiia Negotsiant, 2002.

ben Samuel, Judah. *Sefer hasidim.* Warsaw: Levin Epshtain, 1909.

Berkowitz, Joel, and Jeremy Dauber, eds. *Landmark Yiddish Plays: A Critical Anthology.* Albany: State University of New York Press, 2006.

Berkowitz, Y. D., ed. *Dos Sholem-Aleykhem bukh.* New York: Sholem Aleykhem bukh komitet, 1926.

Berman, L. *In loyf fun yorn: zikhroynes fun a yidishn arbiter.* New York: Farlag Unzer Tsayt, 1945.

Bernstein, Leon. *Ershte shprotsungen: zikhroynes.* Buenos Aires: Gezelshaft far yidishveltlekhe shuln in Argentine, 1956.

Bershadskii, S. A. *Litovskie evrei.* St. Petersburg: M. M. Stas'iulevicha, 1883.

———. *Russki-evreiskii arkhiv: dokumenty i materialy dlia istorii evreev v Rossii.* St. Petersburg: Obshchestva rasprostran. prosveshch. mezhdu evreiami v Rossii, 1882.

Bickel, Shlomo, ed. *Pinkes-Kolomey: geshikhte, zikhroynes, geshtaltn, hurbn.* New York: Rausen Bros., 1957.

Blumental, N., ed. *Sefer Mir.* Jerusalem: Entsiklopedyah shel galuyot, 1962.

Brainin, Reuven. *Fun mayn lebns-bukh.* New York: IKUF, 1946.

Buber, Martin. "Jüdische Renaissance." *Ost und West* 1, no. 1 (January 1901): 7–10.

Cahan, Abraham. *The Education of Abraham Cahan.* Trans. Leon Stein, Abraham P. Conan, and Lynn Davidson. Philadelphia, Pa.: Jewish Publication Society of America, 1969.

Cherikover, I. M. *Istoriia obshchestva dlia rasprostraneniia prosveshcheniia mezhdu evreiami v Rossii (Kul'turno-obshchestvennyiia techeniia v russkom evreistve), 1863–1913.* St. Petersburg: I. Fleitman / I. Lur'e, 1913.

Dan, Hayim, ed. *Sefer Horokhov.* Tel Aviv: Irgun yots'e Horokhov be-Yisra'el, 1966.

Dimov, Osip. *Vos ikh gedenk.* 2 vols. New York: Tsiko bikher-farlaf, 1943.

Dobrushin, Y. *Gedankengang.* Kiev: Kultur-Lige, 1922.

Dubnov, S. M., *Kniga zhizni: vospominaniia i razmyshleniia: materialy dlia istorii moego vremeni.* Ed. Viktor Kel'ner. St. Petersburg: Peterburgskoe vostokovedenie, 1998.

———. "Nahpesah ve-Nahkorah." *Pardes* 1 (1892): 221–242.

———. *Nationalism and History.* Philadelphia: Jewish Publication Society, 1958.

———. "Russko-evreiskaia intelligentsia v istoricheskom aspekte." *Evreiskii mir ezhegodnik na 1939 god.* Paris: Ob'edinenie russko-evreiskoi intelligentsii, 1939.

———, ed. *History of the Jews.* 5 vols. Trans. Moshe Spiegel. South Brunswick: Thomas Yoseloff, 1967.———, ed. *Pinkas ha-medinah o Pinkas Va'ad hakehilot ha-rashiyot bi-medinat Lita.* Berlin: 'Ayanot, 1925.

Edlboym, Meir. *Di yidn-shtot Meziritsh.* Buenos Aries: Mezritsher landslayt fareyn in Argentine, 1957.

Evreiskoe statisticheskoe obshchestvo. *Evreiskoe naselenie Rossii po dannym perepisi 1897 g i po noveishim istochnikam.* Petrograd: Kadima, 1917.

Feierberg, Mordecau Ze'ev. *Kitve M. Z. Feierberg.* Tel Aviv: Keneset, 1951.

———. *Vuhin? ertsehlung.* Trans. Leon. Warsaw: Velt bibliotek, 1909.

Feigenbaum, M., ed. *Sefer Byalah-Podlaskah.* Tel Aviv: Kupat gemilut hesed a. sh. kehilat Byalah-Podlaskah,1961.

Fink, Reuven, ed. *Seyfer Hosht: yizker-bukh.* Tel Aviv: Irgun yotse'e Hosht, 1957.

Firkovich, A. *Sefer Avnei Zikaron: ha-measef reshimot ha-masevot 'al qivrey beney Yisrael be-hasi ha-iqirim.* Vilna: Sh. Y. Fin ve R. A. S. Rosenqrans, 1872.

Ganzfried, Solomon. *Code of Jewish Law (Kitzur Schulchan Aruch): A Compilation of Jewish Laws and Customs.* Trans. Hyman E. Goldin. New York: Star Hebrew Book Company, 1927.

Gessen, Iu. I., ed. *Galleria evreiskikh deiatelei. Literaturno-biograficheskii ocherki.* St. Petersburg: A. E. Landau, 1898.

Ginzburg, Shaul. *Amolike Peterburg*. New York: Tsiko Bikher-Farlag, 1944.

Gordin, Jacob. *Ale shriften fun Yakov Gordin*. 4 vols. New York: Hebrew Publishing Company, 1910.

———. *Yakov Gordins dramen*. 2 vols. New York: Soyrkel fun Yakov Gordins Fraynt, 1911.

Gruzenberg, O. O. *Yesterday: Memoirs of a Russian-Jewish Lawyer*. Trans. Don C. Rawson and Tatiana Tipton. Berkeley: University of California Press, 1981.

Ha'am, Ahad. *Selected Essays of Ahad Ha'am*. Trans., ed., and with an introduction by Leon Simon. Cleveland, Ohio: World Publishing Company, 1962.

Harkavy, Abraham. *Altjüdische Denkmäler aus dem Krim mitgetheilt von Abraham Firkowitsch (1839–1872)*. St. Petersburg: Impr. De l'Acad, 1876.

———. *Ob iazyke evreev zhivshikh v drevnee vremia na Rusi i o slavianskikh slovakh vstrechaemykh y evreiskikh pisatelei*. St. Petersburg: Imp. akademii nauk, 1865.

Heine, Heinrich. *Di hartsrayze*. Trans. Zalmen Reyzen. Warsaw: Velt bibliotek, 1911.

———. *Heynrikh Heynes verk mit zayn biografye*. 2 vols. Trans. Leon. Warsaw: Velt bibliotek, 1909.

Hertz, Jacob Sholem, Grigor Aronson, and Sophia Dubnova-Erlich, eds. *Di geshikhte fun bund*. New York: Unzer tsayt, 1960.

Hilel, K. ed. *Lubats u-delatits*. Haifa: Irgun yots'e lubtse ve-delatits, 1971.

Hirschbein, Perets. *Gezamelte shriften*. New York: Literarish-dramatishe fereynen in Amerike, 1916.

———. *In gang fun lebn*. 2 vols. New York: Central Yiddish Culture Organization, 1948.

Huberman, Nakhman. *Bershad: be-tsel 'ayarah*. Jerusalem: Hotsaat Entsiklopedyah shel galuyot, 1956.

Kagan, Berl, ed. *Luboml: The Memorial Book of a Vanished Shtetl*. Hoboken, N.J.: Ktav, 1997.

Kahanovich, Moshe, ed. *Sefer zikaron li-kehilat Ivyehi*. Tel Aviv: Irgune yots'e Ivyeh be-Yiśra'el uva-Amerikah, 1968.

Kel'ner, Victor Efimovich, ed. *Evrei v Rossii: XIX vek*. Moscow: Novoe literaturnoe obozrenie, 2000.

Khavkina, L. B. *Slovari bibliotechno-bibliograficheskikh terminov*. Moscow: Izdatel'stvo Vsesoiuznoi knizhnoi palaty, 1952.

Kohen, David, and Shelomoh Even-Shoshan, eds. *Minsk, 'ir ve-em, korot, ma'asim, ishim, havai*. Tel Aviv: Irgun yots'e Minsk u-benoteha be-Yisrael, 1975–1985.

Kotik, Avrom. *Dos lebn fun a idishn inteligent*. New York: H. Toybenshlag, 1925.

Kotik, Yekhezkel. *Mayne zikhroynes*. Berlin: Klal, 1922.

Kulischer, M. *Das Leben Jesu: eine Sage von dem Schicksale und Erlebnissen der Bodenfrucht, insbesondere der sogenannten palästinensischen Erstlingsgarbe, die am Passahfeste im Tempel*. Leipzig: Otto Wigand, 1876.

——— *Razvod i polozhenie zhenshchiny*. St. Petersburg: B. M. Vol'f, 1896.

Litvak, A. *Vos geven: etyudn un zikhroynes*. Vilna: B. Kletskin, 1925.

Luninski, Ernest. *Berek Joselevicz i jego sy: zarys historyczny*. Warsaw: Nakl. Tow. Akc. S. Orgelbranda Synów, 1909.

Mahler, Raphael, ed. *Tshenstokhover yidn*. New York: OFG, 1947.

Mandelstam, Osip. *The Noise of Time: Selected Prose*. Trans. Clarence Brown. Evanston, Ill.: Northwestern University Press, 2002.

Margalioth, Hayyim Ze'eb. *Dubna rabati toldot ha-'ir dubna ve ha-at'akot mi-pinkas ha-kahal shelah mi-shenat 475 ve-hal'ah*. Warsaw: Bi-defus ha-Tsefirah, 1910.

Medem, Vladimir. *Fun mayn lebn*. 2 vols. New York: Vladimir Medem Komite, 1923.

Meirovits, Aharon. *Megilat Kurenits: ayarah be-hayeha uve-motah*. Tel Aviv: Irgun yots'e Kurenits be-Yisrael, 1956.

Merimson, Meir. *Zikhroynes fun a Nikolayever soldat*. Vilna: B. Kletskin, 1921.

Morgulis, M. G. *Il'ia Grigo'evich Orshanskii i ego literaturnaia deiatel'nost*. St. Petersburg: A. E. Landau, 1901.

Mukdoyni, A. *Teater*. New York: A. Mukdoyni yubili-komitet, 1927.

———. *Yitshak Leybush Perets un dos Yidishe teater*. New York: Yidisher kultur farband, 1949.

Nahmani, Shimshon. *Pinkas Slutsk u-venoteha*. New York: Hotsa'at Va'ad ha-sefer, 1962.

Niger, Shmuel. *Geklibene shriftn*. New York: Idisher Kultur Farlag, 1928.

———, ed. *Der Pinkes*. Vilna: B. Kletskin, 1913.

Obshchestvo dlia rasprostraneniia mezhdu evreiami v Rossii. *Spravochnik po evreiskomu bibliotechnomu*. St. Petersburg: Tip. I. Fleitmana, 1914.

Orshanskii, I. G. *Evrei v Rossii. Ocherki ekonomicheskago i obshchestvennago byta russkikh evreev*. St. Petersburg: O. I. bakst, 1877.

———. *Russkoe zakonodatel'stvo o evreiakh. Ocherki i issledovaniia*. St. Petersburg: A. E. Landau, 1877.

Oz, Amos. *A Tale of Love and Darkness*. Trans. Nicholas de Lange. Orlando: Harcourt, 2004.

Peretz, Y. L. *Ale verk fun Yitshak Leybush Peretz*. 19 vols. Vilna: B. Kletskin, 1925–1929.

———. *Razskazy i skazki*. Trans. S. G. Frug. St. Petersburg: Pechatnyi trud, 1909.

Perles, Perets ben Barukh Asher. *Geschichte der Juden in Posen*. Breslau: Verlag der Schletterschen Buchhandlung, 1865.

Pervaia vseobshchaia perepis' naseleniia Rossiiskoi Imperii. 1897 g. St. Petersburg: izd. Tsentral'nago statisticheskago komiteta, Ministerstva vnutrennikh diel, 1899–1905.

Polnoe sobranie zakonov Rossiiskoi Imperii. St. Petersburg: Gos. Tip., 1830–1913.

Raban, Y., ed. *Sefer Deretsin*. Tel Aviv: Irgun yots'e Deretsin, 1971 or 1972.

Reyzen, Avrom. *Epizodn fun mayn lebn: literarishe erinerungen*. Vilna: B. Kletskin, 1929.

———, ed. *Yohr-bukh "Progres": A zshurnal fir literature, vissenshaft un kritik*. Warsaw: Progres, 1904.

Riklis, Aaron. *Liev Tolstoy (zayn leben un zayne verk)*. Warsaw: Velt-bibliotek, 1910.

Rosen, Avraham, H. Sarig, and Y. Bernshtain, eds. *Kaminits-Podolsk ve-sevivatah*. Tel Aviv: Irgun yots'e Kaminits-Podolsk u-sevivatah be-Yisra'el, 1965.

Rosenthal, Leon. *Toldot Hevrat marbe haskalah be-Yisrael be-erets Rusya mi-shenat hityasdutah 624 (1863) 'ad shenat 646 (1885)*. St. Petersburg: Bi-defus H. Ts. H. Pines, 1885–1890.

Rubakin, Nikolai. *Etiudy o russkoi chitaiushchei publike: fakty, tsifry i nabliudeniia*. St. Petersburg: Sklad izd. v knizhnykh magazinakh N. P. Karbasnikova, 1895.

———. *Sredi knig*. Moscow: Knigaizdatel'stvo Nauka, 1911–1915.

Rubin, Yosef, ed. *Dubosari: sefer zikaron*. Tel-Aviv: Irgun yots'e Dubosari ba-Amerikah, Argentinah ve-Yisra'el, 1965.

Schmidt, Gilya G., ed. *The First Buber: Youthful Zionist Writings of Martin Buber*. Syracuse, N.Y.: Syracuse University Press, 1999.

Schnitzler, Arthur. *Gezamelte shriften*. 3 vols. Trans. B. K., ed. H. D. Nomberg. Warsaw: Velt bibliotek, 1909.

Sefer Ivenits, Kamin, veha-sevivah. Tel Aviv: Defus Arazi, 1973.

Sefer Lutsk. Tel Aviv: Irgun yots'e Lutsk be-Yisra'el, 1961.

Sergeeva, Irina, ed. "Perepiska barona Gintsburga i S. An-skogo po povodu etnograficheskikh ekspeditsii v cherte evreiskoi osedlosti." *Ab Imperio*, no. 4 (2003): 429–473.

Shamurin, E. I. *Slovar' knigovedcheskikh terminov dlia bibliotekarei, bibliografov, rabotnikov pechati i knizhnoi torgovli*. Moscow: Izdatel'stvo Sovetskaia Rossiia, 1958.

Shatzky, Ya'akov ed. *Pinkes Mlave*. New York: Velt-farband Mlaver yidn, 1950.

Sholem Aleichem. *Ale verk fun Sholem Aleykhem*. 28 vols. New York: Sholom Aleykhem folks-fond oysgabe, 1917–1923.

Shneour, Zalman. *Fertsik yor: lider un poemen, 1903–1944*. New York: Yidishn natsionalen arbeter-farband, 1945.

Shuster, Aaron. *Lipkan fun amol*. Montreal: A. Shuster, 1957.

Shvarts, Betsalel, ed. *Sefer Kobrin: megilat hayim ve-hurban*. Tel Aviv: Hadash, 1951.

Sliozberg, Genrikh. *Delo minuvshikh dnei: zapiski russkago evreia*. 3 vols. Paris: Pascal, 1933–1934.

Slutsky, Yehuda, ed. *Bobroisk: sefer zikaron li-kehilat Bobroisk u-venoteha*. Tel Aviv: Yots'e Bobroisk bi-Medinat Yisra'el uva-Artsot-ha-Berit, 1967.

Stein, Abraham Samuel, ed. *Pinkas Kremnits: sefer zikaron*. Tel Aviv: Hotsa'at irgun 'ole Kremnits be-Yisra'el, 1954.

Stein, Abraham Samuel, Y. Krust, and A. M. Orz'itser, eds. *Sefer ha-zikaron li-kehilat Kamin-Koshirski veha-sevivah*. Tel Aviv: Irgun yot'se Kamin-Koshirski veha-sevivah be-Yisra'el, 1965.

Sudarski, Mendl, Urieh Katsenelbogen, and Y. Kisin, eds. *Lite*. New York: Kultur-gezelshaft fun litvishe yidn, 1951.

Sztokfisz, David, ed. *Sefer Nisviz*.' Tel Aviv: Irgun yots'e Nisviz' be-Yisra'el uva-tefutsot, 1976.

———, ed. *Sefer Zgyerz: mazkeret netsakh li-kehilah Yehudit be-Polin*. Tel Aviv: Irgun yots'e Zgyerz be-Yisra'el, 1975.

Tamari, Moshe, ed. *Kehilat Lenin: sefer zikaron*. Tel Aviv: Vaad yots'e Lenin, 1957.

Teitelbaum, Hanokh Henikh. *Mefa'neach ne'elamim*. New York: A. M. Meisels, 2000.

Tenerama, A. *L. N. Tolstoy vegen Iden*. New York: Di internatsionale bibliotek, 1911.

Tsesler, Shmuel, Yosef Reznik, and Yitshak Tsesler, eds. *Zabludove yizker-bukh: di geshikhte fun der Yidisher kehile Zabludove fun ir breyshes biz ir fartilikung durkh di Natsishe rotshim.* Buenos-Aires: Yizker-bukh komitet, 1961.

Tsitron, Pinhas. *Sefer Kelts.* Tel Aviv: Irgun ole Kelts be-Yisra'el, 1957.

Trus, Alter, and Julius Cohen. *Braynsk sefer ha-zikaron: a bashraybung fun unzer heym.* New York: Braynsker relif komite, 1948.

Uri, Azri'el, and Moredkhai Boneh, eds. *Zvhil (Novogrodvolinsk).* Tel Aviv: ha-Igud ha-artsi shel yots'e Zvhil veha-sevivah, 1962.

Valtser-Fas, Mikhael, ed. *Korolits-Korelitsh: hayeha ve-hurbanah shel kehilah Yehudit=kiyum un hurbn fun a Yidisher kehile.* Tel Aviv: Akhdut, 1973.

Verbitskaia, Anastasya. *Keys to Happiness: A Novel.* Trans. and ed. Beth Holmgren and Helene Goscilo. Bloomington: Indiana University Press, 1999.

Vinaver, M. *Nedavnee (Vospominaniia i kharakteristiki).* Paris: Imp. d'Art Voltaire, 1926.

Weichert, Mikhl. *Teater un drame.* Warsaw: Yiddish, 1922.

———. *Trupe Tanentsap: a Goldfadn-shpil in a Galitsish shtetl.* Tel Aviv: Menorah, 1966.

———. *Zikhroynes.* 4 vols. Tel Aviv: Menora, 1960.

Weissenberg, Samuel. "Südrussische Amulette." *Verhandlungen der Berliner Gesellschaft für Anthropologie, Ethnologie und Urgeschichte* (1897): 367–369.

Wheeler, Joseph L. *The Library and the Community.* Chicago: American Library Association, 1924.

Yanovits, Barukh, ed. *Kapresht 'ayaratenu.* Haifa: Irgun yots'e Kapresht be-Yisra'el, 1980.

Yerushalmi, E., ed. *Pinkas Navaredok.* Tel Aviv: Relif Komitet a. sh. Aleksander Harkavi be-Artsot ha-Berit, 1963.

Yeshurin, Yefim, ed. *Vilne: a zamelbukh gevidmet der shtot Vilne.* New York: Vilner Brentsh 367 Arbeyter Ring, 1935.

Ze'evi, Yosef, ed. *Yizkor kehilot Luninyets/Koz'anhorodok.* Tel Aviv: Irgun yots'e Luninyets ve-Koz'anhorodok, 1952.

Zhitlowsky, Chaim. *Gezamelte shriften.* 10 vols. New York: Dr. Kh. Zhitlovsky Ferlag gezelshaft, 1912–1919.

———. *Zikhroynes fun mayn lebn.* 3 vols. New York: Dr. Kh. Zhitlovsky Ferlag gezelshaft, 1935–1940.

Zolf, Falik. *Di letste fun a dor: heymishe geshtaltn.* Winnipeg: Israelite Press, 1952.

Zweig, Arnold. *The Face of East European Jewry.* Ed., trans., and with an introduction by Noah Isenberg. Berkeley: University of California Press, 2004.

Scholarly Works

Alexander, Jeffrey C. *The Civil Sphere.* Oxford: Oxford University Press, 2006.

Altick, Richard D. *The English Common Reader: A Social History of the Mass Reading Public 1800–1900.* Chicago: University of Chicago Press, 1957.

Altmann, Alexander, ed. *Studies in Nineteenth-Century Jewish Intellectual History.* Cambridge, Mass.: Harvard University Press, 1964.

Altshuler, Mordechai. *Hate'atron hayehudi bevrit ha-mo'atsot.* Jerusalem: Hebrew University of Jerusalem Press, 1996.

Andreeva, T. A., ed. *Sotsial'no-politicheskie instituty provintsial'noi Rossii (XVI–nachalo XX vv)*. Cheliabinsk: Cheliabinskii gosudarstvennyi universitet, 1993.

Apter-Gabriel, Ruth, ed. *Tradition and Revolution: The Jewish Renaissance in Russian Avant-Garde Art, 1912–1928*. Jerusalem: Israel Museum, 1987.

Armborst, Kerstin. "Die Zeitschrift 'Evrejskaja Starina' Wissenschaftlicher Kommunikationsort und Sprachohr der Jüdischen Historisch-Ethnographischen Gesellschaft in St. Petersburg." *Zeitschrift für Religions- und Geistesgeschichte* 58, no. 1 (2006): 29–48.

Ascher, Abraham. *The Revolution of 1905*. Vol. 1. *Russia in Disarray*. Stanford, Calif.: Stanford University Press, 1988.

———. *The Revolution of 1905*. Vol. 2. *Authority Restored*. Stanford, Calif.: Stanford University Press, 1992.

Assaf, Simhah. *Am ha-sefer veha-sefer*. Safed: ha-Muze'on le-'omanut ha-defus, 1964.

Astrinsky, Aviva, Mordekhai Zalkin, and Yermiyahu Taub, eds. *Mattityahu Strashun 1817–1885: Scholar, Leader, and Book Collector*. New York: YIVO Institute for Jewish Research, 2001.

Avisar, Shmuel. *Ha-mahazeh veha-teatron ha-Ivri veha-Yidi*. Jerusalem: Re'uven Mas, 1996.

Balmuth, Daniel. *Censorship in Russia, 1865–1905*. Washington, D.C.: University Press of America, 1979.

Bartoszewski, Wladyslaw T., and Antony Polonsky, eds. *The Jews in Warsaw: A History*. Cambridge: Basil Blackwell, 1991.

Bar-Yosef, Hamutal. "Reflections on Hebrew Literature in the Russian Context." *Prooftexts* 16, no. 2 (1996): 127–149.

Bauman, Richard. *Verbal Art as Performance*. Rowley, Mass.: Newbury House, 1978.

———, ed. *Folklore, Cultural Performances, and Popular Entertainments: A Communications-Centered Handbook*. New York: Oxford University Press, 1992.

Beizer, Mikhail. *The Jews of St. Petersburg: Excursions through a Noble Past*. Philadelphia, Pa.: Jewish Publication Society, 1989.

Belkin, Ahuva. *Ha-Purim shpil: 'iyunim ba-te'a·tron ha-Yehudi ha-'amami*. Tel Aviv: Mossad Bialik, 2002.

Beller, Steven. *Vienna and the Jews, 1867–1938: A Cultural History*. Cambridge: Cambridge University Press, 1989.

Benina, M. A., ed. *Tsenzura v Rossii v kontse XIX–nachale XX veka: Sbornik vospominanii*. St. Petersburg: Dmitri Bulanin, 2003.

Beregovskii, M. *Purimshpil. Evreiskie narodnye muzykal'no-teatral'nye predstavleniia*. Kiev: Dukh i litera, 2001.

Berkowitz, Joel, ed. *Yiddish Theater: New Approaches*. Oxford: Littman Library of Jewish Civilization, 2003.

Berlin, Isaiah. *Vico and Herder: Two Studies in the History of Ideas*. London: Hogarth Press, 1976.

Beukers, Mariëlla, and Renée Waale, eds. *Tracing An-Sky: Jewish Collections from the State Ethnographic Museum in St. Petersburg*. Zwolle: Waanders Uitgevers, 1992.

Biale, David, Michael Galchinsky, and Susannah Heschel, eds. *Insider/Outsider: American Jews and Multiculturalism*. Berkeley: University of California Press, 1998.

Bilski, Emily D., ed., *Berlin Metropolis: Jews and the New Culture, 1890–1918*. Berkeley: University of California Press, 1999.

Binevich, Evgenii. "Gastroliori v Peterburge." Jewish Heritage Society preprints and reprints no. 9. Available at www.jewish-heritage.org/prep9.htm.

———. "Vozrozhdenie: Evreiskii teatr v Rossii, 1896–1904." Jewish Heritage Society preprints and reprints no. 44. Available at www.jewish-heritage.org/prep44.htm.

Birnbaum, Nathan. *Was sind Ostjuden? Zur ersten Information*. Vienna: R. Löwit, 1916.

Black, Alistair. *A New History of the English Public Library: Social and Intellectual Contexts, 1850–1914*. London: Leicester University Press, 1996.

Blackbourn, David, and Geoff Eley. *The Peculiarities of German History: Bourgeois Society and Politics in Nineteenth-Century Germany*. New York: Oxford University Press, 1984.

Blejwas, A. "The Origins and Practice of Organic Work in Poland: 1795–1863." *Polish Review* 15, no. 4 (1970): 23–54.

Blobaum, Robert E. *Rewolucja: Russian Poland, 1904–1907*. Ithaca, N.Y.: Cornell University Press, 1995.

Bonnell, Victoria E. *Roots of Rebellion: Workers' Politics and Organizations in St. Petersburg and Moscow, 1900–1914*. Berkeley: University of California Press, 1983.

Bourdieu, Pierre. "Intellectual Field and Creative Projects." *Social Science Information Bulletin* 8, no. 2 (April 1969): 89–119.

Boyarin, Daniel. "Placing Reading: Ancient Israel and Medieval Europe." In *The Ethnography of Reading*, ed. Jonathan Boyarin, 10–37. Berkeley: University of California Press, 1993.

Bradley, Joseph. "Subjects into Citizens: Societies, Civil Society, and Autocracy in Tsarist Russia." *American Historical Review* 107, no. 4 (October 2002): 1094–1123.

Brenner, Michael. *Propheten des Vergangenen: Jüdische Geschichtsschreibung im 19. und 20. Jahrhundert*. Munich: C. H. Beck, 2006.

———. *The Renaissance of Jewish Culture in Weimar Germany*. New Haven, Conn.: Yale University Press, 1996.

Brooks, Jeffrey. *When Russia Learned to Read: Literacy and Popular Literature, 1861–1917*. Princeton, N.J.: Princeton University Press, 1985.

Brower, Daniel R. *The Russian City: Between Tradition and Modernity, 1850–1900*. Berkeley: University of California Press, 1990.

Brower, Daniel R., and Edward S. Lazzerini, eds. *Russia's Orient: Imperial Borderlands and Peoples, 1700–1917*. Bloomington: Indiana University Press, 1997.

Budnitskii, Oleg V., ed. *Mirovoi krizis 1914–1920 godov i sud'ba vostochnoevropeiskogo evreistva*. Moscow: ROSSPEN, 2005.

———. *Rossiiskie evrei mezhdu krasnymi i belymi: 1917–1920*. Moscow: ROSSPEN, 2005.

Calhoun, Craig, ed. *Habermas and the Public Sphere*. Cambridge: MIT Press, 1992.

Cassedy, Steven. *To the Other Shore: The Russian Jewish Intellectuals Who Came to America*. Princeton, N.J.: Princeton University Press, 1997.

Cavallo, Guglielmo, and Roger Chartier, eds. *A History of Reading in the West*. Trans. Lydia G. Cochrane. Amherst: University of Massachusetts Press, 1999.

Chamberlain, Heath B. "On the Search for Civil Society in China." *Modern China* 19, no. 2 (April 1993): 199–215.

Clowes, Edith W., Samuel D. Kassow, and James L. West. *Between Tsar and People: Educated Society and the Quest for Public Identity in Late Imperial Russia.* Princeton, N.J.: Princeton University Press, 1991.

Cohen, Hagit. *Ba-hanuto shel mokher ha-sefarim: hanuyot sefarim Yehudiyot be-Mizrah Eropah ba-mahatsit ha-sheniyah shel ha-me'ah ha-tesha esreh.* Jerusalem: Hebrew University Magnes Press, 2006.

Cohen, Tova. "'Information about Women Is Necessarily Information about Men': On Iris Parush's 'Reading Women.'" *Journal of Israeli History* 21, no. 1–2 (2002): 169–191.

Corrsin, Stephen D. *Warsaw before the First World War: Poles and Jews in the Third City of the Russian Empire, 1880–1914.* Boulder, Colo.: East European Monographs, 1989.

Crisp, Olga. *Civil Rights in Imperial Russia.* Oxford: Clarendon Press, 1989.

Dalinger, Brigitte. *"Verloschene Sterne": Geschichte des jüdischen Theaters in Wien.* Vienna: Picus Verlag, 1998.

Darnton, Robert. *The Literary Underground of the Old Regime.* Cambridge, Mass.: Harvard University Press, 1982.

de Certeau, Michel. *The Practice of Everyday Life.* Trans. Steven F. Rendall. Berkeley: University of California Press, 1984.

Daxelmüller, Christoph. "Max Grunwald and the Origins and Conditions of Jewish Folklore at Hamburg." In *Proceedings of the Ninth Congress of Jewish Studies, Jerusalem, August 4–12, 1985: Division D, Volume 2, Art, Folklore, Theater, Music,* 2:73–80. Jerusalem: World Union of Jewish Studies, 1986.

Dianina, Katia. "The Feuilleton: An Everyday Guide to Public Culture in the Age of the Great Reforms." *Slavic and East European Journal* 47, no. 2 (2003): 187–210.

Duara, Prasenjit. *Sovereignty and Authenticity: Manchukuo and the East Asian Modern.* Lanham, Md.: Rowman & Littlefield, 2004.

Dubnova-Erlikh, Sophia. *Life and Work of S. M. Dubnov: Diaspora Nationalism and Jewish History.* Ed. Jeffrey Shandler. Bloomington: Indiana University Press, 1991.

Duker, Abraham G. "Evreiskaia Starina: A Bibliography of the Russian-Jewish Historical Periodical." *Hebrew Union College Annual* 8–9 (1931–1932): 523–602.

Ecksteins, Modris. *Rites of Spring: The Great War and the Birth of the Modern Age.* New York: Houghton Mifflin, 1989.

Efron, John. *Defending the Jewish Race.* New Haven, Conn.: Yale University Press, 1994.

Eisenbach, Artur. *The Emancipation of the Jews in Poland, 1780–1870.* Ed. Antony Polonsky, trans. Janina Dorosz. Cambridge: Basil Blackwell, 1991.

Eklof, Ben. *Russian Peasant Schools: Officialdom, Village Culture, and Popular Pedagogy, 1861–1914.* Berkeley: University of California Press, 1986.

El'iashevich, D. A. *Pravitel'stvennaia politika i evreiskaia pechat' v Rossii, 1797–1917.* St. Petersburg: Mosty Kul'tury; and Jerusalem: Gesharim, 1999.

Emmons, Terence. *The Formation of Political Parties and the First National Elections in Russia.* Cambridge, Mass.: Harvard University Press, 1983.

Engelstein, Laura. "The Dream of Civil Society in Tsarist Russia: Law, State, and

Religion." In *Civil Society before Democracy: Lessons from Nineteenth-Century Europe*, ed. Nancy Bermeo and Philip Nord, 23–41. Lanham, Md.: Rowman & Littlefield, 2000.

———. *The Keys to Happiness: Sex and the Search for Modernity in Fin-de-Siècle Russia*. Ithaca, N.Y.: Cornell University Press, 1992.

Estraikh, Gennady. *In Harness: Yiddish Writers' Romance with Communism*. Syracuse, N.Y.: Syracuse University Press, 2005.

Feiner, Shmuel. *Haskalah and History: The Emergence of a Modern Jewish Historical Consciousness*. Trans. Chaya Naor and Sondra Silberston. Oxford and Portland, Ore.: Littman Library of Jewish Civilization, 2002.

———. *The Jewish Enlightenment*. Philadelphia, Pa.: University of Pennsylvania Press, 2004.

Finnegan, Ruth. *Literacy and Orality: Studies in the Technology of Communication*. Oxford: Basil Blackwell, 1988.

Fishman, David E. *The Rise of Modern Yiddish Culture*. Pittsburgh, Pa.: University of Pittsburgh Press, 2005.

Frame, Murray. *School for Citizens: Theatre and Civil Society in Imperial Russia*. New Haven, Conn.: Yale University Press, 2006.

Frankel, Jonathan. *Prophecy and Politics: Socialism, Nationalism, and the Russian Jews, 1862–1917*. Cambridge: Cambridge University Press, 1981.

———, and Steven Zipperstein, eds. *Assimilation and Community: The Jews in Nineteenth-Century Europe*. New York: Cambridge University Press, 1991.

Freeze, ChaeRan Y. *Jewish Marriage and Divorce in Imperial Russia*. Hanover, N.H.: University Press of New England for Brandeis University Press, 2002.

Frieden, Ken, ed. *Classic Yiddish Stories of S. Y. Abramovitsh, Sholem Aleichem, and I. L. Peretz*. Syracuse, N.Y.: Syracuse University Press, 2004.

Frumkin, Jacob, Gregor Aronson, and Alexis Goldenweiser, eds. *Russian Jewry, 1860–1917*. South Brunswick, N.J.: Thomas Yoseloff, 1966.

Funkenstein, Amos. *Perceptions of Jewish History*. Berkeley: University of California Press, 1993.

Gabler, Neal. *An Empire of Their Own: How the Jews Invented Hollywood*. New York: Anchor Doubleday, 1989.

Gassenschmidt, Christoph. *Jewish Liberal Politics in Tsarist Russia, 1900–1914*. New York: New York University Press, 1995.

Gay, Peter. *Freud, Jews, and Other Germans: Masters and Victims in Modernist Culture*. New York: Oxford University Press, 1978.

Gelber, Mark H., ed. *The Jewish Reception of Heinrich Heine*. Tübingen: Max Niemeyer Verlag, 1992.

Geraci, Robert. *Window on the East: National and Imperial Identities in Late Tsarist Russia*. Ithaca, N.Y.: Cornell University Press, 2001.

Gitelman, Zvi, ed. *The Emergence of Modern Jewish Politics: Bundism and Zionism in Eastern Europe*. Pittsburgh, Pa.: University of Pittsburgh Press, 2003.

Gluck, Mary. "The Budapest Flâneur: Urban Modernity, Popular Culture, and the 'Jewish

Question' in Fin-de-siècle Hungary." *Jewish Social Studies* 10, no. 3 (Spring/Summer 2004): 1–22.

Goodman, Susan Tumarkin. *Russian Jewish Artists in a Century of Change, 1890–1990.* Munich: Prestel, 1995.

Gorin, Bernard. *Di geshikhte fun idishen teater.* New York: Idisher farlag far literatur un visenshaft, 1923.

Gottesman, Itzik Nakhmen. *Defining the Yiddish Nation: The Jewish Folklorists of Poland.* Detroit, Mich.: Wayne State University Press, 2003.

Groberg, Kristi, and Avraham Greenbaum, eds. *A Missionary for History: Essays in Honor of Simon Dubnov.* Minneapolis: University of Minnesota, 1998.

Guesnet, François. *Polnische Juden im 19. Jahrhundert. Lebensbedingungen, Rechtsnormen und Organisation im Wandel.* Cologne: Böhlau, 1998.

Gutman, Yisrael, Ezra Mendelsohn, Jehuda Reinharz, and Chone Shmeruk. *The Jews of Poland between Two World Wars.* Hanover, N.H.: University Press of New England, 1989.

Habermas, Jürgen. *The Structural Transformation of the Public Sphere: An Inquiry into a Category of Bourgeois Society.* Trans. Thomas Burger. Cambridge, Mass.: MIT Press, 1989.

———, Sara Lennox, and Frank Lennox. "The Public Sphere: An Encyclopedia Article (1964)." *New German Critique*, no. 3 (Autumn 1974): 49–55.

Hagen, Manfred. *Die Entfaltung Politischer Öffentlichkeit in russland, 1906–1914.* Wiesbaden: Franz Steiner Verlag, 1982.

Haimson, Leopold. *The Politics of Rural Russia 1905–1914.* Bloomington: Indiana University Press, 1979.

Harcave, Sidney. *First Blood: The Russian Revolution of 1905.* New York: Macmillan, 1964.

———. "The Jewish Question in the First Russian Duma." *Jewish Social Studies* 6 (1944): 155–176.

Harshav, Benjamin. *Language in Time of Revolution.* Berkeley: University of California Press, 1993.

———. *Marc Chagall and His Times: A Documentary Narrative.* Stanford, Calif.: Stanford University Press, 2004.

———. *The Meaning of Yiddish.* Stanford, Calif.: Stanford University Press, 1990.

Hoffman, Stefani, and Ezra Mendelsohn, eds. *The Revolution of 1905 and Russia's Jews.* Philadelphia: University of Pennsylvania Press, 2008.

Horowitz, Brian. "The Society for the Promotion of Enlightenment among the Jews of Russia and the Evolution of the St. Petersburg Russian-Jewish Intelligentsia, 1893–1905." In *Studies in Contemporary Jewry.* Vol. 19, *Jews and the State: Dangerous Alliances and the Perils of Privilege,* ed. Ezra Mendelsohn, 195–213. New York: Oxford University Press, 2004.

Horowitz, Rosemary. *Literacy and Cultural Transmission in the Reading, Writing, and Rewriting of Jewish Memorial Books.* San Francisco, Calif.: Austin & Winfield, 1998.

Howe, Irving. *World of Our Fathers: The Immigrant Jews of New York, 1881 to the Present.* London: Routledge and Keegan Paul, 1976.

Hundert, Gershon David. "The Library of the Study Hall in Volozhin, 1762: Some Notes on the Basis of a Newly Discovered Manuscript." *Jewish History* 14, no. 2 (June 2000): 225–244.

———, ed. *The YIVO Encyclopedia of Jews in Eastern Europe*. 2 vols. New Haven, Conn.: Yale University Press, 2008.

Ivenina, T. A. *Kul'turno-prosvetitel'nyie organizatsii i uchrezhdeniia obshchestvennoi i chastnoi initsiativy v dorevoliutsionnoi rossii (1900–1916 gg.)*. Moscow: Frantera, 2003.

Jaffee, Martin S. *Torah in the Mouth: Writing and Oral Tradition in Palestinian Judaism, 200 BCE–400 CE*. New York: Oxford University Press, 2001.

Jelavich, Peter. *Berlin Cabaret*. Cambridge, Mass.: Harvard University Press, 1993.

———. *Munich and Theatrical Modernism: Politics, Playwriting, and Performance, 1890–1914*. Cambridge, Mass.: Harvard University Press, 1985.

Karner, Doris A. *Lachen unter Tränen: Jüdisches Theater in Ostgalizien und der Bukowina*. Vienna: Steinbauer, 2005.

Katz, Dovid. *Words on Fire*. New York: Basic Books, 2004.

Katz, Steven T., ed. *The Shtetl: New Evaluations*. New York: New York University Press, 2007.

Kiel, Mark W. "A Twice Lost Legacy: Ideology, Culture and Pursuit of Jewish Folklore in Russia until Stalinization (1930–1931)." Ph.D. diss., Jewish Theological Seminary, 1991.

Kirshenblatt-Gimblett, Barbara. "The Concept and Varieties of Narrative Performance in East European Jewish Culture." In *Exploration in the Ethnography of Speaking*, ed. Richard Bauman and Joel Sherzer, 283–308. Cambridge: Cambridge University Press, 1974.

———. "Imagining Europe: The Popular Arts of American Jewish Ethnography." In *Divergent Jewish Cultures: Israel and America*, ed. Deborah Dash Moore and Ilan Troen, 166–191. New Haven, Conn.: Yale University Press, 2001.

Klausner, I. "Ha-gezerah al tishbot ha-yehudim." *Gal-Ed: On the History of the Jews in Poland* 6 (1982): 11–26.

Klier, John Doyle. *Imperial Russia's Jewish Question*. Cambridge: Cambridge University Press, 1995.

———. "Russkaia voina protiv Khevra Kaddisha." *Trudy po iudaike* 1 (1993): 109–115.

———, and Shlomo Lombroza, eds. *Pogroms: Anti-Jewish Violence in Modern Russian History*. Cambridge: Cambridge University Press, 1992.

Kligsberg, Moshe. "Di yidishe yugnt-bavegung in Poyln tsvishn beyde velt-milkhomes (A sotsiologishe shtudie)." In *Studies on Polish Jewry, 1919–1939*, ed. Joshua Fishman, 137–228. New York: YIVO Institute for Jewish Research, 1974.

Knight, Nathaniel. "Constructing the Science of Nationality: Ethnography in Mid-Nineteenth Century Russia." PhD. diss., Columbia University, 1995.

Kopytova, G. B. *Obshchestvo evreiskoi nadornoi muzyki v peterburge-petrograde*. St. Petersburg: EZRO, 1997.

Krutikov, Mikhail. *Yiddish Fiction and the Crisis of Modernity, 1905–1914*. Stanford, Calif.: Stanford University Press, 2001.

Kugelmass, Jack, and Jonathan Boyarin, ed. and trans. *From a Ruined Garden: The*

Memorial Books of Polish Jewry. 2nd ed. Bloomington: Indiana University Press, 1998.

Kuznitz, Cecile Esther. "The Origins of Yiddish Scholarship and the YIVO Institute for Jewish Research." Ph.D. diss., Stanford University, 2000.

Kymlicka, Will. *Multicultural Citizenship: A Liberal Theory of Minority Rights.* Oxford: Clarendon Press, 1995.

Lederhendler, Eli. *The Road to Modern Jewish Politics: Political Tradition and Political Reconstruction in the Jewish Community of Tsarist Russia.* New York: Oxford University Press, 1989.

Leich, Harold M. "The Society for Librarianship and Russian Librarianship in the Early Twentieth Century." *Journal of Library History* 22, no. 1 (Winter 1987): 42–57.

Levin, Vladimir. "Russian Jewry and the Duma Elections, 1906–1907." In *Jews and Slavs,* ed. Wolf Moskovich, Leonid Finberg, and Martin Feller, 7:233–264. Jerusalem: Hebrew University of Jerusalem Center for Slavic Languages and Literatures / The Institute of Jewish Studies, 2000.

Levitats, Isaac. *The Jewish Community in Russia, 1844–1917.* Jerusalem: Posner and Sons, 1981.

Liberles, Robert. "Postemancipation Historiography and the Jewish Historical Societies of America and England." In *Studies in Contemporary Jewry.* Vol. 10, *Reshaping the Past: Jewish History and the Historians,* ed. Jonathan Frankel, 45–65. New York: Oxford University Press, 1994.

Lindenmeyr, Adele. *Poverty Is Not a Vice: Charity, Society and the State in Imperial Russia.* Princeton, N.J.: Princeton University Press, 1996.

Loeffler, James Benjamin. "'The Most Musical Nation': Jews, Culture and Nationalism in the Late Russian Empire." Ph.D. diss., Columbia University, 2006.

Lohr, Eric. *Nationalizing the Russian Empire: The Campaign against Enemy Aliens During World War I.* Cambridge, Mass.: Harvard University Press, 2003.

Lokshin, Aleksandr. "Fantasmagoriia ili gesheft? Sionistskoe dvizhenie glazami tsarskoi administratsii." *Rodina,* nos. 4–5 (2002): 95–101.

Löwe, Heinz-Dietrich. "From Charity to Social Policy: The Emergence of Jewish 'Self-Help' Organizations in Imperial Russia, 1800–1914." *East European Jewish Affairs* 27, no. 2 (1997): 53–75.

Lukacs, John. *Budapest 1900: A Historical Portrait of a City and Its Culture.* New York: Grove, 1990.

Lukin, Benjamin. "Ot narodnichestva k narodu (S. A. An-skii—etnograf vostochno-evropeiskogo evreistva)." In *Evrei v Rossii: Istoriia i kul'tura,* ed. D. A. El'iashevich, 125–161. St. Petersburg: Peterburgskii evreiskii universitet, 1995.

Mah, Harold. "Phantasies of the Public Sphere: Rethinking the Habermas of Historians." *Journal of Modern History* 72, no. 1 (March 2000): 153–182.

Mahler, Raphael. *Karaimer: a Yidishe geule-bavegung in Mitlalter.* New York: E. Shulman, 1947.

Manger, Itzik, Jonas Turkow, and Moses Perenson, eds. *Yidisher teater in Eyrope tsvishn beyde velt-milkhomest.* New York: Alveltlekhn yidishn kultur-kongres, 1968.

Mayzel, Nakhman. *Avrom Goldfadn: der foter fun yidishn teater.* Warsaw: Groshn bibliotek, 1935.

McKim, Robert, and Jeff McMahan, eds. *The Morality of Nationalism*. New York: Oxford University Press, 1997.

McReynolds, Louise. *The News under Russia's Old Regime: The Development of a Mass-Circulation Press*. Princeton, N.J.: Princeton University Press, 1991.

———. "Reading the Russian Romance: What Did the Keys to Happiness Unlock?" *Journal of Popular Culture* 31, no. 4 (Spring 1998): 95–108.

———. *Russia at Play: Leisure Activities at the End of the Tsarist Era*. Ithaca, N.Y.: Cornell University Press, 2003.

Meir, Natan M. "Jews, Ukrainians, and Russians in Kiev: Intergroup Relations in Late Imperial Associational Life." *Slavic Review* 65, no. 3 (Fall 2006): 475–501.

Mendelsohn, Ezra. *Class Struggle in the Pale*. New York: Cambridge University Press, 1981.

———. *The Jews of East Central Europe between the Two World Wars*. Bloomington: Indiana University Press, 1985.

———. *On Modern Jewish Politics*. New York: Oxford University Press, 1993.

———. *Painting a People: Maurycy Gottlieb and Jewish Art*. Hanover, N.H.: Brandeis University Press, 2002.

———. *Zionism in Poland: The Formative Years*. New Haven, Conn.: Yale University Press, 1982.

Meyer, Michael. "The Emergence of Jewish Historiography: Motives and Motifs." *History and Theory* 27, no. 4 (1988): 160–175.

———. *Judaism within Modernity: Essays on Jewish History and Religion*. Detroit, Mich.: Wayne State University Press, 2001.

Miron, Dan. *The Image of the Shtetl and Other Studies of Modern Jewish Literary Imagination*. Syracuse, N.Y.: Syracuse University Press, 2000.

———. *A Traveler Disguised: The Rise of Modern Yiddish Fiction in the Nineteenth Century*. 1973; reprint, Syracuse: Syracuse University Press, 1996.

Mishkinsky, Moshe. *Reshit tenu'at ha-poalim ha Yehudit be-Rusyah*. Tel Aviv: Hakibutz Hamechad, 1981.

Mlotek, Eleanor, ed. *S. Ansky (Shloyme-Zanvl Rappoport), 1863–1920: His Life and Work, Catalog of an Exhibition*. New York: YIVO, 1980.

Moore, Donald J. *Martin Buber: Prophet of Religious Secularism*. Philadelphia, Pa.: Jewish Publication Society of America, 1974.

Moseley, Marcus. *Being for Myself Alone: Origins of Jewish Autobiography*. Stanford, Calif.: Stanford University Press, 2006.

Moss, Kenneth. "Jewish Culture between Renaissance and Decadence: *Di Literarishe Monatsshriften* and Its Critical Reception." *Jewish Social Studies* 8, no. 1 (Fall 2001): 153–198.

———. "'A Time for Tearing Down and a Time for Building Up': Recasting Jewish Culture in Eastern Europe, 1917–1921." Ph.D. diss., Stanford University, 2003.

Mosse, George L. "Nationalism and Respectability: Normal and Abnormal Sexuality in the Nineteenth Century." *Journal of Contemporary History* 17, no. 2 (1982): 221–246.

Most, Andrea. *Making Americans: Jews and the Broadway Musical*. Cambridge, Mass.: Harvard University Press, 2004.

Myers, David N. *Re-Inventing the Jewish Past: European Jewish Intellectuals and the Zionist Return to History.* New York: Oxford University Press, 1995.

————, and David B. Ruderman, eds. *The Jewish Past Revisited: Reflections on Modern Jewish Historians.* New Haven, Conn.: Yale University Press, 1998.

Nathans, Benjamin. *Beyond the Pale: The Jewish Encounter with Late Imperial Russia.* Berkeley: University of California Press, 2002.

————. "On Russian-Jewish Historiography." In *Historiography of Imperial Russia: The Profession and Writing of History in a Multinational State,* ed. Thomas Sanders, 397–432. Armonk, N.Y.: M. E. Sharpe, 1999.

————, and Gabriella Safran, eds. *Culture Front: Representing Jews in Eastern Europe.* Philadelphia: University of Pennsylvania Press, 2007.

Niger, Shmuel, and Ya'akov Shatzky, eds. *Leksikon fun der nayer yidisher literatur.* 8 vols. New York: Alveltlekhn yidishn kultur-kongres, 1956–1981.

Ong, Walter J. *Orality and Literacy: The Technologizing of the Word.* London and New York: Methuen, 1982.

————. *Rhetoric, Romance, and Technology: Studies in the Interaction of Expression and Culture.* Ithaca, N.Y.: Cornell University Press, 1971.

Orlov, Alina. "Natan Altman and the Problem of Jewish Art in the 1910s." Ph.D. diss., University of Southern California, 2003.

Otte, Marline. *Jewish Identities in German Popular Entertainment, 1890–1933.* Cambridge: Cambridge University Press, 2006.

Paret, Peter. *The Berlin Secession: Modernism and its Enemies in Imperial Germany.* Cambridge, Mass.: Belknap Press of Harvard University Press, 1980.

Parush, Iris. *Reading Jewish Women: Marginality and Modernization in Nineteenth-Century Eastern European Jewish Society.* Waltham, Mass.: Brandeis University Press, 2004.

Penslar, Derek. *Shylock's Children: Economics and Jewish Identity in Modern Europe.* Berkeley: University of California Press, 2001.

Perlman, Joel. "Russian-Jewish Literacy in 1897: A Reanalysis of Census Data." *Proceedings of the Eleventh World Congress of Jewish Studies, Jerusalem, June 22–29, 1993.* Vol. 2, part 3, 23–30. Jerusalem: World Union of Jewish Studies, 1994.

Pinchuk, Ben Cion. "Jewish Discourse and the Shtetl." *Jewish History* 15, no. 2 (June 2001): 169–179.

Polischuk, M. *Evrei Odessy i Novorosii. Sotsial'no-politicheskaia istoriia evreev Odessy i drugikh gorodov Novorossii, 1881–1904.* Jerusalem: Gesharim; Moscow: Mosty Kul'tury, 2002.

Polonsky, Antony, ed. *Polin.* Vol. 17, *The Shtetl: Myth and Reality* (Oxford: Littman Library of Jewish Civilization, 2004

Prager, Leonard. "Charles Dickens in Yiddish (A Survey)." *Jewish Language Review,* no. 4 (1984): 158–178.

Preston, David L. "The German Jews in Secular Education, University Teaching, and Science: A Preliminary Inquiry." *Jewish Social Studies* 38, no. 2 (1976): 99–116.

Quint, Alyssa Pia. "The Botched Kiss: Abraham Goldfaden and the Literary Origins of the Yiddish Theatre." Ph.D. diss., Harvard University, 2002.

———. "Yiddish Literature for the Masses"? A Reconsideration of Who Read What in Jewish Eastern Europe." *AJS Review* 29, no. 1 (2005): 61–89.

Raba, Joel. *Between Remembrance and Denial: The Fate of the Jews in the Wars of the Polish Commonwealth during the Mid-Seventeenth Century as Shown in Contemporary Writings and Historical Research.* Boulder, Colo.: East European Monographs, 1995.

Ravidowicz, Shimon, ed. *Sefer Shimon Dubnov.* London, Jerusalem, and Waltham, Mass.: Hotsa'at Erret, 1954.

Raz, Joseph. *The Morality of Freedom.* Oxford: Clarendon Press, 1986.

Ringer, Fritz. "The Intellectual Field, Intellectual History and the Sociology of Knowledge." *Theory and Society* 19, no. 3 (June 1990): 269–294.

Roemer, Nils H. *Jewish Scholarship and Culture in Nineteenth-Century Germany: Between History and Faith.* Madison: University of Wisconsin Press, 2005.

Rogin, Michael. *Blackface, White Noise: Jewish Immigrants in the Hollywood Melting Pot.* Berkeley: University of California Press, 1996.

Rose, Jonathan. *The Intellectual Life of the British Working Classes.* New Haven, Conn.: Yale University Press, 2001.

Roskies, David. *Against the Apocalypse: Responses to Catastrophe in Modern Jewish Culture.* Syracuse, N.Y.: Syracuse University Press, 1984.

———. *The Jewish Search for a Usable Past.* Bloomington: Indiana University Press, 1999.

———. "Yiddish Popular Literature and the Female Readers." *Journal of Popular Studies* 10 (1976–1977): 852–858.

Rubin, Adam. "From Torah to Tarbut: Hayim Nahman Bialik and the Nationalization of Judaism." Ph.D. diss., University of California, Los Angeles, 2000.

———. "Hebrew Folklore and the Problem of Exile." *Modern Judaism* 25, no. 1 (2005): 62–83.

Rudd, Charles A. *Fighting Words: Imperial Censorship and the Russian Press, 1804–1906.* Toronto: University of Toronto Press, 1982.

Ruderman, David B., ed. *Preachers of the Italian Ghetto.* Berkeley: University of California Press, 1992.

Safran, Gabriella, and Steven J. Zipperstein, eds. *The Worlds of S. An-sky: A Russian Jewish Intellectual at the Turn of the Century.* Stanford, Calif.: Stanford University Press, 2006.

Sandrow, Nahma. *Vagabond Stars: A World History of Yiddish Theater.* New York: Harper & Row, 1977.

Saperstein, Marc. *Jewish Preaching, 1200–1800: An Anthology.* New Haven, Conn.: Yale University Press, 1989.

———. *"Your Voice Like a Ram's Horn": Themes and Texts in Traditional Jewish Preaching.* Cincinnati, Ohio: Hebrew Union College Press, 1996.

Sargeant, Lynn Mary. "Middle Class Culture: Music and Identity in Late Imperial Russia." Ph.D. diss., Indiana University, 2001.

Schefski, Harold K. "Tolstoi and the Jews." *Russian Review* 41, no. 1 (January 1982): 1–10.

Schorsch, Ismar. *From Text to Context: The Turn to History in Modern Judaism.* Hanover, N.H.: Brandeis University Press, 1994.

Schorske, Carl E. *Fin de Siècle Vienna: Politics and Culture.* New York: Knopf, 1979.

Scott, Donald M. "The Popular Lecture and the Creation of a Public in Mid-Nineteenth-Century America." *Journal of American History* 66, no. 4 (1980): 791–809.

Seltzer, Robert. "Simon Dubnov: A Critical Biography of His Early Years." Ph.D. diss., Columbia University, 1970.

Senn, Alfred Erich. *Nicholas Rubakin: A Life for Books.* Newtonville, Mass.: Oriental Research Partners, 1977.

Sergeeva, Irina, ed. "Khozhdenie v evreiskii narod: etnograficheskie ekspeditsii Semena An-skogo v dokumentakh." *Ab Imperio,* no. 4 (2003): 395–428.

Shatsky, Jacob. *Geshikhte fun Yidn in Vashe.* 3 vols. New York: YIVO, 1947–1953.

———. *Zamlbukh lekoved dem tsvey hundert un fuftikstn yovl fun der yiddisher prese.* New York: YIVO, 1937.

Shavit, David. "The Emergence of Jewish Public Libraries in Tsarist Russia." *Journal of Library History, Philosophy, and Comparative Librarianship* 20, no. 3 (Summer 1985): 239–252.

———. "Pirsumim safranayim be-Yidish lifnei milhemet ha-olam ha-rishonah." *Yad La-kore* 17, no. 1 (December 1977–January 1978): 71–76.

Shils, Edward. "The Virtue of Civil Society." *Government and Opposition* 26, no. 1 (January 1991): 3–20.

Shmeruk, Chone. "Sholem Aleichem un di onheybn fun der yiddisher literature far kinder." *Di goldene keyt* 112 (1984): 39–53.

———. "Yiddish Adaptations of Children's Stories from World Literature." In *Studies in Contemporary Jewry.* Vol. 6, *Arts and Its Uses: The Visual Image and Modern Jewish Society,* ed. Ezra Mendelsohn, 186–200. New York: Oxford University Press, 1990.

Singer, Milton. *When a Great Tradition Modernizes: An Anthropological Approach to Indian Civilization.* New York: Praeger, 1972.

Slezkine, Yuri. *Arctic Mirrors: Russia and the Small Peoples of the North.* Ithaca, N.Y.: Cornell University Press, 1994.

———. *The Jewish Century.* Princeton, N.J.: Princeton University Press, 2004.

Slutsky, Yehuda. *Ha-ʾItonut ha-yehudit-rusit ba-meʿah ha-ʾesrim, 1900–1918.* Tel Aviv: ha-Agudah le-Heker Toldot ha-Yehudim, ha-Makhon le-Heker ha-Tefutsot, 1978.

———. *Haʾ-Itonut ha-yehudit-rusit ba-meʿah ha-teshaʾ-ʿesreh.* Jerusalem: Mosad Byalik, 1970.

———. "Shnat 1905 be-hayeshem shel Yehudei Rusya." *He-avar* 22 (1977): 3–23.

Smith, Douglas. *Working the Rough Stone: Freemasonry and Society in Eighteenth-Century Russia.* DeKalb: Northern Illinois University Press, 1999.

Snape, Robert. *Leisure and the Rise of the Public Library.* London: Library Association, 1995.

Soifer, Paul Eric. "The Bespectacled Cossack: S. A. Bershadskii (1850–1896) and the Development of Russo-Jewish Historiography." Ph.D. diss., Pennsylvania State University, 1975.

Sperber, Jonathan. "Bürger, Bürgertum, Bürgerlichkeit, Bürgerliche Gesellschaft: Studies of the German (Upper) Middle Class and Its Sociocultural World." *Journal of Modern History* 69, no. 2 (June 1997): 271–297.

Stampfer, Shaul. "Gender Differentiation and Education of the Jewish Woman in Nineteenth-Century Eastern Europe." In *Polin*. Vol. 7, *Jewish Life in Nazi-Occupied Warsaw*, ed. Antony Polonsky, 63–85. Oxford: Littman Library of Jewish Civilization, 1992.

———. Review of *Reading Jewish Women* by Iris Parush. *Jews in Russia and Eastern Europe* 52, no. 1 (Summer 2004): 244–248.

Stanislawski, Michael. *Autobiographic Jews: Essays in Jewish Self-Fashioning*. Seattle: University of Washington Press, 2004.

———. *A Murder in Lemberg: Politics, Religion, and Violence in Modern Jewish History*. Princeton, N.J.: Princeton University Press, 2007.

———. *Zionism and the Fin de Siècle: Cosmopolitanism and Nationalism from Nordau to Jabotinsky*. Berkeley: University of California Press, 2001.

Stein, Sarah Abrevaya. *Making Jews Modern: The Yiddish and Ladino Press in the Russian and Ottoman Empires*. Bloomington: Indiana University Press, 2004.

Steinlauf, Michael C. "Fear of Purim: Y. L. Peretz and the Canonization of Yiddish Theater." *Jewish Social Studies* 1, no. 3 (Spring 1995): 44–65.

———. "Jews and Polish Theater in Nineteenth Century Warsaw." *Polish Review* 32, no. 4 (1987): 439–458.

———, and Antony Polonsky, eds., *Polin*. Vol. 16, *Jewish Popular Culture and Its Afterlife*. Oxford: Littman Library of Jewish Civilization, 2003.

Stites, Richard. *Serfdom, Society, and the Arts in Imperial Russia: The Pleasure and the Power*. New Haven, Conn.: Yale University Press, 2005.

———, and Aviel Roshwald, eds. *European Culture in the Great War: The Arts, Entertainment and Propaganda, 1914–1918*. Cambridge: Cambridge University Press, 1999.

Stuart, Mary. "'The Ennobling Illusion': The Public Library Movement in Late Imperial Russia." *The Slavonic and East European Review* 76, no. 3 (July 1998): 401–440.

Swift, E. Anthony. *Popular Theater and Society in Tsarist Russia*. Berkeley: University of California Press, 2002.

Tamir, Yael. *Liberal Nationalism*. Princeton, N.J.: Princeton University Press, 1993.

Taylor, Charles. *Modern Social Imaginaries*. Durham, N.C.: Duke University Press, 2004.

———. *Multiculturalism: Examining the Politics of Recognition*. Ed. and introduced by Amy Gutman. Princeton, N.J.: Princeton University Press, 1994.

———. *A Secular Age*. Cambridge: Belknap Press, 2007.

Teater Bukh: zamlung tsum fuftsikyorikn yubiley funm Idishn teatr (1876–1927). Kiev: Kultur-Lige, 1927.

Thurston, Gary. *The Popular Theatre Movement in Russia, 1862–1919*. Evanston, Ill.: Northwestern University Press, 1998.

Tumanova, A. S. *Obshchestvennye organizatsii goroda Tambova na rubezhe XIX–XX vekov*. Tambov: Tambovskii gosudarstvennyi universitet, 1999.

————. *Samoderzhavie i obshchestvennye organizatsii v Rossii, 1905–1917 gody*. Tambov: Tambovskii gosudarstvennyi universitet, 2002.

Turkow-Grudberg, Isaac. *Di Mame Ester Rokhl*. Warsaw: Yidish bukh, 1953.

Turner, Victor. *The Anthropology of Performance*. New York: PAJ Publications, 1986.

Ury, Scott. "Red Banner, Blue Star: Radical Politics, Democratic Institutions and Collective Identity among Jews in Warsaw, 1904–1907." Ph.D. diss., Hebrew University of Jerusalem, 2006.

Vaneev, A. N. *Razvitie bibliotekovedcheskoi mysli v Rossii v nachale XX veka: uchebnoe posobie*. St. Petersburg: Sankt-Peterbergskaia gos. Akademiia kul'tury, 1999.

Veidlinger, Jeffrey. " . . . Even beyond Pinsk: *Yizker Bikher* [Memorial Books] and Jewish Cultural Life in the Shtetl." In *Studies in Jewish Civilization*. Vol. 16, *The Jews of Eastern Europe*, ed. Leonard J. Greenspoon, Ronald A. Simkins, and Brian J. Horowitz, 175–189. Lincoln: University of Nebraska Press, 2006.

————. "The Historical and Ethnographic Construction of Russian Jewry." *Ab Imperio* 2003, no. 4: 165–184.

————. *The Moscow State Yiddish Theater: Jewish Culture on the Soviet Stage*. Bloomington: Indiana University Press, 2000.

————. "Simon Dubnow Recontextualized: The Sociological Conception of Jewish History and the Russian Intellectual Legacy." *Simon Dubnow Institute Yearbook* 3 (2004): 411–427.

Vital, David. *The Origins of Zionism*. Oxford: Clarendon Press, 1975.

————. *Zionism: The Crucial Phase*. Oxford: Clarendon Press, 1987.

Walkin, Jacob. *The Rise of Democracy in Pre-Revolutionary Russia*. New York: Frederick A. Praeger, 1962.

Walzer, Michael, Menachem Lorberbaum, and Noam J. Zohar, eds. *The Jewish Political Tradition*. Vol. 1. *Authority*. New Haven, Conn.: Yale University Press, 2000.

Warnke, Nina. "Going East: The Impact of American Yiddish Plays and Players on the Yiddish Stage in Czarist Russia, 1890–1914." *American Jewish History* 92, no. 1 (March 2004): 1–29.

Wartenweiler, David. *Civil Society and Academic Debate in Russia, 1905–1914*. Oxford: Clarendon Press, 1999.

Weeks, Theodore R. *From Assimilation to Antisemitism: The "Jewish Question" in Poland, 1850–1914*. DeKalb: Northern Illinois University Press, 2006.

————. *Nation and State in Late Imperial Russia: Nationalism and Russification on the Western Frontier, 1863–1914*. DeKalb: Northern Illinois University Press, 1996.

Wein, Abraham. "'Memorial Books' as a Source for Research into the History of Jewish Communities in Europe." In *Yad Vashem on the European Jewish Catastrophe and Resistance*. Vol. 9. Jerusalem: Yad Vashem, 1973.

Weinberg, David H. *Between Tradition and Modernity: Haim Zhitlowski, Simon Dubnow, Ahad Ha-am, and the Shaping of Modern Jewish Identity*. New York: Holmes and Meier, 1996.

Weinberg, Robert. *The Revolution of 1905 in Odessa: Blood on the Steps*. Bloomington: Indiana University Press, 1993.

Wisse, Ruth R. *I. L. Peretz and the Making of Modern Jewish Culture.* Seattle: University of Washington Press, 1991.

Wolitz, Seth. "A Jewish *Kulturkampf* in the Plastic Arts." In *The Emergence of Modern Jewish Politics: Bundism and Zionism in Eastern Europe,* ed. Zvi Gitelman, 151–177. Pittsburgh, Pa.: University of Pittsburgh Press, 2003.

Yaari, Abraham. "*Ner Tamid* Societies in Poland and Lithuania." *Jewish Social Studies* 21 (1959): 118–131.

Yerushalmi, Yosef Hayim. *Zakhor: Jewish History and Jewish Memory.* Seattle: University of Washington Press, 1982.

Zborowski, Mark, and Elizabeth Herzog. *Life Is with People: The Culture of the Shtetl.* New York: Schocken Books, 1962.

Zdobnov, N. V. *Istoriia russkoi bibliografii do nachala XX veka.* 2nd ed. Moscow, 1951.

Zimmerman, Joshua D. *Poles, Jews, and the Politics of Nationality.* Madison: University of Wisconsin Press, 2004.

Zipperstein, Steven. *Elusive Prophet: Ahad Ha'am and the Origins of Zionism.* Berkeley: University of California Press, 1993.

———. *Imagining Russian Jewry: Memory, History, Identity.* Seattle: University of Washington Press, 1999.

———. "The Politics of Relief: The Transformation of Russian Jewish Communal Life during the First World War." In *Studies in Contemporary Jewry.* Vol. 4, *The Jews and the European Crisis, 1914–1921,* ed. Jonathan Frankel, 22–40. New York: Oxford University Press, 1988.

Zorkaia, N. M. *Na rubezhe stoletii: U istokov massovogo iskusstva v Rossii, 1900–1910 godov.* Moscow: Nauka, 1976.

Zviagintsev, E. *Pravovoe polozhenie narodnykh bibliotek za 50 let.* Moscow: Izdanie knizhnago sklada "dlia samoobrazovaniia biblioteki i shkoli" E. D. Trautskoi, 1916.

Zylbercwieg, Zalmen. *Leksikon fun yidishn teater.* 6 vols. New York, Warsaw, and Mexico City: Elisheva, 1931–1969.

INDEX

Italicized page numbers indicate illustrations.

Abramovitsh, Sholem Yankev. *See* Mendele Moykher Sforim (S. Y. Abramovitsh)

Abramson, Bernard, 234

Abramson, Jacob, 234

Academic Union for the Study of Jewish History and Literature, 127

Academy of the Science of Judaism, 231

acculturation, into Russian language, 15, 82, 87, 115, 127

actors, 55, 173, 185

Adler, Sam, 180, 186

Aggada, 69

Agnon, S. Y., 70, 89

agriculture/agrarian reform, 19, 89

Ahad Ha-Am, xi, 6, 14, 100; on balance of flesh and spirit, 5; Jewish history studies and, 236; liberal nationalism and, 13; libraries and, 43

Ahashverush (Purim play), 199

Aizenstadt, S., 161

Aizman, David, 95

"Al ha-tsipor" [To the Bird] (Bialik), 7

Aleksander (Grand Prince of Lithuania), 275

Alexander II, Tsar, 108, 253, 255, 256, 265

Alexander III, Tsar, 30, 171, 237, 257

All-Russian Librarians' Conference, 44, 47, 126

All-Russian Zionist Organization, xi, 22

Altick, Richard, 24, 67

Amfiteatrov, Aleksandr, 91

An-sky, S., 6, 70, 72, 123; autobiography, 26–27; on canon of Yiddish literature, 79; on celebrity lecturers, 153, 155–56; death of, 288; on destruction of Great War, 283, 284–85; ethnography promoted by, 257–60; on Jewish assimilation in Germanic lands, 39; on Jewish folklore, 22–23; JHES and, 229, 246, 257, 258; language debates and, 129; on theater, 192

Anan ben David, 275

Andersen, Hans Christian, 105, 110, 111, 316n156

Andreev, Leonid, 91, 95, 102

Anokhi (Zalmon Yitshok Aronsohn), 104

anthropology, racial, 276–78

anti-Semitism, 14, 29, 133, 158, 191; libraries and, 63, 64; in Poland, 58; sexual themes in, 93, 109. *See also* pogroms

Ari (Isaac Luria), 36

Aristotle, 68

Arnshteyn, Mark, 200, 215–16

Aronowicz, Joseph, 267

artels, xii

artisans, 54, 56, 64, 89

Artsybashev, Mikhail, 4, 80, 95, 109, 112; cultural impact of, 92; popularity among Jewish readers, 12, 90

asceticism, 1, 4, 5, 208

Asch, Sholem, 7, 58, 129; as celebrity speaker, 156, 162; fund-raising theater and, 206; international fame of, 84; language debates and, 130; "living picture" performances and, 226; poor/ordinary folk as readers of, 70; popularity of, 101; portrait, *128;* in Russian translation, 95, 96; theater and, 174, 181, 185, 194; women readers and, 79; women's roles in plays of, 208

Assaf, Simha, 25

assembly, freedom of, 8, 15, 17, 18, 142

assimilation, 113, 115, 127, 206, 268; cultural hybridity and, 264; failures of, 235; in imperial capital, 136; language question and, 130, 334n3; in Moscow, 174; in Poland, 232; traditional dress and, 264–65

association, freedom of, 15

Austro-Hungarian empire, xiv, xviii, 84, 123, 190; Polish partitions and, 274; revolution (1848), 268–69, 270; theater in, 167, 169

avoyde (service to God), 4

Turgenev, Ivan, 72, 80, 91, 97, 105; popularity of, 101; "this-worldniks" and, 4
Turkow, Zygmunt, 180
Turner, Victor, 166
Twain, Mark, 110, 315n152

Uchebnik evreiskoi istorii dlia shkoly i samoobrazovaniia [Textbook on Jewish History for School and Self-Education] (Dubnow), 108
Ukraine, 58, 196, 256, 287; Chmielnicki rebellion, 268; under Soviet rule, 289; theater, 177
Ukrainian language, 212, 289
Ukrainians, 136, 221
Union for the Attainment of Equal Rights for the Jews of Russia, 116
Union of the Russian People, 133
United States, 3, 39; emigration to, 214, 222, 288; Jewish sermonizing in, 144; libraries in, 41, 47, 51; shtetl life in popular culture of, 11; Yiddish culture in, 82, 187, 190; Yiddish theater in, 14, 180, 186, 199, 214–15
Universal'naia biblioteka Series, 91
Uralic Jews, 276
urban landscapes, xii, 10–11, 99
Uriel Acosta (Gutzkow), 227
Urusov, Prince, 241
Ussishkin, Menachem, 134, 138–39
utopianism, 1

Varshavsky, Mark, 198
vaudeville, 165, 170
Vayter, A., 6, 131–32, 160; death of, 288; theater and, 191, 193, 194
Der veg tsum glik (The Road to Happiness), 108–109
Verbitskaia, Anastasiia, 4–5, 95, 96, 109; popularity among Jewish readers, 90, 91, 92, 110; young Jewish readers of, 110
Verne, Jules, 100–101, 110
Vienna, 10, 25, 184, 268–69; coffeehouses, 39; modern culture in, 290
Vilna (city and province), xx, 31, 123, 220; Bundist circles, 3; celebrity lecturers in, 148; as "Jerusalem of Lithuania,"

xv; Jewish Literary Society, 125; libraries, 47, 52, 53, 61, 75, 81, 88; pogrom (1919), 288; theater, 181
Der vilner balebesl [The Vilna Gentleman] (Arnshteyn), 215
Vilner Trupe, 187, 206, 285
Vinaver, Maksim, 19, 229, 237, 239, 240–41; on historical understanding, 246; JHES and, 244; OPE and, 242
Vishnitser, Mark, 245, 246
Vital, Hayyim, 36
Vitebsk (city and province), xx, 12, 125, 253; libraries, 52, 55, 57; Society of Jewish Literature and Music, 158
Volhynia Province, xiv, xv, xx; fire brigade orchestras, 221; libraries, 52, 89; theater, 169, 207; in World War I, 285
voluntary associations, xi, 16–17, 289, 291; bourgeois formality and, 239; in Central and Western Europe, 229; cultural performance and, 142; in era of reaction, 136, 139; laws regarding, 115; libraries and, 58; public sphere and, 7–9; Russian authorities and, 134; Temporary Regulations and, 19
Volynsky, A. L., 109
Voskhod (journal), 78, 94, 236, 242, 244

Waliszewski, Kazimierz, 107–108
Warsaw, 7, 108, 123, 148; cultural crackdown in, 136; cultural performances, *161;* Hazomir Society, 225, 284–85; Jewish Literary Society, 126; newspapers, 112; as publishing center, 83–84, 113; theater, 177, *179,* 179–80, 185–86, *186,* 188
Warsaw Yiddish Theater (Varshaver idisher teatr), 208
Weichert, Mikhl, 175, 205, 227–28
Weininger, Otto, 4, 93, 109, 112
Weissenberg, I. M., 103, 104
Weissenberg, Samuel, 229, 263–64, 277–79
Wells, H. G., 110, 112
Die Welt (Zionist weekly), 13
"What Is Jewish History?" (Dubnow), 245
"What Is World Literature?" (Niger), 103–104
Wheeler, Joseph L., 66
Whither? (Feierberg), 102–103, 314n127

Jeffrey Veidlinger is Associate Professor of History, Alvin H. Rosenfeld Chair in Jewish Studies, and Associate Director of the Borns Jewish Studies Program at Indiana University, Bloomington. His first book, *The Moscow State Yiddish Theater: Jewish Culture on the Soviet Stage* (Indiana University Press, 2000), received a National Jewish Book Award and the Barnard Hewitt Award for Outstanding Research in Theatre History and was named an Outstanding Academic Title by *Choice* magazine.